JOURNAL FOR THE STUDY OF THE OLD TESTAMENT
SUPPLEMENT SERIES

411

Editors
Claudia V. Camp, Texas Christian University
and
Andrew Mein, Westcott House, Cambridge

Founding Editors
David J.A. Clines, Philip R. Davies and David M. Gunn

Editorial Board
Richard J. Coggins, Alan Cooper, John Goldingay,
Robert P. Gordon, Norman K. Gottwald, John Jarick,
Andrew D.H. Mayes, Carol Meyers, Patrick D. Miller

THE BIBLE IN THE TWENTY-FIRST CENTURY SERIES

5

Editor
Athalya Brenner

The Meanings We Choose

Hermeneutical Ethics, Indeterminacy
and the Conflict of Interpretations

edited by

Charles H. Cosgrove

T & T CLARK INTERNATIONAL
A Continuum imprint
LONDON • NEW YORK

Copyright © 2004 T&T Clark International
A Continuum imprint

Published by T&T Clark International
The Tower Building, 11 York Road, London SE1 7NX
15 East 26th Street, Suite 1703, New York, NY 10010

www.tandtclark.com

British Library Cataloguing-in-Publication Data
A catalogue record for this book is available from the British Library

Library of Congress Cataloging-in-Publication Data
A catalogue record for this book is available from the Library of Congress

Typeset by CA Typesetting, www.sheffieldtypesetting.com
Printed on acid-free paper in Great Britain by MPG Books Ltd, Bodmin Cornwall

ISBN 0–567–08216–4 (hardback)

for our students

CONTENTS

SERIES EDITOR'S PREFACE

This volume is the fifth in the 'The Bible in the 21st Century' series. This is the title of our collective research project in the Biblical Studies Section, within the Department of Art, Religion and Culture at the University of Amsterdam, with the support of NOSTER (Netherlands School for Advanced Studies in Theology and Religion) and ASCA (Amsterdam School of Cultural Analysis). In this research program, as can be seen from its Internet formulations,[1] together with our international research partners, we endeavour to problematize contemporaneous authoritative and cultural meanings of bibles by focusing upon the processes of transmission, readership and actualization of biblical texts up to and including the Twenty-First Century.

We started the project together with our corresponding departments at the University of Glasgow in 2000. The first book of the BTC series, *Bible Translation on the Threshold of the Twenty-First Century: Authority, Reception, Culture and Religion* (A. Brenner and J.W. van Henten [eds], 2002), is a collection of papers problematizing contemporary biblical translations as cultural phenomena. Subsequent BTC volumes, be they collections or monographs by single authors, have followed and will follow a similar pattern and present work done locally as well as by international research partners and colleagues.

The present volume, *The Meanings We Choose*, is edited by Charles Cosgrove (Northern Seminary). It constitutes an engagement with the ethics of responsible bible reading – Hebrew Bible/Old Testament and New Testament texts – for the past as well as for the present and future. Its stated perspectives are multi-denominational Christian. But the implications of such readings go far beyond a specific confessional framework. In the present political climate the aware, responsible 'personal' is meaningful for any community, confessedly religious as well as otherwise. And scholarly roles have to be pondered anew. If postmodernism is to be taken seriously, then voices emanating from a majority deserve at least the same 'hearing' as minority voices. While the articles collected in this volume, broadly speaking, can and perhaps should be compartmentalized as 'ideological criticism', their significance for reading ideologies different from their own is more than considerable.

To quote from our local research program,

> The cultural-historical significance of 'the bible' results from the fact that bibles function as canons, i.e. networks or collections of intensely mediated texts that are considered sources for forms, values and norms by people. The canonical status of

---

1. http://www.theo.uu.nl/noster/ (in Dutch), and http://www.hum.uva.nl/bijbelwetenschappen/english/research (in English).

these texts leads to an ongoing process of re-interpretation and actualization, during which the biblical text is read selectively... Elements that are considered meaningful are being connected with actual views of life. Fragments of biblical texts function as a source of common values and interests. They form a point of attachment for the formulation of common identities and a reservoir of images, archetypes, topoi and model texts that inspire new texts and other forms of expression.

Broadly speaking, this is the mission of the present series. Hopefully, this volume as well as others will explore features and issues that are oriented to contemporary culture and the bible's (and religion's) place within it, issues that are gaining ground but – perhaps – still get less academic attention than they deserve.

Athalya Brenner

ABBREVIATIONS

AARAS	American Academy of Religion Academy Series
ANTC	Abingdon New Testament Commentaries
BibInt	*Biblical Interpretation: A Journal of Contemporary Approaches*
CBQ	*Catholic Biblical Quarterly*
EKKNT	Evangelisch-Katholischer Kommentar zum Neuen Testament
ExAu	*Ex Auditou*
FCB	Feminist Companion to the Bible
Int	*Interpretation*
JBL	*Journal of Biblical Literature*
JPS	Jewish Publication Society
JSNTSup	*Journal for the Study of the New Testament*, Supplemental Series
JSOT	*Journal for the Study of the Old Testament*
LWF	Lutheran World Federation
NICNT	New International Commentary on the New Testament
OBT	Overtures to Biblical Theology
OTL	Old Testament Library
PC	Proclamation Commentaries
SBL	Society of Biblical Literature
SBLDS	Society of Biblical Literature Dissertation Series
SJT	*Scottish Journal of Theology*
SP	Sacra Pagina
ST	*Studia theologica*
TTod	*Theology Today*
ZNW	*Zeitschrift für die neutestamentliche Wissenschaft*
ZTK	*Zeitschrift für Theologie und Kirche*

List of Contributors

A.K.M. Adam, Seabury-Western Theological Seminary, 2122 Sheridan Road, Evanston, IL 60201, USA

Mark G. Brett, Whitley College, The University of Melbourne, 271 Royal Parade, Parkville, Victoria, Australia

Charles H. Cosgrove, Northern Baptist Theological Seminary, 660 E. Butterfield Rd., Lombard, IL 60513 USA

Carole R. Fontaine, Andover Newton Theological School, 210 Herrick Rd., Newton Centre, MA 02459 USA

Dennis T. Olson, Princeton Theological Seminary, P.O. Box 821, Princeton, NJ 08542-0803 USA

Daniel Patte, Vanderbilt Divinity School, 411 21st Avenue South, Nashville, TN 37240-1121 USA

Jeffrey L. Staley, Seattle University, 900 Broadway, Seattle, WA 98122-4340 USA

Robert C. Tannehill, 960 Braumiller Rd., Delaware, Ohio 43015 USA

Frank M. Yamada, Seabury-Western Theological Seminary, 2122 Sheridan Road, Evanston, IL 60201, USA

Khiok-khng Yeo, Garrett-Evangelical Theological Seminary, 2121 Sheridan Rd, Evanston, IL 60201 USA

INTRODUCTION

Charles H. Cosgrove, Northern Baptist Theological Seminary, Illinois, USA

As a lay Christian in the United Church of Christ who teaches New Testament at an American Baptist seminary outside Chicago, I am constantly preoccupied with the question of how I, my church and my students use the Bible to develop and defend our moral and theological convictions. Twenty years ago, as an assistant professor fresh out of graduate school, I understood the constructive use of the Bible as a matter of finding the right interpretation (the historically demonstrable one) and making connections between that interpretation and some contemporary question, problem or need. Even then I knew – but was not yet ready to draw the implications – that 'finding' the demonstrable original meaning was a simplistic way of conceiving the first step in this hermeneutic. Eventually, I began to come to grips with the fact that the biblical writings admit multiple reasonable interpretations of their original sense (not to mention the multiplicity that arises when we use other definitions of the sense of the text). I realized that my own interpretations, however much I cherished them (and had a stake in them owing to all the hours of work it took to work them out and publish them!), were usually at best only equal competitors with other eminently reasonable but competing interpretations. In effect I was beginning to take seriously at least certain forms of what goes by the name 'indeterminacy'. Soon the question of how constructive 'use of the Bible' should take account of indeterminacy became a central concern of my work.[1] This interest has led me to extend invitations to the contributors of the present volume, soliciting their exploration of various moral, didactic and theological approaches to making judgments between competing interpretations of the Bible (Hebrew Bible and New Testament), including choices between interpretations for use in preaching, teaching, theology and ethics. The identities of the contributing biblical scholars give the volume a Christian orientation (broad and diverse), but sensitivities to Jewish and Muslim perspectives are also present in a number of the essays,

---

1. My first published effort along these lines was an article, 'The Justification of the "Other": An Interpretation of Rom. 1.18–4.25', in Eugene H. Lovering (ed.), *Society of Biblical Literature 1992 Seminar Papers* (Atlanta: Scholars Press, 1992); followed by 'Rhetorical Suspense in Romans: A Study in Polyvalence and Hermeneutical Election', *JBL*, 115 (1996), pp. 271–87; *Elusive Israel: The Puzzle of Election in Romans* (Louisville, KY: Westminster/John Knox Press, 1997); and *Appealing to Scripture in Moral Debate: Five Hermeneutical Rules* (Grand Rapids: Eerdmans, 2002), pp. 154–80.

and most if not all of the articles are animated by scholarly as well as wider ecumenical and humanistic concerns.

The intellectual environment of our question is the postmodern (or 'late modern') intellectual context. In particular, two tenets arising out of that context provoke the present exploration. They are (1) that biblical texts are typically open to competing reasonable interpretations, where 'competing' means 'mutually exclusive' and 'reasonable' means 'plausible/defensible' on the basis of a rigorous application of chosen methods; and (2) that this openness of texts to competing construals of meaning makes interpreters morally and theologically responsible for the meanings they choose in representing, describing, using and appealing to the Bible in and for the life and faith of the church.

These two assumptions raise important questions about the use of the Bible in the church. For example, what are Christian preachers, teachers and theologians to do when faced with 'indeterminacy' (modestly or radically conceived)? Do we have a right or responsibility to choose one interpretation over another? If so, what criteria should inform such choices? A 'rule of faith'? A set of moral commitments? A canon-within-the-canon for adjudicating not simply between different voices of scripture but also between different interpretations of scripture? Or is adjudication a matter not of criteria or hermeneutical 'method' but of Christian 'character' and 'wisdom' (*phrōnesis*)? And what is our moral responsibility with respect to plausible interpretations that we reject? How should we conceive the relation, within the hermeneutical task, between retrievalist appropriation and ideological critique of the Bible with respect to conflicting interpretations of the same text?

Hermeneutical Ethics

In recent years increasing attention has been given to the ethical dimensions of interpretation (ethics of interpretation, ethics of reading). Concerns about how to give authors a fair reading continue to be pressed. At the same time other moral aspects of interpretation have been identified and explored. A number of these newer understandings of interpretive ethics arise from the perception that purely objective interpretation – that is, reading unaffected by the identity, assumptions, and commitments of interpreters – is neither possible nor desirable. If biblical texts are often (or always) overdetermined (or underdetermined) and polyvalent, then readers are co-constructors of the sense of the text. In that constructive role, readers are unavoidably shaped by their own experiences and social location. In that case, what matters is not simply what methods are used or whether they are used sincerely and correctly but *who* does the interpreting. Hence, in an influential presidential address to the Society of Biblical Literature in 1987, Elisabeth Schüssler Fiorenza called for a 'decentering' of biblical interpretation, a widening of the circle of readers who 'count' to include women and non-Europeans and an end to the hegemony of ethnically European males as arbiters of good interpretation.[2] The

---

2.   Elisabeth Schüssler Fiorenza, 'The Ethics of Interpretation: De-Centering Biblical Theology', *JBL*, 107 (1988), pp. 3–17.

grounds for decentering are that many heads from different social locations are better than a few heads from a narrow band of cultural experience. Justo Gonzalez' idea of the ethnically-inclusive hermeneutical 'roundtable' calls for a similar kind of inclusion.[3]

If social location shapes reading, then it is important to be honest and self-conscious about one's social location in approaching any act of interpretation. This is not merely a matter of caution, a way of making one's social identity explicit in order to bracket it. It is appropriate to read from a particular 'place'[4] and with particular interests. Not only do interpreters necessarily bring a preunderstanding to the text that enables them to understand at all,[5] they also bring commitments, a stake in the outcome of interpretation, *a will to interpret in a certain direction.*[6]

Discussion of interpretive ethics has also involved criticism of certain postmodern theories of textual indeterminacy, including those associated with deconstruction, radical reader-response criticism, and what is regarded by some as a cynical relativism of interpretation associated with so-called 'identity politics'. Since the 1960s, E.D. Hirsch has pressed the moral responsibility of interpreters to authors, championing the rights of authors to have their words understood as they intend.[7] He has also insisted that the only reason we are (or should be) interested in classic texts is because we believe that they have something to teach us; we do not (or should not) want to discover our 'own' meanings in texts, since then we would learn nothing.[8] Fredric Jameson has attacked deconstruction and other 'contemporary ideologies of pluralism' by accusing their advocates of dedication to a

3. Justo Gonzalez, *Out of Every Tribe and Nation: Christian Theology at the Ethnic Roundtable* (Nashville: Abingdon Press, 1992). See also Jürgen Habermas, *Moral Consciousness and Communicative Action* (trans. Christian Lenhardt and Shiery Weber Nicholsen; Cambridge, MA: MIT Press, 1990).

4. R.S. Sugirtharajah (ed.), *Voices from the Margin: Interpreting the Bible in the Third World* (London: SPCK, 1991); Cane Hope Felder (ed.), *Stony the Road We Trod: African American Biblical Interpretation* (Minneapolis: Fortress Press, 1991); Mary Ann Tolbert and Fernando Segovia (eds.), *Reading from This Place*, vol. 1: *Social Location and Biblical Interpretation in the United States*; vol. 2: *Social Location and Biblical Interpretation in Global Perspective* (Minneapolis: Fortress Press, 1995).

5. Rudolf Bultmann, 'Is Exegesis without Presuppositions Possible?', in Schubert M. Ogden (ed. and trans.), *Existence and Faith: Shorter Writings of Rudolf Bultmann* (London and Glasgow: Collins, 1964), pp. 342–51.

6. Juan Luis Segundo, 'The Hermeneutic Circle', in *Liberation of Theology* (trans. John Drury; Maryknoll, NY: Orbis Books, 1976), pp. 7–38. From the standpoint of liberationist hermeneutics, not all social locations are equal. The liberationist principle of the 'epistemological privilege of the oppressed' implies that the Bible can be rightly read only from the experience of oppression, that is, *by* or at least *in solidarity with* the oppressed. See Daniel Schipani, *Religious Education Encounters Liberation Theology* (Birmingham, AL: Religious Education Press, 1998), pp. 210–60.

7. E.D. Hirsch, 'Three Dimensions of Hermeneutics', in *The Aims of Interpretation* (Chicago and London: University of Chicago Press, 1976), pp. 90–92. See further, the description and analysis of contemporary advocacy of this viewpoint in the essay by A.K.M. Adam in the present volume.

8. E.D. Hirsch, *Validity in Interpretation* (New Haven, CT: Yale University Press, 1967), pp. 25–26.

program designed 'to forestall that systematic articulation and totalization of
interpretive results which can only lead to embarrassing questions' about their
social location and interests.[9]

Hirsch, Jameson and others dispute the claim that all interpretation is necessarily
subjective, reflecting only what interpreters want to see in the text, so shaped by
social location and interest that no interpretation can claim any superiority over
others except by gaining political advantage. Related to this dispute is the recent
application of ideological critique not only to interpreters of texts but to the texts
themselves.[10] If we can see in biblical texts things that we don't like, then we do
not invariably read our own desires into the Bible. If we can recognize ways in
which texts promote, validate or otherwise 'encode' systems and practices of
oppression, then we have also recognized that texts are not wholly indeterminate.
As Carole Fontaine confesses in her contribution to the present volume, 'I have
always encountered the text, even those pericopes I hate, as a genuine *reality* –
almost an "entity"! – over against which I am set (the Hebrew word for this is
neged)...' She refers to this as the 'reality of the text', those stubborn, determinate
dimensions of the text that resist interpretive efforts to treat the text as 'entirely
plastic, a shape-shifting entity that responds like a mood ring to its reader's present
desires'. Moreover, deconstruction is not always license. Practiced at its best, it can
be a form of ideological critique in that it reveals 'what is hidden, repressed or
denied in any ordinary reading'.[11]

Indeterminacy

In genealogies of literary criticism, it has been pointed out that in the late twentieth
century the deconstructionist concept of 'indeterminacy' supplanted mid-century's
New Critical idea of 'ambiguity'.[12] The New Critics argued that literary texts (and
especially poetic texts) are fraught with ambiguity and that ambiguity makes literature rich, complex and open to profound and paradoxical interpretations. Decon-
structionists (notably Jacques Derrida and Paul de Mann) displaced the concept
of ambiguity with that of indeterminacy. They saw reality as fractured (disunified,
radically pluralistic) and therefore saw texts and interpretations as indeterminate.
However, once 'indeterminacy' became a common term of literary criticism and
other disciplines, it acquired a broader and more varied semantic scope. Not everyone who uses the term defines it in accord with its radical, anti-metaphysical,

---

9.   Fredric Jameson, *The Political Unconscious: Narrative as a Socially Symbolic Act* (Ithaca,
NY: Cornell University Press, 1981), pp. 31–32.

10.   Judith Fetterley, *The Resisting Reader: A Feminist Approach to American Literature.*
(Bloomington, IN: Indiana University Press, 1978); David Jobling and Tina Pippin (eds.),
'Ideological Criticism of Biblical Texts', *Semeia*, 59 (1992); George Aichele *et al.*, *The
Postmodern Bible: The Bible and Culture Collective* (New Haven and London: Yale University
Press, 1995), pp. 272–308.

11.   *The Postmodern Bible*, p. 130.

12.   Timothy Bahti, 'Ambiguity and Indeterminacy: The Juncture', *Comparative Literature*, 38
(1986), pp. 209–23.

deconstructionist sense. Many (including me) understand indeterminacy as a matter of degree.[13]

Here's my definition of indeterminacy: the recurring interpretive situation in which I perceive there to be two or more *reasonable* but *competing* interpretations, that is, two or more mutually exclusive interpretations that are plausible/defensible on the basis of a rigorous application of the same methods or what I judge to be appropriate competing methods. Thus, I face indeterminacy when, for example, I become convinced (as I am) that there is no way to resolve by the use of grammatical-historical methods (with due attention to context) the question whether Paul's use of the Greek expression πίστις Χριστοῦ means Christ's own faith (faithfulness) *or* the faith of believers in Christ (or some other alternative).[14] Likewise, I confront indeterminacy when I consider the competing interpretive results of certain literary interpretations of a text, carried out in a New Critical style, and socio-historical interpretations of the same text, because I cannot see that a socio-historical approach is provably more appropriate than a New Critical approach and vice versa.

Indeterminacy applies in different degrees. In addition to displaying combinations of more or less determinate and indeterminate features, texts also present us with interpretive problems we judge to be incapable of resolution by their very nature (including cases where we have reason to think that the ambiguity or openness of the text is deliberate[15]), those for which we may entertain the hope of some future resolution unavailable to us at present, and those for which we allow that compelling resolutions may exist but accessing these resolutions is not feasible for us (the typical situation of a preacher before equally persuasive commentators in conflict).

Indeterminacy also comes in different varieties. These differences cannot be distinguished as neat types; nor is only one conceptualization of types possible. Nevertheless, some schematization may be helpful as a way of organizing the topic. We should begin by distinguishing indeterminacy as a factor in the interpretation of texts from other kinds of indeterminacy, such as ontological, epistemological, and mimetic indeterminacy, to name a few of the categories offered by Stuart Lasine.[16] Using a historical model of indeterminacy in the interpretation of

---

13. Literary critic Gerald Graff observes that we can easily become so preoccupied with what is indeterminate in interpretation that we forget how much we know with ordinary certainty, which is ironic inasmuch as our perception of indeterminacy depends on a 'background of partial determinacy that makes it stand out'. See Gerald Graff, 'Determinacy/Indeterminacy', in F. Lentricchia and T. McLaughlin (eds.), *Critical Terms for Literary Study* (Chicago and London: University of Chicago Press, 1990), p. 174.

14. On the debate over this interpretive question, see E. Elizabeth Johnson and David M. Hay (eds.), *Pauline Theology*, vol. 4: *Looking Back, Pressing On* (SBL Seminar Series, 4; Atlanta: Scholars Press, 1997), pp. 33–92.

15. A text may be designed to be indeterminate, left unresolved, treated as contradictory or paradoxical. Michael Fox thinks we should use the term 'indeterminacy' only for these intentional kinds, not for uncertainties that arise from failure of communication, the passage of time, etc. But in that case we would need a second term to describe the latter types. See Michael V. Fox, 'The Uses of Indeterminacy', *Semeia*, 71.2 (1995), p. 175.

16. Stuart Lasine, 'Indeterminacy and the Bible: A Review of Literary and Anthropological

texts, we can distinguish original, historical-reconstructive, and recontextual (hermeneutical) forms of indeterminacy. That is, a text can be indeterminate in its original context (indeterminate for its original audience); it can be indeterminate for us owing to the limits of our reconstructive abilities; and it can be indeterminate in its signicance when taken into new contexts (due to the uncertainties and flexibilities of analogical reasoning).[17] Using a New Critical or Ricoeurian model, which regards the text as its own world (separate or 'distantiated' from the biography of its author or a particular history), we can distinguish various forms of literary indeterminacy, such as ambiguity arising from multiple possibilities for relating part to whole and whole to part, linguistic ambiguity (ambiguity of words and syntax), uncertainties of form and genre (e.g., whether Jonah purports to be history or satire, to what extent 1 Kings 3–11 involves parody, irony, or hyperbole, what kind of 'law' we have in the legal materials of Exodus or Deuteronomy or the Sermon on the Mount), uncertainty arising from apparent contradictions as well as gaps, polyvalence caused by intertextuality (uncertainty about the presence and role of allusions to other texts, cultural symbols, etc.), and so on. Of course, one can also treat these literary types or causes of indeterminacy within a historical framework of interpretation, particularly one that attends to the socio-rhetorical aspects of the text.

Indeterminacy also arises from the application of different methods that produce competing results. The Bible does not tell us how to interpret it. It does not tell us whether we should adopt a literary-critical approach to Genesis 2–3[18] instead of a socio-historical one,[19] or whether we should use marxist or deconstructionist interpretations and what to do when they conflict.[20] Moreover, in addition to modern critical methods, which at times are complementary and at times compete, there is now a growing interest in what premodern methods or approaches (patristic and rabbinic) can teach us about the nature of hermeneutics. Even so robust a historian as Wayne Meeks has recently called for giving up the historical method as a means of 'umpiring' (resolving disputes between competing interpretations) and using it instead in the role of *advocatus diaboli* to stand up for the past alongside competing 'charismatic' interpretations.[21]

Theories and Their Application to Biblical Texts', *Hebrew Studies*, 27 (1986), pp. 48–80. Lasine examines the work of recent literary critics who see textual indeterminacy as serving to express or point to these other kinds of indeterminacy.

17. Application of a text to a later historical setting requires the use of analogical reasoning, which admits competing possibilities. See Cosgrove, *Appealing to Scripture in Moral Debate*, pp. 51–89. On the open-endedness of texts through recontextualization, see also Graff, who points out that recontextualization need not always be indeterminate ('Determinacy/Indeterminacy', pp. 167–68).

18. See Phyllis Trible, *God and the Rhetoric of Sexuality* (Philadelphia: Fortress Press, 1978), pp. 72–143.

19. See Susan S. Lanser, '(Feminist) Criticism in the Garden: Inferring Genesis 2–3', *Semeia*, 4 (1988), pp. 67–84.

20. Jameson, *The Political Unconscious*.

21. Wayne A. Meeks, 'On Trusting an Unpredictable God', in John T. Carroll *et al.* (eds.), *Faith and History: Essays in Honor of Paul W. Meyer* (Atlanta, GA: Scholars Press, 1990), p. 119.

Indeterminacy also arises from the diverse orientations of different interpreters, owing to differences of preunderstanding and precommitment based on personal experience and social location. Interpretation is a matter of complex judgments about how things fit together, what is plausible, how the world works. Individual interpreters and communities of interpretation bring different assumptions to the text. These assumptions may include the sorts of identifiable opinions that one might bracket, such as certain theological convictions or information from various scientific disciplines. They also include a complex mix of attitudes and sensibilities shaped by personal history and the perspectival wisdom of one's own group. Together, these elements go into producing that *phronēsis* by which we make most of our judgment calls in life (as Aristotle taught). When it comes to deciding, for example, whether Onesimus' freedom is important to Paul and, if so, whether Paul's rhetorical strategies in Philemon are marshaled to that end, it may be an inescapable difference of *phronēsis* about how the world works in slave-based societies that leads interpreters in different directions. But awareness of this – of the other's interpretation and the reasons for it – can make me cognizant of alternate reasonable possibilities. Thus, indeterminacy arises when I recognize that my experience shapes the way I see the text, that yours shapes how you see the text, and that I must take your witness into account in any decisions about how I will appropriate and use the text.

The Meanings We Choose

Many continue to assume that the church's use of the Bible must be 'objective' in the traditional historical-critical sense (i.e., based on demonstrably determinate meaning). Others reject this assumption, asserting that interpretation is inherently subjective and everyone reads unavoidably from his or her own standpoint. As I see it, the *original* meaning is in fact to a significant degree *in*determinate and *that* is something we can discuss and describe in modestly objective ways. At the same time, we do all read from our own place, but it is also possible for each of us to see how the text looks from other social locations. Moreover, we can make informed judgments about the extent to which any reading (our own or someone else's) has a plausible foothold in the text. And we can compare interpretations emanating from different social locations and assess them for their moral and theological merits. These assessments must of their nature be subjective in the sense of culturally located and conditioned by tradition and experience. But here, too, an ecumenical conversation is possible as an avenue to better understanding and an antidote to parochialism. Above all, it is important that we identify and state not just the interpretive reasons for the meanings we choose (reasons based in the various criticisms: historical, literary, socio-rhetorical, etc.) but also the moral and theological reasons for the interpretations we affirm. These and other[22] reasons usually

22. There are, of course, other reasons besides moral and theological ones. I may prefer an interpretation because I perceive that it promotes my interests, even if living by it might put others at risk or disadvantage. This self-centered interest has a better chance of being exposed (to me and to others) if I take responsibility for my interpretations by assuming the obligation of making moral

go unspoken, yet they work powerfully in both scholars and non-scholars to foster a preference for one interpretation over another. Hence, these extra-exegetical[23] criteria for theologically affirming ('choosing') one interpretation over another ought to be made explicit so that we can submit them to examination by ourselves and others.

I hasten to stress that indeterminacy does not always require choosing as the proper response. We are not compelled to choose between interpretations that are different but morally and theologically compatible. Theologians of premodern times held that the Bible contains levels of meaning, each to be accessed by a different logic. In our day, various kinds of compatibility are possible for the integration or peaceful co-existence of results emanating from different methods, approaches, places, and concerns. For example, different interpretations that result from different questions and methods need not be exegetically contradictory. A structuralist exegesis may differ from a socio-rhetorical exegesis without producing contradiction. Further, interpretations that result from the same questions and methods but are exegetically incompatible may turn out to be morally and theologically compatible. For example, if I conclude that it is equally possible that the breaking of bread in the Lukan version of the Last Supper symbolizes *either* Jesus' self-giving death (as it does in Matthew and Mark and in certain Lukan manuscript traditions) *or* the resurrection presence that creates the new community (following the shortest reading of Lk. 22.19-20 and taking the Lukan story of the disciples on the road to Emmaus as the decisive clue), these two different interpretations are exegetically incompatible but not incapable of being theologically combined. Choosing *between* interpretations becomes necessary only where affirming different interpretations that result from the same or different questions and methods would entail moral or theological contradiction. Of course, we will often have to decide about compatibility in the face of gray areas since judging compatibility exegetically, morally and theologically is often not a matter of straightforward logical analysis but requires consideration of possibilities for creative synthesis, paradox, the importance of open-endedness and the impossibility in most situations of tying up all loose ends. Still, there are many hermeneutical situations in which we do choose between interpretations and rightly so.

The essays of this volume examine the intersection of indeterminacy and moral-theological responsibility from various angles. Some are more general hermeneutical essays; others focus on a specific biblical text as a way of exploring the hermeneutical issues of our common agenda. The following summaries of these contributions can only sketch their main lines of argument and hint at their richness and nuance.

---

and theological arguments for them rather than simply claiming that I have arrived at the one correct original meaning.

23. By 'extra-exegetical' I mean simply that when my efforts at interpreting the text lead me to two or more reasonable interpretations and I apply moral and theological criteria as a way of judging between these interpretations, the application of those criteria is 'extra-exegetical' (or 'post-exegetical').

Part One, 'Reflections on Indeterminacy and Hermeneutical Judgment', offers four general treatments of our topic. An essay by *A.K.M. Adam* opens this section with a reflection on two leading hermeneutical questions: 'How are we to understand texts?' and 'How shall we know whose interpretation is right (or 'true' or 'legitimate')?' Adam terms the subject of the first question 'integral' hermeneutics 'because it poses for itself… the task of articulating the positive characteristics of unitary interpretive truth'. He calls the second approach 'differential' hermeneutics because it 'challenges us to explain why the very most knowledgeable and wisest interpreters so often disagree about what a text means'. Adam provides sympathetic descriptions of both hermeneutical philosophies but advocates differential hermeneutics as the better way of accounting for the conflict of interpretations among equally competent interpreters.

Integral hermeneutics, Adam observes, holds that texts *have* meanings, namely, the compositional intentions of their authors. These meanings may be hidden but exist nonetheless objectively as part of the text in the same way that the unseen earthward side of a house's foundation exists objectively as a property of the house. Integralists stress that we owe an ethical obligation to authors to interpret their textual communications as they intended. Moreover, integralists charge that when differentialists reject intentionalism and allow that texts can have multiple meanings, they 'undermine the deeply-held human covenant that makes effective communication possible'. Not only that, differentialists operate with a double standard; seeking to be understood and to correct misunderstandings of their work, differentialists show that they are not non-intentionalists when it comes to their *own* meanings. Adam notes the valid concerns of these integralist critiques but thinks they distort the perspective and practice of differentialists.

Unlike integral hermeneutics, differential hermeneutics does not start with the question of which interpretive method is correct but 'begins from the fact of ineluctable interpretive difference'. Differentialists are not pluralists who eschew all criteria for assessing interpretations. Rather, they seek to work out evaluative criteria that make room for interpretive diversity. Adam shows that differential hermeneutics has certain salient affinities with the hermeneutical approaches of the early church, notably those we meet in Augustine and Irenaeus. Augustine celebrated interpretive plurality and also put forward criteria for choosing between interpretations. Augustine's criteria have to do with effects, whether a particular interpretation promotes God's grace and love. Similarly, Irenaeus criticized interpretations he thought erroneous by appealing not to exegetical principles but to results, as when he famously said that gnostic interpreters rearrange the pieces of the scriptural witness that are supposed to make up the mosaic of a king and produce instead the image of a dog. As this example shows, 'the problem for Irenaeus is with interpretations that misrepresent Jesus, not with a general plurality in interpretation'.

Differentialists are also especially sensitive to the ethical obligation that interpreters have to one another. The integralist position almost invariably leads interpreters to say or at least think that those who disagree with their exegesis must be intellectually or morally deficient in some way. How else to account for difference? Differential hermeneutics challenges this attitude by rejecting its premise that there is only one correct meaning. Differential hermeneutics explains interpretive difference as largely a product of interpretive interest, which arises from identity and experience and is tied to particular social locations. It is not only inescapable but also good to interpret from and for a particular 'place'. This creates a plurality of local families of interpretation. Celebrating this plurality does not mean that one has abandoned all norms for assessing interpretations as better or worse. Criteria for evaluating interpretations are not lacking but plentiful in every local interpretive community. The important thing is to recognize that most, if not all, interpretive criteria are *appropriately local*, not universal.

This notion of local hermeneutical criteria worries advocates of integral hermeneutics because they defend singularity of textual meaning and universality of hermeneutical criteria by presuming that without the assumption of the 'one correct intended meaning' we would have no way of discerning God's communicative intent in or behind the witness of scripture but would in effect be attributing cacophony or communicative failure to God. Against this view, Adam proposes that God's ways of knowing and constituting unity and harmony probably elude our human grasp and that differential hermeneutics wisely 'leaves final answers to questions of rectitude and unity in God's hands and espouses instead the shared endeavor patiently and respectfully to cultivate distinct, concordant testimonies to God's glory, from every tribe and language and people and nation'. Different interpretations can be diverse but, as Augustine believed, harmonious in their effects of promoting God's love and grace.

My contribution to our discussion follows Adam's. I begin with an overview of 'indeterminacy' as both an ancient and a postmodern perception. The ancient rhetor Quintilian, speaking about problems in interpreting legal texts, advises that in cases of ambiguity considerations of 'equity' ought to have a say in determining the meaning of the text. Today we confront indeterminacy as the hermeneutical situation in which 'applying a given interpretive question and a given publicly-shared method (or set of methods) yields more than one reasonable interpretation'. This calls for self-awareness about the way we choose one interpretation over another for constructive Christian use. Here our decisions almost invariably depend on 'extra-exegetical' considerations. Our own sense of 'equity' (or 'justice') is likely to inform our judgments. Adjudicating between competing reasonable interpretations also calls for taking into account other values and interests; in this way we take responsibility for the meanings we choose, subjecting to scrutiny not only our exegetical rationales (as critical methods demand) but also the usually hidden factors that incline us toward one interpretation and not another.

I offer four types of extra-exegetical criteria for judging between competing plausible interpretations: (1) theological, (2) moral, (3) correlational, and (4) ecumenical. I describe these criteria in ways that show connections with premodern hermeneutics and with tacit modern hermeneutical practice. In reaching for a postmodern *hermeneutica sacra*, I aim to build bridges to the premodern church without burning bridges to modernity or lapsing into acritical or anticritical attitudes.

Under theological criteria I discuss the possibility of a contemporary 'rule of faith'. Under moral criteria, I continue my examination of the rule of faith by noting the hermeneutical function of a rule of love in Augustine and certain Reformed confessions. I connect this criterion with the question of prophetic justice and propose that we think of the rule of faith today as 'an emancipatory vision of God's love in Christ'.

I specify two correlational criteria: depth and relevance. Ancient Jews and Christians assumed that scripture is universally relevant and profound and adopted corresponding interpretive attitudes toward the Bible. Today we recognize that profundity is a perspectival judgment, conditioned by identity and social location. Correlational connection with a particular time and place is a legitimate considera-tion in judging between interpretations. Moreover, in reading from our own place (social location), it is also appropriate to read 'for elegance, nuance, weightiness, depth', which are in turn valid criteria for preferring one interpretation over another.

Ecumenical criteria provide a corrective to correlational values that might lock us into ethnocentric or, as I like to put it, 'hemeiocentric' (we-centered) herme-neutics. Ecumenical sensitivity across cultures (including theological sub-cultures and traditions) calls for taking into account the way the text is read in contexts different from our own. In working out an ecumenical path, I consider the merits of hermeneutical tolerance, pluralism, and synthesizing as ways of honoring culturally diverse interpretations. Without claiming that 'universal' synthesizing interpretations are possible or even desirable, I suggest that limited, local efforts at accommodating and adjusting our interpretations to those reflecting other cul-tural locations and concerns are an important way in which we show faithfulness to the communion of saints. All other things being equal, a more ecumenically, culturally inclusive interpretation is better than a purely local and hemeiocentric one.

Daniel Patte has made important contributions to our topic in several recent publications.[24] In his essay for the present volume he approaches the question of indeterminacy and the conflict of interpretations by asking what form a postmodern commentary should take if its purpose is to assist preachers, Bible study groups, and theological students in using the Bible as scripture. For Patte, the purpose of such a commentary should be to '*open the text up* to a multiplicity of readings' rather than limit interpretive possibilities by using the commentary to advance only the reading advocated by the commentator. The postmodern commentary should present preachers with interpretive options in such a way as to encourage them to be 'free to *choose the meaning* that is most appropriate for Christians in their specific time and place and that they will want to proclaim as the Word of God for their congregations today'. At the same time a postmodern commentary should help preachers (and the rest of us) take responsibility for the meanings we choose.

In the opening and closing sections of his essay, Patte addresses the fundamental hermeneutical and epistemological assumptions that inform his conception of a

---

24. Daniel Patte, *Discipleship according to the Sermon on the Mount: Four Legitimate Readings, Four Plausible Views of Discipleship, and Their Relative Values* (Valley Forge, PA: Trinity Press International, 1996); Daniel Patte, *The Challenge of Discipleship: A Critical Study of the Sermon on the Mount as Scripture* (Harrisburg, PA: Trinity Press International, 1999).

postmodern commentary. In the first part he discusses shifting conceptions of the Bible and hermeneutics as a result of postmodern sensibilities. This includes rejection of postmodernism by fundamentalists and others, ambivalence toward postmodernism by biblical critics, and spontaneous embrace of postmodern hermeneutics by 'conscientious preachers'. In the closing section of his essay Patte seeks to 'clarify why, despite the believers' fear, choosing a meaning for the biblical text is not denying "truth", and why, despite their present ambivalence, biblical critics should self-consciously develop a postmodern approach, because it is a responsible way to strive to reach the traditional goals of biblical critical studies'.

In the central part of his essay, Patte sets forth three broad criteria for a postmodern commentary on the Bible as scripture. First, the postmodern commentary should present a *multiplicity of analytical frames* for interpreting the Bible. This means offering 'a series of selected critical interpretations', which Patte organizes under the broad critical headings of historical, literary and rhetorical criticism. The aim here is to examine the text from the standpoints of different tools of analysis and to discover what scholars, working with one or another of these approaches, discovered as 'most signicant' in the text.

Second, the postmodern commentary should *demonstrate the plausibility of multiple theological frames* for interpreting the biblical text. One begins with a focal theological theme or concept about which the text is understood as speaking. Next, one explicates 'the particular choice that each interpretation makes among several possible ways of conceiving this theological concept of the text'. The history of (theological) interpretation provides the clues for this analysis, which Patte illustrates by considering interpretations of the 'atonement' in Romans. Each of the various traditional theories of the atonement 'necessarily chooses among several possible and plausible understandings of atonement' in Romans (and other biblical texts). The postmodern commentary refuses to argue (as many modern commentaries typically do) that one of these views of the atonement was Paul's and therefore that to interpret Romans from the standpoint of a different atonement theory is wrong. The postmodern commentary assumes that we do not know and cannot know 'Paul's view of the atonement' beyond knowing that several ways of understanding the atonement in Paul are reasonable, critically defensible.

Third, the postmodern commentary should articulate the plausibility of *several contextual frames*. This involves consideration of how the text can speak relevantly in different settings, how believers can live by the text in different life contexts. Patte does not imagine that the postmodern commentator can anticipate all the different ways in which the text can speak relevantly to believers in different times and places. Instead, he suggests that the postmodern commentary can illumine the kinds of decisions believers make in finding a relevant word in the text. One way the postmodern commentary can help is by showing how 'the analytical choice of any given interpretation of Romans envisions in its own way the "Roman Christians" to which Paul addressed his letter with the expectation that they would live by it'. For every critical interpretation, working within a particular analytical frame, there are implications for how these readers are to connect the letter to their lives, their relationships, their moral choices and so forth. Thus, a kind of relevance potential is built into choice about which analytical frame to use and the interpretive judgments one makes within that frame.

Khiok-khng Yeo explores the role of 'culture' in interpretation. He begins from the thesis that the interpreter's own culture is always a constructive factor in the reading process. He elaborates this thesis by offering an 'intersubjective' model of reading, which incorporates I.A. Richards' notion of metaphor as constitutive of language and Julia Kristeva's concept of 'intertextuality', which is the meaning-productive force of intersubjectivity in reading that produces multiple interpretations. Texts are part of a fabric of life in which both writer and reader participate. The writer is not in control of how the intertextual dynamics of the environment create possibilities for meaning. Moreover, when texts are loosed from their original contexts and read by later interpreters from other cultures, new possibilities for intertextuality (and meaning production) emerge.

Yeo draws three conclusions from his description and analysis of the intersubjective reading process. First, we are all jointly responsible for the meanings the biblical texts bear for us. Second, no culture has a monopoly on textual meaning. Third, judgments about interpretation can be responsible only if they involve cross-cultural awareness and dialogue. Yeo goes on to illustrate culturally-sensitive dialogue by analyzing several interpretations of Romans 7, pointing out for each the role of the interpreter's cultural location in the construction of the meaning of the text. In the course of this examination, Yeo also works out some general criteria for judging between competing interpretations, and models culturally inclusive interpretation by showing how he has adjusted his own Confucian reading of Romans 7 to take account of the concerns of other interpreters reading from other cultural locations.

Yeo concludes his essay by presenting three fundamental considerations that guide his approach to global hermeneutics. One is an eschatological principle or eschatological 'reservation' about our possibilities for knowing the truth. Indeterminacy is a good and welcome reminder of our present epistemological condition in a world that has not yet been redeemed. At the same time, the inadequacy of our knowledge and methods for obtaining knowledge should spur us to cooperation and reliance on one another as a way of overcoming to some degree the limitations of our own social location. The eschatological future beckons us to global hermeneutics at the same time that it cautions us against any 'overly-realized' eschatology in our hermeneutical quest.

A second consideration is 'fiduciary community', which Yeo takes from the *Analects* of Confucius. Fiduciary community means loyalty to one's own tradition and at the same time openness to others. It requires the art of being 'at ease with humanity' by finding common ground, accepting and accommodating differences. Hence, fiduciary community requires a hermeneutic that is neither imperialistic (one cultural interpretation dominating all others) nor relativistic (all interpretations being equally valid and having no claim on each other). Fiduciary community as a middle way calls for cross-cultural dialogue, transformation and humility.

A third consideration is the 'dialectic of values'. The norms that inform our lives as Christians and our interpretations derive from both the Bible and from our culture. These exist in a dialectic through the hermeneutic circle. We interpret scripture through our cultural lens and we interpret culture through the scriptural lens. The cultural lens is a social construction, and the scriptural lens is always an interpretation of scripture. 'Thus, the relation between scripture and culture is a complex dialectic of values in which we are both recipients, socially constructed persons and peoples (as heirs of culture and tradition) and also hermeneutical agents, choosers of meaning, negotiators of value'.

Part Two, 'Case Studies in Indeterminacy and Hermeneutical Judgment', presents essays that offer methodological reflections by focusing on a particular text or topic. I have organized these contributions under the themes of 'Liberation and Oppression', 'Violence' and 'Exclusion and Embrace'.[25]

Carole Fontaine opens Part Two with a study of the Song of Songs. She observes a politics in debates about textual determinacy/indeterminacy, with some dissatisfied interpreters (including some feminists looking for a way out of traditional patriarchy in the biblical text) celebrating the polyvalence of the text and other, more traditional interpreters, including most churches, seeking 'those Ten Words that would always and everywhere be correct when applied faithfully'. Fontaine sees the matter as more complicated. The Bible is open to competing interpretations but not all interpretations are valid: 'some are uniformed, selective or downright manipulative'. Our postmodern awareness of the nature of texts and interpretation teaches us that generally we ought not be claiming to have found the one, correct meaning of the text; nevertheless, some things in the Bible are stubbornly determinate. Sometimes the biblical text is transparent in what it says. Sometimes it is transparent in what it does *not* say, being 'pretty clear about not giving answers, driving us to come to terms with our lack of certainties'.

Fontaine offers a number of what might be called 'tests' for judging which interpretations are worth defending on grounds not simply of exegetical defensibility but moral-theological probity as well. One test is whether we are grasped by the text in its otherness, its power to surprise us and woo us toward a reality different from our own. A second test is whether what one makes of the text is sufficiently capacious, useful or beautiful. 'Ask of your reading: Is it large enough to express the surprises and ambiguity of the interaction of human and divine realities? Is it beautiful enough to capture something of the joyousness of a creator who calls creation very good indeed, creates Leviathan for the fun of it, and yet hears the cries of the enslaved?' Clearly, beauty here is a moral category. It has its counterpart in 'useful ugliness', the moral uglinesses in the text that we need to consider and question (such as slavery, patriarchy, brutality). A third test is the transformative power of the reading. Fontaine finds a fundamental 'thematic plot' in the Bible, which she describes as 'transformation and generation', a tendency of the Bible to go against the grain of the status quo and complacency about our world and ourselves. A good reading is one that offers possibilities for transformation. A fourth test is whether our interpretation reflects the limits of the text's communication, the ambiguity and limits of both the part and the whole, ambiguities and limits

---

25. I have borrowed this last subheading from Miroslav Volf's superb theological study by that name: Mirosalv Volf, *Exclusion and Embrace: A Theological Exploration of Identity, Otherness, and Reconciliation* (Nashville: Abingdon Press, 1996).

that are not simply impediments to understanding but part of the biblical witness, its transparency about not giving answers and not speaking everywhere with one voice. A fourth test (also a strategy) is whether our reading is informed by the perspective of the Radical Other, 'the one who does not and will not *ever* agree with your notion of the text or its meanings?' In Fontaine's interpretation of the Song of Songs, this 'reading Other-ly' means examining the patriarchal institutions of the Beloved's *brothers*, the *watchmen*, and the *stripping of her garment* (Song 5.7) from the perspective of contemporary Muslim women, for whom institutions of this kind are a brutal present reality.

In the Song of Songs, the codes of patriarchy are the least susceptible to alternative, liberative interpretations, while Fontaine's discovery of love as a protest against patriarchy is an unstable meaning based on textual elements that admit other reasonable construals. Consistent with her hermeneutic, she chooses, being honest about the ambiguities of the Song but finding herself morally bound, within the constraints of reasonable interpretation, 'to partner the text into a reading that affirms life and love in all their forms against the tyrannies of domination and social death'.

Robert Tannehill considers how we should evaluate diverse reconstructions of the historical situations in which a text arose and to which it responds. Those reconstructions influence how we interpret the text by shaping our grasp of both the sense and the rhetoric of the text. As reconstructions change, so do interpretations. Nevertheless, rarely is any historical reconstruction so dominant that it rules out all competitors. Even where there is a 'favored position' among scholars, it is usually 'only... marginally better than alternatives'. Hence, we must reckon with multiple plausible reconstructions of the setting of any biblical text.

The susceptibility of texts to different interpretations based on how our historical imaginations link up bits of evidence and fill in gaps means that interpretation can be viewed as a *strategy* aimed at particular goals, and those goals may in turn be (or include) *moral interests*. Tannehill shows how this model of hermeneutical ethics operates in the recent work of Elisabeth Schüssler Fiorenza. In her discussion of 'seven interpretive strategies' for liberative interpretation, Schüssler Fiorenza speaks of a 'hermeneutics of imagination' that 'seeks to generate utopian visions that have not yet been realized and to "dream" a different world of justice and well-being'.[26] Tannehill stresses the implication that by linking the agenda for liberation with interpretive imagination, Schüssler Fiorenza is at least tacitly suggesting that we are morally obligated not so much to seek the one historically correct interpretation, which is rarely if ever demonstrable, as to seek historically defensible interpretations that illumine and further the quest for liberation and social justice.

Tannehill uses as an illustration recent debates about the meaning of 1 Corinthians in its original historical setting. A 'political' interpretation advanced in the work of Richard Horsley and Neil Elliott sees Paul as an advocate of 'liberation from the power of the Roman empire and the social structures that support it'. A 'feminist' interpretation, represented by the work of Schüssler Fiorenza and

---

26. Elisabeth Schüssler Fiorenza, *Rhetoric and Ethic: The Politics of Biblical Studies* (Minneapolis: Fortress Press, 1999), p. 52.

Antoinette Clark Wire, casts Paul as 'acting to limit the freedom of Corinthian women who have begun to claim their new freedom in Christ'. Tannehill judges both interpretations, based as they are on different historical reconstructions, to be plausible and regards both as valuable. They are both plausible because they depend on substantial historical evidence and arguments. They are both valuable because they show how 1 Corinthians can speak (including the effects of its rhetoric) in different social circumstances, including those in our own time that are analogous to scholarly reconstructions of the ancient Corinthian setting. Paul is liberator or oppressor depending on how we reconstruct the identities and actions of the various groups with whom he interacts in the Corinthian church and in the wider social world. This means that where multiple reasonable reconstructions exist, Paul may be both liberator and oppressor.

Our response to this state of interpretive affairs should involve ethical evaluation guided by the double love commandment, which Jesus announces as a hermeneutical norm in Mt. 22.40 and which finds an echo in Paul as well (Rom. 13.8-10; Gal. 5.14). Tannehill urges that, 'following this fundamental scriptural principle, we give scripture force in our lives in ways that consistently foster love of God and neighbor'.[27] Although the double love commandment is no panacea for resolving questions about which plausible interpretation to endorse in any contemporary context, it does provide a substantive guide, one that we must fill out by our own critical sense of what love demands. Following this approach, we can make judgments about appropriate applications of Paul in our own time and place. Our decisions 'will be influenced by our faith commitments, theological understanding, and ethical values'. As we make our judgments, awareness of a variety of genuine possibilities for conceiving the original situation can assist us by helping us discover the way our interpretation of the force of Paul's words must shift as our conception of the situation changes. 'Multiple experiments in historical reconstruction will help us imagine the range of contexts in which Paul's words might be spoken and gain a sense of good and evil consequences, revealing useful applications we might not have thought of, warning us of dangerous applications we might tend to ignore, and suggesting necessary adaptations so that the words of scripture might fulfil their purpose of promoting love of God and neighbor'.

Dennis Olson looks at the story of Moses slaying the Egyptian in Exod. 2.11-15 and asks whether it supports 'the use of violence for the sake of social justice', as some have argued. After surveying the history of the interpretation of the passage, Olson focuses on the story in its immediate context in Exodus 2. Noting that the story of the slaying 'provides no clear verdict on whether Moses' act was right or wrong', Olson looks to the surrounding narrative for clues. But here, too, the interpreter confronts ambiguity. For example, the juxtaposition of the slaying of the Egyptian narrative with Moses' rescue of the Midianite women from hostile shepherds could suggest a contrast, if we assume that Moses acted non-violently to

---

27. See also Robert C. Tannehill, 'Freedom and Responsibility in Scripture Interpretation, with Application to Luke', in Richard P. Thompson and Thomas E. Philips (eds.), *Literary Studies in Luke–Acts* (Macon, GA: Mercer University Press, 1998), pp. 276–78.

save the women. But our only guide is the verb יש״ע (save, rescue, deliver), which often *but not always* refers to violent defense or rescue. Matters are further complicated by the question of how Moses' identity bears on the moral quality of his act. Is he a Hebrew as Exod. 2.11-15 portrays him, or an Egyptian, as the Midianite women describe him (2.19)? When he acts *secretly* as a *Hebrew* to defend his oppressed people by killing an Egyptian, is he a kind of terrorist? Or is he a freedom fighter? The text gives no clear answer.

Olson observes in the wider context that the Exodus narrative presents morally ambiguous identities, situations and boundary crossings, all of which should discourage us from moral simplification and stereotyping (e.g., taking Hebrews as good and Egyptians as bad). We should resist 'filling in the gaps' and resolving the narrative ambiguities if that means reducing the text to a definitive moral lesson. Instead, we must accustom ourselves to being 'not... fully "at home" with any solution or verdict regarding Moses and his use of violence for the sake of social justice', just as Moses is not fully at home anywhere but remains always an alien and dies before he reaches the Promised Land.

Frank Yamada ponders questions of hermeneutical ethics in how we read another violent tale, the story of the rape of Dinah in Genesis 34. This chilling narrative depicts characters who are confronted with challenging moral decisions when Shechem's sexual aggression sets in motion a series of negotiations between Dinah's family and the men of Shechem's city. As readers we are also drawn into the moral tangle of the tale, not only by our natural readerly tendency to choose sides, identifying with one character or group against others, but also by our choices about how to construe characters and their actions. Yamada examines two competing interpretations of the story, one by Meir Sternberg and the other by David Gunn and Danna Nolan Fewell, to show how these interpreters' differing value systems guide their interpretive decisions, leading them to stress certain elements of the text and to downplay or ignore others, to link ambiguous elements into one pattern and not another, and to interpret characters with charity or suspicion. In the end, neither interpretation has defeated the other; neither has tied up every loose end or satisfactorily answered every challenge to its construal of parts or whole. Is each interpretation to be justified or rejected, then, on the basis of a moral system or by some other method that transcends the interpretive limitations that lead here, as so often in biblical studies, to exegetical impasse?

The story of the rape of Dinah demands a response from us. Inevitably that response is at once a moral reaction to the story and a moral assessment of interpretations of the story, since the story always presents itself to us as our own or someone else's reading of it. We may prefer one reading over another on moral grounds. We may be inclined to adjust this or that reading out of moral considerations. Yamada asks whether we can do so 'within a coherent ethical, moral or interpretive system'. Drawing on the anti-foundationalist work of Stanley Fish and Jacques Derrida, Yamada returns a 'no' to this question. Indeterminacy is the condition not only of texts but of us. Interpretive decisions about the rape of Dinah, moral assessments of any resulting interpretation, and any system or theory meant to provide us with our moral orientation – all of these begin with 'undecidability'. Hence, Yamada invites us to consider a non-foundationalist approach to Genesis 34, one that he develops in conversation with Emmanuel Levinas.

One thing is determinate about Genesis 34: Dinah is raped and every subsequent decision about her is made by men. By excluding her voice, the text marks her as other. In Levinas' categories, she becomes for us the presence or 'face' that calls into question 'my spontaneity', the one who cannot be absorbed into me or into a relation to myself. The text, by its marginalization of the voiceless Dinah, produces an experience of the Other, the Other who stands radically outside me and for that reason calls for a kind of responsibility that is not susceptible to systematizing or theorizing. The Other cannot be reduced to something manageable within 'ethics', cannot be solved as a problem for me. But the violence done to Dinah in Genesis 34 creates the question that opens up the true possibility for ethics, for a moral response that begins with undecidability.

Mark Brett reads Genesis 22 by way of two conversations. One is with Jacques Derrida and Søren Kirkegaard. The other is with modern biblical scholarship, focusing specifically on his own prior work on Genesis and that of Christopher Heard. The two dialogues intersect at the point where Brett's and Heard's debate about the question of election and ethnocentrism in Genesis touches Derrida's claim that Genesis 22 reveals the rupture in ethics that is present in every loyalty. Sacrifice, says Derrida, 'is the most common event in the world'.[28] By choosing or accepting any set of specific responsibilities, simply by giving our time to a specific profession, we sacrifice and betray our duties to the billions of our fellow human beings who also have claims on us. Local duties to family, nation, etc. always violate universal obligations, the moral duty to the 'other others'. And vice versa. Thus, 'everyone is being sacrificed to everyone else in this land of Moriah that is our habitat every second of every day'.[29]

Kirkegaard and Derrida read Genesis 22 in isolation from the rest of Genesis. Brett observes that when we read Genesis 22 in its wider literary context we discover that it is possible to interpret Abraham's story in either of two opposing ways. If we follow Christopher Heard's exegetically-plausible and sociologically-sensitive reading,[30] we will see the final form of Genesis as the product of editors working during the Persian period who redacted the Abraham stories so as to *dis*-elect foreigners (spiritually and economically), specifically to justify dispossession of foreigners in the land, including families that are the product of intermarriage with non-Israelites. On this reading, Isaac is elect; Ishmael stands for all the rejected 'others'. But an equally cogent interpretation, also sensitive to socio-historical setting and the final literary shape of the text, finds clues that tend in the opposite direction, suggesting that the editors have labored to undermine ethnocentric/

---

28. Jacques Derrida, *The Gift of Death* (trans. D. Willis; Chicago: University of Chicago Press, 1995), p. 69 (as quoted by Brett).

29. Derrida, *The Gift of Death*, p. 69 (as quoted by Brett).

30. R. Christopher Heard, *Dynamics of Diselection: Ambiguity in Genesis 12–36 and Ethnic Boundaries in Post-Exilic Judah* (Semeia Studies, 39; Atlanta: Society of Biblical Literature, 2001).

exclusivistic ideology and to invite readers to embrace the tension between loyalties to one's own (the Isaacs) and obligation to all the 'other others' (the Ishmaels).[31]

Brett opts for the second of these two interpretations, justifying his choice by referring to ethical concerns and commitments he has embraced in and for his own local social context. 'In the current political climate in Australia, in which asylum seekers from Muslim countries are subject to paranoid strategies of exclusion, there are especially good reasons not to see Ishmael as subject to divine dis-election... Given the range of possible interpretations that are equally defensible in cognitive terms, I have chosen a reading of Genesis that provides hermeneutical possibilities in the present'. Nevertheless, this interpretive choice, which depends on the judgment that Genesis presents us with something like Derrida's paradox of sacrifice, is necessarily subject to that very paradox. Brett's astute insight is that even when we choose an interpretation for the sake of 'the other', our reading remains 'local', caught in the tension between the claims of those 'others' to whom we have chosen to be loyal and all the countless other others. No reading escapes the land of Moriah, even when it attempts to break the boundaries of ethnocentrism.

Jeffrey Staley writes on apocalyptic as a hermeneutic. Apocalyptic thinking is dualistic, he observes, leaving no room for continuums, in-betweens, grays, ambiguities, indeterminacies of any sort. This dualistic mode of categorization is a pernicious hermeneutic, distorting reality by reducing it artificially to simple opposites and, at least in the extreme, demonizing those who do not share its view. Staley's moral assessment of apocalyptic dualism leads him to regard 'indeterminacy' as a good thing insofar as it undermines the dualistic ideology of apocalyptic. Therefore, speaking for himself and others who find apocalyptic binarism morally repugnant but embrace the Bible as a canonical text, Staley asks whether it is possible to reread biblical apocalyptic as indeterminate or, in the alternative, whether possibilities for freedom from apocalyptic dualism reside not in reinterpreting biblical apocalyptic but in reinterpreting the concept of 'canon'. Is the authority of the Bible a determinate concept, confronting the believer with the same kind of dualistic choice that apocalyptic demands – accept and submit or reject and make oneself an enemy (of the canon? of God?)? Can the Christian befriend biblical apocalyptic as scripture without submitting to its dualistic hermeneutic?

Staley sees the question of apocalyptic dualism as especially urgent because apocalyptic replicates itself in contemporary settings of all different sorts and is not a habit of sectarians alone. Apocalyptic dualism permeates the thinking of not only the radical Christian Right but also mainstream science fiction films and the Left-leaning scholarship typified by the Jesus Seminar. All three of these otherwise 'very different contemporary responses to ancient biblical apocalyptic have adopted its dualistic perspective on the world'. Staley devotes much of his essay to substantiating this claim, conducting us on an engaging tour of apocalyptic thinking in our time and challenging us to consider whether our own habits of thought and ways of reading the Bible as scripture are dualistic.

---

31. Brett has advanced this interpretation in a previous study, *Genesis: Procreation and the Politics of Identity* (Old Testament Readings; London: Routledge, 2000).

Concluding Observations

'We all seek the center that will allow the senses to rest', Frank Kermode remarks, 'at any rate for one interpreter, at any rate for one moment'.[32] In *The Genesis of Secrecy*, from which these words come, Kermode describes interpretation as bound for disappointment after each fleeting luminescence of closure, and he doubts that many of us are ready to embrace indeterminacy by refusing the quest for the center and rest. Nevertheless, anyone who seeks that repose but grants with Kermode that it can only be fleeting is obligated to ask not simply whether this state of affairs is tolerable but what our responsibility is to the text, to ourselves and to others. Particularly when it comes to scripture, we must ask what moral and theological obligations we have before God and neighbor in responding to indeterminacy and the conflict of interpretations. Much of *The Genesis of Secrecy* treats brilliantly of Gospel texts, above all the Gospel of Mark in which discipleship, *following Jesus*, is a central theme. Yet, Kermode suggests, the text (or interpretation) is an 'unfollowable world', just like the world we live in.[33] Does indeterminacy preclude discipleship? The authors of the present volume see our honest and responsible engagement with indeterminacy, with the semantic openness of text and interpretation, as part of the call of discipleship.

I have no intention of trying to synthesize the insights of the contributors, much less to play them off against each other. Instead I offer a few closing observations about the essays in connection with Kermode's perception that we invariably seek some kind of interpretive closure even when we know there is no such thing. A first observation is Olson's point that sometimes it may be important to keep the senses open so that the text can do its proper work, leading us away from neat moral solutions and encouraging us to learn how to be ill at ease in a moral world where the perception of perspicuity in the choices we face is often the result of misleading oversimplication. Moreover, Staley challenges us to seek with him a way out of the tendency to 'binarism', whether of the Left or of the Right (and I'm sure also of the middle), that makes us read apocalyptically according to the logic that every text and every interpreter we meet must be identified as friend or foe and dealt with accordingly.

It is also possible to keep the senses open as a matter of acknowledging that interpretations of the same text can be diverse but not contradictory, incompatible but equally reasonable or different but complementary. One can hold to this view and do one's part to defend and preserve the wide range of interpretations (in a commentary of the sort Patte envisions), yet at the same time opt for the interpretation that we think best – best for the here and now or best in some larger sense. No doubt we all find it difficult to interpret without making sure that what

---

32. Frank Kermode, *The Genesis of Secrecy: On the Interpretation of Narrative* (Cambridge, MA: Harvard University Press, 1979), p. 72.

33. Kermode, *The Genesis of Secrecy*, pp. 125–45.

we value above all about our own lives is not put at risk by our interpretations. But interpretive discipleship also calls for choosing interpretations with the interests of our neighbors in mind, a concern of all of the essayists. Tannehill and I stress the importance of the double love commandment in its Matthean form as a hermeneutical norm. Brett, Fontaine, Yamada and Staley press our hermeneutical obligation to the 'other'. Yet even when guided by these laudable aims, it is important that we preserve the dialectic between the sense we choose and the other possibilities of the text. As Brett points out, when we opt hermeneutically for the sake of 'the other' in our midst, we invariably choose against the 'other others'. In life and in interpretation, closure is sacrifice because we choose to devote our time, resources *and our interpretations* to one set of causes and not the innumerable others that could rightfully claim us. We must choose if we are to offer anything. Part of choosing responsibly is to acknowledge and ponder the sacrifices inherent in our choices.

We bring the sense to rest in order to preach, to champion a particular textual possibility, to work up theologically the meanings that engage us and fit our sense of the larger pattern of God's revelation in Christ. We do so often as 'one interpreter... for one moment', knowing that in a different place and time we would probably bring the senses of the text to rest at a different 'center' and recognizing that 'center' itself is a relative term in a world where centers are social constructions and one of the tasks of hermeneutics today is to 'decenter' biblical interpretation. The text is supposed to come to rest not in anticipation or imitation of the sort of final rest that eschatological resolution promises but contingently and locally, as Adam, Patte and Yeo emphasize. Not only that, interpretation does not have to be the solitary enterprise that Kermode imagines. It probably does little good beyond fleeting aesthetic and intellectual satisfaction when the senses of a biblical text come to rest only for one interpreter, for one moment, since the Bible as the church's book functions effectively only in shared interpretations that persist long enough to shape the identity and practice of a Christian community. So the church wisely seeks to settle on interpretations that nurture the community, foster love of God and neighbor, and engender courageous and charitable responsiveness to insiders and outsiders.

How we treat others, whether insiders or outsiders, includes how we treat one another as interpreters and what we do with each others' interpretations. Adam comments that integral hermeneutics fosters interpretive attitudes that inevitably require one to insinuate or boldly charge that advocates of competing interpretations are 'either ignorant, less intelligent, misguided, perverse or insane'. It is important to stress that this is a comment on the logic of integral hermeneutics, not the character of those who practice it, many of whom are gracious and gentle. Nevertheless, the contrast with differential hermeneutics is important because it has to do not only with etiquette (which should not be underappreciated) but also with how we value and make use of the interpretations of others. Differential hermeneutics may at times require us to choose between interpretations but even then to value the interpretation of the other in which the voice of God may also be heard, whether in another time and place or in another way. I am reminded here of the rabbinic spirit exemplified in the following story of a dispute between the House of Hillel and the House of Shammai about a point of law. When no agreement could be reached, a voice spoke from heaven declaring that the law is according to Hillel but 'both are the words of the living God'.[34]

---

34.   *'Erub.* 13b. *The Babylonian Talmud, Seder Mo'Ed in Four Volumes,* II (English translation under the editorship of I. Epstein; London: Soncino Press, 1938), pp. 85–86.

Part I

REFLECTIONS ON INDETERMINACY AND HERMENEUTICAL JUDGMENT

Integral and Differential Hermeneutics[1]

A.K.M. Adam, Seabury-Western Theological Seminary, Illinois, USA

There are at least two leading questions in the study of hermeneutics and the ethics of interpretation. The first and more familiar is 'How are we to understand texts?' The second is 'How shall we know whose interpretation is right (or 'true' or 'legitimate')?' In the course of this essay, I will describe this first approach as 'integral' hermeneutics. The second, less familiar question challenges us to explain why the most knowledgeable and wisest interpreters so often disagree about what a text means. This approach I will characterize and advocate under the name 'differential' hermeneutics.

Differential hermeneutics receives less vigorous attention in debates over meaning and interpretation. Essays in hermeneutics rarely address interpretive difference at all, and those that broach the topic typically elide the distinction between interpretive *difference* and interpretive *error*. If, by contrast, we were to make the study of interpretive difference a more prominent focus of hermeneutical discussion, we would be in a better position to characterize and weigh the differences among interpreters. Then we might acclimate ourselves to a hermeneutical ecology in which difference, far from implying error on one or another part, constitutes a positive contribution toward a fuller understanding of textuality and (in the sphere of biblical interpretation) revelation. For these and other reasons, interpreters who care particularly about the convergence of ethics and interpretation ought to think twice before simply adopting a hermeneutic of 'correctness' or 'legitimacy'. A hermeneutic that focuses on interpretive difference offers strengths that avail mightily to help interpreters make sense not only of the texts they study but also of the ways those texts inhabit and inform ethical and theological deliberation.

In the summaries of integral and differential hermeneutics that follow, I synthesize a variety of positions on each side. By synthesizing, I try in brief scope to articulate and interweave the leading characteristics of each position, but this allows the possibility, perhaps the likelihood, that my synthesis misrepresents the thought of the particular authors whom the summary covers. Readers should not for a moment mistake a heuristic overview for a detailed analysis of a particular scholar's thought. Still less should they suppose that if I identify weaknesses in a

1. This essay owes much to conversations with principals in the discussion on which it reports, especially Stephen Fowl, Francis Watson and Kevin Vanhoozer. As the essay took shape, Thomas Matrullo, Philip Cubeta, David Weinberger, Trevor Bechtel and Margaret Adam teased, probed, challenged, encouraged and refined the ideas that I propose here, and I heartily thank them all.

particular (summarized) approach, then each of the scholars whose work I summarize partakes equally in that weakness. Those interested in further examining these issues should turn to the specific works of the authors in question. I am a thoroughly interested party in the arguments over the merits of integral and differential hermeneutics. I have devoted considerable energy to articulating the case for differential hermeneutics and neither could nor would want to write an objective essay on the topic. This essay endeavors to sketch the terrain of the disagreement between integral and differential hermeneutics and to propose evaluations of the strengths and weaknesses of these two positions in the field in order to make clear the rationale for a differential hermeneutic.

The first of these lines of investigation – integral hermeneutics' search for a legitimate path to correct interpretation – has motivated most studies of hermeneutics. A moment's reflection reveals the reason that such studies often display a fervor that far outweighs the extent of their contribution to the debate over hermeneutics, a debate whose broad outlines have remained largely constant for decades. Once a scholar has figured out how to reach true understandings, he or she naturally feels disinclined to depart from that approach or even to entertain seriously the possibility of changing direction. Such a scholar may see colleagues who hesitate to adopt his or her new-found (or newly-reaffirmed) 'true' approach as recalcitrants who threaten the very structure of knowledge, the academy, even the church's teaching. In order to stave off such threats, scholars have long sought the definitive answer to the urgent question of how to interpret texts correctly. They have offered accounts of insight, understanding, empathy, intention and various other features of legitimate hermeneutics. I call this search that emphasizes correct interpretation 'integral' hermeneutics because it poses for itself (and for the domain of all meaning, over which it usually claims dominion) the task of articulating the positive characteristics of unitary interpretive truth.

Integral hermeneutics grounds its claim to pre-eminence on a number of premises. Some theories of integral hermeneutics posit a unique divinatory *sympathy* or *understanding* or *meaning* at which the interpreter must aim in order to qualify as methodologically legitimate. Some theorists, however, make an explicitly ethical defense of integral hermeneutics. This case – enunciated and elaborated by E.D. Hirsch[2] – maintains that textual interpretation by its very nature owes an ethical debt to the author's compositional intent. Any interpretive deviation from attention to the author's intent may count as a more or less valuable significance of the text[3]; we do the author an injustice, however, if we say that the text in question means anything other than what the author intended. Proponents of this interpretive ethic argue that readers should grant primary authority to interpretation that coheres with the author's intent as it took specific shape in the composition of the text (whether

---

2.   E.D. Hirsch, *Validity in Interpretation* (New Haven, CT: Yale University Press, 1967); 'Three Dimensions of Hermeneutics', in *The Aims of Interpretation* (Chicago and London: University of Chicago Press, 1976).

3.   Hirsch distinguishes the (original) verbal 'meaning' of the text, as a property of the text, from the later 'significances' the text can acquire in new contexts, significances that are valid only insofar as they are based on and cohere with the verbal meaning.

that author be construed as a human wordsmith or the Spirit that gives illumination and provocation to write). Because an author intended that we construe words in a single way, we as interpreters stand under an obligation to accede to the author's intent. Unless we acknowledge the determinative role of the author's compositional intent, we lack the criteria for distinguishing genuine meaning from counterfeit, exegesis from eisegesis, true divine teaching from hermeneutical legerdemain.

The case for integral hermeneutics has developed into a finely-nuanced complex of integrated arguments. While E.D. Hirsch presented the foundational work for this position in his studies in literary and philosophical hermeneutics, Anthony Thiselton,[4] Francis Watson[5] and Kevin Vanhoozer[6] stand as pre-eminent mediators of this approach to the field of biblical interpretation. The cogency of their arguments has built upon a more generally-held intuition that texts simply mean single things. They have reinforced this beginning with sophisticated philosophical, theological and ethical arguments on behalf of the premise that texts mean one thing, that which the text's author intended to mean. Their work has staked out and refined the integralist approach, responding thoughtfully to any serious challenge to their enterprise. When opponents argue, for instance, that 'the author's intention' is unsuitable as a criterion for assessing interpretations – perhaps it is unavailable or insufficiently distinct – the practitioners of integral hermeneutics respond by developing an account of their field that takes into consideration and overcomes their critics' objections by refining their conception of 'intentionality' or defining more precisely their criteria of legitimate interpretation. Their conception of *how* to attain correct interpretation has shifted in response to challenges, but their impulse to attain the proper approach remains undeflected.

The philosophical case for integral hermeneutics proposes that 'meaning' is a property of things called 'texts', so that 'meaningless text' is a contradiction in terms. A text has a meaning built-in; that meaning is the effect of the author's intentionality in composing the text. A text's meaning need not be obvious, although it can be. An octagonal red placard with the white letters 'S–T–O–P' almost surely demands that approaching vehicles halt their forward motion at that point. But the meaning of a text such as Romans 7 has defied centuries of efforts to make it unambiguously clear. Nevertheless, Romans 7 does have a meaning – interpreters simply haven't yet arrived at a shared determination of that meaning with a degree of certainty that matches their certainty that octagonal red road signs require automobiles to stop. The text does not lack meaning, but interpreters lack agreement about what the meaning is.

4.   Anthony C. Thiselton, *New Horizons in Hermeneutics: The Theory and Practice of Transforming Biblical Reading* (London: HarperCollins, 1992; Grand Rapids: Zondervan, 1992).

5.   Francis Watson, *Text, Church, and World: Biblical Interpretation in Theological Perspective* (Grand Rapids: Eerdmans, 1994; Edinburgh: T. & T. Clark, 1994); Francis Watson, *Text and Truth: Redefining Biblical Theology* (Grand Rapids: Eerdmans, 1997; Edinburgh: T. & T. Clark, 1997).

6.   Kevin J. Vanhoozer, *Is There a Meaning in This Text? The Bible, the Reader, and the Morality of Biblical Knowledge* (Leicester, England: Apollos, 1998; Grand Rapids: Zondervan, 1998); Kevin J. Vanhoozer, 'Body Piercing, the Natural Sense, and the Task of Theological Interpretation: A Hermeneutical Homily on John 19.34', *ExAu*, 16 (2000), pp. 1–29.

According to these premises, a text's meaning subsists even though hidden, just as the back of a refrigerator continues to exist when no one observes it, or as the earthward side of a house's foundation continues to exist even when no one observes it (and when no one can state with certainty how far below the visible surface that earthward side lies or what it looks like). The presence of a cement floor in my basement provides sufficient evidence for me to infer the existence of its opposite side; the presence of a text in my hand provides sufficient evidence for me to infer the existence of its meaning. The intentional dimension of the text is its meaning, and when a text's meaning remains concealed, interpreters deploy a variety of devices to ascertain that hidden meaning.

The interpreter bears an ethical obligation to respect the authorial intention of the text because the meaning resides there. An interpreter who treats the text as though it meant something other than its authorial intent distorts the truth about the text. Such interpretations are unjust to the author (who imbued the text with its meaning) and are capriciously inconsistent with the stability we expect of textual meaning in our everyday lives. A meaning inherent in texts demands our interpretive deference.

Moreover, a text exemplifies a type of communicative action: a meaningful action between an author and an auditor by means of a particular expression. The essence of communication rests on the premise that something controllable and specific is being conveyed from author to audience. If an interpreter wilfully ignores the author's communicative intent (while relying on their own readers to acknowledge *their* communicative intent), that interpreter transgresses against the author and the reader both. Interpreters who flout the integrity of communicative action saw away the ethical limb on which they perch and undermine the deeply-held human covenant that makes effective communication possible. An ethics of communicative action obligates all participants in the social bonds that permit communication with the necessity of respecting an author's communicative intent.

The tight integration that binds together participants in the communicative act and the text/meaning heightens the importance of the ethical question, 'How then ought we interpret texts?' From the perspective of integral hermeneutics, the clear answer is that we should interpret texts in a way that expresses the meaning that constitutes the intentional dimension of the text as the author composed it. Likewise, we ought to interpret texts within the context of the author-text-audience configurations that inform them. To the extent that we treat texts (correctly, on this account) as communicative acts, we should observe the authorial and audience-oriented constraints at work on communication in order to find the perspective that correctly illuminates the meaning subsistent in the text, that connects the author and the audience.

Thus, the ethical case for integral hermeneutics rests to a great extent upon exegetical analyses of the natures of 'text' and 'communication'. The advocates of this position find that neither the term 'text' nor the notion of 'communication' can sustain the possibility that texts not possess the property of 'having a meaning'. If texts lack this property, we lack the leverage necessary to account for the innumerable messages that humanity successfully composes and effectively

responds to from moment to moment. The vast preponderance of clarity in
communication testifies to the soundness of supposing that meaning subsists,
somehow, in textuality.

The case for integral hermeneutics has dominated discussions of biblical hermeneutics in part because of this sophisticated reasoning that backs it up, but also in
part because it tends to confirm a colloquial tendency to assume what should be
demonstrated in this sort of argument. Common experience seems to confirm the
premise that texts mean a single thing and that recipients of texts can usually
determine that meaning with a high degree of confidence. So powerful is this
intuition that detractors of integral hermeneutics have been reproached for performative contradiction if they endeavor to correct misapprehensions about their
work. If an interpreter suggests that human communication admits of various
interpretations but suggests that another critic has *mis*understood her work, she
frequently encounters the charge that her own premise should allow others to
interpret her work as they choose ('Now you're trying to say that there's only one
correct way to understand your position!'). Some indeed have endured the less
imaginative tactic of being told, 'You have broccoli between your teeth', by a sly
boots who thinks that one's impulse to check one's reflection in a mirror for stray
vegetable matter 'proves' that utterances have meanings as their property.

The debate over interpretation thus falls out with opponents to integral hermeneutics ostensibly holding up as a positive goal just exactly the interpretive
wilderness that defenders of integral hermeneutics warn against. The principal
counterposition to integral hermeneutics has typically been one or another mode of
pluralism. While 'pluralism' itself may stand for many different things, practitioners of integral hermeneutics have often represented pluralists as advocating
divergence in interpretation as a positive value. A pluralist, on this account, would
suppose that the more different interpretations one could devise, the better for all
concerned. Moreover, a pluralist would have no particular ground on which to
object to alleged misconstruals of his work.

Theorists of integral hermeneutics have (rightly) pointed out many philosophical, theological and practical weaknesses of the pluralist case for meaning. Pluralism as a positive program for interpretation devolves rapidly into an uninteresting
exercise in improbable, unsatisfying fancy. As long as pluralism (or 'relativism')
has stood as the only distinguishable alternative to integral hermeneutics, the
integral program in hermeneutics has held center stage, especially with regard to
interpretation of the Bible.

Recently, however, certain scholars have tried to outline a basis for a hermeneutics that begins from the ineluctable fact of interpretive difference. If, as a moment's
perusal of the most respected journals of biblical scholarship will attest, the wisest
and most careful interpreters have not been able to attain unanimity in ascertaining
the meanings of the texts they examine, perhaps hermeneutics went wrong in
supposing that 'meaning' should be constrained to singularity, no matter how
painstakingly defined or remotely deferred. Whereas recent interpretive discourses
wrestle and bite to attain and hold pre-eminence over other approaches, in a former
age – an era that modern scholars have dismissed as 'pre-critical' – plurality in

interpretation constituted a tolerable condition, indeed a positive dispensation from God. Augustine's *On Christian Doctrine* represents the sterling example of a theological celebration of plurality in interpretation (plurality that did not diminish the scriptures' testimony to the One God of love and grace). Likewise, the varying traditions of spiritual exegesis affirm that readers might find an inexhaustible plenitude of quite legitimate interpretations of scripture. When early Christian teachers criticize erroneous interpretations – as in Irenaeus famously saying that the Gnostics take the mosaic of a king and rearrange the pieces to form the picture of a dog – the argument doesn't insist on a single text-immanent meaning but relies on what we might call a physiognomy of legitimate interpretation. Those interpretations of scripture that point toward the Jesus whom the church recognizes in scripture, that depict the subject of the mosaic as a king, in other words, would not fall under Irenaeus' anathema. The problem for Irenaeus is with interpretations that misrepresent Jesus, not with a general plurality in interpretation.

Today's theorists of interpretative difference follow the early church in not simply creating plurality as a good in and of itself. Instead, they have begun putting together a way of deliberating about hermeneutics that offers an explanation for interpretive variety and complexes of criteria for evaluating better and worse interpretations. This hermeneutics of difference does not resolve every interpretive problem but offers ample advantages that may attract interpreters dissatisfied with both pluralistic and integral hermeneutics. A differential hermeneutic permits practitioners to see in interpretive variety a sign of the variety in human imagination (in establishing historical facts as well as in drawing theological inferences), to account positively for difference among interpreters, to envision the practice of biblical interpretation less as a contest of experts and more as the shared effort of Christian communities, and at the same time to provide clearer, more specific and more modest criteria for correctness and legitimacy in interpretation.

The differential riposte to integral hermeneutics' ethical claim shifts attention away from interpreters' ethical obligation to the author and toward their ethical obligation to their readers and one another. Instead of supposing that the nature of textuality involves a hermeneutical trinity of author, text and reader, such that all readers must strive to articulate an author's intentional meaning in the text, practitioners of differential hermeneutics observe that the act of offering an interpretation involves not only the author and the text but also one's interpretive colleagues and the audience of the interpretation. Hence, interpreters must devise interpretations that are accountable not only to text and author but also to rival interpreters and audiences. Moreover, the divided churches have sought justification for their sides of various ecclesiastical disputes by appealing to scripture; yet this tactic loses much of its force if one allows that scripture may also offer support for the opposite party's opinion. The integral-hermeneutic quest for single textual meaning feeds on, and in turn itself feeds, theological conflicts. Finally, integral hermeneutics benefits from its advocates having made their premises so familiar that any alternative approach to interpretation must either justify itself on terms indigenous to integral hermeneutics (terms that strongly favor the outlook that generates them) or suffer the dubiety that accompanies the impression that the alternative hermeneutic neglects apparently necessary aspects of hermeneutical reasoning. Familiarity with a dominant point of view breeds contempt for alternative ways of considering an issue.

Integral hermeneutics derives further strength from theological buttresses to its philosophical ramparts. Inasmuch as God is One and God's will cannot err or equivocate ('For God is not a God of confusion but of peace', as the Apostle said in the Revised Standard Version), so the written communication of God's word must not permit ambiguity in expression or plurality in interpretation. God's will is perfectly expressed in the words of scripture. Interpreters, therefore, stand under the obligation to seek and promulgate that singular divine intent. Likewise, the communicative triad of Author, Text, and Reader matches the theological trinity of Father, Son, and Spirit. Finally, many scholars identify the necessity of 'interpretation' with the fall from grace in Eden. The prelapsarian humans enjoyed unambiguous, 'uninterpreted' converse with one another and with God. Since interpretation manifests itself as a consequence of sinful rebellion, faithful readers should strive for the true meaning as they strive to resist sin. The congruence of God's unitary purpose and triune identity with the text's (alleged) singular meaning and triadic appropriation, along with the apparent sinfulness of multiplicity in interpretation, reinforces the integral-hermeneutic case for singularity in meaning and for the obligation to aim for that meaning in our encounter with texts.[7]

All these reasons combine to give integral hermeneutics the high ground in debates over interpretation. The alternative case for differential hermeneutics rests on reasoning every bit as sophisticated as that for integral hermeneutics, but the differential side lacks the support of conventional wisdom and ecclesiastical approval. Its force depends on readers stepping outside what they have taken for granted about hermeneutics and considering the hermeneutical problem differently from the start. But familiarity does not by itself constitute an argument in support of integral hermeneutics. The unfamiliarity of alternative approaches to hermeneutics should not count against the case their proponents argue.

A practitioner of differential hermeneutics does not begin by wondering what the correct interpretive method (or 'approach' or 'perspective') might be or even by assuming that the question itself makes sense. Differential hermeneutics arises from the observation that people interpret constantly and interpret so successfully that they manage extremely complex lives in indifferent (or even hostile) social environments. On the whole, people seem remarkably skillful at interpretation. The proponents of integral hermeneutics should welcome this aptitude; it tends to underscore the weight of their argument from communicative action. But at this point the differential interpreter raises the frustrating question, 'Why do the most erudite, pious, intelligent and expert interpreters of scripture so rarely agree with one another?'

---

7.   My summary of the trinitarian case for integral hermeneutics grossly oversimplifies – but does not, I think, parody – Kevin Vanhoozer's arguments (*Is There a Meaning in This Text?*, pp. 455–57).

Just this ubiquity of interpretive difference motivates a heterogenous scattering of scholars – Daniel Patte,[8] Charles Cosgrove,[9] James K.A. Smith,[10] Stephen Fowl,[11] and myself,[12] perhaps the most recent work of Elisabeth Schüssler Fiorenza as well,[13] among others[14] – to press ethical questions that concern not just the author and the text alone. Instead, the differential interpreters ask how we can account for the differences among rivals' interpretations, especially when those interpreters show all the signs of extraordinary intelligence, wide and deep acquaintance with relevant historical and literary context, and even genuine reverence for the subjects of the texts in question.

Consider more closely this blind spot of integral hermeneutics. When Hans Dieter Betz,[15] Donald Carson,[16] and Amy-Jill Levine[17] interpret the Sermon on the

8. Daniel Patte, *Ethics of Biblical Interpretation: A Reevaluation* (Louisville, KY: Westminster/John Knox Press, 1995); Daniel Patte, *Discipleship according to the Sermon on the Mount: Four Legitimate Readings, Four Plausible Views of Discipleship, and Their Relative Values* (Valley Forge, PA: Trinity Press International, 1996).

9. Charles H. Cosgrove, *Elusive Israel: The Puzzle of Election in Romans* (Louisville, KY: Westminster/John Knox Press, 1997); Charles H. Cosgrove, *Appealing to Scripture in Moral Debate: Five Hermeneutical Rules* (Grand Rapids: Eerdmans, 2002), pp. 154–80.

10. James K.A. Smith, *The Fall of Interpretation: Philosophical Foundations for a Creational Hermeneutic* (Downers Grove, IL: InterVarsity Press, 2000).

11. Stephen Fowl, *Engaging Scripture: A Model for Theological Interpretation* (Oxford: Basil Blackwell, 1999); Stephen Fowl and Gregory L. Jones, *Reading in Communion: Scripture and Ethics in the Christian Life* (Grand Rapids: Eerdmans, 1991).

12. A.K.M. Adam, 'The Future of Our Allusions', *Society of Biblical Literature Seminar Papers*, 31 (1992), pp. 5–13; A.K.M. Adam, *Making Sense of New Testament Theology: "Modern" Problems and Prospects* (Studies in American Biblical Hermeneutics, 11; Macon, GA: Mercer University Press, 1995); A.K.M. Adam, 'The Sign of Jonah: A Fish-Eye View', *Semeia*, 51 (1990), pp. 177–91; A.K.M. Adam, 'Twisting to Destruction: A Memorandum on the Ethics of Interpretation', *Perspectives in Religious Studies*, 23 (1996), pp. 215–22; A.K.M. Adam, *What Is Postmodern Biblical Criticism?* (Minneapolis: Fortress Press, 1995).

13. Elisabeth Schüssler Fiorenza, 'The Ethics of Biblical Interpretation: Decentering Biblical Scholarship', *JBL*, 107 (1988), pp. 3–17; Elisabeth Schüssler Fiorenza, *Rhetoric and Ethic: The Politics of Biblical Studies* (Minneapolis: Fortress Press, 1999).

14. Two others are Trevor Bechtel, 'How to Eat Your Bible: Performance and Understanding for Mennonites', *Conrad Grebel Review* (forthcoming) and Margaret B. Adam, 'This Is My Story, This Is My Song... A Feminist Claim on Scripture, Ideology, and Interpretation', in Harold C. Washington, Susan Lochrie Graham and Pamela Thimmes (eds.), *Escaping Eden* (Sheffield: Sheffield Academic Press, 1998), pp. 218–32.

15. Hans Dieter Betz, *The Sermon on the Mount: A Commentary on the Sermon on the Mount, including the Sermon on the Plain (Matthew 5.3–7.27 and Luke 6.20-49)* (Hermeneia; Minneapolis: Augsburg Fortress Press, 1995).

16. Donald A. Carson, *The Sermon on the Mount: An Evangelical Exposition of Matthew 5–7* (Grand Rapids: Baker Book House, 1978); Donald A. Carson, *Jesus' Sermon on the Mount and His Confrontation with the World: An Exposition of Matthew 5–10* (Toronto and Grand Rapids: Global Christian Publishers, 1999).

17. Amy-Jill Levine, 'Matthean Jesus, Biblical Law, and Hemorrhaging Woman', in D.R. Bauer and M.A. Powell (eds.), *Treasures Old and New: Recent Contributions to Matthean Studies* (Symposium Series, 1; Atlanta: Scholars Press, 1996), pp. 379–97; Amy-Jill Levine, 'Anti-Judaism and the Gospel of Matthew', in William R. Farmer (ed.), *Anti-Judaism and the Gospels* (Valley

Mount, they bring to bear all the capacities of spirit and intellect to which a biblical interpreter might aspire. Their interpretations of that text, however, diverge in numerous important ways. By the theory of integral hermeneutics, only one of them has truly interpreted the Sermon; the other two propound more or less gravely erroneous interpretations (unless all three have gone astray!). This state of affairs constitutes a troubling ramification for integral hermeneutics, since we who have not attained to the frontmost ranks of biblical interpretation must try to discern which of these three interpreters offers the soundest interpretation. Moreover, we do so without the full extent of the knowledge that each of these interpretive leaders brings to bear (else we would stand with them at the cutting edge). We must decide which of the three has correctly interpreted Matthew's Gospel, but we lack the scholarly standing requisite to adjudicate the question. If even these three leading scholars disagree, we would need to know more than they do in order to make an authoritative decision for or against their positions. But under the circumstances we do not know even as much as they do, still less do we possess the deeper understanding that would enable us to determine on which scholar we should rely.

More troubling still, a proponent of integral hermeneutics can in the end offer no respectful account of why anyone would disagree with him or her. The most honorable explicit explanation of difference under the integral approach runs more or less as follows: 'She doesn't understand the text (or the history or the culture or the background influences) as well as I do'. We mask such pretensions with claims such as 'He does not take full account of' or 'He doesn't show acquaintance with' or 'He doesn't consider' or 'She accords inappropriate weight to this and insufficient attention to that'. But these all amount to claiming that *I* have the soundest insight into this text and all *others* have fallen short in one way or another.

Sometimes interpreters offer less charitable explanations of interpretive difference. We sometimes describe others' divergence from our conclusions to their succumbing to inappropriate influences. They are fundamentalists or radical skeptics or feminists or patriarchs or racists or 'politically correct' or traditionalists or victims of brainwashing by the dominant cultural environment. (Thanks be to God that 'we', or perhaps just 'I', have escaped such pernicious influences!) Sometimes we chalk up divergence to ignorance or moral weakness (a desire for publicity or approval, let us say, or financial greed, or the hunger for a biblical rationale for indulging other unspiritual appetites). Explanations such as these fit the assumptions of integral hermeneutics perfectly but leave other pivotal questions unanswered. How did one scholar avoid the subtle pitfalls that so confound others? Does a reader who is interpreting under the influence of something bad know that he or she is beclouded and, if not, how can we be sure that interpreters who vigorously proclaim their innocence of ideological determination are not simply unconscious of the deeper influences bearing down on them?

Forge, PA: Trinity Press International, 1999), pp. 9–36; Amy-Jill Levine, 'Matthew's Advice to a Divided Readership', in David E. Aune (ed.), *The Gospel of Matthew in Current Study: Studies in Memory of William G. Thompson, S.J.* (Grand Rapids: Eerdmans, 2001), pp. 22–41.

At the end of a debate conducted under the auspices of integral hermeneutics, however, one is left only with the alternatives of saying that one's rival is either ignorant, less intelligent, misguided, perverse or insane. If she knew the relevant factors as well as the correct interpreter – me, or you – and if she understood the proper weight to ascribe to each bit of evidence, she, too, would assent to our interpretation. At the most polite, one can decline to speculate as to why one's rival disagrees; in more candid moments, practitioners allow that their interlocutors simply work with their vision narrowed by commitments that the (correct) interpreter doesn't hold. Yet without a strong account of how it is that wise, learned interpreters come to disagree with one another, a theory of how *correctly* to understand a text risks serving flatly as a justification for one interpretive party's efforts to shout louder than all others. Each participant in an interpretive disagreement arrives at the point of dissent by way of confidence that he or she has pursued the correct understanding with a legitimate method. That which an advocate of integral hermeneutics proposes as a diligent effort to ascertain the true meaning of the text, a supporter of differential hermeneutics may see as a mystified expression of an interpretive will to power (an example of what Elisabeth Schüssler Fiorenza might diagnose as 'kyriarchy', the unholy union of power-over with spiritual leadership[18]).

On the account of differential hermeneutics, on the other hand, the explanations for interpretive difference proliferate. These by no means exclude ignorance, intellectual limitation, error, perversity or madness, but they include positive characteristics as well. The differential interpreter can frankly admit that presuppositions make knowledge possible but also that they limit knowledge, such that our capacity to sympathize with ancient perspectives on the nature of reality may, for instance, inhibit our capacity to note and acknowledge our complicity with contemporary oppressive political forces. Or, to give another example, our profound acquaintance with recent scholarship on postcolonialism and subaltern literature may overshadow our attention to the grammatical nuances of the text. Most scholars have observed some of their colleagues riding interpretive hobby-horses, solving every exegetical conundrum with a single interpretive device, whether it be chiasm, honor/shame dynamics, deconstruction, reader-response criticism, etymology or whatever. Pertinent though these all may be to interpretive discernment, it is doubtful that any one of them resolves every dilemma. To a less obvious degree, however, all interpreters favor a particular limited range of exegetical explanations and depreciate others. Just as the hobby-horse jockey may be faulted for adhering to too limited a range of interpretive tools, so we all may advocate a range of interpretive preferences that, while generally sound, undervalues contributions from the fields we do not ourselves prefer. In short, differential hermeneutics begins from the recognition that different interpreters have good reasons for adopting different interpretations, reasons that cannot be exhaustively or even thoroughly evaluated. The criteria by which we evaluate our rationales are themselves, after all, subject to evaluation – and so on to an infinite regress.

---

18. On Schüssler Fiorenza's notion of kyriarchy, see her book, *Rhetoric and Ethic*, p. ix and passim.

Proponents of integral hermeneutics are liable quickly to respond that on this account of differential hermeneutics, no interpretation can be better than another, or that differential hermeneutics renders all interpretive decisions radically subjective. They collapse differential hermeneutics into a purely pluralistic hermeneutic in which all interpretations are merely interpretations, none better than another, with no reason to adopt one rather than another. One can offer an immediate practical rebuttal to this objection by observing, once again, that practitioners of differential approaches simply do not behave or argue as this objection presumes. At this point, most proponents of integral hermeneutics insist that differential interpreters must be pluralists or that they have no reason for approving one interpretation rather than another. On the premises of integral hermeneutics, this may be true, but the practitioners of differential hermeneutics do not assent to the premises of integral hermeneutics.

Differential hermeneutics proceeds by identifying the criteria by which an interpretation claims validity, the soundness of that claim, and the scope of that claim and those criteria. All criteria, on this account, are local criteria. Some criteria are narrowly local (as particular schools of biblical interpretation exemplify; an interpretation that would be warmly received at Harvard might reasonably and appropriately be less welcome at Fuller – and vice versa). Other criteria extend to groups so expansive as to seem universal, although in such cases one should remember that 'universal' includes many more interpreters than 'everyone I can think of', however often confident interpreters ignore this fact. The claim that a premise holds universally can be disconfirmed, after all, if a single interpreter dissents.

Interpretive agreement indicates not the discovery of a hitherto-concealed 'true meaning' but the convergence of interpreters' priorities and sensibilities, such that two interpreters share a sense of which aspects of the text count and how to associate the pertinent aspects of the text to cultural, grammatical, theological and other such correlates in the broader communicative environment. Agreement arises most readily among readers who learned about the Bible from the same teachers, who share interests, whose theologies (or lack thereof) converge and so on. Such convergence doesn't dissolve agreement into 'congruent formation', as though identical (academic, theological) twins would automatically agree on interpretive issues simply because of their training; one need not look far to find examples of classmates and denominational colleagues who disagree bitterly with one another. When readers agree, however, they attest a common evaluation of a variety of dimensions of interpretation. These common evaluations are made more likely when readers inhabit common educational and theological spheres.

Moreover, the local criteria that derive from identity and experience intersect, envelope and overlap each other. My outlook on interpretation has been informed by my adherence to Anglican ecclesial identity and to the catholic wing of that expansive communion. But my interpretations have likewise been formed by the institutions at which I have studied (and taught), by writings of and friendships with scholars at schools where I have not studied, by my upbringing in a home redolent of respect for the English literary canon (especially of Shakespeare and the English novel), by my undergraduate philosophy major, by my ministries in inner-city parishes, by my familiarity with a variety of languages, by my partici-pation in ministries to people affected with AIDS, and so on indefinitely. No single set of interpretive priorities always takes precedence over all others, although my perspective shows enough consistency that readers who are well-acquainted with my work can suggest that such-and-such an interpretation was 'predictable' or that another is 'surprising'. In other words, although no single criterion (or set of criteria) determines a particular interpreter's perspective on a text, the problem of assessing interpretations derives not from the paucity of available criteria but from the superabundance of possible criteria.

One can legitimately criticize my postmodern predilections, for instance, either on the basis that my whole entanglement with postmodern theory is misguided and dangerous from the outset, or on the basis that I do not understand the scholars whom I pretend to draw on, or on the basis that my postmodern premises (although neither intrinsically misguided nor misconstrued) are simply wrong. If I make a technical argument that the history of first-century Judaism, the grammar and rhetoric of the ancient texts, and the canons of historical plausibility that pre-dominate among the practitioners of historical reasoning in the major academies of Europe and North America all support my claim that Jesus of Nazareth most closely resembles a wandering Jewish cynic-like figure, then the bounds of my argument's authority extend just as far as my audience assents to my premises. Somebody who dissents from Euro-American scholarly norms or who cares not a bit about first-century Judaism or who relies on the King James Version of the Bible may not be interested in my argument. (We can argue about whether such a person *should* demur from my priorities, but for now, granted the possibility of such a person's existence, we will allow him or her these predispositions.) Differ-ential hermeneutics does not banish judgments about correctness but ties these judgments to specific premises that constitute the particular interpretive process.

Whereas integral hermeneutics falters over the question of whence disagree-ments arise, on the account of differential hermeneutics, reasons for adopting one interpretation rather than another abound. A differential hermeneutic can stipulate explicitly what counts as a good reason within a particular interpretive discourse without demanding that every interpretive discourse adhere to that criterion. Thus, African-American hermeneutics will produce interpretations that vary from those produced under hermeneutical approaches that do not attend specifically to racial contingencies. Literary-critical interpreters will advance exegetical results that derive their cogency not necessarily from attention to the historical background of the text in question but from observations about the interplays of character, plot, diction and so on (which may themselves interweave, to varying degrees, with historical discourses). Anglican interpreters will, with sound reason, propose inter-pretations that differ from those offered by Southern Baptist interpreters – and this, not because of a pernicious influence that clouds the minds of theologically-motivated interpreters but precisely because the cast of mind that inspires one to sympathize with the Southern Baptist tradition may incline one to weigh interpre-tive decisions differently from one's Anglican colleagues. Scholars who adhere to no particular ecclesiastical tradition are not thereby uninfluenced, but are influenced by a different array of ideals. Were such denominational, philosophical or cultural alliances subject to disinterested comparison and criticism, one might attain to an intellectual clarity that permitted the sort of judgment that integral hermeneutics requires; under the conditions of mortal knowledge, however, advocacy of integral hermeneutics amounts to a kind of interpretive ethnocentrism.

From the perspective of differential hermeneutics, the limitations of human understanding and interpretation do not derive from sin and the fall but, like diversity in human constitution and identity, signal the human distinction from God and serve to give God glory precisely by the harmonious expression of their difference. As parts of the body are not all eyes, feet, hands or nose, so interpretations of scripture are not all historically-warranted assertions about the original intent of a human (or divine) author; nor is interpretive differentiation any more a result of sin than is corporal differentiation. Again, the very existence of difference serves the positive purpose of enabling human beings, whose individual limitations cannot satisfactorily represent God, to begin to represent truth by the harmonious ordering of differentiated bodies and interpretations.

Similarly, the claim that the interpretive triad of Author, Text and Reader reflects God's triune identity in a sort of literary *vestigium trinitatis* fails to account for the possibility that the constitutive elements of interpretation number some quantity other than three. Perhaps 'context' should be reckoned among the characteristics of the interpretive situation. Indeed, the author's context and the reader's context may both make fair claims to stand among the definitive elements of an interpretive act. Moreover, other numbers than 'three' carry theological significance within the Christian tradition. 'Four' might be a more appropriate number for theological constituents of interpretive practice, since four gospels interpret the identity of Jesus to his disciples. Without multiplying examples indefinitely, the argument from triunity should be granted ornamental, not probative, force.

Last, although God's will is perfect, singular and unconfused, our appropriation of these terms should attend to the likelihood that these attributes function differently with regard to God's intentions than with regard to ours, with regard to God's thoughts than with regard to our thoughts. While we might assent to the proper unity of God's literary intent in inspiring scripture, could we but see with God's eyes, we ought not simply assume that 'singularity' in human interpretation reflects fittingly the complex unity of God's purpose. Integral hermeneutics provides one coherent way of positing a connection between meaning, interpretation, divine identity and the Christian theological tradition; differential hermeneutics proposes another coherent approach to connecting these dots and does so without some of the problematic implications that characterize integral hermeneutics.

The extent to which local cultural currents determine interpretation, for example, motivates some proponents of differential hermeneutics to pay particular attention to interpretive discourses in Africa, Asia, Latin America and among indigenous peoples, discourses to which the dominant European and North American schools typically pay only cursory attention, when they attend at all. Proponents of integral hermeneutics certainly do not cultivate a deliberate policy of excluding

interlocutors based on race or culture, but when they interact only with interpretations from other Euro-American interpreters (or with interpreters from outside
Europe and North America only to the extent that those interpreters reflect Euro-
American critical priorities), they effect a culturally-colored exclusion, whether
deliberately or inadvertently. Moreover, since integral hermeneutics allows for
only a single standard of legitimacy, if a practitioner of integral hermeneutics
excludes any particular groups of interpreters, that exclusion implies the group's
lack of legitimate interpretive authority.

Differential hermeneutics, on the other hand, describes interpretive practices as
always necessarily imbued with cultural specificity, such that Euro-American
interpreters would not ordinarily be expected to interact with interpreters from non-
Western cultures. If Euro-American interpreters do scan more distant cultural
horizons, they may legitimately do so without justifying their research as seeking
the correct interpretation but seeking to learn critically from readers whose angle of
vision enables them to see texts in ways that customary Western approaches
exclude. Differential interpreters may pursue such illumination in the name of
inclusivity or of liberation from theology's Constantinian captivity of Western
culture. Or they may do so out of their humble appreciation that interpretive wisdom dwells with interpreters without academic training as well as with those who
hold advanced degrees, with inhabitants of any continent, indeed with illiterate as
well as erudite readers ('I thank you, Father, Lord of heaven and earth, because you
have hidden these things from the wise and the intelligent and have revealed them
to infants; yes, Father, for such was your gracious will'[19]).

That humility does not necessitate a romantic inerrancy-of-the-primitive. One
can assess non-academic readings critically without either dismissing them for
failure to meet the local standards of twenty-first century Northern, Western culture
or abjectly deferring to the privilege of a romanticized Outsider. In order critically
to evaluate non-academic (or non-Western or non-historical) readings, however,
one should learn to recognize non-academic criteria without prejudging them as
'pre-critical' or 'naive'. Interpreters from all times and places exercise critical
judgment and will always appraise critically interpretations from other contexts. A
richly critical, ethical, theologically-sound practice of interpretive discernment will
develop the capacity to distinguish stronger from weaker interpretations by a
variety of different sets of criteria.

The geo-cultural aspect of differential hermeneutics entails momentous implications for missional theology. Past generations of evangelists and expositors have
often sought to inculcate an authoritative version of integral hermeneutics along
with inviting their neighbors to share in the welcoming grace of God. On their
assumptions, the unity of the presence of Christ, made manifest in the singular
meaning of the text, requires learning not only the stories, the laws, the wisdom
and counsel of scripture but also the authorized mode for interpreting. If the presence of Christ abides not in the 'letter', however, but in the Spirit that integrates
separated people and nations into one body, then a differential hermeneutic may

---

19. Mt. 11.25-26 (NRSV).

more fitly acknowledge the Spirit's freedom to make the meaning of scripture active in various peoples in various ways.

Differential hermeneutics provides a way of thinking about correct interpretation that respects the relevance of particular criteria and the necessity of attending to the applicable criteria at all times and in all places. A practitioner of differential hermeneutics can comfortably uphold some interpretations as right and reject others as wrong without self-contradiction. Since criteria and contexts always infuse interpretation, interpreters will always encounter canons by which critics distinguish better from worse interpretations. At the same time, differential hermeneutics does not extrapolate from the criteria that one critic applies in one situation to a universal set of norms for distinguishing valid from invalid interpretations. Integral hermeneutics practically implies ongoing interpretive conflict among Christians. What, shall we wonder, is the single correct meaning of, for example, Jesus' blessing of Simon Peter in Mt. 16.18, the prohibition of a woman having 'authority over a man' in 1 Tim. 2.12, the New Testament descriptions of baptism, the genocidal wars of God in the conquest narratives? Differential hermeneutics, by contrast, recognizes that disciples will always adopt divergent interpretations of the Bible (and of their life-worlds as well), so that the unity by which believers bespeak their allegiance to the one God derives not from their consensus about the textual meaning of scripture but from the obligation to bear with one another, to testify to the truth as we have received it, and to continue to show forbearance and patience in the shared hope that when all things are revealed, the Revealer will also display the manner in which our diverse interpretations form a comprehensive concord in ways that presently elude our comprehension.

In expressing such a hope, this advocate of differential hermeneutics draws near again, I think, to the proponents of integral hermeneutics. The advocates of integral hermeneutics do not, after all, deny the existence of varying interpretations; nor do they repudiate faith in a wisdom greater than human interpretive insight. As readers who operate under the sign of differential hermeneutics can stoutly argue for the correctness of a particular interpretation, so readers who adhere to the premises of integral hermeneutics can allow that no mortal interpretation will attain finality and that advocates of various competing interpretive claims can each usually cite a cornucopia of reasons in defense of their respective interpretations.

The operative distinction between differential and integral hermeneutics involves a particular sort of ethical argument. In this case, the ethical question concerns not so much 'Who's right and who's wrong?' as 'What sort of lives and interactions should our hermeneutics engender?' The integral quest for rectitude and unity bespeaks the unique identity and perfect will of God but with the consequence of setting readers over against one another in an interpretive contest without end. The differential vision of hermeneutics leaves final answers to the questions of rectitude and unity in God's hands and espouses instead the shared endeavor patiently and respectfully to cultivate distinct, concordant testimonies to God's glory, from every tribe and language and people and nation.

Toward a Postmodern *Hermeneutica Sacra*: Guiding Considerations in Choosing between Competing Plausible Interpretations of Scripture

Charles H. Cosgrove

The idea that authoritative texts can be open to multiple interpretations is an ancient perception. The conviction that methods can and should be devised to deal with this multivocality is equally ancient. Ancient jurists and rhetors considered the problem of how to treat the unclear legal text. Quintilian comments on this problem as follows: 'the only questions which confront us will be, sometimes which of the two interpretations is most natural, and always which interpretation is most equitable, and what was the intention of the person who wrote or uttered the words' (*Institutio Oratoria* 7.9.15).[1] The histories of the responses lodged in this laconic formulation could be a study in itself. Of special significance is the fact that the three responses became at various points separated from each other. The third – that of determining intention – reached its dominance with the application of historical methods to the meaning of texts as authorial communications. Under modern historical-critical assumptions, arriving at intention is supposed to settle the meaning of an ambiguous text. But for Quintilian, intention is only one of three considerations. One must also weigh the natural sense of the words and whether a given interpretation is equitable. The splitting off of 'natural sense' from intent and equity also has a long tradition in law. According to one school of jurisprudence, the ordinary sense of the words is what governs, apart from considerations of legislative intent or whether the result seems equitable or not.[2] In the Anglo-American tradition, the separation of equity from the canons of legal interpretation is seen vividly in the creation of courts of equity, that is, legal forums for doing justice where the law would otherwise do injustice. Nevertheless, there have always been advocates of a place for moral judgment in legal interpretation,[3] and it

---

1. *Institutio Oratoria of Quintilian*, III (trans. H.E. Butler; Loeb Classical Library; Cambridge, MA: Harvard University Press, 1921; London: William Heinemann, 1921), p. 161.
2. The most famous recent advocate of a version of this view is US Supreme Court Justice Antonin Scalia. See his *A Matter of Interpretation: Federal Courts and the Law* (Princeton, NJ: Princeton University Press, 1997).
3. A most recent and forceful advocate of moral interpretation of the law is Ronald Dworkin. He argues that proper interpretation of the law requires imputing a moral theory to the law and deciding between competing interpretations on the basis of that moral theory. See Ronald Dworkin, 'The Model of Rules', *The University of Chicago Law Review*, 35 (1967), pp. 14–46 (reprinted in *Taking Rights Seriously* [Cambridge, MA: Harvard University Press, 1977]), pp. 41–45; Ronald Dworkin, *Law's Empire* (Cambridge, MA: Harvard University Press, 1985), pp. 53–63.

is widely acknowledged in law that whether they should or not, judges do use their own moral sense or their understanding of community moral norms as factors in working out what the law means in a given case.

The ancient Christians lived in a world where the kind of integrated approach Quintilian advises for dealing with textual ambiguity was an ideal, not a sign of hermeneutical confusion (as a modern might view it). Early Christians also lived in a world where people regarded sacred texts as semantically extraordinary, possessing meanings on multiple levels and requiring special methods of interpretation. Moreover, it was widely assumed that theological and moral criteria should guide discriminations between competing interpretations of scripture. One function of the ancient Christian concept of the 'rule of faith' was to provide norms for interpreting scripture.

In recent years interest in the ethics of interpretation has confronted the growing recognition that the use of exegetical method,[4] however rigorous, cannot overcome or eliminate 'indeterminacy', that hermeneutical situation in which applying a given interpretive question and a given publicly-shared method (or set of methods) yields more than one reasonable interpretation (as an answer to that question). Indeterminacy in this sense is not about the fact that we can put an almost limitless number of questions to texts or that we can apply many different methods. It is what happens when we put a single question, rigorously apply a common method, work out reasonable interpretive arguments on the basis of that method, and come up with more than one plausible result. I refer to this typical hermeneutical situation as one of 'bounded indeterminacy'. The text, if fairly treated, is not open to any and all interpretations, but to a limited range.

In response to the perception of bounded indeterminacy, a number of biblical scholars (myself included) have proposed that those of us who interpret scripture for Christian faith and practice need to become self-aware and disciplined about the criteria we use in judging between competing interpretations of scripture.[5] A first step is to recognize that decisions about which interpretation to adopt almost invariably depend, at least tacitly, on 'extra-exegetical' considerations.

By 'extra-exegetical' I mean considerations taken up on the assumption of certain given results of exegesis. For example, if I am persuaded that it cannot be settled exegetically whether, in Paul's instructions to slaves, the expression μᾶλλον χρῆσαι in 1 Cor. 7.21 means 'avail yourself of the opportunity' for freedom (RSV; NRSV alternative translation) or the contrary, 'make use of your present condition' of slavery (NRSV; RSV alternate translation), then in choosing between these two interpretations for preaching or other constructive theological use, I must depend on judgments that come into play after the exegetical situation has been clarified as

---

4. Under 'exegetical method' I include traditional historical interpretation in its various forms and outfitted with more recent tools (sociological interpretation, rhetorical interpretation, ideological criticism, etc.), as well as other methods that may be less historically oriented, depending on how they are conceived (certain forms of literary criticism, canonical criticism, structural criticism, etc.).

5. In addition to the introduction to the present volume, see ch. 5 of my book, *Appealing to Scripture in Moral Debate: Five Hermeneutical Rules* (Grand Rapids: Eerdmans, 2002).

indeterminate. Even if I decide to honor both interpretations in some way, that, too, is a judgment that can be justified (if at all) only by extra-exegetical considerations.[6]

None of this is to say that the interests and values of these considerations do not guide and inspire exegetical insights or influence choice of method and approach. They do. Nevertheless, it is not only possible but also crucially important to keep these extra-interpretive values from overwhelming interpretation in a way that makes us incapable of seeing or unwilling to recognize the plausibility of inter-pretations that do not advance our moral and theological interests. Hence, I reject the position of those who hold that any person's or group's moral and theological convictions will be determinative for their interpretation from start to finish, as if exegesis were completely 'subjective', wholly controlled by what we want to get from the text. The very fact that criticism – including ideological criticism – is possible shows that interpretation need not be purely subjective and solipsistic. In fact, it is often very hard to get the text to say what we want it to say! Most of us are able to recognize the difference between the text and ourselves, to distinguish reasonable interpretations from those that are forced or far-fetched, and to discover the flaws and limitations of our own interpretations by being confronted with the interpretations (and critiques) of others.

For those of us who hold that biblical texts, when fairly treated, display inde-terminacy, it is important to advocate and practice forms of exegesis that stake out ranges of interpretation. Our capacity for rigorous application of exegetical methods and reasoned discourse about competing interpretations allows us to make judg-ments about which interpretations are plausible and which are not. We will not always agree in these judgments, but in many cases we may be able to achieve some rough consensus about what the reasonable range of interpretation is for a given text (regarding a given interpretive question). Moreover, we can develop styles of exegetical argument and analysis (in speech and writing) that lay out the range of plausible exegesis and avoid giving the impression that there is only one correct exegetical result.

The critical task of setting forth ranges of interpretive possibility disturbs the established modernist conception of the relation between exegesis and theology. On the modernist understanding, exegesis provides the correct interpretation and the theologian is to work with that interpretation by analogizing and drawing the inferences that make for theological doctrine attuned to a new time and place. This way of construing the relation of exegesis to theology is essentially the program inaugurated in the late eighteenth century by Johann Philipp Gabler, who argued for the discipline of 'biblical theology' as the mediating step between exegesis of individual texts and the work of dogmatic theology.[7] But few theologians have

---

6. Of course, I can elect not to make constructive use of this passage on the grounds that its meaning is uncertain. But if I take this approach to every instance of indeterminacy, the Bible will quickly become a closed book. I hold that it belongs to the nature of scripture that it becomes operative for us only when we become co-responsible for its meaning, that is, when we apply extra-exegetical criteria in adjudicating between competing reasonable interpretations.

7. Johann Philipp Gabler. 'An Oration on the Proper Distinction between Biblical and Dog-matic Theology and the Specific Objectives of Each', trans. John Sandys-Wunsch and Laurence Eldridge, *SJT*, 33 (1980), pp. 133–44.

operated in accord with Gabler's protocol by using the specific results of biblical scholarship or 'biblical theology' as foundational for their work. Theologians who seek biblical foundations have typically done their own exegesis (Barth, for example!) and usually without concern for constructing a 'biblical theology' as a middle step between exegesis and systematics.[8] Moreover, even those in the habit of consulting commentaries must have noticed that the commentators typically disagree and that usually more than one interpretive theory about what the text means is consistent with the evidence. At this point extra-exegetical factors naturally come into play to guide the choice of which interpretation to follow as a basis for analogizing and extrapolating for contemporary theological application.

I say that extra-exegetical factors 'naturally' come into play, meaning by this *not only* that they have always played this role for the preacher, theologian or anyone interested in appropriating scripture for Christian faith and life but also that they *should* play this role. It is important that they not play this role in a tacit and hidden way. Taking responsibility for our interpretations requires identifying the extra-exegetical considerations that guide our hermeneutical judgments and subjecting them to critical examination through dialogue with others.

In identifying some of the questions we should consider in judging between competing interpretations I have made a special effort to build bridges to premodern hermeneutics. One salutary trend of postmodern theology is a renewed interest in premodern traditions of interpretation as models or at least inspirations for contemporary hermeneutics. One sees this, for example, in theologians like David Steinmetz who affirms '[t]he medieval theory of levels of meaning' against 'the modern theory of a single meaning',[9] in Paul Ricoeur's idea of moving through criticism to a 'second naiveté' beyond criticism,[10] in the discovery that postmodern hermeneutical approaches (and even certain brands of deconstruction) resonate in uncanny ways with traditional rabbinic hermeneutics,[11] in the great work of Wilfred Cantwell Smith on what the concept of 'scripture' means,[12] and in renewed

---

8. On systematic theologians' disinterest in and even opposition to 'biblical theology', see James Barr, *The Concept of Biblical Theology: An Old Testament Perspective* (Minneapolis: Fortress Press, 1999), pp. 240–52.

9. See, for example, David C. Steinmetz, 'The Superiority of Pre-Critical Exegesis', *TTod*, 37 (1980/81), pp. 27–38.

10. The expression 'second naiveté' first appears in Paul Ricoeur, *The Symbolism of Evil* (Boston: Beacon Press, 1967), p. 352, and has become a programmatic hermeneutic term for a post-critical (but not anti-critical) retrieval of the wisdom and spiritual power of the premodern heritage, including the Bible.

11. See, for example, Beth Sharon Ash, 'Jewish Hermeneutics and Contemporary Theories of Textuality: Hartman, Bloom, and Derrida', *Modern Philology*, 85 (1987), pp. 65–80; Susan Handelman, *The Slayers of Moses: The Emergence of Rabbinic Interpretation in Modern Literary Theory* (Albany, NY: SUNY Press, 1982). For important cautions about seeing the rabbis as proto-deconstructionists, see Kenneth Dauber, 'The Bible as Literature: Reading Like the Rabbis', *Semeia*, 31 (1985), pp. 27–48 and William Scott Green, 'Romancing the Tome: Rabbinic Hermeneutics and the Theory of Literature', *Semeia*, 40 (1987), pp. 147–68.

12. Wilfred Cantwell Smith, *What Is Scripture? A Comparative Approach* (Minneapolis: Fortress Press, 1993).

attention to the history of pre-critical exegesis for its theological and spiritual value.[13] But I am not advocating a 'postmodern' disposition that is 'antimodern', any more than I am calling for an uncritical use of the premodern. For me the challenge for a viable postmodern hermeneutic – one that wishes to stay 'in communion' with ancient, medieval, modern and postmodern saints – is how to move forward by *building* bridges to premodernity without *burning* bridges to modernity. Meeting this challenge involves looking for ways in which the postmodern theological spirit is in tune (at least analogically) with premodern sensibilities and being attentive to unacknowledged or even suppressed ways in which modern exegesis resembles the ancient hermeneutical heritage it claims to disavow.[14] Here, a postmodern style of interpretation reveals the staging of modern interpretive practice, which, for all its concerns for honesty, created styles of interpretive discourse that masked much of what the interpreter knew (or should have known) about what he or she was doing. Hence, just as the postmodern television camera exposes the trappings of the studio, so the postmodern interpreter exposes the motivations and strategies of hermeneutical argument. The postmodern chapter of our 'turn to the subject' brings us now to a place where it is not enough merely to assert (or celebrate) that different perspectives produce different interpretations and that the ambiguity of language conspires to multiply multivocality. An *ethical* turn to the subject requires that we take responsibility for our interpretations, our role as co-producers of meaning, and our obligation to identify, state and deliberate about the moral and theological criteria by which we choose one interpretation over another.

It is important to stress that biblical texts do not all require hermeneutical adjudication in the same way. Not only are there some things in biblical texts that are exegetically clear ('determinate'), there are also enigmas, silences, and ambiguities in texts that can plausibly be taken as invitations to resist adjudication, to keep the text and its problems open. Two of the essays in this volume judge that

---

13.   Some notable examples are the immense project being carried out under the direction of Daniel Patte and Cristina Grenholm, 'Reading Romans through History and Culture' (an SBL seminar whose work is being published in a series of volumes by Trinity Press International); and Brevard Childs' agenda for recovering traditional theological exegesis from the medieval and early modern period (before the rise of historical-critical hegemony in biblical studies), an interest that is also being pursued in a variety of publications by Childs' student Gerald T. Sheppard.

14.   On the resemblance between the practice of exegesis in much modern scholarship and premodern hermeneutics, see James Barr, 'The Literal, the Allegorical, and Modern Biblical Scholarship', *JSOT*, 44 (1989), pp. 3–17. 'From roughly the Enlightenment on', Barr observes, 'everyone (except fundamentalists) agreed that the Bible, if taken literally, was sometimes untrue, perhaps often untrue' (p. 8). In response to this recognition, some rejected the Bible as a source of truth; others said that 'although the Bible was not always literally true, its basic truth was not affected by this fact since its basic truth lay on a different level. *A different level: a level different from the literal sense*' (p. 8). This idea that the truth of scripture lies on a different level from the literal puts modern biblical scholars in agreement with premodern interpreters. The modern interest in the 'theological sense' beyond the literal is a kind of allegorizing. Barr also points out important differences between ancient and modern allegorizing.

their chosen biblical subjects have this character.[15] Moreover, the argument has been made that for Jacques Derrida, deconstruction (as a strategy for keeping all interpretation open) is ethically necessary as a way to be radically receptive to what we do not comprehend, to what lies beyond us, including our neighbor who constantly exceeds the categories of our understanding. Deconstruction seeks to avoid a kind of idolatry and oppression of interpretive closure.[16] 'Deconstruction', Derrida insists, 'is not enclosure in nothingness [a form of nihilism], but an openness towards the other'.[17] I think there are interpretive moments when this is the right attitude, although in putting my response in this way I show that I am not a deconstructionist but at most a borrower of deconstructionist insights.

Guiding Considerations in Judging between Competing Reasonable Interpretations

The following proposals are not a set of keys for resolving all interpretive disputes or a set of formulas that can be applied mechanically. They are considerations to be taken into account and require weighing, comparison and judgment. In setting forth these considerations I have divided them into four categories – theological, moral, correlational and ecumenical – but do not mean to suggest that these categories are neatly distinct. Certainly, they overlap at points and bear on one another.

Theological Considerations

I begin with the ancient concept of the 'rule of faith', a widely-held hermeneutical guide during the patristic age. Among its advocates were Irenaeus (*Adv. Haer.* 1.10), Tertullian (*Praescr. Haer.* 13), and Augustine (at various points in *De Doctrina Christiana*) to name some of its most notable early proponents.[18] Owing in part to the influence of Augustine's *De Doctrina Christiana*, the hermeneutic of a rule of faith persisted through the medieval period. It also continued under the Reformation doctrine of *analogia scripturae* (interpreting scripture in light of scripture), since from ancient times the rule of faith was thought of as the central,

15. See Dennis Olson's discussion of Moses' slaying of the Egyptian, and Frank Yamada's treatment of the rape of Dinah.

16. I am following John Caputo's interpretation of Derrida. There are certainly other ways to read Derrida and deconstruction. Caputo's aim is to correct what he thinks are misinterpretations of Derrida's work as nihilistic, anti-religious, and in the end amoral. For purposes here, I am referring only to Caputo's take on Derrida and Caputo's interpretation of the implications of deconstruction for theology and ethics. See John D. Caputo, *The Prayers and Tears of Jacques Derrida: Religion without Religion* (Bloomington, IN: Indiana University Press, 1997).

17. As quoted by Caputo, *The Prayers and Tears of Jacques Derrida*, p. 17.

18. On the rule of faith in patristic times, see further Nils A. Dahl, 'Trinitarian Baptismal Creeds and New Testament Christology', in Donald H. Juel (ed.), *Jesus the Christ: The Historical Origins of Christological Doctrine* (Minneapolis: Fortress Press, 1991), pp. 165–86; Georges Florovsky, 'The Function of Tradition in the Ancient Church', in *Bible, Church, Tradition: An Eastern Orthodox View* (Belmont, MA: Norland Publishing Company, 1972); R.P.C. Hanson, *Tradition in the Early Church* (Philadelphia: Westminster Press, 1962); Bengt Hägglund, 'Die Bedeutung der "regula fidei" als Grundlage theologischer Aussagen', *ST*, 12 (1958), pp. 1–44.

clear teachings of scripture as a whole. Although it is probably fair to think of certain ancient creeds as efforts to encapsulate the rule of faith, the use of this concept in the fathers suggests they thought of it as the clear and paramount teachings of scripture and not any particular secondary formulation of these teachings in a creed or catechism. We are more sensitive today to the difficulties of speaking of the 'clear' and 'central' (or 'most important') teachings of scripture. At the same time we recognize that there are multiple plausible conceptions of a rule of faith. Nevertheless, one reason for stating a rule of faith is to make explicit to ourselves and others what theological and ethical assumptions guide our interpretive strategies and hermeneutical judgments.

For example, it would be an interesting story to consider and trace out how certain elements belonging to patristic conceptions of the rule of faith have fared over the centuries not only as theological doctrines but also as hermeneutical norms. The incarnation offers an instructive illustration for modern theology. Adolf von Harnack observed over a hundred years ago the 'intoxicating impression' that later generations would derive from the Fourth Gospel's assertion, 'The Word became flesh'.[19] In neo-orthodoxy, incarnational theology came to mean that God affirms and enters fully into the world in all its concreteness. One implication of this was that we meet God in our neighbor and especially in those in need. A related implication was that we are called by the incarnation to be present in and for the world, morally and spiritually engaged in the this-worldly domain with all its tasks and responsibilities as opposed to taking a 'flight from the body'. This conception of the incarnation has served at least two hermeneutical functions. First, it has provided a way to interpret life – to make claims about God's presence in particular circumstances, to work out understandings of Christian responsibility, and so forth. Second, but almost always *tacitly*, it has influenced the interpretation of scripture. Whatever biblical sources may have inspired the development of the modern incarnational principle, once the doctrine acquired normative status it became a guide for interpreting the Bible. It is probably fair to say that in twentieth-century neo-orthodox circles, any interpretation gained extra appeal if it served incarnational theology. But one did not usually make explicit appeals to theological principles, the incarnation or any other doctrine, as reasons for preferring one interpretation over another; instead one argued that the 'best exegesis' supports this or that theological principle. The time has come to apply theological principles not tacitly but openly to choices between interpretations.

Consider, for example, how the incarnational principle might compete with other theological principles in our adjudication between contrary interpretations of the Last Judgment in Matthew 25. The incarnational idea that we meet Christ in our neighbor weighs in favor of the interpretation of 'the least of these' as any human beings who are in the kinds of extremity signified by nakedness, imprisonment,

19. Adolf von Harnack, 'Über das Verhältnis des Prologs des Vierten Evangeliums zum ganzen Werk', *ZTK*, 2 (1898), pp. 189–292 [228]. According to Harnack, the author of the Fourth Gospel was not enthralled (like later generations) with his incarnational statement but focused far more on Jesus' divine or heavenly identity and status.

hunger and thirst,[20] but the ecclesial principle of the church as the body of Christ may incline us to prefer the interpretation that takes 'the least of these' as followers of Jesus.[21] Moreover, a community of interpreters that holds evangelism and *not* social service to be the primary mission of the church has a theological reason for preferring the ecclesial interpretation of 'the least of these'. The meaning of Mt. 25.31-46 is ambiguous, with the consequence that Christian readers are co-responsible with scripture for what they take this passage to mean. But only by being explicit about the theological norms that inform our judgments about how to 'take' Mt. 25.31-46 can we subject those judgments to the discipline and scrutiny they deserve. We should be ready to state and defend the convictions that lead us to embrace the incarnational interpretation over the ecclesial interpretation or vice versa.

Another example of how theological commitments guide interpretive choices is the law/gospel distinction in Lutheran interpretation. This distinction, epitomized in the doctrine of justication by faith, has enjoyed an important place in Lutheran theology as a theological norm. Luther himself also used the law/gospel distinction hermeneutically, developing from it something like a canon-within-the-canon approach to the Bible. At the beginning of the twentieth century, the hermeneutical potential of justication by faith was rediscovered, beginning with a set of insightful studies by Karl Holl.[22] One learned to judge both theology and life by the doctrine of justification and to weight parts of the Bible according to the degree to which they expressed it. But I contend that there was and has continued to be another, usually unacknowledged function of the doctrine: those committed to it worked out interpretations of scripture and judged between competing interpretations *under the guidance of this norm*. They typically argued that their interpretations were simply what the text itself teaches as demonstrated by careful exegesis. But in fact, some interpretations were preferred over others because they better served the doctrine of justification by faith.

---

20. I recently encountered two incarnational interpretations of Mt. 25.31-46 in ministry publications, one a Sunday School lesson on the incarnation as an advent theme (which included Mt. 25.31-46 as one of its focal passages) and the other a guide from a non-profit Christian organization serving the homeless, that equated touching the homeless with touching Christ (citing Mt. 25.44-45). Commentators who interpret 'the least of these' as any human beings in need include Frank W. Beare, *The Gospel according to Matthew: Translation, Introduction, and Commentary* (San Francisco: Harper & Row, 1981), p. 495; W.D. Davies and Dale C. Allison, Jr, *A Critical and Exegetical Commentary on the Gospel according to Matthew*, vol. 3: *Commentary on Matthew XIX–XXVIII* (Edinburgh: T. & T. Clark, 1988), pp. 428–29.

21. Among the interpreters who interpret 'the least of these' as Christians are Craig S. Keener, *A Commentary on the Gospel of Matthew* (Grand Rapids: Eerdmans, 1999), pp. 604–605; Robert H. Gundry, *Matthew: A Commentary on His Handbook for a Mixed Church under Persecution* (Grand Rapids: Eerdmans, 2nd edn, 1994), pp. 514–15; Daniel J. Harrington, SJ, *The Gospel of Matthew* (SP Series, 1; Collegeville, MN: Liturgical Press, 1991), pp. 357–58.

22. Karl Holl, 'Die Rechtfertigungslehre im Lichte der Geschichte des Protestantismus', in *Gesämmelte Aufsätze zur Kirchengeschichte*, III (Tübingen: J.C.B. Mohr, 1922), pp. 525–57; Karl Holl, 'Was hat die Rechtfertigungslehre dem modernen Menschen zu sagen?', in *Gesämmelte Aufsätze zur Kirchengeschichte*, III, pp. 558–67.

Let me illustrate with an anecdote. A number of years ago I co-taught with a theologian of Wesleyan extraction and sentiments a course on 'Justification by Faith and Social Justice'. We invited a Lutheran theologian from a nearby seminary to one of our class sessions to speak with us about Lutheran perspectives on this topic. Somehow we got into a debate over the interpretation of the story of the Rich Young Ruler in Mk. 10.17-31 (Lk. 18.18-30; Mt. 19.16-30). My Wesleyan colleague argued that the point of the story is that the man missed the way to life because he failed to abandon his wealth and care for the poor. As my colleague understood the teaching of the story, it was more or less that apart from participation in Jesus' kingdom work for the poor and the oppressed there is no true salvation. Our Lutheran guest insisted that the aim of the story is to show the dead-end of works as a way of salvation by confronting the man with the impossible demands of the Law (not just conventional keeping of commandments but true obedience and self-renunciation) in order to drive him to despair and ultimately to grace. Clearly in this debate two different theological conceptions of the gospel (or rule of faith) were at work as competing hermeneutical norms. Now, assuming that, perhaps with some adjustments, both interpretations can be reasonably defended, this conflict suggests the necessity and appropriateness of taking *theological* factors into consideration when judging which interpretation is more valuable or suitable for application to the church's faith and practice. (I leave aside the question whether the two interpretations might in some way be dialectically combined.)

Moral Considerations

For the ancient theologians – and especially for Augustine – the rule of faith included teachings about affections and practices that contemporary theologians group under the theological disciplines of ethics and spirituality (spiritual formation). Augustine is explicit that the double love commandment should guide judgments about whether an interpretation is acceptable or not. According to Augustine, love of God and neighbor is the purpose of scripture; therefore, one should aim at love in one's interpretation of the Bible and discriminate between interpretations on the basis of love as a hermeneutical norm central to the rule of faith.[23]

A number of documents in the Reformed tradition follow Augustine in identifying love as a hermeneutical norm: the Second Helvetic Confession of 1566 (drafted by Heinrich Bullinger), a pronouncement from the Synod of Berne (1528), the Scots Confession (1560), and, more recently, the 1983 consensus statement 'Presbyterian Understanding and Use of Scripture'.[24] In contemporary scholarship, it has been argued that Mt. 22.34-40 presents Jesus advocating the double love

---

23. On Augustine's understanding of love as a hermeneutical principle, see Cosgrove, *Appealing to Scripture in Moral Debate*, pp. 158–59. In Book 3 of *De Doctrina Christiana*, Augustine states that in Book 1 he had set forth the rule of faith (3.3[II]); a principal focus of Book 1 is the double love commandment (as the purpose of scripture), which indicates that for Augustine the rule of love lies at the heart of the rule of faith.

24. See Cosgrove, *Appealing to Scripture in Moral Debate*, pp. 160–61.

commandment as a hermeneutical principle.[25] In a previous publication I have appealed to this Matthean passage as a warrant for hermeneutical adjudication.[26]

Love as a hermeneutical norm is no magic formula for resolving the conflict of interpretations. Its very generality as a moral concept is both an advantage and a limitation. It provides a broad orientation and direction for any interpretive question and is thus a unifying hermeneutic principle, but it goes only so far in application to most specific cases. Even as a general principle, love has limitations. It is not self-evident what love means. The concept is used in so many different ways that one can easily despair of its usefulness as a moral or hermeneutical criterion.[27]

Certainly any claim that the love commandment is a central hermeneutical principle for the interpretation of scripture must begin with a biblical approach to the concept of love. In the New Testament the 'love chapter' of 1 Corinthians (ch. 13) provides a classic definition for the church. So do certain parables of Jesus as well as various forms of moral exemplification – above all the gift of God in Christ but also the gospel portrayals of Jesus. Furthermore, both Jesus and Paul call for seeing the law as summed up by love. At many points, however, New Testament writers assume that their audiences already know what love is, regarding the good and right as matters of general human knowledge.[28] This justifies at least a kernel insight in Rudolf Bultmann's exaggerated remark that Paul calls for 'nothing that the judgment of pagans would not also recognize as good'.[29] The same can also be said generally of the moral witness of the Old Testament. Its teachings have distinctive elements and patterns, but the Old Testament also derives moral bearings from the ethos of its wider environments. In story after story, the Hebrew Bible assumes that the reader can make the appropriate moral judgments. Even when it makes ethical pronouncements, it presumes to share common ground with its audience (as in the judgment oracles of the prophets). Hence, the task of defining love requires a constructive synthesis of what we know from experience and what we learn from the wide range of biblical teachings.

25. Günther Bornkamm, 'Das Doppelgebot der Liebe', in *Neutestamentliche Studien für Rudolf Bultmann* (Berlin: Alfred Töpelmann, 2nd edn, 1957), pp. 85–93; Birger Gerhardsson, 'The Hermeneutic Program in Matthew 22.37-40', in Robert Hammerton-Kelly and Robin Scroggs (ed.), *Jews, Greeks, and Christians* (Leiden: E.J. Brill, 1976), pp. 129–50; Terence L. Donaldson, 'The Law That Hangs (Matthew 22.40): Rabbinic Formulations and Matthean Social World', *CBQ*, 57 (1995), pp. 689–709; Klyne R. Snodgrass, 'Matthew's Understanding of the Law', *Interp*, 46 (1992), pp. 368–78; Wolfgang Schrage, *The Ethics of the New Testament* (trans. David E. Green; Philadelphia: Fortress Press, 1988), pp. 48–50.

26. Charles H. Cosgrove, *Elusive Israel: The Puzzle of Election in Romans* (Louisville, KY: Westminster/John Knox Press, 1997), pp. 43–45. See also Robert C. Tannehill, 'Freedom and Responsibility in Scripture Interpretation, with Application to Luke', in R.P. Thompson and T.E. Philips (eds.), *Literary Studies in Luke–Acts* (Macon, GA: Mercer University Press, 1998), pp. 276–78.

27. See Richard B. Hays, *The Moral Vision of the New Testament: A Contemporary Introduction to New Testament Ethics: Creation, Cross, and New Creation* (San Francisco: HarperSanFrancisco, 1996), pp. 200–203.

28. Wayne A. Meeks, 'Understanding Early Christian Ethics', *JBL*, 105 (1986), pp. 3–11.

29. Rudolf Bultmann, 'Das Problem der Ethik bei Paulus', *ZNW*, 23 (1924), pp. 123–40 (138).

Jesus and Paul teach that love is the fulfilment of the law, which covers both personal and social relations. This teaching implies that love is the foundation of justice[30] and invites us to explore their relationship. One way to put that relationship is to say that love requires what it also exceeds through mercy and forgiveness; the one who loves demands that the neighbor be treated fairly but is also ready to extend grace beyond the demands of fairness. It is also possible, however, to interpret justice in the light of love's demands and gifts by seeing love in all its forms and domains as so essential to human well-being that a justly ordered society – one where the goods of the common life are fairly distributed – must be a society ordered by love.[31] For purposes here it is not necessary to decide between these two ways of conceiving love's relation to justice – love as presupposing yet exceeding justice and love as the form of justice. It is enough that both conceptions define love in ways that include justice.

If the rule of faith entails a rule of love and if love requires justice, then the rule of faith includes the claims of justice. Biblically defined, this is the love that seeks justice in Jesus' kingdom works and in his death under Pontius Pilate (the powers that be). It is the motive principle of what Walter Brueggemann calls the 'Mosaic revolution' whose primary aim is 'to establish justice as the core focus of Yahweh's life in the world and Israel's life with Yahweh'.[32] It is what Rosemary Radford Ruether calls the 'prophetic-messianic' witness of the Bible that protests on behalf of the oppressed against 'sacred canopy' religion and its justifications of the status quo.[33] 'New Testament' love is not a sentimental, individualistic retreat from the justice concerns of 'Old Testament' law; nor is it a superior order of being beyond law and justice.

We live in an age of liberation, a period in history when distributive justice is defined according to an emancipatory model and considerable philosophical, theological and political thinking about justice focuses on identifying forms of oppression and conceptualizing new social arrangements and practices of freedom and equality. To a significant degree, one can trace the moral and spiritual sources of the emancipatory vision to the Judeo-Christian tradition, even if traditions of liberation inspired by these sources have in many settings and currents of development become secularized. From a host of religious and secular avenues, liberationist concerns and tools of analysis now inform much contemporary biblical interpretation. Moreover, in many circles of contemporary theology – both academic and popular – liberation is regarded as a central part or aim of the love of

30. So also Paul Tillich, *Love, Power, and Justice: Ontological Analyses and Ethical Applications* (Oxford: Oxford University Press, 1954), pp. 57, 71.

31. One can make this plausible claim without pronouncing on whether the legal arrangements of such a society ought to provide for an equitable distribution of *all* the goods of love that are necessary for human well-being, an idea that strikes me as absurd, inasmuch as some of love's 'goods' must be free and unconstrained in order to be themselves.

32. Walter Brueggemann, *Theology of the Old Testament: Testimony, Dispute, Advocacy* (Minneapolis: Augsburg-Fortress, 1997), p. 735.

33. For a detailed description and analysis of Ruether's biblical hermeneutic, see Jeffrey S. Siker, *Scripture and Ethics: Twentieth-Century Portraits* (New York and Oxford: Oxford University Press, 1977), pp. 170–202.

God in Christ, which is to say that for many of us *the rule of faith includes an emancipatory vision of God's love in Christ.*

The analytic tools of this modern emancipatory vision include the concept of ideology and three related ideas that define its operation: hierarchy, marginalization and 'otherness'. Outfitted with these concepts, the liberationist analytic helps us to see and encourages us to choose liberative possibilities in the biblical text.[34] A liberationist reading of the parable of the Good Samaritan provides a nice illustration. It is about the definition of love – its nature, agents and objects. The following interpretation of this parable aims to display a constructive synthesis of what a liberationist hermeneutic helps us discover when we apply it to a familiar biblical text, a text that teaches in certain straightforward and obvious ways but also harbors puzzles, clues and provocations that invite a more discerning look.

In Luke Jesus tells this parable in answer to the lawyer's question 'Who is my neighbor?' (Lk. 10.25-37). Hence, the parable helps to define for constructive biblical theology what love of neighbor means in the double love commandment, including its meaning as a hermeneutical guide in Mt. 22.37-40. Of special significance is the fact that the story about the Samaritan is the only example of a parable as an interpretation of the law (Lev. 19.18 being the legal text in question), which makes it especially apposite as a hermeneutical complement to Mt. 22.37-40.

A common way to interpret the parable as an answer to the question 'Who is my neighbor?' is to see Jesus saying that the one who fulfills the commandment does so by making himself a neighbor even to outsiders and 'enemies'. In that case, *everyone is my neighbor* and *I am to be a servant neighbor to all my neighbors.* But a liberationist reading can go further, using the concept of ideology to discover a hermeneutical or epistemological dimension in the story. Ideology is a set of 'ruling ideas' about social structures that serve the interests of the powerful (elites) at the expense of the less powerful and yet are embraced by all (or the vast majority) unquestioningly as simply a description of how things are ('rightly', 'naturally'). Regarded from this perspective, Jesus' parable can be seen as challenging a Jewish ideology that casts Samaritans as outsiders and enemies, unworthy of trust. This attitude toward Samaritans serves the interests of the Jewish aristocracy in Jerusalem by helping to protect the tenet that Jerusalem is the supreme, exclusive, and indispensable place of sacrifice for all true descendants of Abraham, which guarantees the Jerusalem commerce connected with the temple (from which the priestly aristocracy benefits) and also helps maintain the aristocracy's relationship with the Romans as broker between Rome and the Jewish populace.

---

34. There is an ancient antecedent for this kind of interpretation in the Western legal tradition. Already in Roman times, in cases involving questions of freedom where there was legal or factual uncertainty, the matter was to be resolved *'in favorem libertatis'*. This principle entered into English law and was invoked in American slavery cases. See Max Kaser, *Roman Private Law* (trans. Rolf Dannenbring; Pretoria: University of South Africa, 4th edn, 1984), pp. 79, 87–88; Ex Parte Simeon Bushnell v. Ex Parte Charles Langston, 9 Ohio St. 77, 115 (1859). The Ohio court wrote that according to 'a rule older than the constitution – older than the Declaration of Independence, older than magna carta, older even than the common law itself – wherever the right of man to his liberty is the subject of question, every doubt is to be resolved in favor of liberty'.

Moreover, Pharisees have a stake in the Samaritan question because Samaritans present a rival theology and hence a threat to Pharisaic pretensions to hegemony in the interpretations of Israel's sacred traditions (the Law). Hatred of Samaritans can also be analyzed along the axis of an ideology of otherness, whereby Jews (not only the wealthy and politically connected but ordinary Jews as well) derive psychological benefit from seeing Samaritans (along with gentiles) as outsiders to God's covenant.[35]

If ideology is distortion, the ideology that governs ancient Jewish perceptions of the Samaritan 'other' distorts by casting the Samaritan not only as a morally inferior human being (lacking virtue) but also as a deluded human being, a spiritually blind person. The shock of Jesus' parable is therefore not only that a Samaritan of all people should do something *good* but that a Samaritan should know – in a way the Jewish lawyer did not know – *what the good is* and therefore *what the Law is* in its deepest aims. In Jesus' parable, an outsider neighbor teaches insiders. According to this reading, the kind of love of neighbor Jesus requires excludes condescending forms of charity and requires meeting the other on equal terms, with willingness not only to give but also, in humility, to receive and to learn. Above all, the 'outsider' must be treated as one who is hermeneutically (epistemologically) competent. Love seeking justice is therefore possible only through a restructuring of social, political and hermeneutical relationships; it cannot be achieved merely through acts of kindness that accept the status quo with its overt and covert systems of oppression. On moral-theological grounds, I think the preceding is a good way to read the parable and to let it shape our conception of the rule of love.

The preceding interpretation of the parable of the Good Samaritan is not the only plausible one. I advocate it because it makes sense of my experience, as a Christian, of the religious witness of non-Christians. This suggests another moral criterion that deserves mention, namely, honesty about ourselves and our neighbors. In some of my previous work on hermeneutical adjudication, I have focused on the question of Paul's view of Judaism. In this connection I like to quote the remark by Lloyd Gaston that if it is *possible* to interpret Paul as Judaism-affirming, it is also *necessary* to do so after Auschwitz.[36] Gaston does not discuss the hermeneutical assumptions of this claim, but they seem to involve at least the following: (1) that one can make a plausible case that Paul is Judaism-affirming (in Gaston's words 'that Paul has no left hand'), even though one can also make out plausible interpretations that cast the apostle as one of the Christian roots of antisemitism;[37] and

---

35. This interpretation of the parable depends on the insight that ancient Jews lived by ideologies of ethnocentrism, which has been generally true of human societies and is not anything unique to ancient Jews. That the dominant first-century Jewish attitude toward Samaritans amounts to blindness and prejudice is a central point of the parable, a point aimed by a Jewish teacher at his Jewish compatriots; it is therefore intramural prophetic critique. In another place (e.g., in Samaria) one could tell such a parable with the roles reversed. For Christians, the parable can and should also be heard theologically through a retelling in which the church is the priest or Levite and Israel is the 'Samaritan'.

36. Lloyd Gaston, 'Paul and the Torah', in Alan T. Davies (ed.), *Antisemitism and the Foundations of Christianity* (New York: Paulist Press, 1979), pp. 48–71 (67).

37. See Rosemary Radforth Ruether, *Faith and Fratricide: The Theological Roots of An-*

(2) that our moral interest in avoiding the kind of theology that led to antisemitism and its horrific expressions (exemplified by Auschwitz) is an argument for preferring those interpretations that cast Paul as Judaism-affirming. Entailed in our moral condemnation of antisemitism is the conviction that it has not only proven to lead to morally bad consequences (persecution of Jews) but also that it involves *falsehoods* about Jews (the falsehoods becoming part of the propaganda inspiring and justifying persecution of Jews). For example, there has been a growing consensus over the last thirty years or so that the traditional Protestant picture of first-century Jews as legalists bound by a spirit of works-righteousness distorts the ancient evidence for Jewish theology, self-understanding and practice.[38] One way to view the alternatives created by this new perception is to say that either (1) Paul misinterpreted the Judaism of his day, thus leading Christian interpreters of Paul into a false understanding of Judaism, or (2) Paul did not misinterpret his Jewish faith, we misinterpreted Paul. But the matter is in fact hermeneutically more complex. As it happens, Paul is susceptible to more than one reasonable interpretation on the question of Israel, Judaism, the law, works-righteousness, etc. Honesty requires frankness about this. The question of honesty also impinges on our *appropriation of Paul*. For purposes of using Paul in constructive Christian theology, we have a moral interest in opting for those reasonable interpretations of Paul that do not commit us to distorting what we otherwise know about ancient Jews and Judaism.[39]

The same goes for the use of scripture as inspiration and warrant for constructive theological positions involving other subjects. In judging between competing interpretations, it is always important to ask whether a given interpretation will lead us to bear false witness against our neighbor. Making these assessments does not mean suppressing those plausible interpretations that we disfavor. We can *reject* them as guides for our lives without suppressing them. It is as important to acknowledge, describe and criticize for the record not only the twisted interpretations of the Bible advanced by past (and present) generations *but also the exegetically defensible interpretations that we judge unworthy for use in Christian theology.*[40] Hence, a hermeneutic of suspicion is as important as a hermeneutic of charity; scriptural criticism ought to include ideological critique of the gamut of plausible interpretations of any biblical text.

tisemitism (New York: Seabury, 1974), pp. 95–107. Those who trace 'antisemitic roots' to Paul should (and often do) qualify this attribution by pointing out that the roots do not have a racial character in Paul and that any ostensibly 'anti-Jewish' polemic is intramural (Paul the Jew speaking to other Jews).

38. The decisive book in bringing about this recognition among Pauline scholars is E.P. Sanders, *Paul and Palestinian Judaism: A Comparison of Patterns of Religion* (Philadelphia: Fortress Press, 1977).

39. See my essay, 'Advocating One Reasonable Interpretation of Paul against Other Reasonable Interpretations: A Theological Approach to the *Sonderweg* Question', in Robert Gagnon (ed.), *Another Way? Pauline Soteriology for Jews and Gentiles in Romans* (Grand Rapids: Eerdmans, forthcoming).

40. See further, my discussion of this in *Elusive Israel*, pp. 97–100.

My organization has separated out 'moral' from 'theological', which can misleadingly suggest that moral considerations are non-theological. In fact, moral concepts must be analyzed from multiple perspectives, including the theological. Hence, I conclude my illustration of moral criteria by examining a pair of concepts that closely integrate the moral and the theological.

Walter Brueggemann speaks of two competing tendencies in the Bible, which he terms iconic and aniconic.[41] Iconic impulses are tendencies toward consolidation and stability based on a need for social order. Aniconic tendencies are socially transformative, liberative. The iconic interest is the preservation of identity through time. And although the aniconic is opposed to the iconic as a 'status quo' that falls short of God's purposes in history, the aniconic also depends on the iconic impulse to preserve the progress of those purposes. Brueggemann sees the aniconic impulse in the service of social justice as the most characteristic and distinctive feature of the Old Testament's witness to Israel's vocation and partnership with God.[42]

In another place I have described the ways in which a hermeneutical principle of 'counter-cultural witness' warrants giving greater weight to the aniconic voices of scripture that speak for the less powerful than to those voices that merely reflect the dominant tendencies of the culture.[43] To the extent that a special aniconic concern for social justice can be said to be essential to the witness of scripture as a whole, the aniconic principle is also a reason for preferring not only certain voices of scripture over others but certain *interpretations* over others. Carole Fontaine, for example, judges interpretations according to their power for personal and social transformation, their success at presenting the divine Presence as the Other who grasps and woos us into new ways of being and living. As she puts it in her essay for this volume (see p. 109), 'Whether one says "Exodus" or "Resurrection", the [plot of the biblical story] is one of possible *change* and growth of something new in the wake of that transformation'. Likewise, Daniel Patte argues that an interpretation that does not disclose something new but simply repeats what we already know lacks the transformative power that the Bible as scripture is to exercise in the church.[44] Moreover, newness is not always something novel; it may be seeing the familiar in a new and transformative way.

My own impatience with the state of the world and the church often inclines me toward an almost unqualified affirmation of the aniconic witness. Nevertheless, the importance of order and conservation as a hedge against chaos should not be underrated. It is an important caution to all utopian projects. We ought to ask of any interpretation not only whether it serves the interests of transformation but also whether it serves legitimate interests of conservation. Among these concerns are, for example, the conservation of Christian identity through time (so that the communion of saints is an intelligible historical concept), the protection of the natural world (creation), and the preservation of the works of the kingdom of God in history.

41. Walter Brueggemann, *Theology of the Old Testament*, pp. 71–72.
42. Brueggemann, *Theology of the Old Testament*, p. 424.
43. Cosgrove, *Appealing to Scripture in Moral Debate*, ch. 3.
44. Daniel Patte, *The Challenge of Discipleship: A Critical Study of the Sermon on the Mount as Scripture* (Harrisburg, PA: Trinity Press International, 1999), pp. 29, 140–43.

Paul Lehmann has characterized God's purpose in history this way: 'to make and keep life human'.[45] To *make* life truly human in accord with the full purpose of the image of God is a transformative work. To *keep* life human is a conservative work. Many debates between 'liberals' and 'conservatives' over the interpretation of scripture involve competing perceptions of what God is seeking to make (the aniconic work of God) and what God is seeking to keep (the iconic work of God) in the world today. And because we form our views of what God is making and keeping by consulting scripture, we cannot avoid the hermeneutical circle involved in using our understanding of scripture to judge between competing interpretations of scripture.

Correlational Criteria: Depth and Relevance
In a study of ancient Jewish and Christian conceptions of scripture, John Barton sets forth a number of ancient shared assumptions about the Bible as sacred text that entail corresponding hermeneutical imperatives. Ancient Jews and Christians assumed that it was the nature of scripture to be relevant to every time and place and that therefore one should read the Bible as relevant to one's own situation.[46] They also assumed that scripture is everywhere profound, not trivial, and that one should bring a corresponding attitude to the interpretation of scripture.[47] We are today in a better position to see that these ancient hermeneutical principles of relevance and profundity are closely related since attributing profundity to an interpretation of scripture is a perspectival judgment dependent on the identity and situation of the interpreters. What one community greets as profound, another may object to as merely abstruse. 'Relevance', then, is a necessary condition of profundity, for when we say that something is profound we mean that it touches us deeply.

The ancient assumptions that scripture is profound and relevant for every time and place engendered interpretive practices, such as spiritual (or allegorical) interpretation familiar to us from Philo, Paul and the church fathers, and the *pesher* style of interpretation known to us from the Dead Sea Scrolls and Paul. At the same time, these assumptions also express criteria for judging interpretation. A good interpretation is one that displays relevance and profundity.

Not only ancient Christians but the church through the ages has regarded the qualities of depth and relevance as definitional (or 'analytic') to the concept of scripture[48] in a way analogous to how most if not all cultures regard their scriptures

---

45. As far as I have been able to discover, this way of defining God's activity in the world appears for the first time in Lehmann's writings in an address he gave at Instituto Evangélico de Estúdios Teológicos and published in Spanish as '¿Que está haciendo el Dios en el mundo?', *Cuadernos teológicos*, 10 (1961), pp. 243–68.

46. John Barton, *Holy Writings, Sacred Text: The Canon in Early Christianity* (Louisville, KY: Westminster/John Knox Press, 1997), pp. 137–38.

47. Barton, *Holy Writings*, p. 136.

48. David Kelsey writes perceptively that 'authority' is analytic to the concept of the Bible as Christian *scripture* (David H. Kelsey, *The Uses of Scripture in Recent Theology* [Philadelphia: Fortress Press, 1975; reprinted by Trinity Press International under the title *Proving Doctrine*], p. 97). By the same token, relevance is analytic to the concept of the authority of scripture.

and other literary classics.[49] Sacred writings and literary classics are by definition texts that a community or culture regards as possessing permanent value, inviting profound interpretations. Thus, we treat sacred writings and classic texts differently than other writings, including other literary writings. Gerald Graff offers a nice example from the field of English literature. He quotes a poetic fragment from the Keats corpus and considers the implications of certain evidence and arguments that the fragment may be a forgery. Graff asks whether this makes any difference for our interpretation of the meaning of the fragment and observes, no doubt rightly, that 'by virtue of Keats' stature as a major poet, the lines take on a weight and pathos that they would surely lose if we knew they were the product of a forgery'.[50] They take on this weight and depth *because* treating the poem as stemming from Keats brings into play certain interpretive attitudes, along with various assumptions and approved interpretive strategies, all of which work together to produce profound readings. Hence, it matters whether or not a work is counted as a classic not simply because classic status means inclusion in the literary canon but also because classic status brings with it certain attitudes on the part of interpreters that affect how they construe the meaning of the work and condition their judgments about what counts as a good interpretation.

That scripture is profoundly relevant is a theological judgment based on a dialectical combination of the church's encounters with scripture and the way the church reads scripture creatively and constructively on the assumption that it mediates God's Word. Hence, reading the Bible as scripture calls for certain attitudes toward the text, among them a predisposition to read for elegance, nuance, weightiness and depth. Accordingly, we rightly judge the value of any interpretation by its success at bringing out hidden depths of the text.

Of course, one can read the Bible as nothing more than a collection of ancient writings. One can read the Bible 'like any other book'[51] and subject it to forms of interpretation that aim exclusively at identifying and explaining its original sense. There is an important place for this kind of biblical interpretation and it can and should inform the task of reading the Bible as scripture. But these two kinds of reading are not the same, and reading the Bible as scripture or classic should not be collapsed into reading the Bible as a collection of ancient artifacts.

---

49.   Classics are by definition 'profoundly relevant', whether one uses T.S. Eliot's notion of the classic as a fixed cultural pinnacle from which to illumine and to judge life and culture henceforth or one follows Frank Kermode in seeing the classic as the ever-renewed object of creative interpretive engagement, by which the classic speaks meaningfully to succeeding generations by retaining its identity even as it changes. See Frank Kermode, *The Classic: Literary Images of Permanence and Change* (New York: Viking Press, 1975), which describes and takes its point of departure from Eliot's idea of the classic.

50.   Gerald Graff, 'Determinacy/Indeterminacy', in Frank Lentricchia and Thomas McLaughlin (eds.), *Critical Terms for Literary Study* (Chicago and London: University of Chicago Press, 1990), pp. 163–76 (163–64).

51.   This famous expression is used to characterize the rationalistic approach to scripture advocated by Baruch Spinoza in chapter seven of his *Tractatus Theologico-Politicus* (1670). The phrase has come to refer to any approach that treats the Bible's status as scripture as immaterial to the methods appropriate for interpreting scripture. Usually, the historical-critical approach to the Bible is in view.

Some who distinguish reading the Bible like any other book from reading the Bible as scripture are nevertheless wary of talk about 'making the Bible relevant'. They think that this preoccupation with relevance is misleading and does an injustice to the Bible as self-sufficient in its capacity to touch us with God's grace and transforming power. Those who make this claim are not against interpretation; they are simply wary of forms of interpretation that they suspect 'make the Bible relevant' by accommodating it to the modern spirit.[52] I am sympathetic with the concerns and many of the insights of those who approach the question of hermeneutics from this perspective of suspicion about postmodern trends and methods. Nevertheless, I am convinced that interpretation of the Bible is a constructive endeavor in which the interpreter *necessarily* contributes to the creation of meaning. Hence, my doctrine of scripture says that the Bible *is* relevant, possessing powers under the operation of God's Spirit to enliven and transform us. At the same time, the operation of these powers depends on interpretation, which is inherently co-creative, a partnership of text and reader. Therefore, the Bible that *is* (potentially) relevant must also be *made* (actually) relevant through interpretation.

In the language of theological method, 'making scripture relevant' can be termed an act of correlation. I mean this in a modified form of Paul Tillich's definition of the 'method of correlation'. For Tillich the method proceeds as follows: systematic theology 'makes an analysis of the human situation out of which [humanity's] existential questions arise, and it demonstrates that the symbols used in the Christian message are the answers to those questions'.[53] We may adjust this by saying that the method of correlation involves judgments *between competing interpretations of the Christian symbols (including the Bible) as to which of those interpretations best speak to the questions arising out of the human situation in a particular place and time.*[54] Depth and relevance are correlational criteria of good interpretation of scripture.

---

52. I think here especially of Hans W. Frei, 'The "Literal" Reading of Biblical Narrative in the Christian Tradition: Does It Stretch or Will It Break?', in Frank McConnell (ed.), *The Bible and the Narrative Tradition* (New York: Oxford University Press, 1986), pp. 36–77 (challenging the agenda of philosophical hermeneutics).

53. Paul Tillich, *Systematic Theology*, I (3 vols. in one; Chicago: University of Chicago Press; New York and Evanston: Harper & Row, 1967), p. 62. Tillich gives the impression that the analysis of the human situation takes place apart from the Christian symbols. Whether this is his intention or not, I hold that one ought to use all the sources of critical reflection in a disciplined way – *including the Christian tradition* with its competing voices – in identifying and analyzing the 'questions' arising out of the 'situation'.

54. Compare Daniel Patte's concept of 'epistemological judgments' – considerations about how well an interpretation fits the setting to which it is addressed in Christian teaching and preaching. An epistemological judgment is, in Patte's terminology, a 'plausibility' judgment, a determination of the suitability of an interpretation for a particular cultural context. See Patte, *The Challenge of Discipleship*, pp. 18–21. I prefer to reserve the term 'plausibility' as a description of reasonableness, methodological soundness, consistency with evidence, etc. (in judgments about exegesis), and to use the term 'relevance' for what Patte calls 'plausibility'.

Ecumenical Considerations

The idea that scripture is everywhere relevant and therefore should be interpreted as relevant 'to my time and place' involves a tension for anyone who recognizes that different times and places may be so different (and different in contradictory ways) that 'my interpretation' excludes 'yours'. What is the proper scope of relevance? Is it enough to say that each interpreter has a hermeneutical right to construe the text in ways that are relevant to his or her context? Or does every interpreter's obligation to the body of Christ as a whole require some effort to study and accommodate other contextually-relevant interpretations?

One way in which we refer to context as an integrated reality is through the term 'culture'. The recognition that no culture can claim universality as the normative omega point toward which all other cultures should strive is the basis for commitment today to culturally-sensitive interpretation, whether that is described as 'constructing local theologies',[55] 'reading from one's own place',[56] or 'dynamic translation'.[57]

In anthropology the term 'culture' refers to an integrated symbolic and material world of systems of communication, shared practices, institutions, histories, artifacts, etc. But the term culture is also used of various subcultures and traditions that are not in themselves complete symbolic and material worlds but nevertheless have their own integrity, history and traditions: ethnic subcultures within a larger culture, 'school culture', 'corporate culture' and so forth. For purposes here I use the term 'culture' in this broader sense to include not only ethnic or national culture but also theological traditions and other ways in which communities of interpretation may be defined by their histories, shared practices, social location and interests. In this sense, ecumenical sensitivity is a kind of cultural awareness or intelligence.

The following rough – and, for our discussion, provisional – typology suggests something of the gamut of hermeneutical stances that might be taken toward the question of ecumenically-sensitive interpretation:

> Hermeneutic of intolerance: reject other interpretations that compete with one's home-group reading.

> Hermeneutic of tolerance: respectfully acknowledge, without accepting or affirming, other interpretations that conflict with one's home-group reading.

> Hermeneutic of robust pluralism: affirm competing interpretations as equally valid and good for their respective times and places and immune from judgment by any outsider.

---

55. Robert J. Schreiter, *Constructing Local Theologies* (Chicago: Catholic Theological Union, 1977).

56. Mary Ann Tolbert and Fernando Segovia (eds.), *Reading from This Place* (2 vols.; Minneapolis: Fortress Press, 1995).

57. Eugene Nida's concept of dynamic translation (or functional equivalency) was worked out on a cross-cultural model of translation and can be applied to culturally-sensitive hermeneutics as well. See Eugene A. Nida and C.R. Tabor, *The Theory and Practice of Translation: Helps for Translators* (Leiden: E.J. Brill, 1969), pp. 5, 173, 202.

Hermeneutic of qualified pluralism: affirm that in many cases competing interpretations may be equally valid for their respective times and places but not that all interpretations are valid simply because they are valued in a particular time and place.

Hermeneutic of limited ecumenical synthesis: accommodate one's home reading to other interpretations (especially those occupying the same social context) through a higher-level synthesis by engaging in *collaborative intercultural interpretation* to achieve more inclusive local interpretations.

Hermeneutic of global synthesis: attend to interpretations from around the world and seek to develop universal interpretations that integrate the wide range of culturally-sensitive interpretations, modifying indigenous interpretations for the sake of universal unity.

In what follows, it will become evident that I advocate a hermeneutic of qualified pluralism together with a hermeneutic of limited ecumenical synthesis, seeking to hold these two together in a dialectic or healthy tension.

The historical record is long and at times bloody that recounts how ethnocentrism or what may be termed *hemeiocentrism* ('we'-centeredness) has inclined various communities (and 'nations') of Christians to devise interpretations of the Bible that promoted their own perceived interests to the exclusion and often the detriment of other people's legitimate interests, often in the guise of claims to universality. A hermeneutic of tolerance is a healthy antidote to hemeiocentric hermeneutics. But the values of ecumenism call for more than that – ideological critique of cherished parochial interpretations and corresponding efforts toward appreciation of interpretations not one's own. This can be done by embracing a hermeneutic of pluralism, which affirms but does not integrate competing interpretations. It can also be pursued through efforts at *inclusive relevance*, that is, working out interpretations that take account of the experience, situation, tradition, cultural perspectives, etc. of others in the wider human community and offer integrated interpretations that the greater body of Christ can share.[58]

A hermeneutic of pluralism can mean different things. It may mean that mutually exclusive interpretations of the same text can be affirmed so long as they do not conflict morally and theologically. For example, Hos. 6.7 may speak of a covenant with Adam or 'Adam' may be a place name here, depending on which textual tradition we follow. These two interpretations are exegetically incompatible but they do not produce theological contradiction. By contrast, in making hermeneutical judgments about Mt. 16.13-20, one probably cannot theologically affirm both the interpretation that Peter himself is the foundation of the church and that *not* Peter but only his confession is the foundation of the church without getting into theological contradiction. Then there are differences that are momentous whether

---

58. In her contribution to the present volume, Carole Fontaine calls this 'reading "Other-ly"' (see pp. 109–10), which includes for her the effort to 'read alongside and make meaning in the presence of the Radical Other, the one who does not and will not *ever* agree with your notion of the text or its meanings'. In her essay, she seeks to do this by reading the Song of Songs from the perspective of Afghani Muslim women.

they produce moral-theological contradiction or not. Elisabeth Schüssler Fiorenza's argument that 'laborer' and 'coworker' are titles applied to women that carry authority[59] is exegetically incompatible with competing interpretations of this language, but choosing one of these competing interpretations for theological construction would not logically require a non-egalitarian theology of gender. Nevertheless, given the overwhelmingly patriarchal cast of biblical literature, Schüssler Fiorenza's discovery of a radically egalitarian way of construing the 'laborer' and 'coworker' language in Paul is very significant for the egalitarian cause in theology, and (for egalitarians) that is a powerful reason to embrace her interpretation theologically and not to treat the theological appropriation of its opposite as a neutral alternative to be celebrated under the banner of pluralism.

A hermeneutic of inclusive relevance can leave room for a hermeneutic of pluralism that affirms the validity of exegetically incompatible interpretive results that suit different social locations and moments and do not involve moral-theological contradiction. But faithfulness to the communion of saints in all its diversity also calls for practices of interpretation that work toward ecumenical synthesis through collaborative intercultural interpretive practice.

No doubt there are limits to inclusive relevance, a concept that raises the question of how far any interpretation can be general. Much well-placed criticism has been directed against Western biblical interpretation – scholarly and non-scholarly – for assuming that its readings of scripture offered everything that Christians in every part of the world could possibly need, as if the social location of the interpreter had no effect on (much less any constitutive importance for) interpretation. If it is wrong to treat a culturally-specific interpretation as universal on the unexamined assumption that one's own culture is universal (or is superior to all others in ways that make it the standard of aspiration for others), the question still remains to what extent cross-cultural dialogue and partnership can produce interpretations that are not culturally-specific in narrow, hemeiocentric ways. Short of universal interpretations, perhaps there can be instances of intercultural synthesis that accommodate some of the diversity of interpretations worked out from different cultural contexts and traditions. One can adopt this attitude toward intercultural interpretation, I believe, without insisting that the goal must be some utopian (Hegelian!) synthesis that includes and transcends every local interpretation. (I regard the 'hermeneutic of global synthesis' from my typology as 'utopian' in the bad senses of that word.) There can be modest efforts at cross-cultural dialogue and interpretive accommodation, along with respectful and humble acceptance that there will always be unbridgeable differences.

The value of ecumenicity is a warrant for a hermeneutic of intercultural synthesis where accommodation to other perspectives is possible; ecumenicity is also a reason for a hermeneutic of pluralism where accommodation is not possible. Moreover, ecumenical considerations must compete with the other interests and values that guide hermeneutical adjudication, including those theological and

---

59. Elisabeth Schüssler Fiorenza, 'Missionaries, Apostles, Coworkers: Romans 16 and the Reconstruction of Women's Early Christian History', *Word and World*, 6 (1986), pp. 420–33 (428–30) (in connection with the discussion of Prisca and Aquila as coworkers).

moral criteria that belong to our conception of the rule of faith. Where ecumenical interests and our own conception of that rule collide, we must always ask whether in that instance we should revise our understanding of the rule of faith so as to adjust it to the experience, perspectives and judgments of others in the wider church or subordinate our ecumenical interest to the rule of faith as we know it.

An example of ecumenical synthesis is the organized effort of Lutherans and Catholics in the 1980s to read the Bible in ways that maximize the possibilities for agreement between their two traditions. An important outcome of this dialogue is the joint volume on justification by faith,[60] which illustrates the possibilities for ecumenical synthesis that the indeterminacy of biblical texts offers to those seeking interpretations that accommodate their respective traditions. Not that the participants in this venture subscribed to the concept of indeterminacy. The group's Common Statement on justification by faith speaks in traditional historical-critical terms about the results of historical-critical exegesis, as if most of the exegetical differences between Lutherans and Catholics could be cleared up once the historical-critical method arrived, was accepted by both sides, and yielded up mature scholarly results.[61] I don't deny that some basic agreements about interpretive methodology have helped the dialogue, but this in itself cannot explain the consensus since biblical scholarship remains, in fact, more divided than ever on many of the exegetical questions that are resolved by the Common Statement. The degree of consensus in the Common Statement rests to a large extent, I contend, on willingness to work out agreements about which plausible interpretations of scripture to support and how to integrate competing interpretations into a larger conceptual scheme. The warrant for doing so is not, in the end, a set of exegetical arguments so powerful that they defeat all other interpretations but the legitimate interests of relying on plausible exegesis that serves the *value of ecumenical unity*.

Another example of an effort at ecumenical synthesis – in this case a synthesis involving cross-cultural sensitivity – is found in the contribution by K.K. Yeo to the present volume. From the perspective of his own Chinese identity and his experience growing up in Malaysia, Yeo explores the way in which the so-called 'new perspective on Paul' as advanced by James Dunn provides resources for a theological critique of ethnocentrism and the violence that often goes with it. This interpretation assumes that Paul attacks Jewish privilege and ethnocentrism in Romans. But Yeo also considers the concern of certain Western interpreters who seek, in a post-Holocaust context, to avoid anti-Jewish readings of Paul. Yeo aims to fashion an interpretive accommodation, within his own version of the 'new perspective' reading, that does justice to the interests of these post-Holocaust rethinkings of Paul. It is important to add, lest anyone get the wrong impression, that Dunn in no way supports any form of anti-Jewishness and that he has his own ways of working out legitimate concerns to avoid anti-Jewish readings of Paul with what he sees as Paul's attacks on Jewish enthnocentrism. But my focus here is on

---

60. H. George Anderson, T. Austin Murphy, and Joseph A. Burgess (eds.), *Justification by Faith* (Lutherans and Catholics in Dialogue VII; Minneapolis: Augsburg, 1985).

61. The Common Statement as much as says so in §122 (*Justification by Faith*, p. 158).

Yeo's development of the new perspective interpretation, a development guided by perceptions and concerns arising from his Malaysian and Chinese standpoints. From that vantage Yeo reflects on his own obligation, despite the fact that he has no cultural connection in his Malaysian/Chinese background to anti-Jewishness, to take seriously the post-Holocaust rethinking of Paul, which is informed by the specific history of relations between Jews and Christians in the West, as well as by specific cultural histories in the West of reading Paul in anti-Jewish ways.

Concluding Summary

In this essay I have sought to show how the modern 'turn to the subject' must now involve us in a hermeneutical process of identifying, stating and deliberating about the interests and values that guide us in choosing between interpretations that have more or less equal grounding in the text. Biblical texts display indeterminacy of a limited or 'bounded' sort in the sense that for innumerable exegetical questions more than one reasonable solution can be developed based on rigorous application of shared methods. Hence, judgments about how to appropriate the Bible for faith and practice necessarily entail choices between competing reasonable interpretations, choices that can be made only on the basis of 'extra-exegetical' considerations.

We owe it to ourselves and others to scrutinize the extra-exegetical interests and values that guide our choices between interpretations, so that these considerations and criteria can be examined, criticized, revised and enlarged. This calls for something like a 'rule of faith' that we make explicit and continue to examine and develop in dialogue with others. To my mind, all four categories of hermeneutical considerations that I have presented – theological, moral, correlational and ecumenical – belong to such a rule because they all involve convictions of faith and thus embody a critical *hermeneutica sacra* suitable to the interpretation and use of the Bible as scripture to guide the thinking and practice of the church.

Daniel Patte, Vanderbilt Divinity School, Tennesse, USA

The task of writing a commentary on Romans is far from self-evident in an ambivalent postmodern context in which many acknowledge that interpreting is choosing a meaning and many more are horrified by this thought. Yet, this is our context. For better or for worse, globalization is confronting all of us with a postmodern outlook, whether we are in the Western World or in the post-colonial and neo-colonial Two-Thirds World. Thus, as I prepare a commentary, I find myself confronted by basic questions regarding the practice of critical biblical studies and its goals, and consequently regarding my ethical responsibility for this practice.

In the first part of this essay, I will examine the different kinds of responses that contemporary readers of the Bible have to postmodernism. As we shall see, beyond the fundamentalists' loud rejection of postmodernism, and the biblical critics' ambivalence toward it, conscientious preachers spontaneously adopt a postmodern outlook by deliberately choosing one interpretation among the several they consult. Because such preachers (together with leaders of Bible study groups and students who prepare themselves for both roles) will be the primary users of my commentary, I believe I must write a postmodern commentary. But what does this mean? In the second part, I will explore the broad characteristics such a postmodern commentary needs to have so as to *open the text up* to a multiplicity of readings, rather than closing it down by exclusively focusing upon the reading that I would like to advocate. Then, the preachers using this commentary will be free to *choose the meaning* that is most appropriate for Christians in their specific time and place and that they will want to proclaim as the Word of God for their congregations today. The third and concluding part of this essay will clarify why, despite the believers' fear, choosing a meaning for the biblical text is not denying 'truth', and why, despite their present ambivalence, biblical critics should self-consciously develop a postmodern approach, because it is a responsible way to strive to reach the traditional goals of biblical critical studies.

Reading the Bible in a Postmodern Context

Rejection of Postmodernism by Fundamentalists and Other Believers
A first kind of response to postmodernism is found among the many readers of the Bible who strongly reject the postmodern view that interpretation is necessarily inculturated and contextual. They adopt this negative attitude because they view

the fluidity of a postmodern outlook as a threat – indeed, an antithesis – to the certitude of faith. This first group includes 'fundamentalists', for whom the biblical (or koranic) text as Word of God *contains* and conveys 'fundamental' teachings that are the basis of the true Christian (or Jewish or Muslim) faith. Yet, it also includes many other Christian readers of the Bible (especially Protestants, but also many Catholics), who hold that the truth of the Christian faith is solidly grounded in scripture and thus who have a hard time distinguishing their position from that of fundamentalists. I will argue below that this rejection of a postmodern outlook for reading the Bible involves a theological choice that these Christian believers might want to assess. What are the views of 'biblical truth' and of 'God's revelation' that this rejection of inculturated and contextual biblical interpretations entails? To what extent are these theological views in tension with an understanding of God involved in human history and, therefore, in tension with the theological concepts of sacred history and of the incarnation? I will come back to these important questions in the concluding part of this essay.

Ambivalence of Biblical Critics Toward Postmodernism
A second kind of response to postmodernism is represented by the large majority of biblical critics: ambivalence, with the result that postmodernism does not really affect their practice of biblical criticism. This is the response that the guild expects – 'the default setting of critical biblical studies'[1] – and that all of us have as long as we do not self-consciously question it. I agree: critical caution is necessary. Yet, I want to question the knee-jerk reaction that risks to lead us, biblical critics, to replicate in another key, but with similar effects, the fundamentalist response. Obviously biblical critics would give different reasons for their ambivalence. Yet, from my readings of these colleagues' works and from many conversations with them, I believe it is fair to give the following composite picture of the reasons they invoke to justify their ambivalence toward postmodernism.

On the one hand, these biblical critics have three basic reasons for welcoming postmodernism. First, they applaud the postmodern denunciation of fundamentalist interpreters for their denial of the cultural and contextual character of the meaning of biblical texts, as well as for their failure to recognize that they read into the text (*eisegesis*) their own beliefs. Second, most biblical critics have been trained to acknowledge the legitimacy of a plurality of critical methods. Thus, they recognize that one can make sense of a text by selectively focusing on one or another of its signifying dimensions, be it one of its historical dimensions (meaningfulness is located 'behind the text', including its authorial, social, economic, political or cultural dimensions), or one of its literary dimensions (meaningfulness is located 'in the text', including its narrative, structural, figurative dimensions), or again, one of its rhetorical dimensions (meaningfulness is located 'in front of the text', in the meaning effect of the text upon its past or present readers, including its

---

1.   A phrase repeatedly used by James Dunn in his SNTS presidential address, August 2002, 'Altering the Default Setting: Re-envisaging the Early Transmission of the Jesus Tradition', *NTS*, 49 (2003), pp. 139–75. Dunn applied this concept to the 'literary' (rather than 'oral') perspective of biblical criticism. I use it in a much broader way.

illocutionary, rhetorical, discursive dimensions). Third, biblical critics acknowledge their own role in the interpretive process, as they take note of the role of cultural, theological or religious preunderstandings in the hermeneutical circle. Hence, these biblical critics can affirm: Yes, meaning is chosen by readers.

On the other hand, in their own interpretive practices, these same biblical critics often find themselves repeatedly ignoring the hermeneutical circle and the diversity of critical methods. This is what happens as long as, in their practices, they keep the modern 'default setting of critical biblical studies'. Accordingly, they view their task as seeking to establish '*what* the text meant' (when using a historical approach), or '*what* the text says' (when using a literary approach), or '*what* the effect of the text is' on certain readers (when using a rhetorical approach). Even as they argue against fundamentalist interpretations, in many instances they find themselves adopting a fundamentalist-like attitude by claiming, 'this is what the text says', as if the interpretation they defend did not reflect an interpretive choice made because they obscurely felt it directly addresses important issues in their context. Strangely enough, this is also the case in 'advocacy interpretations', when feminist, liberation, and/or post-holocaust biblical critics claim that a book 'is' patriarchal, or oppressive or anti-Jewish. By their very practice, they implicitly deny their self-conscious effort to present one particular contextual reading among several plausible ones.[2] As James Gustafson recently noted, 'I have ceased to be surprised, since it happens so frequently, by how celebrators of radical Christian particularism seem to have utter confidence in the objectivity of their interpretations of texts they do not like'.[3]

Spontaneous Adoption of Postmodern Practice by Conscientious Preachers
The third kind of response is represented by the many readers of the Bible who spontaneously adopt a postmodern outlook and acknowledge that interpreting a biblical text, such as Paul's letter to the Romans, involves choosing a meaning. These include conscientious preachers (followed by many leaders of Bible study groups) who consult several commentaries and deliberately 'choose' a particular interpretation that they then proclaim as 'Word of God for us today'.

Cristina Grenholm and I have claimed[4] that biblical critics should take as models for our practice these conscientious preachers who spontaneously accept postmodernism by deliberately choosing a meaning of the text upon which they focus their

---

2. For instance, Jane Schaberg, 'Luke', in Carol A. Newsom and Sharon H. Ringe (eds.), *The Women's Bible Commentary* (Louisville, KY: Westminster/John Knox Press, exp. edn, 1998), pp. 363–80. She opens her remarkable feminist commentary on Luke with these words: 'The Gospel of Luke is an extremely dangerous text' (p. 363). She then goes on to substantiate this judgment by exploring 'the oppressive dynamics of the Gospel of Luke' as 'Luke's intent'. Her concluding invitation to read Luke in a 'positive and promising' way is then necessarily understood as 'reading with new eyes against Luke's intent' (p. 380) and thus against 'what the text says', rather than recognizing that we can choose to focus on other dimensions of Luke.

3. James M. Gustafson's concluding statement in his 'letter to the editor' about 'Christ and Culture Clash', *The Christian Century*, 119 (July 3–10, 2002), p. 44.

4. Cristina Grenholm and Daniel Patte, 'Overture: Receptions, Critical Interpretations, and Scriptural Criticism', in Cristina Grenholm and Daniel Patte (eds.), *Reading Israel in Romans:*

sermon. This is all the more appropriate for writing a commentary, since it is primarily for such preachers that commentaries are written. A postmodern commentary departs from the traditional way of conceiving commentaries. Yet, I want to argue, it does not deny critical biblical studies. It simply requires from us as biblical critics that we acknowledge and make explicit in our practice what we have been doing all along. Those who use critical commentaries, the end-products of critical biblical studies, are here to remind us of the necessary and healthy limitations of our works.

Writing a Commentary that 'Opens the Text Up' for Conscientious Preachers

The primary users of commentaries are conscientious preachers and leaders of Bible study groups who imitate them, as well as students who prepare themselves for both of these roles. Therefore, as I strive to envision how to write a commentary, I find it essential to keep in mind how these preachers proceed in their preparation of a sermon. Who are these 'conscientious preachers'? How do they 'choose a meaning' as they prepare to preach a sermon on a biblical text? To what extent should their practice be reflected in my practice as a biblical critic and therefore shape my commentary? Cristina Grenholm and I have addressed these questions at length.[5] It is enough to summarize the main points we made.

Conscientious preachers assume responsibility for their scriptural reading. This is why we called their practice, 'scriptural criticism'. They do so in three ways.

> 1) They closely read (often in the original Greek or Hebrew) and *analyze the biblical text*. They do so by consulting a plurality of commentaries and other tools of critical biblical studies. They have a twofold goal: ensuring that their interpretation will be properly grounded in the text and becoming aware of the different potential teachings offered by the text. Through their consultation of a diversity of critical biblical studies of their focal passage, they 'open the text up' to a multiplicity of interpretations, rather than 'closing the text down' by exclusively focusing on one interpretation.

> 2) In order to conceptualize the teaching of the scriptural text for Christians in their congregations, conscientious preachers seek to *identify theological categories* that account for the way in which the text relates to the (positive, negative or absent) religious experiences of these believers. How is their religious experience perceived when contemplated from the perspective of the text? Is it challenged or affirmed by the text? Conversely, what is most significant in the text when it is read in terms of these believers' religious experiences?

> 3) Furthermore, in order to develop their sermons, conscientious preachers seek to *discern how the scriptural text engages the life-contexts of the members of their congregations*. Does it address actual needs they have in each of their particular life-contexts? How is this life-context perceived when contemplated from the

Legitimacy and Plausibility of Divergent Interpretations (Romans Through History and Cultures Series, vol. 1; Harrisburg, PA: Trinity Press International, 2000), pp. 1–54.
    5.   See Grenholm and Patte, 'Overture', pp. 12–14.

perspective of the text? Conversely, what is most significant in the text when it is read in terms of this particular life-context and the actual needs of people in that context?

In so doing, following a common postmodern practice, conscientious preachers read traditional commentaries 'against the grain'. While 'modern' commentary strives to present 'the' (only true) interpretation, conscientious preachers deny its implicit claim to present a universal interpretation that would be a-contextual and a-cultural, simply by their practice of reading several commentaries and giving them similar status. By assessing the extent to which the particular interpretation they read engages the specific life-contexts of their congregations, conscientious preachers presuppose that each commentary offers a *contextually framed interpretation*. Similarly, by assessing the extent to which the interpretation proposed by a commentary relates to the religious experiences and the theological outlook of the members of their congregations, conscientious preachers presuppose that each commentary offers a *theologically framed interpretation*. And as they choose to follow one scholarly interpretation rather than another one, they adopt a certain *analytical frame* for their interpretation; that is, they emphasize as particularly significant a certain dimension of the text, as the scholarly interpretation did through its use of a specific critical method (usually explicitly discussed).

It follows that a commentary will be most helpful to these conscientious preachers if it includes three features that would support the three aspects of their practice.

A Commentary Making Explicit a Multiplicity of Analytical Frames for Interpreting the Biblical Text

First, an ideal commentary should 'open the text up' by presenting the multiplicity of significant dimensions of the text, each of which can be the textual grounding for a plausible and legitimate interpretation, instead of advocating one of these dimensions as the most significant (or even as the only truly significant) one. In brief, it should offer *a multidimensional analysis* (or exegesis)[6] of the text.

Multidimensional analysis amounts to presenting a series of selected critical interpretations. In the case of Romans, speaking in very general terms, one can distinguish, to begin with, between the two broad types of interpretations confronting each other in '*The Romans Debate*'[7]: those that view as most significant 'what is *in the text*' (when Romans is read as a doctrinal treatise) and those that view as most significant 'what is *behind the text*' (when Romans is read as a contingent letter addressing particular issues in the church in Rome). Even though historical approaches require focusing on what is behind the text, the former approach remains very influential even among historically-minded scholars, as J. Christiaan

6. The term 'analysis' is more appropriate than 'exegesis' since analysis does not mean extracting meaning from a text as meaning-container but rather bringing to bear analytical tools – be they historical, literary or rhetorical – on the text, and in the process elucidating dimensions of the text that are 'meaning-producing' as readers in their life-context interact with these.

7. Karl P. Donfried (ed.), *The Romans Debate: Revised and Expanded Edition* (Peabody, MA: Hendrickson, 1977 and 1991).

Beker has noted.[8] This is appropriate. After all, Paul's theological argument is and will remain meaningful, and, indeed, will be regarded as what is the *most* meaningful for many interpreters, as James Dunn's commentary and essays illustrate.[9] But the second edition of *The Romans Debate* begins to suggest a greater variety of interpretations, including those that find as most significant 'what is *in front of the text*'. Among these, rhetorical and socio-rhetorical interpretations are concerned with the effect of Romans on its readers/hearers.[10]

As the multidimensional analysis of the commentary opens the text up, I will, of course, make a selection of major options, since each of the three types of interpretations includes many sub-types. I do not want to give the confusing impression that anything in the text can be 'most significant' by presenting too many possibilities. Yet a broad range of possibilities – what the text historically meant, what it literarily says, and how it rhetorically affects its readers – needs to be presented.[11]

A Commentary Making Explicit the Plausibility of Several Theological Frames for Interpreting the Biblical Text
Second, this ideal commentary should clarify the *theological perspective* that frames each of these several potential interpretations. For this, it needs to make explicit the theological concept (or set of concepts) that provides the thematic theological frame of each of the interpretations. No difficulty here. It is simply a matter of identifying the theme(s) upon which the interpretation is focused and which could be the topic of a thematic study: for example, the christology of Romans or its theology (e.g., the righteousness of God), its eschatology, its ecclesiology, its moral teaching, its view

8. Thus, Beker seeks to balance the role of 'contingency' (*behind the text* as most significant) and 'coherence' (*in the text* as most significant). J. Christiaan Beker, *Paul the Apostle: The Triumph of God in Life and Thought* (Philadelphia: Fortress, 1980), pp. 23–36.

9. See James D.G. Dunn, *Romans 1–8* and *Romans 9–16* (WBC 38a and b; Waco, TX: Word Books, 1988–89) and James D.G. Dunn, 'The Formal and Theological Coherence of Romans', in Karl P. Donfried (ed.), *The Romans Debate*, exp. edn (Peabody, MA: Hendrickson, 1977 and 1991), pp. 245–50, and, in the bibliography, the many works Dunn cites about either the coherence or lack of coherence of Romans.

10. This use of rhetorics, illustrated by Wuellner's essay, is to be contrasted with the use of rhetorical categories for understanding the unfolding of the argument of the letter (i.e., 'what is in the text'). Wilhelm Wuellner, 'Paul's Rhetoric of Argumentation: An Alternative to the Donfried-Karris Debate over Romans', in Karl P. Donfried (ed.), *The Romans Debate* (Peabody, MA: Hendrickson, exp. edn, 1977 and 1991), pp. 128–46. This essay foreshadows the works of Stanley K. Stowers, *The Diatribe and Paul's Letter to the Romans* (Chico, CA: Scholars Press, 1981); Stanley K. Stowers, *A Rereading of Romans: Justice, Jews, and Gentiles* (New Haven and London: Yale University Press, 1994); Neil Elliott, *The Rhetoric of Romans: Argumentative Constraint and Strategy and Paul's Debate with Judaism* (JSNTSup, 55; Sheffield: Sheffield Academic Press, 1990); Neil Elliott, *Liberating Paul: The Justice of God and the Politics of the Apostle* (Maryknoll, NY: Orbis Press, 1995); and William S. Campbell, *Paul's Gospel in an Intercultural Context: Jew and Gentile in the Letter to the Romans* (Frankfurt and New York: Peter Lang, 1991).

11. Presenting these multiple interpretations in a single commentary is a challenge, yet not as difficult as it looks. Each pericope can be defined in terms of the approach that requires the broader section of text, namely, a literary approach. Then, it is a matter of successively presenting a historical, a literary and a rhetorical analysis as three independent analytical interpretations that identify as most significant different features of this pericope.

of faith or its view of atonement. The challenge is in the next step: the elucidation of the particular choice that each interpretation makes among several possible ways of conceiving this theological concept. Yet, one can readily recognize this choice when one is aware of the different ways in which the given theological concept has been constructed in the history of biblical interpretations and indeed in the history of Christian thought. Let us take the example of 'atonement'.

'Atonement' is one of the theological concepts that is legitimately chosen to frame interpretations of Romans. Many aspects of Paul's letter can be related to this theme. Yet, each of these interpretations necessarily chooses among several possible and plausible understandings of atonement. Here it is helpful to go to a dictionary of Christian thought designed to underscore the diversity of understandings of each theological concept, such as *The Oxford Companion to Christian Thought*[12] and the forthcoming *Cambridge Dictionary of Christianity*.[13] Then it becomes clear that there have been, through history, what Philip Quinn calls three basic types of 'theories of the atonement': satisfaction theories, ransom theories and exemplar theories.[14] In all cases, atonement refers to the liberation of humans from evil in a unique way by the life, suffering, death and resurrection of Jesus Christ.

The 'satisfaction' understanding of the atonement was most clearly presented by Anselm: 'human sin offends God's honour, so sinners owe God a debt of honour… Hence the Atonement consists of Christ's making satisfaction for human sin';[15] it was also understood, by Martin Luther and other theologians, as Christ paying a 'debt of punishment owed to divine retributive justice'[16] by human sinners. The satisfaction view of atonement is found in the many 'forensic' interpretations of Romans, in particular in those that are directly or indirectly influenced by Luther. This specific theological frame leads these interpretations to relate atonement to the gospel as the good news addressed to a Christian believer: 'You are "justified by faith", i.e., "reckoned as righteous" by faith in Christ who died for your sins (Rom. 3.21-28)'. Thus, the cross is understood in a sacrificial way.[17]

---

12. Adrian Hastings (ed.), *The Oxford Companion to Christian Thought* (Oxford: Oxford University Press, 2000).

13. Daniel Patte (ed.), Enrique Dussel, Cristina Grenholm, Kwok Pui-lan, Archie Chi Chung Lee, Vasile Mihoc, Jesse Mugambi and Eugene TeSelle (assoc. eds.), *The Cambridge Dictionary of Christianity* (Cambridge and New York: Cambridge University Press, forthcoming). As is clear from the list of associate editors, it will have a more global perspective than Hastings' dictionary.

14. Philip L. Quinn, 'Atonement, theories of', in Adrian Hastings (ed.), *Oxford Companion to Christian Thought* (Oxford: Oxford University Press, 2000), pp. 51–52. For more details, see Gustaf Aulén, *Christus Victor: An Historical Study of the Three Main Types of the Idea of Atonement* (trans. A.G. Herbert; New York: Macmillan, 1951). To these three traditional (Western) 'theories of atonement', one might need to add a fourth formulated in a community-centered religious context, such as the view of atonement in Bishop Colenzo's *Commentary on Romans* (ed. Jonathan Draper; Pietermarzitzburg: South Africa: Cluster Publications, 2003; originally published 1874) written in Zululand on the basis of his translation of Romans in Zulu.

15. Quinn, 'Atonement', p. 51.

16. Quinn, 'Atonement', p. 51.

17. It is not the place to discuss further each of these interpretations. While this view of the atonement is found in the corresponding commentaries, it is most visible in formulations of Paul's theology such as the following: Günther Bornkamm, *Paul* (trans. D.M.G. Stalker; New York:

The 'ransom' understanding of atonement is that the life and death of Christ were a victorious struggle against personal or impersonal forces of evil – the devil, Satan or Sin as power – that keep human beings (sinners) in bondage. Thus, atonement (or redemption) is the liberation of sinners from these evil powers. This 'ransom' view of atonement is found especially in the 'apocalyptic' interpretations of Paul's theology and of Romans.[18] While this interpretation still focuses on 'justification by faith' as the center of Paul's gospel, it now emphasizes that being *'justified by faith' is being 'made righteous'*, that is, being transformed, by being freed from a state of bondage. 'The problem is not the disposition of God but the condition of humanity',[19] namely, that all human beings are under the power of sin (Rom. 3.9-18; when πάντας ὑφ' ἁμαρτίαν εἶναι is translated 'all are under the power of sin'). The good news addressed to Christian believers is: 'Christ is... the beginning of the New Age' when you can be freed from the bondage of sin; by believing/trusting that the cross occurred 'for our sins' and that the resurrection of Jesus was the prototype of our own transformation, we are 'in Christ' and are 'participants in new creation'.[20]

The 'exemplar' understanding of atonement should not be dismissed because of the secular form it took after the Enlightenment, a form underscored by Quinn: 'Christ's life and death are nothing more than an inspiring example of love and obedience... Sinners are moved by the example of Christ to repent of their sins, improve their lives, and become more loving'.[21] Actually, the exemplar understanding of atonement helps us to make sense of interpretations of Romans that do not find helpful either a 'satisfaction-forensic' or a 'ransom-liberation' view of atonement. I want to refer to those interpretations that James Dunn has called 'the new perspective on Paul'.[22] In this line of interpretation, the predicament (i.e., the

Harper & Row, 1971); Rudolf Bultmann, *Theology of the New Testament*, I (trans. Kendrick Grobel; New York: Charles Scribner's Sons, 1951); Hans Conzelmann, *An Outline of the Theology of the New Testament* (trans. J. Bowden; New York: Harper & Row, 1969); James D.G. Dunn, *The Theology of Paul the Apostle* (Grand Rapids: Eerdmans, 1998); Werner Georg Kümmel, *The Theology of the New Testament according to Its Major Witnesses: Jesus, Paul, John* (trans. J. Steely; Nashville: Abingdon Press, 1973).

18. These apocalyptic interpretations of Paul are clearly presented in John Riches, *A Century of New Testament Study* (Valley Forge, PA: Trinity Press International, 1993), pp. 32–49, 125–49 (it is also Riches' own perspective). This was the prevalent view in the patristic period. In modern times, it was brought to the attention of the critical world by Albert Schweitzer, *Paul and His Interpreters: a Critical History* (trans. W. Montgomery; London: A. & C. Black, 1912), and is found in different ways in the interpretations of Paul by Ernst Käsemann, *New Testament Questions of Today* (trans. W.J. Montague; Philadelphia: Fortress Press, 1969); Ernst Käsemann, *Perspectives on Paul* (trans. Margaret Kohl; Philadelphia: Fortress Press, 1971); Ernst Käsemann, *Commentary on Romans* (trans. Geoffrey W. Bromiley; Grand Rapids: Eerdmans, 1980); Leander E. Keck, *Paul and His Letters* (PC; Philadelphia: Fortress Press, 2nd edn, 1988); and by J. Christiaan Beker, *Paul The Apostle: The Triumph of God in Life and Thought* (Philadelphia: Fortress Press, 1980); J. Christiaan Beker, *Paul's Apocalyptic Gospel: The Coming Triumph of God* (Philadelphia: Fortress Press, 1982).

19. Keck, *Paul and His Letters*, p. 37.

20. Keck, *Paul and His Letters*, pp. 48, 78.

21. Quinn, 'Atonement', p. 52.

22. James D.G. Dunn, 'The New Perspective on Paul', in Karl P. Donfried (ed.), *The Romans*

primary problem) that is overcome by Christ's life, death and resurrection is neither a debt toward God that needs to be satisfied nor a bondage from which humans need to be freed. Rather, what Paul expresses through his emphasis on 'justification through faith' concerns the overcoming of the separation between Jews and Gentiles, as Stendahl insisted already in his 1976 book.[23] What does this mean concerning the interpretation of the atonement? These interpreters are hesitant. Stendahl directly relates his reinterpretation of 'justification through faith' to his rejection of the satisfaction-forensic view of atonement as an inadequate 'introspective' interpretation of Paul.[24] Beyond Stendahl, Stowers, for instance, emphasizes on the basis of his rhetorical reading of Rom. 3.19-26 that it is through the 'faithfulness of Christ' (rather than through 'faith in Christ') that God's righteousness has been shown, because God provided a 'way for the gentiles to be made righteous'.[25] Even though Stowers still presupposes a satisfaction-forensic view of atonement (e.g., when speaking of the anger of God that needs to be satisfied in the last judgment), commenting on Romans 6 and 12 he reorients it to underscore that what Christ has done through his faithfulness becomes effective for Gentiles when they view it as a model-exemplar that they are to reenact so as to be freed from the tyranny of sin.[26] This same view of atonement as exemplar can be found in interpretations that underscore Paul's typological way of thinking. In this perspective, Christ's life, death and resurrection and their transformative effects on some of his contemporaries – including Paul – are a type or model that is transformative (liberating) for other people in other times when it is 'fulfilled' or 'imitated' in these people's experience.[27] In this typological perspective, 'imitation' is not primarily a moral attitude, but a recognition that the same things that happened to Christ (his being crucified and resurrected by God) happen to believers (including being under death-like powers and God's interventions overcoming their bondage to these powers). Here, the exemplar view of atonement reorients the ransom-liberation view of atonement. Actually, this exemplar understanding of the

---

Debate (Peabody, MA: Hendrickson, exp. edn, 1991), pp. 299–308. Among the interpretations included in this new perspective one can list Krister Stendahl, *Paul Among Jews and Gentiles* (Philadelphia: Fortress Press, 1976); E.P. Sanders, *Paul and Palestinian Judaism: a Comparison of Patterns of Religion* (Philadelphia: Fortress Press, 1977); Stowers, *Diatribe* and *Rereading Romans*; Elliott, *Rhetoric of Romans* and *Liberating Paul*; Campbell, *Paul's Gospel*; Mark D. Nanos, *The Mystery of Romans: The Jewish Context of Paul's Letter* (Minneapolis: Fortress Press, 1996); and John G. Gager, *Reinventing Paul* (New York: Oxford University Press, 2000).

23. What Paul was concerned with were the questions: '(1) what happens to the Law (the Torah, the actual law of Moses, not the principle of legalism) when the Messiah has come? (2) what are the ramifications of the Messiah's arrival for the relation between Jews and Gentiles?' (Stendahl, *Paul*, p. 8).

24. 'Paul and the Introspective Conscience of the West' in Stendahl, *Paul*, pp. 78–96.

25. Stowers, *Rereading Romans*, pp. 37–38, passim.

26. Stowers, *Rereading Romans*, pp. 39–40, 324–26, passim.

27. See Daniel Patte, *Paul's Faith and the Power of the Gospel* (Philadelphia: Fortress Press, 1983), pp. 122–54, 232–96. Note that in this typological perspective, 'imitation' is not primarily a moral attitude but first of all a recognition that the same things (including God's interventions) happen to you as happened to Christ. This exemplar view of atonement is quite distinct from another understanding of atonement as exemplar, which reduces the atonement to a moral teaching.

atonement opens the way to a much more radical, and yet almost self-evident, re-orientation of both the satisfaction and ransom understandings of atonement. As Stendahl has recently suggested,[28] the good news of the atonement concerns those who are not Christian believers, outsiders to the people of God, among whom today's Christians would include Muslims, Hindus, atheists, etc., and even Jews. All of them have been reconciled with God, have been saved, are set in the right relationship with God, or are being transformed and liberated from bondage by God's powerful intervention. Thus, the role of Christians as members of the body of Christ is to manifest this atonement of those around them by following the example of Christ among them.

In sum, when one is aware that there is a diversity of ways of constructing any given theological concept – such as the atonement – one can readily recognize that by choosing to deal with this concept any interpretation, including a most sophis-ticated scholarly one, has also chosen a particular view of this theological concept. This means in our example that each interpreter, because of her or his theological preunderstandings (reflecting a certain kind of religious experience), has come to the text with one or another theory of the atonement. Thus, she or he has read Romans for what it has to say about either 'satisfaction-forensic', or 'ransom-liberation', or 'exemplar' atonement. A commentary will be most helpful to consci-entious preachers if it presents, as equally plausible choices, several theological understandings of the teaching of Romans about atonement.

To put it bluntly, this ideal postmodern commentary would renounce arguing – as modern commentaries do – a) that Paul held one of these views of atonement and b) that reading Romans in terms of another view would be wrong.

Objections to such a practice abound. Is it not the task of biblical scholarship to establish what is 'Paul's view of the atonement'? Is not the problem with the interpretations by ordinary believers that they 'read into the text' what they already believe? Is it not the task of critical biblical scholars to denounce 'eisegesis' and overcome it by establishing 'what the text actually says' or 'what Paul meant'?

None of these objections holds, as soon as one examines actual scholarly inter-pretations and the receptions of these scriptural texts by believers through history and today through cultures. I took the time to refer in some detail to several scholarly interpretations of Paul's letters, especially Romans. Why? Because it then becomes clear that knowledgeable scholars disagree about what view of the atonement Paul held, yet each is able to make a defensible case for the interpreta-tion he or she proposes. And one can repeat this experiment with all kinds of theological and ethical themes, as I did at length with the concepts of discipleship and of morality in different scholarly interpretations of the Sermon on the Mount.[29]

---

28. Krister Stendahl, 'A Last Word', in Daniel Patte and Eugene TeSelle (eds.), *Engaging Augustine on Romans: Self, Context, and Theology in Interpretation* (Harrisburg, PA: Trinity Press International, 2002), pp. 270–72. 'If Paul is about how to deal with communities and their relation to each other in a world that is a community of communities, does he by implication have something to say toward the construction of a Christian theology of religions?' (p. 272).

29. Daniel Patte, *Discipleship according to the Sermon on the Mount: Four Legitimate Read-ings, Four Plausible Views of Discipleship, and Their Relative Values* (Valley Forge, PA: Trinity Press International, 1996).

Shall we say that the last scholarly interpretation is the true one, and that all the preceding ones were wrong? On what ground? Because it is à la mode and trendy? Or because we are supposed to believe in a progress of biblical interpretation comparable to progress in the natural or the medical sciences? Obviously not.

We must rather acknowledge that each of these is an interpretation of a religious discourse – in this case, Paul's discourse addressed to the Romans – and that as such each interpretation is necessarily involved in a hermeneutical circle. This should not be viewed as a 'problem' to be overcome but rather as the necessary condition for interpreting such documents; otherwise no interpretation takes place. Interpretation involves entering in dialogue with the text about a subject-matter chosen by the interpreter.[30] Thus, any interpretation of Romans concerning the atonement necessarily starts with the interpreter's view on the atonement – be it a particular view of atonement as satisfaction, ransom or exemplar – and unfolds as a dialogue with the text on this subject matter. Through this dialogue, the interpreter's original view of atonement as satisfaction (or as ransom or as exemplar) is challenged, affirmed, modified or completely rejected – to the point that this interpreter might find that she/he should envision another view of atonement (let us say, a ransom view). In such a case, one should not conclude and say: 'Paul did not have a view of atonement as satisfaction, but rather a view of atonement as ransom'. Rather, one should say: 'Paul did not have the *particular view* of atonement as satisfaction *that I brought to the text*; a view of atonement as ransom that I can now conceive of seems to be supported by the text'. Thus, the interpreters, especially the scholarly interpreters, learn from the text. The text affects and at times radically transforms the views they bring to the text and through which they read it. Reading into the text one or another view of the atonement ('eisegesis') is therefore not a problem in itself. It becomes a problem only when it is denied, either by those believers who claim that their interpretation establishes the fundamentals of the teaching of the text or by biblical scholars who, while rejecting positivism and fundamentalism, practice critical biblical studies as if its goal were to establish what the text meant or what the text says (a narrow meaning of 'exegesis').

Conscientious preachers in their practice acknowledge that scholarly biblical interpretations are framed by a diversity of theological perspectives and therefore consult different interpretations out of which they choose the one that opens up a theological outlook with which they resonate and which they feel would be meaningful for the hearers of the sermon they prepare. This is what they do *in practice*, even though, if pressed, they might join other believers and express their trust that biblical scholars establish for them 'the truth' that the biblical text conveys.

---

30. I do not need to demonstrate this point that has long been made by specialists of hermeneutics and semiotics. Suffice it to refer to the concise presentation of the history of hermeneutics by David Tracy, 'Interpretation of the Bible and Interpretation Theory', 'Theological Interpretation of the Bible Today', and 'Theological Interpretation of the Scriptures in the Church: Prospect and Retrospect', in Robert M. Grant with David Tracy, *A Short History of the Interpretation of the Bible* (Minneapolis: Fortress, 2nd edn, 1984), pp. 153–87; see also my presentation of major semiotic theories in Daniel Patte, *The Religious Dimensions of Biblical Texts: Greimas's Structural Semiotics and Biblical Exegesis* (SBLSS; Atlanta: Scholars Press, 1990), pp. 1–72.

A Commentary Making Explicit the Plausibility of Several Contextual Frames for Interpreting the Biblical Text

Before addressing this essential question of 'the truth' that the biblical text conveys, I want briefly to underscore the third aspect of the conscientious preachers' practice. As they prepare their sermons, they self-consciously choose an interpretation that, they hope, will address issues and needs that their parishioners have in their specific life-context. Do they need to have (additional) *knowledge* of the will of God that they should carry out in their particular situation (e.g., a complex cultural context where confused people do not know how to discern what is good and evil)? Or maybe they know very well what is God's will, but do not want to do it – lacking the *will* to do it – because of some aspects of their life-context (e.g., bad influences, laxity)? Or maybe, while they know God's will and truly want to do it, they are totally *powerless, unable* to do it, because they are in bondage to oppressive powers, e.g., sickness, disability, addiction or physical and psychological abuse, or debilitating poverty or social, economic, political oppression? Or maybe they lack *faith*, not having in their life-context either a vision of God's presence or a sense of God's love and of belonging to God's family? Conscientious preachers are quite aware that their sermons will miss the mark if they address the wrong need. For instance, it is useless to repeat again and again 'what' is God's will about a particular issue to believers who know quite well what it is but do not want to do it, or vice versa. Hence, as they read scholarly interpretations, these preachers choose the one that they feel will best address the contextual needs of their parishioners. By this choice, they show their pragmatic sense that each scholarly interpretation is contextually framed; its analytical and theological choices are intertwined with concerns for the needs that believers have in a certain life-context.

This contextual character of interpretation is quite visible when one considers the use of scripture in moral arguments. As Charles Cosgrove has shown, one can readily discern very different 'hermeneutical assumptions' or rules that govern appeals to scripture in moral arguments which are 'persuasive only if speaker and audience share the same hermeneutical assumptions'.[31] By analyzing five different kinds of appeals to scripture in moral arguments (different ways to live by scripture), Cosgrove illustrates five different kinds of contextual framing of biblical interpretations in moral debates, that he summarizes as follows:

> 1. The Rule of Purpose: The purpose (or justification) behind a biblical moral rule carries greater weight than the rule itself.
> 2. The Rule of Analogy. Analogical reasoning is an appropriate and necessary method for applying scripture to contemporary moral issues.
> 3. The Rule of Countercultural Witness. There is a presumption in favor of according greater weight to countercultural tendencies in scripture that express the voice of the powerless and the marginalized than to those tendencies that echo the dominant culture of their time.
> 4. The Rule of the Non-Scientific Scope of Scripture. Scientific (or 'empirical') knowledge stands outside the scope of scripture.

31. Charles H. Cosgrove, *Appealing to Scripture in Moral Debate: Five Hermeneutical Rules* (Grand Rapids: Eerdmans, 2002), p. 3.

5. The Rule of Moral-Theological Adjudication. Moral-theological considerations should guide hermeneutical choices between conflicting plausible interpretations.[32]

Are such contextual readings of the biblical text as scripture, i.e., as a book to live by, a second step of a hermeneutical process? Are they the application of 'what the text meant' to today's life so as to discern 'what it means'? No, as I suggested above, any interpretation of a biblical text is implicitly or explicitly contextually framed from its inception.

This contextual frame cannot be isolated from the analytical frame of the interpretation that chooses one aspect of the text or another as most significant. This analytical choice involves an implicit or explicit construction of encoded readers who are envisioned as living by the given text. For instance, the analytical choice of any given interpretation of Romans envisions in its own way the 'Roman Christians' to whom Paul addressed his letter with the expectation that they would live by it. These encoded readers are urged to apply the teaching of this letter to the various aspects of their life-context: their relations with other believers within their Christian congregations and beyond, including Jews; morality issues in society (the world) and the church; as well as economic and political realities of their time, including the Roman emperor. One might want to ask: How did Paul expect the Roman churches to be affected by his letter and to live by it? And/or: How were the Romans affected by Paul's letter? How did they receive it and live by it? In both cases, the analytical reconstructions that the interpreters end up proposing also depend on *theological choices* they made, this time, among different ways of envisioning how one 'lives by' a religious text. Is scripture to be conceived, for instance, as a 'Lamp to My Feet' (Ps. 119.105) , as 'Canon', as 'Good News', as 'Testament' (i.e., as 'Book of the Covenant'), as 'Prophetic Word', as 'Holy Writ'? Each of these metaphors refers to theological concepts concerning the relationship between these books and the divine, as well as to views of revelation, of inspiration, of God's interactions with humans. Yet, each of these metaphors also represents a particular way to live by scripture and consequently provides a particular contextual frame for the way in which this text addresses certain kinds of needs that believers might or might not have in their life-context.

If a biblical text is read as *Lamp to My Feet*, one presupposes that scripture teaches believers what they should do, step by step, because the problem in their life-context is that they lack direction for their lives and do not know what is good or evil. The biblical text provides *knowledge* of what believers are called by God to do.

If a biblical text is read as *Canon*, one presupposes that scripture shapes the believers' moral life as an implementation of God's will, so that the church may fulfill its mission. The problem in their life-context is that at the community level one lacks either knowledge of the will of God or the will to do God's will. Thus, scripture provides a means to recognize who does or does not belong to the community of believers and thus provides either *knowledge* of what believers must do to belong to the community or, through threats and demands, influences

32. Cosgrove, *Appealing to Scripture*, p. 3.

a believer's *will* to act in a certain way and to contribute to the mission of the church.

Yet, if a biblical text is read as *Good News* or as a *Book of the Covenant* (a 'Testament' or 'Family Album'), one presupposes that scripture is primarily a revelation of God's love. It is a comforting, encouraging, merciful word for believers who in their life-context do not know or experience God's love, grace and mercy. Here, the Bible might provide believers with *knowledge* of God's love or may influence their *will* to serve God, as a response to God's love. But, as it gives believers a true sense of their relationship to God and to others, the Bible more commonly provides them with *faith* or a *vision* of their identity as members of God's people.

If a biblical text is read as a *Prophetic Word*, scripture speaks to believers who are discouraged, lack faith and/or feel powerless because of the dire situation that prevails in their life-context. As 'corrective glasses' this prophetic Word allows them to see their lives or experiences through eyes of faith, discerning in the midst of evil 'what is good and acceptable and perfect' and what God is doing. As 'empowering word', this prophetic Word of scripture conjures a new reality for believers. For example, it provides preliminary manifestations of the kingdom and of God's justice in a broken world and thus gives hope. In this role, scripture provides *faith or a vision* of God's presence in the lives of believers and *empowers or enables* them.

Similarly, if a biblical text is read as *Holy Writ*, one presupposes that the problem believers face in their life-context is the experience of the absence of God, a common experience in the secular world today, but also in more religious eras. Scripture confronts believers with the holy. The Bible provides a 'goose bumps' experience – a sense of awe, mystery and wonder – because it shatters a believer's expectations and confronts him or her with something radically different and awe-inspiring.

The conscientious preachers are right in recognizing that each given scholarly interpretation has presupposed one or another kind of contextual problem. Thus, in the ideal postmodern commentary I envision, in the process of making explicit how different interpretations have made analytical and theological choices, I will also need to signal the contextual choices involved in each interpretation.

Conclusion

This is not the place to explain how all this can be done concretely in the pages of a commentary, although it is simpler than one might think. Rather, in conclusion, I need to address two issues: (a) an epistemological question that believers, preachers and scholars alike readily ask: Where is 'truth' in all this? and (b) an ethical question concerning what is at stake in this choice of a postmodern form for critical biblical commentaries.

Where Is 'Truth' in This Postmodern Conception of a Commentary?
At this point it is important to keep in mind that this commentary (as any commentary on Romans) will be primarily used by Christian believers who read the New

Testament and the Hebrew Bible as scripture. Recent statistics show that far from shrinking – as one might think in the Western world – the number of such believers is on the increase; almost two-thirds of the 2.1 billion Christians are now in the Two-Thirds World. Hence, a commentary is to be written for believers and preachers in very different life-contexts who need 'comments' on biblical texts to help them when they read the Bible as scripture.

What kinds of 'comments' on biblical texts do believers need from a critical commentary? Here there are theological and contextual disagreements concerning what is 'the truth of scripture'. The commentary I envision chooses one option, which is puzzling and confusing for many believers and preachers who have chosen the opposite option.

Unlike the conscientious preachers described above, many believers, preachers, lay-leaders and students consult a commentary with the hope that it will authoritatively establish what is 'the truth' – that is, 'the true teaching' – expressed and contained by the given biblical book. From their perspective, the biblical 'truth' – the Word of God – communicated by the text is a 'propositional truth' (as some like to say), a cognitive entity that can be apprehended and studied as an object. Some might conceive the truth of the gospel presented by Paul in Romans as similar to a platonic idea, a disembodied idea that needs to be appropriated before being applied in one's life. For these believers, the ideal commentary should present the best scholarship available concerning 'the true meaning' of the text, which they often identify with 'what the text meant' (when they are historically minded) and at times as 'what the text says' (when they are more theologically or literally minded). For them, this truth is universal in the sense that it is a reality that everyone everywhere and in every time should recognize and appropriate. 'What the text meant' or 'says' should serve as the necessary and solid foundation for determining 'what the text means' in particular contexts today, that is, how this universal truth can be applied to concrete situations today.

Obviously, it is possible to read Romans and other books of the Bible for this kind of truth. Many do! Yet, one has to recognize that in so doing one has made *a contextual choice*: one has presupposed that the human predicament is a lack of knowledge – of cognitive entity, of propositional truth, to be appropriated – regarding God, God's will, Christ and all kinds of theological realities, eventually encompassing all that the biblical text speaks about. This kind of 'biblical truth' might also address people whose predicament is primarily a lack of will: knowledge about God's love can entice them to want to do the will of this loving God, convincing them that God's will is good for them; conversely, a knowledge about God's wrath and threats of punishment might have a similar effect. But it does not really help them if the human predicament is a lack of ability (powerlessness) that requires a transformation of their personal or collective situation or if the human predicament is a lack of faith-vision that requires an encounter with God as the wholly Other who is beyond comprehension (and thus, beyond knowledge). Similarly, as a comparison of several commentaries that claim to present 'the' truth – the true teaching – of Romans reveals, each of these commentaries has made theological choices (as discussed regarding the views of atonement) as well as analytical choices.

Should this be a devastating blow to Christian believers, threatening their faith? Why should it be? Many other believers – and especially many preachers – do not consult commentaries with the expectation of finding in them a presentation of the universal, eternal truth of the biblical text. They are fully aware that 'the true teaching' of a scriptural text is not a cognitive entity contained in the text that believers would simply need to appropriate and then to apply to their lives – as one learns a mathematical formula so as to apply it to resolve a concrete problem. A biblical teaching is 'true' when it interacts with the believers' lives. The truth of the gospel is always incarnated and therefore always contextual. It is the way in which the biblical text affects believers in their particular contexts by affirming, challenging, transforming or rejecting aspects of their religious or cultural world-views and their concrete relational life in society and community. The truth of the gospel is therefore always inculturated, because its truth is in the difference it makes for the believers-readers and thus in how different it is as compared with these believers' original religious and cultural views. The truth of scripture is in the new vision of their life that it gives to the believers-readers, including allowing them to discern the presence of God in concrete situations and experiences. The truth of the gospel is in its transformative power, through which people are set free from bondage and entrusted with particular vocations and missions. Thus, the truth of a biblical text as scripture is always how it affects believers in their lives. I could argue this point regarding any religious discourse, using semiotic theories. But, to anyone who wants to speak to me about 'the truth' of a biblical text, I can make this same point much more forcefully by asking a pair of simple questions from the perspective of scriptural criticism: 'It is fine to tell me what the text says. But tell me: What difference does this text make in the believers' ways of thinking? What difference does this text make in their lives?'

What Is at Stake in My Choice of a Postmodern Form for My Commentary?
My choice of a particular form for my commentary is, of course, both contextual and theological. I will not repeat here what I have already argued in *Ethics of Biblical Interpretation*.[33] But, in concluding, I want to point out the contextual problem that writing a postmodern commentary seeks to address.

Let me first state that, for me, *the primary goal of critical biblical studies is to help people to read the Bible in a responsible way*. It follows that we, biblical critics, must also assume responsibility for our own critical studies of the Bible.

I suggested above that a part of our role is to ask: 'What difference does this text make in the believers' way of thinking? What difference does this text make in their lives?' I believe these questions are an essential step in helping people to read the Bible in a responsible way and to assume responsibility for their own interpretations. Yet, prior to taking this step, people need to read the Bible and to interpret it.

The problem – a problem with far-reaching consequences – is that our 'default practice' of critical biblical studies discourages and even, as an ideological effect,

33. Daniel Patte, *Ethics of Biblical Interpretation: A Reevaluation* (Louisville, KY: Westminster/John Knox Press, 1995).

prevents other people from reading the Bible and interpreting it for themselves. Let me explain briefly.

In my experience, an increasing number of people that we biblical critics address – students in religious studies classes, seminarians and lay people in main-line churches – have never read the Bible and do not read it. My suspicion is that critical biblical studies exacerbates, rather than addresses, this problem of biblical illiteracy. James Smart noted long ago that one effect of critical biblical studies is 'the strange silence of the Bible in the church' (or more exactly, in the mainline churches that are open to critical scholarly biblical studies).[34] But contrary to Smart's assessment, I want to say that this is not a hermeneutical (or theological) problem. It is a matter of 'praxis' and thus a contextual problem. Let me explain.

My intention as a biblical critic is clear: through my critical studies I intend to facilitate the reading of the Bible. I am pretty sure that the large majority of biblical critics have a similar goal. But, in view of Smart's book and many other signs, I am afraid that, against our best intentions, the way we traditionally practice critical biblical studies actually prevents others from reading the Bible. We are surprised. How could we prevent the reading of the Bible by others, when all our efforts and diligence are devoted to helping people read it by clarifying whatever might be difficult to understand in the text and by contributing to bridge the historical gap that separates present-day readers from it? Yet, it is nevertheless the case. This is an unintended, systemic effect that common practices of 'scholarly' biblical studies have upon 'ordinary' readers of the Bible. It results from the structure of authority that these practices of critical biblical studies establish between 'scholarly' and 'ordinary' readings. By positing that scholarly studies are the only ones that can hope to be legitimate, these practices convey to other people that as long as a reading is not informed by critical scholarship it is at best inappropriate or inadequate, and, more often than not, simply wrong-headed. Therefore, these practices of critical biblical studies convey the following message to 'ordinary' readers: 'Stop reading the Bible, because without an expert to tell you what it says you will certainly be wrong'.

As critical readers of the Bible, whether in the pulpit, in the classroom or in our research library, we readily conceive of our scholarly task as the formulation of 'new and better' interpretations, i.e., informed interpretations. Is it not the case that our interpretations are more solidly grounded in the text than those by readers who do not have our training? Then the structure of authority mentioned above is clear. Biblical critics as scholars provide the informed interpretation that, accordingly, ordinary readers would be unable to reach on their own. Scholars read '*for* ordinary readers', '*instead of* them', and in the process prevent them from reading the Bible on their own.[35] This is true even when scholars invite people to read the Bible 'by

---

34. James Smart, *The Strange Silence of the Bible in the Church* (Philadelphia: Westminster Press, 1970).

35. Treat ordinary readers as subalterns. See Gayatri C. Spivak, 'Can the Subaltern Speak?', in G. Nelson and L. Grossberg (eds.), *Marxism and the Interpretation of Culture* (London: Macmillan Publishers, 1988), pp. 277–313.

themselves', because the hierarchical context of this invitation also conveys: 'read the text by yourself following the interpretation I just gave you'.

A brief illustration is helpful to show how pervasive this practice of critical biblical studies is: *The Access Bible*.[36] This annotated Bible 'for beginning Bible students' is very conscious of the fact that these students have not read the Bible and need to be enabled to do so: 'The Access Bible is designed to provide study helps that enable the reader to engage the biblical text directly and not simply read about the Bible. That is, the study helps are designed to lead readers into their own careful and reflective reading of the biblical text'.[37] In sum, this annotated Bible sees the reading of the Bible by the students themselves as the ultimate goal of critical biblical studies. Yet, when one examines the diverse kinds of 'study helps', one soon discovers that the editors propose a specific informed reading – informed by 'the best resources of biblical scholarship' – of each book, paragraph by paragraph. The basic presupposition is that, without these 'study helps' that outline the argument of each book, the biblical text would be inaccessible to students as 'ordinary readers'. The *Access Bible* is a clear example of critical studies that prevent the reading of the Bible by ordinary readers by giving to scholars a veto power over all readings that depart from theirs, in effect saying: 'Read the text by yourself following the interpretation we just gave you'.

This authority structure is present – at times welcomed and at other times resented as academic arrogance by ordinary readers of the Bible – even when we would never dream to claim authority for our scholarly interpretations. Whether we like it or not, regarding biblical interpretation, we biblical critics as scholars are in a position of power.[38] When we present our argument for a 'more informed' interpretation of a text, students, people in the pews and whoever does not have our level of scholarly training, readily view our interpretation as authoritative, that is, as the interpretation they should adopt by abandoning the one they had previously formulated. Indeed, they should wait for or consult such informed interpretations, rather than read the text by themselves and formulate their own interpretations.

I do not suggest that having authority is in itself problematic. I question the kind of authority commonly projected by this type of structure of our 'scholarly' practices of critical biblical studies. As I suggested in *Ethics of Biblical Interpretation*, it is enough for us, biblical critics, to make our claim to authority our knowledge of a greater number of interpretations of each given biblical text. This is the type of authority I want to claim as author of a postmodern commentary that *opens the text up* by presenting a plurality of interpretations as equally legitimate and plausible.

---

36. Gail R. O'Day and David Petersen (eds.), *The Access Bible: New Revised Standard Version with the Apocryphal/Deuterocanonical Books* (College Edition; Oxford and New York: Oxford University Press, 1999).

37. O'Day and Petersen (eds.), *The Access Bible*, p. 1.

38. See the repeated warnings regarding this issue in Gerald O. West, *Contextual Bible Study* (Pietermaritzburg, South Africa: Cluster Publications, 1993) and Gerald O. West, *The Academy of the Poor: Toward a Dialogical Reading of the Bible* (Sheffield: Sheffield Academic Press, 1999).

Of course, there are interpretations that are, 'in some sense' better than others. The question is: In what sense? Assuming responsibility for our interpretations, whoever we might be, involves discerning which interpretation is 'better' than others or which are totally unacceptable because of their devastating direct or indirect effects upon certain people (women, Jews, people of other races, of other cultures or of other social, economic, political or intellectual aptitudes). But I, as a biblical critic, do not have the authority to make this assessment on my own; this has to be a collective, communal judgment. The only thing I can do is facilitate this assessment by helping readers of the Bible be aware of the options they have. This is what a postmodern commentary seeks to do through a presentation that makes explicit the interpretive choices involved in several plausible and legitimate interpretations.

CULTURE AND INTERSUBJECTIVITY AS CRITERIA FOR
NEGOTIATING MEANINGS IN CROSS-CULTURAL INTERPRETATIONS

Khiok-khng Yeo, Garrett-Evangelical Theological
Seminary, Illinois, USA

The purpose of this essay is to identify the role 'culture' plays in contributing to the indeterminacy of meanings in a biblical text as well as the way 'culture' serves as one of the most significant criteria in evaluating competing plausible interpretations of scripture. Biblical interpretation in any cross-cultural context, in the good and robust sense, must allow the historical meaning(s) of the text to speak to the contemporary interpreters and their modern audiences. Yet, besides overlapping and commonalities that pose no problem of conflicting interpretations, biblical scholars often confront genuinely competing interpretations of the same text. The discipline of judging between reasonable interpretations constitutes an important part of the ethics of interpretation.[1] It involves putting forth a legitimation of one's preferred reading over other plausible meanings as an act of faithful interpretation in community, where the reading of scripture cannot be confined to merely individual interest but is a matter of community judgment. My aim in this essay is to consider how culture shapes (and ought to shape) our choices between competing interpretations of scripture in the interests of Christian faith and practice.

Autobiographical Interests in Cross-Cultural Hermeneutics

I grew up in Malaysia, a multicultural setting that taught me to value the co-existence of various ethnic and religious groups. Malaysians pride themselves on celebrating cultural diversity and respecting uniqueness. Once I reached the environment of the postmodern academy, concepts (and values) such as 'indeterminacy', 'ambiguity', 'openness' and 'plurality' sounded good to my ears because they resonated with the Malaysian reality. I have also accepted that ongoing historical and cultural changes are powerful factors in creating our experience of

---

1. On indeterminacy and hermeneutical adjudication between competing plausible interpretations, see Charles H. Cosgrove, *Appealing to Scripture in Moral Debate: Five Hermeneutical Rules* (Grand Rapids: Eerdmans, 2002), pp. 154–80; also Charles H. Cosgrove, *Elusive Israel: The Puzzle of Election in Romans* (Louisville, KY: Westminster/John Knox Press, 1997), pp. 38–45; Daniel Patte, *Discipleship according to the Sermon on the Mount: Four Legitimate Readings, Four Plausible Views of Discipleship, and Their Relative Values* (Valley Forge: Trinity Press International, 1996).

indeterminacy, ambiguity and pluralism.[2] From my first year of theological study in the US, while I was being trained to read the Bible as any Westerner would, I was constantly thinking about my Chinese culture. I kept asking the question: What has the Bible to do with my people and the Chinese culture? This question and the studies it sparked eventually led me to produce a monograph that brought the Bible and Chinese culture into dialogue: *What Has Jerusalem to Do with Beijing? Biblical Interpretation from a Chinese Perspective.*[3]

Culture changes across space and time. Hence, the cultural identity of persons and peoples also changes. Culture, context and people are in constant interaction. My cultural identity is located, in part, in the Confucianist ethical tradition and the modern intellectual quest. Even though my family does not have a Confucian altar (that would be treating Confucianism as a religion), for us Chineseness means that to be human is to be social and ethical beings who establish themselves so that they can contribute toward the goodness and prosperity of their community. Confucianism, at least the kind of Confucian ideals that my family embraces, is an accommodating way of being. It gives me the best it has to offer without the obligations of its religious rituals. My family and I have never considered Confucianism a religion; it is a way of life for us. But Confucianism does have significance for my religious faith. Since my cultural identity matters to me, Confucian ideals guide my reading of the Bible. Confucianism provides some of the questions and the norms by which I make sense of scripture and adjudicate between competing interpretations.

The Intersubjective Process of Cross-Cultural Hermeneutics

Over the last fifteen years I have done extensive cross-cultural reading of the Pauline epistles. I have also carried out a critical reflection on my reading process, which I have come to understand as 'intersubjective'. My intention in this section is not to give a survey of methods in biblical interpretation or to describe intersubjectivity in a general way[4] but to discuss the intersubjective and rhetorical-hermeneutical elements of my cross-cultural interpretation process in order to delineate the role of culture in interpretation.

The Rhetorical-Hermeneutical Reading Process
An intersubjective reading assumes a rhetorical-hermeneutical reading process that is interactive and persuasive. In *Rhetorical Interaction in 1 Corinthians 8 and 10*, I spelled out in detail the significance and process of an interactive model in biblical reading and cross-cultural hermeneutics based on rhetorical theories.[5] What needs

2. Wendy Griswold, *Cultures and Societies in a Changing World* (London/Thousand Oaks/ New Delhi: Pine Forge Press, 1994).

3. Khiok-khng Yeo, *What Has Jerusalem to Do with Beijing? Biblical Interpretation from a Chinese Perspective* (Harrisburg, PA: Trinity Press International, 1998).

4. On the methodology of intersubjectivity, see Michael Morton and Judith Still (eds.), *Intertextuality: Theories and Practices* (Manchester and New York: Manchester University Press, 1991); George Aichele and Gary A. Phillips (eds.), 'Intertextuality and the Bible', *Semeia*, 69/70 (1995).

5. Khiok-khng Yeo, *Rhetorical Interaction in 1 Corinthians 8 and 10: A Formal Analysis*

further explication is the rhetorical nature of the reading process on at least three planes. A rhetorical reading of any biblical text observes the interaction of these planes within the larger whole and articulates the way that interaction brings out a persuasive argument to the readers. We can use a series of diagrams to present the various planes of rhetorical reading of a biblical text.

First, a rhetorical reading at the broadest plane happens at a meta-spatiotemporal level of sophistication:

Signified

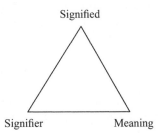

Signifier   Meaning

The philosophical plane concerns the use of language in relation to reality. Philosophers of language seek to explore the relationship between linguistic signs and physical worlds. The typical question asked at this plane is whether language represents (expresses) or *re*-presents (creates) reality, or both? I have argued in my previous work that language, by means of metaphor, is both descriptive and prescriptive, communicative and creative.[6] At this representational or ideational plane, the rhetorical interaction happens between the language (sign, signifier), the rhetor and reality (signified).

Language is limited in the sense that it is not able to represent the signified with perfect clarity. Language works in metaphors, which have both descriptive and creative functions of 'is and is not' *and* 'is and is more'. It is this 'something more' that makes language creative and open-ended. Metaphor is the power of this 'more' of language. I.A. Richards contends that metaphor is not a matter of using words in a special way but an omnipresent principle of speech and thought. Hence, metaphor is not a deviation from literal or ordinary language. Rather, it is constitutive of our ordinary conceptual structure and is therefore cognitively irreducible.[7]

At the second plane, the triangle of utterance is the rhetorical communication of the rhetor with the audience. A rhetorical reading observes the argumentation, the rhetorical force and the meaning conveyed by analyzing the genre, context, structure, intention, rhetorical skills and devices.[8]

The third plane of rhetorical reading involves the interaction among the interpreter, the text and the meaning. As modern readers read on the first and second

with Preliminary Suggestions for a Chinese, Cross-Cultural Hermeneutic (Leiden: E.J. Brill, 1995), ch. 3.

6.   *Rhetorical Interaction*, pp. 31–37.

7.   I.A. Richards, *The Philosophy of Rhetoric* (New York: Oxford University Press, 1965), pp. 108–109. See also Mark Johnson, *Philosophical Perspectives on Metaphor* (Minneapolis: University of Minnesota Press, 1981), pp. 63–82.

8.   The rhetorical criticism in my previous work focuses on this plane of interaction (Yeo, *Rhetorical Interaction in 1 Corinthians 8 and 10*, pp. 50–74).

planes, they themselves become the interpreters who are drawn into the rhetorical process of interpersonal communication with the text. In this plane, the interpreter cannot assume that he or she will fully participate in the reality of the original interaction among the rhetor, audience and utterance. The interpreter should rather recognize that reading/interpretation is always constructive: the interpreter plays a significant role in the meaning-producing process. Reader-response approaches have revealed to us that the creative, constructive work of the reader *cannot* be absent from the reading process. To understand meaning based on the text is both limited and creative – limited in the sense that we can never go back to the original communicative event and creative in the sense that it is precisely in the limitation as well as in the textuality that new meaning can evolve out of the interaction between the text and the interpreter. Whether that meaning (M^1) is the original intention of the original rhetor is impossible to ascertain. The best that we can say is that there is probably often a certain *continuity*, but the textuality is the enduring character of the utterance, the locus of its meaning for succeeding generations of readers.

Interpretation of biblical texts always takes place through a dialogical process.[9] The text can be a living text in a rhetorical transaction only as it interacts with its successive audiences, from ancient to modern times.[10] Therefore, drawing out hermeneutical implications is not a peripheral task of biblical interpretation but one of the necessary links in the hermeneutical circle. It is especially imperative because those perceived implications can also be reasons for choosing one interpretation over another.

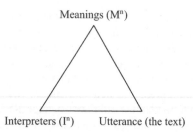

Meanings (M^n)

Interpreters (I^n)　　　　Utterance (the text)

Here, in summary, are the three planes we have talked about, laid out to show the linear reading-movement.[11]

---

9. Hans-Georg Gadamer, *Truth and Method* (rev. trans. Joel Weinsheimer and Donald G. Marshall; New York: Crossroad, 2nd edn, 1994), p. 364.

10. The notion of the Bible as the living text can be seen in the translation process. For an excellent account of the transmission process and a theory of how God works as translator, see Willis Barnstone, *The Poetics of Translation: History, Theory, Practice* (New Haven: Yale University Press, 1993), pp. 124–31 (God as the translator of the Bible), pp. 135–216 (Bible as the translation paradigm).

11. I have adapted Geoffrey N. Leech's study of pragmatics based on Halliday's three functions of hierarchy of instrumentality. See Geoffrey N. Leech and Michael H. Short, *Principles of Pragmatics* (London and New York: Longman, 1983), p. 59; Geoffrey N. Leech, 'Stylistics and Functionalism', in *Style in Fiction: A Linguistic Introduction to English Fictional Prose* (London and New York: Longman, 1981), pp. 81–83.

1. Representation   6. ideational / spatiotemporal meaning of signifiers and signified
2. Text   5. textual meaning / utterance of rhetor to audience
3. Discourse   4. interpersonal / meaning of interpreter in discourse with text

Though the actual reading process might be multi-planar (the three planes in confluence with each other), *understanding* that process and the way one *communicates* that understanding are always limited by the linear movement of thought. Hence, numbers 1–3 indicate the reading process that begins with the representational plane and moves to the textual plane, then to the discourse plane. Numbers 4–6 indicate the reverse process of moving from the micro to the macro planes as one's reading progresses to complete the interpretive circle. Paying attention to the movements from 4 to 6 can help critical interpreters make necessary adjustments to their interpretations on the three different planes as they take into account their understanding of language, text, self and audience.

Since any reading essentially involves at least these three planes, we can assume that there is only one text and one rhetor, but many interpreters. Hence, the meanings produced will be M^1, M^2, M^3... M^n. Not only do we attempt to discover the communication of the rhetor in the representation of reality, we also engage in the cross-cultural endeavor as we use a second language system, our own, to understand the second plane of textual meaning. Because of this cross-spatiotemporal nature of reading, the third triangle can be more accurately drawn as follows:

Meanings (M^1)

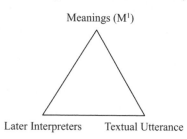

Later Interpreters   Textual Utterance

The reading process on the third plane gets complicated when we add another factor, which, in a real-life setting, is very much part of our meaning-producing process: the audience. As we communicate the same text to different audiences, the message will necessarily differ.

Meanings (M^n) (based on text)

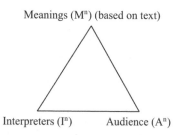

Interpreters (I^n)   Audience (A^n)

In other words, a reading that is rhetorically interactive assumes the reading process to be a complex interaction between the text, the writer and the readers/audience. A rhetorical-interactive reading model accounts for factors in the reading process such as the physical situation, the subject of the discourse, the intention of the speaker (psychological context), the participants' social context, the linguistic code, the rhetorical techniques, the genre of the message and text and the complex horizons of the readers. Any biblical text is therefore simultaneously rhetorical (in the sense of aiming at persuasion), interactive (in the sense of communicative), hermeneutical (in the sense of meaningful) and theological (in the sense of its substantive theological content).

The Intersubjectivity of a Rhetorical Reading

I wish now to supplement the preceding model of the rhetorical interaction of text, writer and reader by drawing on the notions of intertextuality and intersubjectivity.

Julia Kristeva coined the term 'intertextuality' to indicate that a text exists not in a closed system of its own but in interrelation with other texts through quotations, references, allusions and influences of various kinds.[12] The intersubjective influence conveyed through the medium of a 'text' is clearly seen in the 'various cultural discourses'[13] because 'the text is a tissue of quotations drawn from innumerable centers of culture'.[14] The assumed locus of meaning-production in this intersubjective process has shifted from the author to the reader because 'multiplicity is focused [on]... the reader... [who] is the space on which all the quotations that make up a writing are inscribed...'[15] Both axes of intertextuality – via the writer (who is the first reader) and the readers (who are co-producers of textual meaning) – allow the 'dialogism' or 'heteroglossia' (exchange of language in M. Bakhtin's notion) of texts to work in the genesis of meaning.[16] For example, the double-voiced discourse, or even the polyphonic literary novel, serves the intentions and interaction of two speakers' worldviews.

The processes of reading and meaning-production are always dialogues between the writers and the readers. The authority of interpretation does not reside in the frozen text or in the first writer but is to be found in the interactive process of the text, involving both the writer and the reader, which I have previously called 'rhetorical interaction'.[17] Various thinkers have used different terms for this: intersubjectivity in Kristeva and 'communicative action' in Jürgen Habermas.[18] Both of these ideas have the notion of dialogical relation and reciprocal recognition as one critically reflects on, and engages in, one's life history. For example, Dilthey argues that the three classes of 'life expressions' (*Lebensäusserungen*) –

---

12. Julia Kristeva, 'Word, Dialogue and Novel', in Tori Moi (ed.), *The Kristeva Reader* (New York: Columbia University Press, 1986), pp. 34–61.

13. Jonathan Culler, *On Deconstruction: Theory and Criticism after Structuralism* (Ithaca, NY: Cornell University Press, 1982), p. 32.

14. Roland Barthes, *Image, Music, Text* (New York: Hill & Wang, 1977), p. 146.

15. Barthes, *Image, Music, Text*, p. 148.

16. Dialogism and heteroglossia are M. Bakhtin's terms from his work, *The Dialogic Imagination* (ed. Michael Holquist; trans. Caryl Emerson and Michael Holquist; Austin: University of Texas Press, 1981).

17. Yeo, *Rhetorical Interaction in 1 Corinthian 8 and 10*, pp. 15–49.

18. Jürgen Habermas, *Knowledge and Human Interests* (trans. Jeremy J. Shapiro; Boston: Beacon Press, 1971), p. 198.

linguistic expressions, actions and experiential expressions – mutually interact and interpret one another.[19] Similarly, Gadamer, in line with that tradition, writes of the intersubjective and inter-interpretive understanding process that is productive and reproductive.[20]

This reproductive and productive process of reading allows and requires text/writer and reader/interpretation to be intersubjective. A text not only carries meaning but allows readers to create meanings. Similarly, readers not only interpret texts, they are being 'read' by texts, that is, their stories are made meaningful by the texts. Because understanding and reading processes are reproductive and productive, a writer cannot control the meaning of a text and limit that meaning to *just* his or her own 'original' intention.

If we assume that meaning is contained and carried through various media of writing, writer and reader, then understanding is to be located not so much in the static being of media but in the interaction and interrelationship of writing, writer and reader. In other words, the text itself is not static; it is dynamic and fluid in projecting meaning, depending on how a writer uses it and how a reader will read it. In that case, the meaning of a text is not obvious in the explicit signifiers of the language. Meaning is implied and suggested by the clues or traces of signifiers as well as the lack of signifiers.

Texts are fluid also because they are social reality, a reality that is interdependent with social constructs, events and history. The traditional understanding of the text as an independent entity inherent with objective meaning is inadequate for explaining the vitality of a text. Historically-situated and culturally-conditioned semantic domains shape and multiply the communicative possibilities of the text. Stephen Tyler speaks of discourse as a 'weaving or "stitching together" (cf. *rhapsode*, "stitch together")... a "seamless web"'.[21] Or, as Derrida puts it, '... a "text" that is henceforth no longer a finished corpus of writing, some content enclosed in a book or its margins, but a differential network, a fabric of traces referring endlessly to something other than itself, to other differential traces'.[22] In other words, texts are not merely symbols to be used and manipulated by writers/rhetors, with their meaning extracted by interpreters. Texts are parts of 'the "fabric" of a tale, the "thread of discourse"... the "clothing of thought"... the "network" of ideas'[23] that coexist with writers and readers. A text cannot be frozen in its initial historicity, nor restricted to one meaning of the author. A text, even in the first writer's production, incorporates a complex process of multi-textual influences. The hermeneutical process, therefore, becomes even more complicated when later readers bring their multi-layers of effective traditions and influences to the reading process.

19.   Wilhelm Dilthey, *Selected Writings* (ed. and trans. H.P. Rickman; New York: Cambridge University Press, 1976), pp. 218–20.

20.   Gadamer, *Truth and Method*, p. 261.

21.   Stephen A. Tyler, *The Unspeakable: Discourse, Dialogue, and Rhetoric in the Postmodern World* (Madison: University of Wisconsin Press, 1987), p. 35.

22.   Jacques Derrida, 'Living on/Border Lines' (trans. James Hulbert), in Harold Bloom *et al.* (eds.), *Deconstruction and Criticism* (New York: Seabury, 1979), pp. 75–176 (84).

23.   Tyler, *The Unspeakable*, p. 35.

Adjudicating between Competing Readings:
Towards Cross-Cultural and Global Interpretations

In the preceding section I have presented a model for analyzing the reading process, which I call intersubjective. This intersubjective process involves three planes or factors that interact with one another. Among the three planes of reading, the nine points of the triangles (in the models) also interact. Based on this fluid and interactive reading process, I am arguing that a global, communal and cross-cultural interpretation is the right path, for we are all jointly responsible for the meanings the biblical texts are to bear. While the Bible can speak to all cultures, no culture should have a monopoly on the meaning of scripture. This brings me to the question of adjudication procedures.

The practice of biblical interpretation in a global context does not mean that all interpretations are valid simply because we are paranoid of hegemony. We must make judgments about plausibility, whether the interpretation has a real basis in the text. Furthermore, shared responsibility in intersubjective reading involves communities of interpreters subjecting their readings to mutual ideological critique so that none of us are blinded by our cultural assumptions. For me, a hermeneutic of respect and cross-cultural integration offers a way to this kind of cross-cultural learning and critique. I will illustrate by looking at a series of interpretations of Romans 7.

In what follows I present my own interpretation along with four others. I regard all of these interpretations as plausible in the sense that they are exegetically defensible, but I want to inquire into how each one approaches the text from the interpreter's own socio-cultural location and reading interests, paying special attention to the question of assumptions. When I speak of exegetically plausible interpretations, I do not mean that all five are equally convincing in argumentation. A few of the five interpretations are defended exegetically in greater detail, so they appear to be more convincing to me. I will point out exegetical weaknesses of the less-developed arguments. In looking at my own and the other interpretations, my aim is to examine each to see what assumptions of cultural location and interests lie behind it and to ask how interpretive judgments about the text can be more cross-culturally sensitive and globally inclusive.

In analyzing the five interpretations for ways in which they are rooted in or sensitive to particular socio-cultural locations and interests, I am forced to make some educated guesses at points. Not all of the interpreters state their relation to their cultural contexts or speak of their guiding interests. In preferring my own interpretation, I also allow that some of these interpreters might have been more persuasive (and therefore might have had a greater influence on me in the dialogic reading process), if they had stated clearly the cultural assumptions and values that shaped their readings of Romans 7.

Adjudicating between Competing Interpretations of Romans 7
In Rom. 7.7-25 Paul speaks in the first-person singular ('I') about the operation of sin and the law/commandment in 'his' life. Whether he is talking about himself or

is using the 'I'-style rhetorically has long been a subject of debate. Interpreters also divide over the identity of the 'law' (also called the 'commandment') and the precise nature of the relations between law, sin and the 'I'.

I will comment first on two sample interpretations of Rom. 7.7-25 and make the point that the three planes of the reading process are not always clearly articulated or processed by scholars who use historical approaches. Precisely missing in the following two readings is sensitivity to the interaction between the cultural context of the text and that of the interpreter.

D. Martyn Lloyd-Jones,[24] a conservative minister who wrote a popular commentary on Romans that is much-used by Chinese pastors, takes a grammatical-historical approach to scripture but rejects the thoroughgoing historical-critical brand of scholarship. His aim is to produce edifying exegesis. Lloyd-Jones understands the 'I' of Romans 7 as an immature Christian who has not yet embraced the power of new moral life through the Spirit, a Christian who is convicted of sin as he/she sees the holiness of the law but who is not living the sanctified life. Ambiguous features of Romans 7 (and Romans 5–8 in general) permit Lloyd-Jones to do a 'sanctification' reading, but Lloyd-Jones does not make a very persuasive exegetical argument for his view. A stronger exegetical argument could be made to support some of Lloyd-Jones' theological conclusions, but he is using his third plane to read the second plane of the intersubjective reading-process. The theological context of Lloyd-Jones – his tradition and theological sub-culture – guides him to read Romans 7 as a struggle of an immature Christian, one whose life has not yet been transformed by Christ. This example raises the question whether a valid interpretation must include both sound exegesis and culturally relevant interpretation. My answer is *yes*.

Where Lloyd-Jones carries out an edifying spiritual exposition on Romans 7, Robert Gundry offers an interpretation expressed in the language and arguments of historical-critical interpretation. Lloyd-Jones' exposition is strong in cultural relevance and weak exegetically, but Gundry's is strong in exegesis with no evident interest in cultural relevance. Gundry understands this pericope as Paul's *bar mitzvah* experience, which symbolizes his dawning awareness of the conflict between God's commandment and his own awakening sexual desire. Speaking of v. 9, Gundry writes, 'The commandment Paul singles out prohibits lust, the very sin which, in its sexual sense, is dead prior to puberty but springs to life in a lad about the time he becomes bar mitzvah and therefore legally and morally responsible'.[25] Gundry takes the words 'covet' (ἐπιθυμέω) and 'covetousness' (ἐπιθυμία) in Romans 7 as referring to sexual lust. He argues that 'I was once alive apart from the law' in Rom. 7.9 refers to the time prior to Paul's *bar mitzvah* – *bar mitzvah* occurring about the time of puberty and puberty being the time when sexual lust is, theoretically, first awakened. J.A. Ziesler criticizes Gundry by pointing out that

---

24. D. Martyn Lloyd-Jones, *Romans: The Law – Its Functions and Limits (Romans 7:1–8:4)* (Grand Rapids: Zondervan, 1974).

25. Robert H. Gundry, 'The Moral Frustration of Paul before His Conversion: Sexual Lust in Romans 7.7-25', in Donald A. Hagner and Murray J. Harris (eds.), *Pauline Studies: Essays Presented to F.F. Bruce* (Grand Rapids: Eerdmans, 1980), pp. 228–45 (332).

neither Exod. 20.17 nor Deut. 5.21 (the Hebrew Bible formulations of the tenth commandment, which Paul quotes in v. 7) limits ἐπιθυμέω to sexual desire and that in the New Testament and the Septuagint the words ἐπιθυμία and ἐπιθυμέω 'lack a specifically sexual reference'.[26] Gundry never fully justifies his limitation of ἐπιθυμέω and ἐπιθυμία in vv. 7-8 to sexual lust. Nevertheless, I think Gundry's reading is plausible if we grant that Paul perhaps exploits the ambiguity of the term ἐπιθυμία, which could refer to a specific passion (such as sexual lust) or to passion more generally.[27]

Moreover, using my intersubjective and cross-cultural reading process to understand Gundry, I question whether he is simply doing a purely historical-critical work. I suspect he is not, based on my understanding of the three-plane interactive reading process. But I simply do not have any clues to tell me about the third plane of reading in Gundry's interpretation, that plane where the meaning potential of the text interacts with the interests and social context (cultural presuppositions) of the later interpreter. But one question raised by Gundry's analysis is whether he sees the problem of Romans 7 as a specifically and exclusively 'Jewish' problem. In that case – and here we are considering possibilities that go beyond anything Gundry himself says – does his interpretation harbor anti-Jewish potential? A purely historical-critical work such as Gundry's may not be concerned with the implication that Romans 7, in his interpretation, casts the Jewish law as inferior to the Christian law or moral way. But a culturally-sensitive evaluation of Gundry's interpretation for a post-holocaust context requires that we think this issue through, as I will do at a later point in this essay.

The interpretations of Lloyd-Jones and Gundry both stress the struggle of the 'I'. In the history of interpretation of Romans 7, this emphasis on 'struggle' or 'conflict' is not uncommon. Many interpreters have seen Romans 7 as describing the Christian moral struggle, and a number of Pauline scholars have interpreted the passage as reflecting the flesh-Spirit conflict of two aeons or two existences within the process of salvation history.[28] Clearly, there has also been a deep interest in connecting Romans 7 with the experience of the interpreters and/or their communities. But little is said about this. Yet this is a crucial hermeneutical factor, deriving from the interactions of the third triangle. And, for me, the interpretive arguments of Gundry, Lloyd-Jones and others would be more powerful if they were explicit about the cultural presuppositions, interests and experiences that shape their interpretations.

For example, scholars who are interested in finding 'the Christian moral struggle' in Romans 7 often use Gal. 5.16-18 to support their readings of Romans 7, seeing in Galatians 5 a description of a continuous tension between the flesh and

---

26. J.A. Ziesler, 'The Role of the Tenth Commandment in Romans 7', *JSNT*, 33 (1988), pp. 41–56 (45).

27. Gundry's argument would also be stronger for me if, in addition to offering a more careful treatment of Paul's use of the term ἐπιθυμία, he also explained how the sexual interpretation of the encounter of the 'I' with the law fits with the larger argument of Romans regarding the law.

28. C.K. Barrett, *The Epistle to the Romans* (London: A. & C. Black, 1973), pp. 151–53; F.F. Bruce, *The Epistle of Paul to the Romans* (NICNT; Grand Rapids: Eerdmans, 1963), pp. 150–53.

the Spirit, which are opposed to each other in every Christian's life. This interpretation makes a significant moral and theological contribution to many Christian communities. It is also exegetically defensible. But in order to be more persuasive in their interpretations of Romans 7, scholars in this camp need to take account of the absence of the word 'Spirit' from Rom. 7.14-25 and to show that Galatians 5 serves as an exegetical bridge. My intersubjective conception of interpretation explains this reading as a case of intertextuality between Romans 7 and Galatians 5. Recall that writers are already readers of many texts who bring with them other textual influences (e.g., traditions of linguistic usage, worldview) and their social-historical backgrounds, producing texts that are intertextual moments open to multiple interpretations. At the same time, the reading process never involves only a text and a reader but always that text and the many texts the reader brings. All of these texts interact in multiple ways and no one can dictate precisely how they should interact. Therefore, we can say that Galatians 5 is part of the intertextual matrix for Paul and for us. Although these two passages, taken independently, might not be construed as being about the same experience, an intertextual reading allows one to interpret them together as a description of the moral struggle of the Christian.

We cannot know for certain what Paul actually means in the text but can only test for plausibility and acknowledge that more than one interpretation can be reasonable. Choosing between interpretations requires that we use additional criteria – including criteria of a hermeneutic of global and cross-cultural process – to move beyond exegetical impasses. Such a process will differentiate competing interpretations and bring them into dialogue with a commitment to global co-existence. This dialogue entails negotiating the boundaries of competing interpretations to move them beyond their original vantage points. The intended result is a more richly interpreted Pauline text. This globally-sensitive hermeneutic process does not aim to reduce interpretation to general principles or abstractions, for differentiation and integration will happen with honesty and respect only when we engage one another in depth and specificity. The goal of cross-cultural interpretation is not agreement but mutual transformation. I can make exegetical arguments and adjudicate hermeneutically between competing interpretations only from my particular context. But my cross-cultural reading of Romans 7 can offer insights that other scholars have perhaps not seen. Likewise, my horizon can be expanded by interpretations worked out in cultural settings different from mine. Although we can move toward one another in efforts of interpretive accommodation, there will always be points where we cannot agree. It is wise to state clearly our disagreements and still treat other interpretations with respect.

Let me further illustrate the cross-cultural hermeneutic process I envision by moving on to three more readings of Romans 7: a Lutheran reading, a post-holocaust interpretation, and my own Confucian reading of Romans 7.

The traditional Lutheran interpretation of Romans 7 views it from the standpoint of the doctrine of 'justification by faith', as Lutherans understand this Pauline teaching.[29] This interpretive approach sees the 'I' as the individual struggling to be

---

29. Scholars in the Lutheran tradition (and non-Lutherans persuaded by the Lutheran inter-

righteous through works but failing and ending up in despair. The classic Lutheran interpretation regards this struggle as expressive of a universal human condition, even if Paul couches it in terms more specific to his own Jewish past (or Christian present).

The Lutheran perspective has shown exegetically the plausibility of taking the 'I' of Romans 7 in an autobiographical sense to describe a condition of spiritual and psychological frustration arising from any human effort to achieve salvation by works. The frustration of the 'I' under (the) law is a providential moment that makes the person open to God's grace. I see the attractiveness of the Lutheran interpretation for those who experience guilt as part of what Krister Stendahl calls 'the introspective conscience of the West'.[30] Hence, I affirm that the Lutheran interpretation of Romans 7 has exegetical plausibility *and* cultural-contextual relevance. This Western reading, valued by so many, is no less a 'cultural' reading than my own Chinese reading, which, as I will present it below, correlates Paul's terms not with an inner psycho-spiritual experience but with communitarian social values. A cross-cultural dialogue between 'East' and 'West', between a Confucianist reading and a Lutheran reading, will reveal limitations of both and perhaps push us towards a creative synthesis of individual righteousness and communal righteousness, something that both Lutherans and Confucianists care about. Taking the Lutheran reading seriously helps me to become aware of the ways in which my communitarian reading may lose sight of the individual. While I have no doubts that the Lutheran tradition has a good sense of community, just as the Confucianist teaching has a good sense of individuality, a cross-cultural dialogue about Romans 7 can help each interpreter rediscover the text from a fresh cultural vantage point, to see the bigger picture, and to help us interpret in ways that are more inclusive of both the range of plausible readings and the cultural experiences that those readings reflect and illumine.

I turn now to Charles Cosgrove's post-holocaust reading of Romans 7, which is part of his treatment of the question of a *Sonderweg* for Israel[31] in Paul.[32] Cosgrove

---

pretation of Paul) interpret the following pairs as oppositions: law and Christ, faith and works. They hold that an individual obtains righteousness (often termed 'forensic' righteousness) not by doing the law (or by any other work) but by believing in Christ. Romans 7 is Paul's confession of the impossibility of keeping the law as a way of being truly righteous before God, an impossibility that applies to both the non-Christian and the Christian. Moreover, the very effort to achieve righteousness by works is sinful. See Rudolf Bultmann, *Theology of the New Testament*, I (trans. Kendrick Grobel; New York: Charles Scribner's Sons, 1951), pp. 243–53 and 330–52; Ernst Käsemann, *Perspectives on Paul* (London: SCM Press, 1971), pp. 60–78. A recent full-scale treatment of Paul in support of this Lutheran perspective is Hans Hübner, *Law in Paul's Thought* (trans. James C.G. Greig; Edinburgh: T. & T. Clark, 1984).

30. Krister Stendahl, 'The Apostle Paul and the Introspective Conscience of the West', in *Paul among Jews and Gentiles and Other Essays* (Philadelphia: Fortress Press, 1976), pp. 78–96.

31. The issue of a *Sonderweg* for Israel in Pauline scholarship concerns various forms of the thesis that, according to Paul, the way of salvation for the gentiles is through Christ while the way of salvation for Israel is through God's own special work apart from the church and in a fashion that assumes and affirms Israel's ongoing life in the Torah.

32. Charles H. Cosgrove, 'Advocating One Reasonable Interpretation of Paul against Other Reasonable Interpretations: A Theological Approach to the *Sonderweg* Question', in Robert

does not examine the *Sonderweg* question as a matter of 'cultural' hermeneutics, but his essay can be regarded as an effort to address concerns in the West growing out of the history leading to and following the Holocaust. His interpretation of Paul is self-consciously guided by moral and theological criteria, which he sets forth explicitly. These include (1) honesty about the moral history of Christians and Jews (looking honestly at Christian triumphalism), (2) faithfulness to classical Christian identity (including the traditional teaching that the way of salvation is unified, not divided), (3) consideration of the moral consequences of interpretation (e.g., the effects of interpretations that foster anti-Judaism and antisemitism), and (4) doing justice to Judaism (seeking interpretations of Paul that do not lead the church to distort Judaism). Guided by these criteria Cosgrove seeks to test how far one can make a plausible exegetical case from Paul for the Judaism-affirming theology of so many Christians who have recast their views of Israel through Jewish/Christian dialogue. Cosgrove adopts theologian Paul van Buren's 'theology of the Jewish-Christian reality' as representative of this new Christian view of Jews and Judaism[33] and tests a series of theological theses advanced by van Buren. In the course of this discussion Cosgrove comments on Romans 7.

Cosgrove treats Romans 7 in connection with the question of the moral capacitation of Jews and Christians. His aim is to develop a plausible exegetical argument from Paul against the Christian presumption that the church is morally superior to Israel. This leads him to prefer certain interpretations of Romans 7 over others. Cosgrove proposes that we take the 'I' as a rhetorical device for describing the relations between self, sin and law wherever these are found together. According to this interpretation, Romans 7 does not target Israel as morally incapacitated or morally undeveloped in comparison to the church. Instead, Romans 7 is relevant to both Jews and Christians, whatever forms sin and law assume in their lives. Cosgrove calls for keeping in mind 1 Cor. 10.1-4, as we read Romans 7 (just as Stendahl and Kümmel have reminded us to keep Phil. 3.6 in mind). In 1 Cor. 10.1-4, Paul attributes to the wilderness generation of Israel the same spiritual sustenance or resources that believers have in Christ: 'our ancestors... were all baptized into Moses in the cloud and the sea, and all ate the same spiritual food, and all drank the same spiritual drink... the spiritual rock that followed them, and the rock was Christ'. If we read Romans 7 with this assumption in mind, says Cosgrove, we can avoid drawing the conclusion that Jews, according to Paul, lack spiritual resources that are given only with the revelation of Christ and the creation of the church. The spiritual gifts of that revelation are already with Israel going back to the time of Moses. Hence, we can read Paul as saying that the church and Israel are gifted by God with the same moral and spiritual powers.

Gagnon (ed.), *Another Way? Pauline Soteriology for Jews and Gentiles in Romans* (Grand Rapids: Eerdmans, forthcoming).

33. Cosgrove stresses that Paul is open to more than one reasonable interpretation regarding the *Sonderweg* set of questions. Hence, Cosgrove presents extra-exegetical criteria in favor of the reading of Paul that he develops. Cosgrove's aim is not to argue for only one 'correct' reading of Paul but to present plausible exegesis in support of a viable Paul for use in theological construction in our time.

My Confucianist Christian reading empathizes with Cosgrove's post-holocaust hermeneutical sensitivity. In my interpretation of Romans 7, cultural boasting in one's sacred tradition is the sin that Paul primarily combats, just as it is also attacked by Confucius. As Cosgrove rightly fears, many Christian readings of Romans 7 have produced attitudes of Christian superiority over Jews and the way of life in the Torah. Increasing numbers of biblical scholars in the West have examined the history of interpretation to see how Christian exegesis has been part of the legacy of antisemitism. This is an appropriate cultural concern for Western readings of Paul today. As a Confucianist living in Malaysia, I did not encounter antisemitism, but I did witness and experience racism, including racial violence, in my religiously and culturally diverse homeland. This is part of the background that has led to my commitment to read Paul as an opponent of cultural boasting. Furthermore, one of my primary purposes in doing intersubjective, cross-cultural hermeneutics is to counter racism and ethnocentrism in all their forms, with the hope of working towards a global hermeneutic. A global hermeneutic, however, should not take the form of hermeneutical 'tribalism' in the sense that we each go our separate ways, seeking at best only segregation and tolerance. A global hermeneutic must be committed to mutual transformation, as we each bring to the roundtable of interpretation our own contributions while at the same time modifying our understandings as we listen to others. It takes honesty and courage to be interactive with each other in ways that change us.

I take the 'I' in Romans 7 as Paul the Pharisee who seeks to obey the Torah (which I liken to propriety as a cultural ideal, specifically, *li* in Confucianism) with zeal but finds out in light of his present 'in-Christ' experience that his blamelessness before the Torah (i.e., Jewish law) does not necessarily indicate his righteousness (which I liken to holiness or *yi* in Confucianism) before God and people (the community). This 'I' also represents something of the experience of the Jewish and gentile Christians in Rome; that is, Paul describes his Pharisaic self in a way that interprets their relationships and attitudes.

Romans 7 describes not the typical behavior of a Pharisee but the distorted zeal of Paul the Pharisee whose strict conformity to the Torah resulted in his persecution of the Christian church, the body of Christ. This behavior, viewed retrospectively, does not reveal a fault of the Torah. Paul affirms the holiness and goodness of the Torah/cultural ideal and attributes his frustrated experience to the power of sin working through the Torah. His devotion to the Torah, his own cultural and religious traditions, blinded him to the new act of the righteousness of God in Christ, who has opened up salvation to the (gentile) world. Looking back, Paul arrives at a new view of the Torah, which has now become for him the new law of the Spirit. Paul finds victory over his dilemma in 'the law of the Spirit of life in Christ Jesus' (Rom. 8.2), which is more inclusive than Paul's old conception of the law and is essential for the co-existence and salvation of both Jews and gentiles (all people).

Rom. 7.7-25 serves to remind Jewish Christians not to abuse the Jewish law (like Paul once did with the Jewish law) but to live in the Spirit before God and with gentile Christians. It encourages gentile Christians not to take pride in their own traditions and consider themselves strong and Jewish Christians weak (cf.

Romans 14). The law of the Spirit has led both Jewish and gentile believers to victory over sin and death (8.1-13), and to the confession that they are all children of God (8.14). Those in Christ (7.25) and in the Spirit (8.2) do not abrogate but fulfill the Torah (8.4).

I am aware that my interpretation is not the most obvious reading of Romans 7, since the text, when it describes Paul's intention to be righteous by means of the Torah, does not explicitly mention that this intention leads him to persecute the church or reject Christian belief in the Messiah without Torah. The text, especially in 7.7-8, speaks of 'covetousness' (ἐπιθυμία). Here Paul states a general irony that becomes more specific as he moves on to vv. 13-25. We may call this the irony of holiness, the irony of the law captive to sin and also the irony of one's good intention expressed in unrighteous acts. Philippians 3 speaks of Paul's blamelessness before the Torah. I think that the covetousness argument in vv. 7-8 is to prove how the power of sin can gain control via the Torah and cause religious people to sin. The tenth commandment is mentioned in 7.7-8 mainly 'because in some Jewish tradition covetousness, or wrong desire, was held to be the sin from which all others flow'.[34] Hence, I take covetousness in vv. 7-8 as a general example of sin captivating Torah and frustrating the 'I'. But by the time we arrive at v. 18, Paul's language admits a more specific interpretation expressing Paul's experience as a persecutor of the church – Paul's pharisaic experience of wanting to love the Torah but seeking to destroy the church created in Jesus Christ by the God who gave the Torah. This experience of wanting to do good but doing evil fits the narration in v. 18. What Paul means by 'nothing good' in v. 18 is the fact that Paul the zealous Pharisee knows what is good and can will the good but fails to do it. He wanted all to be the people of God through obedience to the Torah (which was good), but his action turned out to be persecution of the church (which was bad). Paul's strong passion or zeal to conform to the Torah as a Pharisee was thus at odds with his performance (see v. 15). The tension between the desire and the performance of a culturally arrogant and ethnocentric Pharisee in vv. 13-25 reminds readers of the parallel tension between desiring to observe the commandment and coveting in vv. 7-8. The reason for the tension is not 'the Law's inability to deliver what it demands',[35] but the indwelling sin in the 'I'.

The term ταλαίπωρος ('wretched', 'miserable', 'distressed') in Rom. 7.24 indicates that Paul despairs over his effort to grasp God's will in the law and live it out. This is neither an anthropological tension nor a generic tension between one's new faith in Christ and one's former faith or tradition. Paul is not saying that he was unable to do the law (see Phil. 3.6). His despair is that of a former Pharisee who now realizes he has misunderstood the will of God for the salvation of Jews and gentiles and has become caught by sin into cultural boasting through the law. Worse still, his blind loyalty to the Torah as the absolute standard for inclusion among God's people resulted in his persecution of the church. The death of Christ revealed to him that God's righteousness was available to all according to the

---

34. Ziesler, 'The Role of the Tenth Commandment', p. 47.
35. Ziesler, 'The Role of the Tenth Commandment', p. 49.

principle of faith (trust) rather than strict conformity to a cultural or religious value-system.

From the preceding it should be clear that I understand the word νόμος ('law') as it is used in Rom. 7.7-25 to mean a cultural and a religious code. Stephen Westerholm has appropriately described the Torah as 'a collection which spells out Israel's covenantal obligations'.[36] These covenantal obligations have their basis in Deuteronomy (4.8; 30.10; 32.46). In short, Torah to Paul is a cultural and religious code that identifies him as a Jew, more particularly as a Pharisee (cf. Acts 23.6; 26.5; 22.3; 5.34). As a loyal Pharisaic Jew, Paul was concerned with how gentiles could come into the full citizenship of the people of God – by adopting the Torah of Israel.

In the Jewish tradition, the gentiles are sinners. Lloyd Gaston has shown that some of the writings of Paul's rabbinic contemporaries express the view that both Jews and gentiles will have a relationship with God, especially in the end-time, but only through the Torah (directly or indirectly).[37] E.P. Sanders has rightly observed that 'in the entire body of Palestinian Jewish literature between Ben Sirach and the redaction of the Mishnah, with only the exception of 4 Ezra, membership in the covenant is considered salvation'.[38] Both Jews and gentiles can achieve and maintain their status in the membership of God only by observing the Torah. And that is the conviction of Paul as a Pharisee before he knew Christ's inclusion of gentiles. Paul's previous zeal for the Torah in persecuting the church should be seen in this light. Paul was concerned for gentiles to be members of the people of God; hence, as a Pharisaic Jew, most probably of the House of Shammai, Paul was zealous to see that his cultural and religious tradition (i.e., the Torah) be accepted by all so that they could be saved. For Paul the follower of Jesus, the Torah is Israel's great privilege (Rom. 2.17-20; 3.1-2; 9.4-5), but it should be understood as a covenantal relationship whereby it leads to obedience in a life of faith. Only Paul the former Pharisee could affirm, 'I delight in the law of God, in my inmost self' (Rom. 7.22). This is why Paul was known for his 'strictness' (or 'exactness') in observing the law (cf. Gal. 1.14).

The preceding interpretation is not exegetically airtight (no interpretation ever is), but it is, I think, exegetically plausible. I also regard it as a valid interpretation because of its cultural relevance for Chinese Christians like myself. More specifically, the unrighteous act of a zealous Pharisee speaks to the moral dilemma and spiritual problem of a Confucian. I understand law as a symbol of an essential part of every group's life, their fundamental sense of identity (religious, national or cultural). Law or sacred tradition is also what society counts as upright. Hence, viewed through the lens of Romans 7, as I have interpreted it, that which is genuinely good

36. Stephen Westerholm, *Israel's Law and the Church's Faith: Paul and His Recent Interpreters* (Grand Rapids: Eerdmans, 1988), p. 140.

37. Lloyd Gaston, *Paul and the Torah* (Vancouver: University of British Columbia Press, 1987), p. 26.

38. E.P. Sanders, 'The Covenant as a Soteriological Category and the Nature of Salvation in Palestinian and Hellenistic Judaism', in Robert Hammerton-Kelly and Robin Scroggs (eds.), *Jews, Greeks and Christians* (Leiden: E.J. Brill, 1976), pp. 11–44 (15).

morally is often used by sin to get the 'I' to violate the good, whether that 'I' is a Pharisee, a Christian or a Confucianist. How does my third plane influence my second plane? In Confucian tradition, it is believed that the observances of *li* (rules/propriety/ritual) can generate *yi* (righteousness/holiness). The Chinese consider their sacred tradition as best couched in the word *li*, the proper and holy way of doing things ('propriety'). *Li* indicates the act or ritual whereby spiritual beings are properly served and human happiness is obtained. Neither Paul nor Confucius wishes to discard traditions altogether. What both advocate is to live a life of *li*, a cultured yet natural pattern of interpersonal relationship that 'works through spontaneous coordination rooted in reverent dignity'.[39] We could say that one should use the Torah/*li* but not impose it on others. Confucius and Paul pinpoint the greatest danger of religious people. It is that those who inherit long and sacred religious traditions often through their piety and religiosity hurt and persecute people in the name of the very God they seek to please.

In Confucian thought, *li* is good and perfect and holy, but Confucius laments that '[n]owadays filial piety means being able to feed one's parents', which amounts to doing no more for one's parents than is done for dogs and horses (*Analects* 2.7).[40] In other words, merely doing the expectation of *li* is not sufficient. One must also fulfill a higher principle, which is *jen* (benevolence). Confucius is deeply concerned that humans live in *jen*, for *jen* is more basic and crucial than the rule of propriety. He insists that each human being is to actualize the mandate of Heaven (*Tien*) by committing himself/herself to *jen*. *Jen* is what makes human beings human.

Paul and Confucius understand human nature not in terms of intrapersonal conflict between flesh and spirit, but in terms of interpersonal socialization between self and group. So *li* without *jen* can degenerate into formalism, violence or pride (cf. *Analects* 3.3). *Li* is the morally good command of *Tien* (Heaven) that produces *yi* (righteousness) to the faithful. But just as sin uses the law to cause those who seek to be faithful to the law to break the Law, lack of *jen* causes inhumanity and brings about conflict in community. Confucius says, 'Virtue or righteousness does not exist in isolation; there must be neighbors' (*Analects* 4.25; my translation). 'In order to establish oneself, one helps others to establish themselves; in order to enlarge oneself, one helps others to enlarge themselves' (*Analects* 6.28; my translation). The process of learning to be a sage (a righteous one) is human participation with others in communal ceremony. The mandate of Heaven is that all live in righteousness and orderliness in relation to others as a society of sacredness. To live a life of righteousness is to ask not whether one has fulfilled the requirement of the law, but how one must relate to others and to God in a way that manifests God's grace and love. A life of righteousness, which is new life in Christ, is to be understood not simply as a transcendent source of life poured into humans from outside but as a process directed toward the ultimate goal of the realization of the

---

39. Herbert Fingarette, *Confucius: The Secular as the Sacred* (New York: Harper & Row, 1972), p. 8. Cf. *Analects* 2.3, 13.3.

40. Confucius, *The Analects of Confucius (Lun Yu)* (trans. Chichung Huang; New York: Oxford University Press, 1997), p. 53.

image (glory) of God in humans, initiated in this life as a life of faith and love. This life of faith and love towards neighbors is an expression of a life of faith and love towards God. For Chinese Christians then, it is natural to read Romans 10.4 as Torah being fulfilled in Christ through love, just as *li* is not negated but subsumed under *jen* so that *li* might have its full force. Christ fulfills the Torah by means of love, thus giving the Torah its validity and full force as well. The implication is that Confucianist tradition can be taken up into Christ for Chinese Christians.

In my Confucianist interpretation, I have interpreted the 'I' as a specific reference to Paul's Pharisaic past, seen from his perspective in Christ. From this specificity, I drew analogies between the interactions of sin, law and righteousness in Paul's social world and the interactions of sin, *li* and *yi* in a Chinese social world shaped by Confucian self-understanding. By contrast Cosgrove does not assign a specific identity to the 'I' but takes the 'I' as a rhetorical device for speaking about how sin and law function in human existence, whether for the Jew or for the follower of Jesus. Cosgrove opts for this interpretation because it helps him avoid certain anti-Jewish implications. I appreciate this concern and have worked out my interpretation of Romans 7 in the light of it. My Confucianist reading seeks to avoid anti-Judaism by making clear that the 'I' of Romans 7 does not stand for Jews in general but represents Paul's distorted practice of the law when he was a Pharisee who persecuted the church. The law became a form of cultural arrogance for Paul, rather than the way of righteousness that it should have been. Thus, I reach a result similar to Cosgrove's. But an important difference is that Cosgrove does not draw analogies from his reading of Romans 7 to other religious traditions and cultural settings, while I relate Romans 7 to a Chinese context and Confucian self-understanding and am open to other such cross-cultural analogies. However, it appears that Cosgrove's reading could be open to analogical connections with other cultural contexts, since Cosgrove takes the 'I' as a rhetorical device for describing the interactions of sin, the law and the self wherever these interactions are found. Cosgrove assumes that Paul is speaking about the operation of the Mosaic law in the life of Jews, but what law is used by sin in the lives of Christians? It cannot be the Mosaic law as such, literally, since those in Christ are not under the Mosaic law. It must be God's moral requirements in some other form (as 'the just requirement of the law' Paul refers to in Rom. 8.4, or the law of Christ or Christian paraenesis expressing the requirements of God's righteousness) that is comparable to the Mosaic law and can function in similar ways (can also be used by sin, etc.). This suggests that there is an implicit analogizing in Cosgrove's interpretation, an analogizing from Jewish experience under the Mosaic law to Christian experience under another form of law. Are there analogues for sin and the law of Moses in other cultural and religious traditions? I say *yes* and have given an example with my Confucianist reading. In addition, where Cosgrove sees Paul's description of God's spiritual gifts to Israel in the wilderness as a paradigm of how God nourishes the Jewish people through history, I affirm this and also see a basis for analogy to other cultures and peoples.

My cross-cultural hermeneutic presses me to ask another question that Cosgrove does not address because of his narrower focus. Are the Torah (for Israel), the 'just requirement of the law' (for Christians, see Rom. 8.4), and *li* with *yi* for Chinese

Confucianists three *separate* ways of righteousness? My cross-cultural hermeneutic does not advocate for each group to have its own way of righteousness, separate
from the others. Torah, Christ and *li* are intersubjective to each other, thus mutually
transforming each other as Jews, Christians and Confucianists enter into dialogue
with each other, including the internal dialogue of the Christian who is a Chinese
Confucianist or the Christian, like Paul, who is also a Jew, or the Chinese who may
be a Jew. From my Christian faith commitment, I affirm that Torah and *li* are taken
up and subsumed under Christ so that Torah and *li* find their cultural vitality in full
force. But I also affirm that Christ and his work are constantly renewed through the
diverse cultural lenses of Torah and *li*. Our understanding of the salvation of Christ
for people and all creation is constantly transformed through the reinterpretation
that comes through cross-cultural dialogue.

Because of the bad legacy of racism and ethnocentrism, many living in our
postmodern age want to argue that the Torah is valid for Jews apart from Christ, *li*
for Chinese apart from Christ and so forth. I agree with many of the reasons behind
this view. We need to resist cultural boasting and the violent hierarchical relations
that often go with it. Jews and Confucianists are not morally and spiritually blind
because they have not converted to Christ. Rather all parties can learn from and be
mutually enriched by one another. It is not my place to speak about how a Jew may
learn from a Christian, but as a Chinese I want to learn from the Jewish tradition
and still remain loyal to my identity as a Chinese, a Confucianist, and a Christian.
My awareness of this – of how culture is inherent to identity and is therefore also
inherent to Christian identity – leads me to appreciate the importance of global
interpretation of the Bible.

Guiding Considerations in Global Interpretation

I approached the interpretation of Romans 7 in this essay with my own Confucianist reading in mind. My effort to read cross-culturally in a way that works toward
global interpretation led me to adjust my interpretation so as to accommodate
the insights of other perspectives, including the classical Lutheran reading and
especially Cosgrove's post-holocaust reading. The preceding descriptions of my
interpretation and the others reflect the result of this dialogue and accommodation.

I have been guided by three fundamental conceptions in my approach to and
practice of global hermeneutics. The first is an eschatological principle or eschatological 'reservation' about the possibilities for knowing the truth. This principle
has three aspects: (1) that complete knowledge of the truth cannot be attained, (2)
that all truth is God's truth, wherever it is found, and (3) that provisional knowledge of the truth can be known by all peoples (not just Christians). Therefore, the
Christ event, which discloses the eschatological dawning of God's truth also signals
the open-endedness of truth and the limitations of our present knowledge. This
eschatological reservation and call invites us into a dialogical process between
cultures, a dialogue in which we can both accept but also transcend the limits of
our specific cultural locations. The ambiguities and uncertainties of our culturally-
conditioned and religiously-relative historicities are partially clarified and

expanded through the process of global interpretation. This is especially important because culturally-contingent interpretation often has blind-spots and prejudices that we ought to discover and overcome. Hence, every effort to read with self-conscious cultural sensitivity should also seek cross-cultural and global sensitivity and accountability. Although we cannot hope to achieve any kind of perfect global interpretation, we might think of this aim toward the cross-cultural and global as the eschatological impulse of hermeneutics in the interest of the good of all human beings who must live together in our global village.

A second and related guideline is a prophetic principle, which I take from the *Analects*, namely, 'fiduciary community'. The *Analects* does not teach that all will agree, if given enough time for dialogue. On the contrary, the *Analects* assumes that it is natural for different persons to have differing visions of the Way. Nevertheless, it is possible for those who differ to be in genuine community with one another and to be shaped by each other. 'The person of humanity', Confucius says, 'is naturally at ease with humanity' (*Analects* 4.2, my translation). In Paul's understanding, the Spirit urges the faithful to become fully human in loving relationships with each other, not erasing all differences but accommodating difference.

Fiduciary community means keeping faith with the values from our own culture that we cherish and believe to be true, while taking seriously and opening ourselves up to the values and perspectives of other peoples. We must keep faith with them, too, which requires seeking the truth together under the eschatological reservation. Hope of authentic community in interpretation is not possible on the assumptions of cultural imperialism or cultural relativism but only through cultural dialogue, transformation and humility.

A third consideration is the *dialectic of values*. In the hermeneutic process, both the scripture text and the culture provide norms of evaluation for Christians, norms that are often in tension. In the hermeneutical circle by which we choose between competing plausible interpretations based on our prior understandings of scripture and the visions and values that are part of our cultural lens, both our understanding of scripture and our cultural self-understanding can be transformed. The hermeneutical circle of scripture criticism – reading scripture through the lens of culture – also includes culture criticism – reading culture through the lens of scripture. In both cases the 'lens' we use is a construction – the social construction of culture as a lens, an *interpretation* of scripture as a lens. Thus, the relation between scripture and culture is a complex dialectic of values in which we are both recipients, socially constructed persons and peoples (as heirs of culture and tradition); and also hermeneutic agents, choosers of meaning, negotiators of values.

Part II

CASE STUDIES IN INDETERMINACY AND HERMENEUTICAL JUDGMENT

WATCHING OUT FOR THE WATCHMEN (SONG OF SONGS 5.7): HOW I HOLD MYSELF ACCOUNTABLE

Carole R. Fontaine, Andover Newton Theological School, Massachusetts, USA

It might seem odd to some that anyone wishing to address the general questions of competing readings and the ethics of hermeneutics would set out as their model text the little book of erotic poetry that is the Song of Songs. It may not be so astonishing as all that, however. I take the Song of Songs as a 'test case' because for centuries the church and the synagogue have advanced normative, competing meanings for this wayward collage of love poems. These normative meanings have each resisted and redefined the 'plain sense' of the text.[1] Likewise, with the growth of feminist interest in this text where a woman's voice dominates that of her male lover,[2] there are modern issues of liberationist interpretations being raised by the presence of the Song (or SoS, as some feminists like to dub it, not without irony) in our canons.[3] I will not be commenting here on the 'will-to-allegorize' a text whose content seems, at face value, to have little to do with the dicta of the Christian and Jewish theology. Instead, I want to reflect on the way that even seemingly *positive* texts carry along with them an inscription of violence and injustice that no commentator or believer can afford to ignore.

Standard Feminist Statement of Disclosure

It is common among my branch of biblical studies that commentators 'come clean' about their 'social location' and personal expectations or biases, since feminist biblical hermeneutics rightly notes that no one is 'objective' and that such specific, personal elements figure strongly in our subconscious desires to create and collate meanings in the text and of the text. I am a 52 year old white woman who has been

---

1.   Carole R. Fontaine, '"Go Forth Into the Fields": An Earth-Centered Reading of the Song of Songs', in Norman C. Habel and Shirley Wurst (eds.), *The Earth Story in the Wisdom Traditions* (Earth Bible, 3; Sheffield: Sheffield Academic Press, 2001), pp. 126–44 (126–27).

2.   André Lacocque, *Romance, She Wrote: A Hermeneutical Essay on Song of Songs* (Harrisburg, PA: Trinity Press International, 1998).

3.   Alicia Ostriker, 'A Holy of Holies: The Song of Songs as Countertext', in Athalya Brenner and Carole R. Fontaine (eds.), *The Song of Songs: A Feminist Companion to the Bible* (FCB, Second Series, 6; Sheffield: Sheffield Academic Press, 2000), pp. 36–54; and J. Cheryl Exum, 'Ten Things Every Feminist Should Know about the Song of Songs', in Brenner and Fontaine (eds.), *The Song of Songs*, pp. 24–35.

married to the same man for over thirty years; I am not a mother. Though white, I was raised in close contact with poverty and especially the oppression in the African American, Jewish and Caribbean communities of the South I remember from my youth. Today, I am employed in a 'free-standing' (no associated university) protestant seminary whose fiscal lifeblood is the support of individual churches and founding denominations. My students do not want to hear 'bad' things about the Bible, any part of it. Their churches do not want them to preach on such topics, and their ordination papers do not regularly feature their skills in critiquing the biblical text, though our seminary doggedly teaches the methods.

Athough I was raised Southern Baptist, I parted ways with conservative and fundamentalist theologies as a teen working on civil rights in the 60s in Project Head Start in a black southern ghetto. Recognizing that I could not (and did not want to) pass the conservative litmus test so routinely administered by those who style themselves as the 'real' Christians, my journey into theological honesty continued, landing me in the welcome haven of the Unitarian Universalist Association. Not as well known as we would like to be outside of New England and Transylvania, we are the group of Yankees who 'just said "No"' during the founding of this country under Puritan theological traditions that re-inscribed many of the old problems of Northern Europe onto an already inhabited 'new' world. We hold ourselves to the ethical bar of the worth and dignity of every person, as well as that of an interdependent ecosystem; we regard reason as a guide in the journey of faith and submit ourselves to the chaos of democratic polity in a denomination characterized by our refusal to agree on much of anything. Feminist analysis is welcomed warmly.

Out of the Past: Reading as a Member of a Professional Guild

As a visual artist, somehow translated into biblical studies by a whimsical cosmos, I have struggled for many years to find a satisfying, reliable hermeneutic I could call my own. We all began as historical critics in the olden days, but the confidence in that method's ability to produce stable meanings collectively waned. I experimented with all the tried-and-true approaches for teaching, knowing my students were more interested in 'living' by the Bible than studying where and how it came into being. The original intent of the author – ah, we were taught to be *so* confident that we could know that and proclaim it objectively! – was the Holy Grail for interpreters. Find that meaning and you're done, which is fine for the *Journal of Biblical Literature*, but what about the world beyond? Ah, 'dynamic analogy' rode in on a white (yes, white) charger to help us battle the dragons of the world – find a similar social setting in the modern world that 'matches' or is at least moderately congruent with the original context and intent of the author and take a flying 'leap of faith' from 'then' to 'now'. By insisting on congruence in social settings, we were able to teach students to critique rich white churches with prophetic texts and support struggling minority communities with messianic or Exodus-oriented traditions.[4] So far, so good.

---

4. Two standard statements on these theological developments can be found in Krister

However, the naiveté of this position was becoming increasingly transparent to some critics. Many feminist interpreters began to agree that there was no *one* pristine reading of a text that pointed us in the direction of an unproblematic code of morality. The polyvalence of the text was a blessing to the dissatisfied interpreter but a curse to churches and denominations looking for those Ten Words that would always and everywhere be correct when applied faithfully to the world of the believer. Critical awareness of competing readings only egged on competing readers, and the stakes were high. Not only were we less sanguine that we could know the past objectively or that there was only *one* past to be known, the readings inscribed within the text itself were becoming problems themselves.[5] Are women or homosexuals really *people* (suitable for ordaining), not failed males or moral deviants? Why do we follow only the *sexual* regulations of the Bible (not that they are all *that* explicit and straightforward) while simultaneously ignoring the Bible's fairly clear witness on the topic of wealth and poverty? Slavery, roundly reported and supported everywhere in the Bible, is judged by critics to be a 'cultural' contaminant from the time and place of the biblical authors. Why is slavery discarded by theologians as a betrayal of the gospel when patriarchal hierarchy and androcentrism are *not*? The lack of logical coherence in the application of the Bible to the world of believers was exacerbated by the purported postmodern position of 'anything goes'!

One problem, it seems to me, is that biblical scholarship was not necessarily developed as a wing of constructive theological inquiry; if anything, we were glad to be 'scientific' in our descriptive study of the Bible and the *theological meaning* of 'what really happened' was beyond the scope of our research. If, in the early years of biblical criticism, historical critics had been the enemies of believers for casting doubt on the 'historicity' of biblical miracles as revelations, now as born-again literary critics or postmodernists we were friend to all, proclaiming 'your reading is as good as mine!' Everybody is invited to the interpretative task, and all efforts are welcome and equal, to be negotiated with civility and appreciation.

Are *All Readings Created Equal?*

But all readings are *not* equal. Some are uninformed, uncontextualized, selective or downright manipulative. We may have taught ourselves to look suspiciously upon coherence as some winning editor's attempt to silence divergent opinions buried below the surface of the text, but we have had nothing to put in its place. In current construals of textual meaning, it sometimes seems that there are more 'gaps' in the

Stendahl's 'Biblical Theology, Contemporary', in *The Interpreter's Dictionary of the Bible: An Illustrated Encyclopedia*, I (Nashville: Abingdon Press, 1962), pp. 418–32; and Elizabeth Achtemeier, *The Old Testament and the Proclamation of the Gospel* (Philadelphia: Westminster Press, 1973), especially pp. 144–59.

5.   See, for example, Itumelang J. Mosala, 'The Use of the Bible in Black Theology', in Itumelang J. Mosala and Buti Tlhagale (eds.), *The Unquestionable Right to be Free: Black Theology from South Africa* (Maryknoll, NY: Orbis, 1986), pp. 175–99; R.S. Sugirtharajab (ed.), *The Postcolonial Bible* (Sheffield: Sheffield Academic Press, 1998).

text (empty spaces in which some critics abjure us to insert ourselves midrashically) than stable pathways. In fact, we are searching for a 'meta-hermeneutic' to guide us from grammar-and-lexicon to city hall and Congress. Who *says* that the Book of Joshua should outweigh the books of Ruth and Esther in shaping our understanding of what to do with that pesky Other in our midst? It behooves interpreters to make clear how and why they interpret as they do and to keep a rigorous eye on one's own interpretive biases and outcomes. On what grounds does one say *No!* to white supremacist readings of the text that cast the white race as God's eternal chosen, while saying *Yes!* to a feminist or other liberationist readings that are aimed at deconstructing the whole parcel of dualistic and ideologically-tainted ideas that suggest God loves some and not others?[6]

Many theologians throughout history have recognized the need to be able to 'update'[7] the text if it is to be applied fruitfully to their times and communities.[8] One method was based on using an appeal to 'tradition' to determine a group's 'canon-within-a-canon'; other options included adding 'reason' and/or a theology of ongoing revelation to the mix. But do such approaches *really* do the trick? Not only is 'reason' captive to socialization, teaching us *not* to see what needs to remain hidden for ideological purposes, but the so-called 'tradition' to which one appealed for answers was by no means inclusive or any less culturally captive than the biblical text itself. White supremacists have their own traditions of reading the texts to which they can appeal and feel justified, as does the male-exclusive Roman Catholic hierarchy in its failure to address the realities of human sexuality in all its variations. So, faith, reason, tradition and revelation provide no sure yardstick; these will vary, because they are human constructs and humans are situated within a matrix of shifting values, authorities and experience. No wonder New Testament critic Daniel Patte argues so forcefully for the adoption of 'androcritical multi-dimensional exegesis', similar in nature to what is offered below.[9]

A Faith-Based Initiative: An Intertextual Hermeneutic

Perhaps the most successful meta-hermeneutic for the church has been the appeal to the gospel and the person of Jesus of Nazareth whose story is narrated there. Evangelicals are always asking themselves, 'What would Jesus do?'[10] Certainly, the story of a Palestinian Jew, a sage-healer-prophet-exorcist, going up against imperial Rome with nothing but the Hebrew Bible and some great parables in his hand thrills us in the same way the tale of David toppling Goliath with some smooth stones does. Expect the unexpected, the content of the gospels counsels us; look for God on the margins and redraw the circle so that the despised Other

---

6. This critique reflects a classically 'Universalist' position.

7. Or 'discard'?

8. Clearly, the New Testament's 'Call no man your father' (Mt. 23.9, RSV) was *never* a big hit within some hierarchies.

9. *Ethics of Biblical Interpretation: A Reevaluation* (Louisville, KY: Westminster/John Knox Press, 1995).

10. Or 'What would Jesus drive?'

('sinners', 'gentiles', whatever) are within its boundaries of humanity. The igno-
minious death as a convicted criminal proclaimed as some kind of a *victory*? Well,
that's unexpected, all right! But does it leave some of us wondering if the Osama
bin Ladens of the world merit a bit more theological analysis than an angry government and its public are prepared to grant? If we construct the Bible as an overall
story of the plucky underdogs whom God protects, nourishes and grants victory
under unexpected circumstances, then are we willing to see ourselves as the rich
stratified Canaanite city-states, the hard-hearted Pharaoh or the Roman Empire?
Can believers in the rich nations of the world see themselves as Job, a wealthy man
suddenly encountering the underside of his society, when they would be so much
more comfortable thinking of themselves as Suffering Servants carrying the White
Man's Burden? We must de-colonize our own methods, identities and interests
before we can ever expect to do justice to either the Bible or society.

Aside from the persistent problem of 'who's who' in mapping the gospels onto
the modern world, we have a few other kinks in using the Jesus of the gospels as
our measuring rod for all truth. First, are we so *very* sure Jesus said this or that?
Certainties are just as scarce in the study of the New Testament as they are in the
world of the Hebrew Bible. Next, there are things upon which Jesus is never said to
have pronounced a final position: *in vitro* fertilization, the ordination of women,
homosexuality and cloning are topics that immediately spring to this interpreter's
mind. Finally, there are things that *are* attributed to Jesus or found in the New
Testament writers that are worthy of critical dispute and whose ethics must be
addressed. It's not fair making Jesus into a feminist, if the point of contrast is based
on Christian constructions of alleged Jewish misogyny and legalism![11] Should the
Passion Narratives *ever* be read liturgically without some gesture toward the legacy
of anti-Judaism they created and perpetuate, yea, even unto the death of Jewish
communities throughout the Christian world in medieval and modern times? I
think not.

Toward a Multidimensional Aesthetic Theology

Embracing the Gaps

The wonder of the disciplines of biblical studies and 'biblical theology' in such a
time of critical uncertainty is that we are all invited to play along, alter the rules of
game or even find a new game board on which to play. While this may make
zealots at either end of the continuum a bit queasy, it at least has the advantage of
getting more people involved in the critical issues of how the Bible relates to a
historical past, to the church and synagogue, to society and to a pluralistic world.
Perhaps the meanings of our meanings are to be found in the *struggle* to create and
live by them, as well as in the *content* of those meanings we choose. If we remember that the Sacred, as known through the Bible, is a dynamic Presence that is often
marked by an absence – no idol in the Holy of Holies![12] – perhaps we may learn

---

11. Katharina von Kellenbach, *Anti-Judaism in Feminist Religious Writings* (Atlanta: Scholars
Press, 1994), pp. 57–90.
12. This is very different from the ancient Egyptian view: there is no greater insult to a god

to take our gaps in certainty *as* pathways in and of themselves, a well-traveled approach to understanding that the Bible itself endorses. The text is that 'gap' in the oppressive discourse of despair that piles up on either side of us[13] like mountains of water in the parting of the Sea of Reeds; we go through in the empty space the Redeemer creates. In this gap, we discover that God is with us in our journey to something more wholesome. The gap itself should be treated as an invitation to redeem a text.

The Reality of the Text

I have always encountered the text, even those pericopes I hate, as a genuine *reality* – almost an 'entity'! – over against (the Hebrew word for this is *neged*) which I am set as reader and artist.[14] As I would say of a piece of art I just *had* to purchase[15] or a new tool I *had* to learn to use, the text 'grabs' me. It's got 'carrying power'. Even from across the room, it captures the eye and engages the heart.[16] One is drawn, willy-nilly, to stand before it and gaze into a different reality than one's own. The text really exists. There are words in a certain order and syntax, and content to be had from it. The text is, in my opinion, *not* entirely plastic, a shape-shifting entity that responds like a mood ring to its reader's present desires. Like it or not, it can't and doesn't say just *anything*, and it says *certain* things very forcefully indeed, for good or ill! The text is not the Presence itself, but it witnesses to it. We know we are in the presence of a Presence when the text takes us in its grasp. But, as C.S. Lewis wrote in *The Screwtape Letters*, this Presence cannot ravish; it can only woo.[17] We are not forced into submission; we are invited to 'turn aside' and see this great sight. We read the text and reread it, and it is not exhausted of meaning or surprise, or as the rabbis said of the Torah, 'Turn her and turn her; find everything in her' (*m.Avot.* 5).[18]

---

than to proclaim 'Your shrine is empty!' See 'The Contendings of Horus and Seth', in William K. Simpson (ed.), *The Literature of Ancient Egypt: An Anthology of Stories, Instructions, and Poetry*, new ed. (New Haven: Yale University Press, 1973), p. 112.

13. '... nothing will ever change... nothing can be done... nothing *you* do will ever change anything... why even try?... why not just give up and enjoy your piece of the pie?...'

14. All great art has the potential to engage its audience in a powerful, personal way. For some of us, life can be divided into 'before' and 'after' participating in such an event. For a ghetto teenager, it was the sculpture of Rodin, regardless of content (a nude Balzac) and Walt Whitman's *Leaves of Grass* that transformed me forever.

15. Glass – molten, shifting, light-made-concrete glass!

16. Jews reading the Talmud might conclude that the Torah is a Lover who beckons and fulfills, demanding complete allegiance. See Ari Elyon, 'The Torah as Love Goddess', in Michael Chernick (ed.), *Essential Papers on the Talmud* (New York: New York University Press, 1994), pp. 463–76. Talking about the text this way – as Person – in Christian feminist circles will get you labeled a Neo-Orthodox collaborator, however! See Elisabeth Schüssler Fiorenza, *In Memory of Her: A Feminist Theological Reconstruction of Christian Origins* (New York: Crossroad, 1983), pp. 14–21.

17. *The Screwtape Letters and Screwtape Proposes a Toast* (New York: Macmillan, 1966), p. 38.

18. I find the power of the text to be manifested in its ability to create communities charged with the quest of un-masking the powers of oppression. Hence, I argue based more on the *function* of the text for its communities, not its origin ('divine') or content (unique revelation).

A Hermeneutic of Beauty and Useful Ugliness

For me, taught as a child to read the biblical text as a paean to white Christian privilege, my readings today stand in striking opposition to the meanings I inherited and now resist at every opportunity. Problems there are, but gifts and joy are found there, too. In asking questions of my own interpretive strategies, I have taught myself and my students to take experience of art and the drive to creativity[19] seriously as tools for meaning-making in interpretation. Paraphrasing William Morris of the Arts and Crafts movement, I tell students: Have nothing in your interpretation of the text that you do not know to be useful or believe to be beautiful! Ask of your reading: Is it large enough to express the surprises and ambiguity of the interaction of human and divine realities? Is it beautiful enough to capture something of the joyousness of a Creator who calls creation very good indeed, creates Leviathan for the fun of it and yet hears the cries of the enslaved?[20]

As a feminist critic, I readily admit that parts of the text are both ugly in the original and devastating in later, real-world application.[21] If our texts have possessed us and expressed us, then even what is ugly and evil in them can be considered useful when employed critically in the service of justice. We *need* to question slavery, sexual oppressions and our constructions of reality: *all* people do, anywhere and in every time. Yet, such difficult topics do not 'play' very well in a materialist, 'free' (rather than 'fair') market society that seeks moral and metaphysical capsules of meaning as a medicine for despair.[22] You may hear the occasional sermon on the sufferings (but more likely, the 'patience') of Job, but you will seldom hear about the gang rape of a nameless woman in Judges 19. Yet those things happen to women everywhere around the world without much comment or public outrage. Our text 'authorizes' us to raise such painful topics – requires it, even when we feel that the text itself does not sufficiently critique the causes of suffering. The text invites us to make the ugly beautiful, transforming and redeeming it in the real world of experience by making us see what we would prefer to leave in shadow. This is very useful indeed.[23]

---

19. I privilege these aspects not just because of an artist's personal preference (though that subject location certainly informs my textual sympathies), but because of the text's statement about the *imago dei* of the Creator in humanity and our role as caretakers and co-creators of a good earth. The rationale for this is, however, beyond the scope of this essay.

20. I know of no other deity of the ancient Near East who holds regular conversation with those on society's margins.

21. Carole R. Fontaine, ' "Many Devices" (Qoheleth 7.23–8.1): Qoheleth, Misogyny and the *Malleus Maleficarum*', in Athalya Brenner and Carole R. Fontaine (eds.), *A Feminist Companion to Wisdom and Psalms* (FCB, Second Series, 2; Sheffield: Sheffield Academic Press, 1998), pp. 137–68.

22. Walter Brueggemann, 'A Text That Redescribes', *TTod*, 58 (2002), pp. 526–40.

23. I learned the principle of beauty as a hermeneutic from the sages who wrote the Bible's wisdom literature (see 'Concluding Semi-Scientific Postscript', in Carole R. Fontaine, *Smooth Words: Women, Proverbs and Performance in Biblical Wisdom* [London: Sheffield Academic Press, 2002], pp. 263–71), and from conversations with Claus Westermann, who knew a thing or two about beauty in the Bible ('Beauty in the Hebrew Bible', trans. Üte Oestringer and Carole R. Fontaine, in Athalya Brenner and Carole R. Fontaine (eds.), *A Feminist Companion to Reading the Bible: Approaches, Methods, Strategies* [Sheffield: Sheffield Academic Press, 1997], pp. 584–602).

Transformational, Generative Content

Along with my notions of beauty as a hermeneutic and its correlate of 'useful ugliness', I find the Bible's thematic 'plot', if you will, to be one of transformation and generation. The text speaks of a Presence whose presence and absence transform the life of the world and generate a new way of being.[24] Interpretations should strive to do the same. If the outcome of meaning-making is nothing more than reinforcement of the status quo or self-congratulation, we would do well to be suspicious of our desires for such readings. Who or what are we trying to exclude, and how shall we transform our blindness into sight? Whether one says 'Exodus' or 'Resurrection', the story is one of possible *change* and growth of something new in the wake of that transformation.

Textual Transparency

I also counsel my students to observe closely the 'how's' of the text's delivery of its message and to strive for an apprehension of the text that understands the limits and the possibilities of the internal textual aesthetic. What does it *mean* that so much of the Bible is poetry or story and not simply historical documentation? Much is made of ambiguity and the open-ended nature of the ancient, alien text, but it seems to me that there is a suggestive *transparency* about that ambiguity. That is, in spots the text is pretty clear about *not* giving answers, driving us to come to terms with our lack of certainties. The ambiguities left for us to puzzle out are presented with the same aplomb that other texts (the much proclaimed 'Gospel Truth' of Deuteronomy or the New Testament) reiterate *exactly* what we are to take as True and Proved! Our hermeneutics should be likewise transparent; no one should be claiming the one, correct, inevitable meaning of any text. The best we can do is rule out some meanings on lack of textual markers that might support our reading. We cannot ever be certain we are wholly correct; nor should we speak as though we are! To achieve this, I juxtapose the regulations and creedal statements about the morality and necessity of something like 'holy war' with all those places in the text where the Other has become a blessing to the self-styled 'chosen'. Such a strategy demonstrates that even those things clearly and unanimously proclaimed as patently 'true' didn't seem quite so certain for the original communities or later faithful interpreters.[25]

Reading Other-ly: Opening the Circle of Readers

In recent days as I have become swept up in interfaith struggles to make a more just and peaceful world, I find that I have added a new question that I must ask of

---

Beauty is an 'event' wherein the human becomes most fully human by encountering the Creator in the mode of 'blessing' (rather than 'saving'). Taking Westermann's view a little further, this artist finds that beauty can also be related to that 'redeeming' aspect also.

24. I also endorse a theology that understands that the life of the world equally transforms the Presence, at least in the ways It makes Itself known to the world.

25. Hosea's reinterpretation of the incident in the valley of Jezreel, believed by the authors/editors of the Book of Kings to have been commanded by God, is a biblical example of reinterpretation *within* the text. Compare 1 Kgs 19.16-17; 2 Kgs 9.24; 10.11 with Hoseas's reinterpretation (Hos. 1.4-5, 2.22).

my interpretations: have I read this text 'Other'-ly? What happens when you read alongside and make meaning in the presence of the Radical Other, the one who does not and will not *ever* agree with your notion of the text or its meanings? If we read along and interpret only with others *inside* Christendom or our professional guild, we will never surmount the death struggles caused by the sometimes mutually exclusive claims of the other Peoples of the Book. So one must ask, how do Jews read this text? (Which Jews? When?) How do Muslims do it? Which ones? Where? Native Americans? People from the Southern Hemisphere? Reading with the Radical Other is no easy thing, but it is a necessary task if we do not want to be unwitting contributors to the sorrows of the planet. For she who would stand between Jerusalem and Jenin and defend the basic human rights of both, the ability to 'read around' with many partners is critical. For myself, reading midrash with Jewish lesbians or studying Hebrew with Guatemalan immigrants is an ethical discipline. Studying with Jewish colleagues teaches one to add new questions: 'What does the Talmud say?' needs to appear alongside of 'What would Jesus do?' so that we are not left with the feeling that we are uniquely alone and unpartnered in our attempts to read the text for livable meaning in later times. The very shape of a rabbinic Bible or page of Talmud provides an 'eyeful' for Christians, offering a visual lexicon of the plethora of voices, often disagreeing, which surround any text's interpretation.

Reading the Quran with Muslim feminists, joining them in their struggles to transform the place of women in popular Islamic practice requires more from me than the discipline of History of Religions ever suggested. I can only be grateful that such contact has turned my scholarship upside down, ripping the self-imposed critical veils from my face,[26] leaving me exposed for all to see.[27] I am a better and more responsible reader because I read Other-ly. If, by nature of my expertise, I am to be a 'watchman' charged with watching out for the integrity of interpretation with an eye to both scholarship and faith, then it is only fair that Others ought to be watching out for *me!* Which brings us to the Song of Songs.

Watching Out for the Song of Songs

The Song is probably best understood as an anthology of love poems united by the presence of similar themes (seeking, finding, romantic love versus an ideology of male control of female sexuality, praise of the beloved's physical attributes, erotici-

---

26. I use the term 'veil' with extreme care, as it has been clearly demonstrated that the veil functions as a symbol of Islamic inferiority to the West within colonial discourse. As such, it is a powerful ideological tool of colonialism for perpetuating all sorts of oppressions. Homa Hoodfar explores this dynamic in her 'The Veil in Their Minds and on Our Heads: Veiling Practices and Muslim Women', in Elizabeth A. Castelli (ed.), *Women, Gender, Religion: a Reader* (New York: Palgrave, 2001), pp. 420–46, where she points out that 'veiling is a lived experience full of contradictions and multiple meanings'. She continues: 'While it has clearly been a mechanism in the service of patriarchy, a means of regulating and controlling women's lives, women have used the same social institution to free themselves from the bonds of patriarchy' (p. 412).

27. As with any dropped garment, whether this loss spells freedom, dishonor or enhanced political options for its wearer remains to be seen!

zation of the landscape of the lovers, etc.), none of which are grounded overtly in a 'covenant' theology or christology that is anywhere explicit. God is not routinely invoked in the songs in any clear way, though euphemistic mediations of the Sacred Name may appear in Song 2.7, 3.5 and 8.6, thereby drawing a cloak of pious theology over the lovers' yearning bodies. We have love songs that praise the Other for their 'difference' (the so-called *waṣfs* genre of 4.1-7; 5.10-16; 6.5a-7; 7.1-9), and dream sequences (3.1-5 and 5.2-8), wedding songs for Solomon (3.6-11) and philosophical reflections on the nature of erotic love (8.6-7). With such a disparate collection of material from different times (?) and places (?),[28] it is almost certain that someone would find *something* about which to be concerned; that is the way of publication and career-building in our discipline, is it not? My concerns center around violence in the Song, especially as mediated by the character motifs of the 'watchmen' (RSV; 'sentinels', NRSV) and the 'brothers' of the Beloved, and the way commentators studiously ignore or trivialize these issues.

Now, overall it is hard for many of us *not* to love the Song. This is true despite warnings like those from Cheryl Exum[29] that the Song represents not a *real* female voice but one *constructed* by male authors or worries about the theological gyrations involved in making theology out of poetic, erotic traditions rather than narratives of salvation history. Cary Ellen Walsh writes:

> ...this Song is affirming, even boldly so, of human sexuality. Given the taciturn nature of other biblical materials on sex, the Song is startling, refreshing, even flamboyant. Both the anticipation and the pleasure of sex are celebrated, lingered over, and nowhere decried. Sexuality and desire are not viewed as problems to repress or punish; nor are they sources of shame. More striking still, they are not areas to be legislated in any way or controlled through patriarchal customs such as the bride negotiation through the father, marriage dowries, bride prices and the like.[30]

While some critics might wonder if the world of erotic lyrics actually can be taken as an index of social practice or genuine female affect, for the most part even the inclusion of a *hypothetical* female voice that rejects patriarchal restrictions on her body and her choices is hailed as a bit of unlooked-for intertextual critique in support of the full agency of women as persons. We may not endorse every aspect of that hypothetical voice, but that some author could even *conceive* of a poem in which a woman spoke in such a way is miracle enough. Those who find themselves in this camp[31] are usually quite impressed with the female voice's lack of 'shame' over her desire, her public searches for her lover and her clear indication of

---

28. Scholars vary enormously in their conclusions on these topics; only compare the work of O. Keel, *The Song of Songs: A Continental Commentary* (trans. F.J. Gaiser; Minneapolis: Fortress Press, 1994); Roland E. Murphy, *The Song of Songs: A Commentary on the Book of Canticles or the Song of Songs* (Hermeneia; Minneapolis: Fortress Press 1990); and Marvin Pope, *Song of Songs* (AB; Garden City, NY: Doubleday, 1977) on these issues!

29. See n. 3.

30. *Exquisite Desire: Religion, the Erotic, and the Song of Songs* (Minneapolis: Fortress Press, 2000), p. 136.

31. I would place myself in this group, with some minor variations and nuances.

enjoyment of sex with her lover without benefit of a formal marriage contract. At the same time, there may be a concomitant desire by those who love the Song and see it as hopeful to *downplay* what I see to be clear indications of social restraint imposed on the Beloved for the very behavior on her part that we praise.[32] These elements, along with much of the military imagery applied to the female, receive polite but scant attention from commentators who find the inclusion of these motifs outside of the Song's *Tendenz*. Hence, these textual markers seldom figure in theologies made from the Song.

Oddly, later allegorists, Jewish or Christian, have found no trouble acknowledging the violence in the Song, whether it be little foxes (Song 2.15), night terrors, beatings by the watchmen (3.2; 5.7) or brotherly 'love' (1.6; 8.8-9).[33] For most Jews, these textual markers represented hostile surrounding nations and their attitudes towards God's chosen Beloved, Israel (the land) and its people (the Jews). For some Christians, those markers were clear indices of the existence of their *own* carping detractors within Christianity or worldly enemies of Christendom in general. Wherever the allegorists found God as the Hidden Referent in a violent passage, the view immediately switched to something more positive – divine violence *for our own good*: those whom He loveth, he chasteneth (Heb. 12.6)![34] In this theology, God beats us because (1) '*He*' loves us, and (2) we made '*Him*' do it. We know what we would say about these kinds of motivations for abuse if we were working in a Women's Shelter; why do we shy away from the same kind of critique when it is the Bible or theologies made from it that are being discussed?

While never specifically addressing the abuse of the watchmen in Song 5.7, Bernard of Clairvaux treats the parallel dream sequence with the watchmen in 3.3 in Sermons 77 and 78 on the Song. After first warning us that not *all* watchmen are guarding the church properly,[35] he goes on to ponder the Bride's peculiar statement that she was 'found' by those she did not seek, the 'apostolic men':

> And so it was; she sought the bridegroom, and this was not hidden from him, for he himself had urged her on to seek him, and given her the desire to fulfil his commands and follow his way of life. But there must be someone to instruct her and teach her the way of prudence. Therefore he sent out as it were, gardeners to

---

32. So, too, Exum, 'Ten Things', pp. 30–32; Fiona C. Black, 'Nocturnal Egression: Exploring Some Margins of the Song of Songs', in A.K.M. Adam (ed.), *Postmodern Interpretations of the Bible – A Reader* (St. Louis, MO: Chalice Press, 2001), pp. 93–104 (100–101).

33. Pope, *Song of Songs*, pp. 322–23, 678–82; Murphy, *The Song of Songs*, pp. 12–18.

34. No, thank you. The patriarchal bias of this kind of exegesis and its tragic effects on real women have been amply deconstructed by those paying attention. See Joanne Carlson Brown and Carole R. Bohn (eds.), *Christianity, Patriarchy and Abuse: A Feminist Critique* (Cleveland: Pilgrim Press, 1989); Renita J. Weems, *Battered Love: Marriage, Sex, and Violence in the Hebrew Prophets* (OBT; Minneapolis: Augsburg-Fortress, 1995); Athalya Brenner, 'Introduction', in Athalya Brenner (ed.), *A Feminist Companion to the Latter Prophets* (FCB, 8; Sheffield: Sheffield Academic Press, 1995), pp. 21–37.

35. 'Now this (watching) is not to adorn the Bride but to despoil her; not to guard her but to destroy her. It is not to defend her but to expose her to danger; not to provide for her, but to prostitute her' (*On the Song of Songs IV* [trans. Irene Edmonds; Kalamazoo, MI: Cistercian Publications, 1980], p.122).

cultivate and water his garden, to train and strengthen her in all truth, that is, to teach her and give her sure tidings of her beloved, since he is himself the truth which she seeks and which her soul truly loves...[36]

Bernard 'normalizes' the traditions of abuse on the part of the very ones set to guard over the woman's well-being by associating it with God's righteous work in the world on behalf of Woman (= the church). Indeed, it is the Groom who, by implication, sends physical abuse in order to 'teach' his Bride. With guardians and lovers like these, no woman needs enemies!

In interpreting the two searching episodes or dream sequences, feminist critic Fiona C. Black is neither willing to tell us that 'all attachment is suffering/love is pain' nor to allegorize as Bernard and other commentators do. Instead, she calls our attention to our repeated denials of the disturbing dimensions of this text, the diminution of its experiential authenticity by labeling it a 'dream', even though Hebrew knows words for 'to dream' and 'dreams', and they do not appear here. For her, the 'plain sense' of the text clearly includes the possibility of gang rape.[37] Speaking of the beating, she names it for what it is – 'transgressive':

> As keepers of order and preventers of violence, they use disorder and violence to repress the actions of the woman. Their treatment of her is unexpected and inappropriate both to the amorous designs of the Song and to the 'right' sexual relation that the protagonist seeks with her lover. The woman's acts, however, are also transgressive, and this appears to be the reason for her treatment. In return for leaving her house (the 'proper' environ for women in the patriarchal order), she is 'reminded' by the keepers of patriarchy just where she should be at night. In return for her sexual license, she is reminded to stay covered, and she is reminded, painfully, to guard the boundaries of her own body and its desires. She is pushed from the center of the Song as a speaking, loving subject.[38]

It seems to me that Black's reading is clear-eyed and well-grounded in the text itself. She does not make the text say something other than what it says, and she is attentive to what the text does *not* say. Her methods are postmodern, depending heavily on the work of critic Julia Kristeva for their attempt to explore the 'counter-coherence' set up in the text by the actions of the watchmen. There is nothing to quarrel with here. Black has delineated the contours of a text of useful ugliness; she makes her method of interpretation transparent to her readers. One presumes that she hopes to generate questions in modern communities of readers that will change the way we read both the Bible and the world of future experience. By reading Other-ly, however, she could have gone even further.

Listening through the Textual Veils
What happens if we read our text alongside women who actually wear veils (whether over their face, around their hair or draped flowingly over the neck as a gesture toward custom), women for whom the seeking of a lover not chosen by their male relatives may be tantamount to a death sentence? In our own time

36. Bernard, *On the Song of Songs IV*, pp. 125–26.
37. Black, 'Nocturnal', p. 101; see especially n. 27.
38. Black, 'Nocturnal', p. 102.

reports of violence against women as forms of social control of female sexuality in traditional society can serve as a helpful referent for some of the troubling silences of the song. If we have been willing to consider late nineteenth- and twentieth-century wedding practices in Muslim Palestinian villages as likely analogues for the original social context of the Song (as some interpreters still do), then we should also look at the sexual practices of those villages in other venues besides the wedding feast.[39]

I refer here to the practice of so-called 'honor killings' in popular Muslim practice, wherein the men of a family, often egged on or joined by their older female relatives, murder the allegedly offending female of their house. This is done in order to restore their own male 'honor', which can be destroyed by any female action deemed inappropriate.[40] While *never* prescribed in the Quran or considered normative Islamic teaching, such murders are wretchedly common, nevertheless,[41] and most especially in tribal settings. It is telling indeed that in Pakistan, the woman to be murdered is declared by her male relatives to be *kari* ('black' = evil) and so becomes a non-person whose life can be taken with impunity in front of witnesses. The male partner who supposedly had a hand in 'dishonoring' the *kari*-woman is punished, too: he is declared *karo*, 'black', but typically suffers only the punishment of paying a fine of money and supplying a 'replacement' female from his own family to restore the property of the outraged male – father, brother, uncle – who was 'forced' to murder his sister after she refused the mate chosen for her,[42] spoke a *'salaam'* to her cousin or bore a female child! Such murders usually go unreported to the police, and even when they are, investigation of the crime is

---

39. In order not to add further fuel to the fire of odious comparisons, given the present ongoing crisis in Israel-Palestine, I will not use the phenomenon of honor killings in Palestine, where tribal women exist in conditions resembling the Iron Age when it comes to values, culture, health care and human rights. It should be noted, however, that honor killings are customary in the Palestine of the West Bank (in some statistics, second only to Pakistan), and that these common occurrences form a major piece of evidence for some Israelis who suggest that peace may be impossible because their opponents have 'no respect for life'.

40. Some critics caution us that our 'feminist' outrage is insufficiently respectful of other cultural standards and inattentive to standards of cross-cultural methodology. See John J. Pilch, 'Family Violence in Cross-Cultural Perspective: An Approach for Feminist Interpreters of the Bible', in Brenner and Fontaine (eds.), *A Feminist Companion to Reading the Bible*, pp. 306–25. But for activists such a position of purported critical neutrality smacks of 'standing idly by in the presence of your neighbor's blood' (Lev. 19.16). See Hina Jillani's report for Amnesty International, http://web.amnesty.org/ai.nsf/Index/ASA330201999?OpenDocument&of=COUNTRIES\ PAKISTAN, as well as their most recent report, available at http://web.amnesty.org/ai.nsf/recent/ ASA330062002?OpenDocument#top.

41. Riffat Hassan, *Women's Rights and Islam: From the I.C.P.D. to Beijing* (Louisville, KY: NISA Publications, 1995); 'Women in Muslim Culture', in M. Darrol Bryant (ed.), *Muslim-Christian Dialogue: Problems and Promise* (New York: Paragon Press, 1998), pp. 187–201; 'The Issue of Woman-Man Equality in the Islamic Tradition', in K.E. Kvam, L.S. Schearing and W.H. Ziegler (eds.), *Eve and Adam: Jewish, Christian and Muslim Readings on Genesis and Gender* (Indianapolis: Indiana University Press, 1999), pp. 463–76.

42. The Quran requires women to be consulted and to give their consent to marriages arranged for them by family members. See Sura 4, 19; in hadith, see Sahih Bukhari, Vol. 9, Book 86, no. 98, Book 85, no. 79, and Sahih Muslim, Book 8, no. 33.5.

treated with a casual or humorous disregard.[43] When challenged about these atrocities by human rights activists, the patriarchal system claims that it is both a religious and indigenous cultural practice and, as such, cannot be critiqued. Those who *do* offer such critique must expect to pay the price – the need to hire body-guards in order to move from office to home, dismissal from access to power, exile or other forms of harassment. In societies where rape is considered 'consensual', illegal sex on a woman's part,[44] reporting of which is likely to cause her death at the hands of her family, it is no wonder that the stories of the scant survivors of these practices do not afford much space to the emotional or narrative 'aftermath' of such events'.[45] Not only do survivors have considerable difficulty articulating these deep, traumatic invasions of their bodies, often there is no audience willing to hear them when they do speak. Once a culture has silenced a women on the subject of her oppression, it then uses her silence to presume that 'nothing happened' or that, if something did happen, it is not a matter of critical importance to the victim's self-understanding.

Reading with someone who knows these conditions to be true in feudal, tribal societies of present time suggests, at least to this critic, that our interpretation of sexual customs in the ancient world against the background of a biblically ideal-ized twelve-tribe structure of interrelated tribes needs to be wary of the gaps we find and how we choose to fill them. Violence against women is part and parcel of tribal control of the economics of marriage. We can see this clearly in well-docu-mented modern contexts; our question must be whether such evidence is relevant for our reading of an ancient text. The Bible *does* speak of such practices directly in its stories of the tribal period, and the culture of violence against women does not substantially improve during monarchic times or in colonial times.[46] It is a violence so typical that it customarily goes unobserved by those who participate in it and unaddressed by the legal traditions of the societies that condone it.[47]

---

43. There are, of course, wonderful and brave men in official positions who provide an exception to the societies' prevalent failure to take such family violence against women seriously. We fear for them as we fear for imams who are moderate.

44. The Zina laws, found in the Hodood Ordinances enacted under fascist dictator General Zia. Amnesty International writes, 'Legal scholar and secretary of the Pakistan Law Commission, Dr Faqir Hussain, said at a seminar in Islamabad in October 2000 that the Hudood Ordinances (which includes the Zina ordinance) had been enacted as a 'political ploy' and not in fulfillment of a genu-ine mission aimed at enforcement of Islamic law... Enforcement of Zina Ordinance was contrary to Islamic injunctions, as had been agreed by many Islamic scholars' (http://web.amnesty.org/ai.nsf/recent/ASA330062002?OpenDocument).

45. The lack of any sustained discussion of the impact of the Beloved's violent experiences at the hands of the watchmen, along with the Song's failure to incorporate the outcome of this episode into its loose structure, are routinely cited by critics as a reason to discredit the Beloved's report as a dream, fantasy or trivial incident of no import for the reading of the text.

46. This dynamic has been explored by Mieke Bal, *Death and Dissymmetry: The Politics of Coherence in the Book of Judges* (Chicago: University of Chicago Press, 1988).

47. The Bible knows all about the force of 'honor and shame' codes of justice in the treatment of its females. See Tikva Frymer-Kensky, 'Virginity in the Bible', in Victor H. Matthews, Bernard M. Levenson and Tikva Frymer-Kensky (eds.), *Gender and Law in the Hebrew Bible and the Ancient Near East* (JSOTSup, 262; Sheffield: Sheffield Academic Press, 1998), pp. 79–96; Victor

Contextualizing the Beloved's encounter with the watchmen, whom Black characterizes as guardians of patriarchal ideology, we find that the nature of her 'veil/mantle' (רדיד) is actually indeterminate. Elsewhere in the Song, we hear her lover speak of her veil (צמה, 4.1,3; 6.6,7), from behind which at least her eyes are visible (6.5,7). In Genesis, Rebeccah and Tamar both present us with a mantle or veil (צעיף, Gen. 24.65; 38.14,19), yet its gendered usage is not clear. Rebeccah puts *on* her veil to meet someone, as a good girl should, but Tamar puts *off* her garments of widowhood, putting on her veil to trap her father-in-law Judah by posing as a prostitute. From this act we can infer that her mantle/veil does not allow the man to recognize a woman who lived for years in his own house. What precisely is being covered up here and in what circumstances? Our term, רדיד, occurs elsewhere only in Isa. 3.23, where it is found at the end of a long list of elite women's clothing and is one of the things God will take away, putting shame and rottenness in its place. There it is distinguished from an 'over-tunic' (מעטפה*, Isa. 3.22) and a 'cloak' (מטפחת*, in the same verse). Loss of this garment is a sign of punishment in Isaiah and fits in with all the 'stripping' motifs visited upon 'bride' Israel by God and his angry prophets. In addition to 'veil', translators have also used the words 'mantle' or 'wrapper' for these Hebrew terms, suggesting an outer garment that signals the boundary between the woman inside it and the world outside. It is certainly not clear whether the wearing of the רדיד signals the status of a modest or married woman, while its absence marks the female as disreputable and an available target – just as prostitutes remain the favored victims of choice for serial killers. What *is* clear is that this garment is as variable in shape as any Muslim woman's: from *burqah* or *hijab* to elegant silk scarf, a compulsory garment can be whatever a woman and her culture make of it – the ultimate answer to a bad hair day or just a traditional item of clothing that symbolizes no special state of inferiority to the women who wear it. Further, any removal of a compulsory outer garment by force can only be taken as a move to intimidate and shame.

The brothers, the watchmen and the stripped garment.[48] These are all *real* features in the Song, just as they are in some women's lives today. When the brothers in the Song are angry at their sister, it has an impact on her life and marks her very skin with 'blackness' in 1.6. She represents an economic resource to them, one they intend to guard carefully and use flagrantly for their own financial purposes (8.8-9).[49] They do not stop at placing their sister in a kind of *purdah*, a forced seclusion enlivened only by assigned drudgery and regulated by the family's desires. They hint at violent retribution should she prove to have eluded their control. The Beloved's repeated statements of a wish for privacy – taking her lover

H. Matthews, 'Honor and Shame in Gender-Related Legal Situations in the Hebrew Bible', pp. 97–112 and Carol L. Dempsey, 'The 'Whore' of Ezekiel 16: The Impact and Ramifications of Gender-Specific Metaphors in Light of Biblical Law and Divine Judgement', pp. 57–78, in the same volume.

48. Or perhaps 'mantle', which Pope explains as a light flowing garment covering head and shoulders and going almost down to the feet (*Song of Songs*, p. 527).

49. For a discussion of sisters as an economic resource of brothers in the ancient world, see Fontaine, *Smooth Words*, pp. 22–23.

to her mother's inner chamber (8.2), going away into the fields with him (7.10-13) – these motifs are not motivated only by the simple desire for privacy. There is *fear* at work here, too. Given her brothers' fixation on control over her, she knows perfectly well that she is at risk when she steps outside of the constraints set for her.

Having one's outer wrapper forcibly stripped away in the Beloved's social context is no little matter of dress or manners; it is a stunning humiliation designed to evoke terror and fear of further violence. It 'dishonors' her and her family by making publicly visible her shameful act of uncovering herself (for her lover), which she has supposedly done in private. Both the socio-cultural context of this act and the Beloved's report about it require something more than a simple hop, skip and jump to allegory. Only death-dealing allegories can be built from such episodes, and these in service of keeping the dirty little secrets of male anxiety over female sexuality well hidden from critical view. We must not overlook this startling incident just because our ugly text does not tell us that the Beloved went immediately into therapy for traumatic shock. This is one 'gap' we may not fill with hearts and flowers. Acquiring sensitivity to the power of the stolen veil for women in societies where veiling is the custom[50] adds a dimension of understanding to the Beloved's silence that we who are Western readers might otherwise overlook.

The 'Other-ly' reading of the loss of one's culturally assigned coverings has implications for other texts besides the Song, of course. We might think of Hos. 2.3,10-13, as well as many other prophetic texts that strip the female 'Israel' publicly as a sign of God's displeasure with the people's idolatry. Clearly, stripping in these texts is an ominous prelude to even more stringent punishments for the metaphorical adultery of the group and has the added by-product of shaming men by forcing them to see themselves in the female 'subject' position.

Another text takes on new interpretive force when read in this light, though it does not explicitly mention the removal of a veil or clothing: the ritual ordeal of the Soṭah found in Num. 5.11-31. When a husband 'suspects' his wife of adultery, his whole household and, by extension, his village are subjected to shame and conflict. Lacking witnesses to his wife's 'defilement' yet tormented by the specter ('spirit of jealousy', Num. 5.14, RSV) of his own loss of honor, a husband may take recourse in the rite of the Soṭah, a 'drinking ordeal'. The suspected adulteress is brought before the priest (and God) who loosens her hair, prepares a cereal offering and forces her to take an oath while drinking the 'waters of bitterness'. If she is guilty, the bitter waters and the oath will bring harmful physical results, public for all to see. If nothing happens, then she is justified and acquitted, and the husband,

---

50. 'Oh, it is a dreadful nuisance!', said one beautifully garbed Pakistani woman as I admired the sheer scarf around her neck. 'It gets into everything – the batter you are cooking, the children's toys, the flower arrangement – but you can't go out without it!' It is not unusual to find many fallen veils at the side of unmarked graves or in out-of-the-way groves where the bodies of *kari*-women have been left, since strangulation with one's own veil is a common form of honor killing. Though no one acknowledges these deaths with grave markers, occasionally women of the villages sneak out to leave memorials of flowers or prayers for the fallen at these sites.

although proven to have harbored false suspicions, need not pay any damages to the woman's family, which has been dishonored by the husband's unfounded accusations against her. Because she has been 'cleared' of the slanders against her and her husband's fears have been dealt with in a ritual way, one could even imagine a basis in the ritual for a restoration of the marital relationship.

It is fair to say that the Soṭah text has usually been despised by feminist interpreters, even as it is prized by those who study ritual and legal traditions.[51] Reading against the background of violence used to control female sexual infractions of traditional codes of conduct, we may note some features of the proceedings we might otherwise dismiss. First, the unbinding of the woman's hair by the priest is a shaming event on par with the stripping of the Beloved: the priest does in public what the lover has supposedly done in private. Although the woman is forced to participate in the ritual – and one can hardly think of her as eager to submit to a magically effective ordeal, since these acts would have had real power in her world – the entire proceeding is left up to God as judge. Here it is helpful to remember a snippet from Hosea, a divine oracle in which God proclaims '… I am God and not man, the Holy One in your midst, and I will not come to destroy' (Hos. 11.9b; RSV). In theory, a woman may expect a just God to give a more fair and empathetic hearing than she is likely to get from a man consumed by a spirit of jealousy or a priest called upon to resolve the matter in a way that enforces the status quo. As unpleasant as this ritual experience looks to moderns, it *does* have the effect of limiting both the husband's and the village's ability to enforce their sexual codes with terminal violence against the unfortunate accused. (I make the assumption here that the priest would not poison the brew beforehand 'under the table', so to speak, since the table belongs to Yahweh, and such an act might have serious repercussions; others would not agree!) Instead of a life of repeated private beatings to induce a confession or a public execution at the hands of those who would eliminate the source of potential shame, the woman has legal 'standing' before the Divine Assembly, and only then can the sentence be pronounced. It is no wonder that some rabbis noted that a woman with knowledge and understanding of the Torah would find protection from God even in the most dire of situations!

From There and Back: The Song Renewed by Reading

If one is forced to a new 'seeing' by reading with the Other, the textual landscape now revealed is highlighted in both its glories in love and its depths of violence. With a sense of the real violence that many traditional societies exercise against their females, we hear the Beloved's yearning with a new accompaniment. We gain a sense of her astonishing bravery and an appreciation of the unique qualities in her lover that inspire such devoted, dangerous actions on her part. My reading proceeds to a final understanding that her statements about love and desire are uttered not just as heated romantic nonsense spoken by inflamed teenagers but as a

---

51. Alice Bach, 'A Case History: Numbers 5.11-31', in Alice Bach (ed.), *Women in the Hebrew Bible: A Reader* (New York: Routledge, 1999), pp. 459–522.

deliberate *choice* to confront death with the only power that can equal it – love (Song 8.6).

The Bible reminds me of beautiful things I have allowed to be forgotten in the overwhelming impact of the visions from the Pit that pervade my daily life as an activist against violence. It provides me with insights into motivation, cultural value and divine compassion that are often lost in a postmodern world that is sure of very little. It partners both my attempt to understand the past and to change the future. I have often wondered as I review the latest news reports sent to activists around the world by the faithful women of Pakistan and Afghanistan,[52] what on earth could drive these poor little girls to such treacherous choices as defying their male relatives,[53] given the terminal consequences? When feudal lords and the tribes they control trade in prestige and power based on their ability to deploy female relatives in advantageous alliances, then a woman as a 'desiring subject' becomes a threat to the very infrastructure of society. She has no intrinsic value apart from the use her male relatives have for her. How did she *ever* even begin to desire, to choose? What is at work here in this day-to-day subversion of the will to control?

Only powerful, elemental forces can prevail against the hegemony of male violence toward women. Though the Song speaks of a kind of 'sisterhood' in the form of the Daughters of Jerusalem, it is not the approval or support of her girl-friends that motivates the Beloved and moves her from safety inside the home out into the dangerous world. It is the very Other-ness of her lover, male to her female, key to her lock,[54] that one who can be full companion to a whole person like the Song's Beloved. Male/female relations can be a source of *strength* for a woman, even as they can be the origin of much pain. Like fire and water, love and death are at war in the Song, and love – though never quite fully experienced as total presence – wins (Song 8.6-7):

> … for love is strong as death, passion fierce as the grave.
> Its arrows are arrows of fire, flames of the Divine.
> Many waters cannot quench love, neither can floods drown it.
> If someone offered for love all the wealth of his house, it would be utterly scorned. (RSV)

The economics of patriarchy are discarded in favor of acknowledgment of another kind of authority governing male/female relations: freely chosen partnership is the only proof against the powers of death. The text suggests this dynamic was true for the Song *then*; it is true for some of us *now* – and there inheres the authenticity of

---

52. You too, Gentle Reader, can have the casualty reports of the daily female Holocaust delivered right to your computer (http://www.inrfvvp.org; http://www.rawa.org). You can even help!

53. Very often, the *kari*-woman has done nothing whatsoever, shown no defiance, transgressed no custom – she is simply inconvenient, or her murder covers up another (reportable) crime, or the murderer was actually trying to obtain a desirable 'replacement' female from the *karo*-family, to whom he would not otherwise have access or could not have afforded.

54. I make no moral or essentialist judgments here concerning the authenticity, sanctity and complementarity of same-sex committed relationships. Other-hood may be constructed and understood in a variety of ways. In the Song, though, the erotic tension displayed in the celebration of the Other's body suggests a very intense heterosexual construction of erotic Otherliness.

an interpretation that chooses to partner the text into a reading that affirms life and love in all their forms.

Epilogue

At the last, biblical interpreters – the self-constituted 'watchfolk' who strive to guard against 'wrong' readings – make choices. I am well aware that in privileging the voice of the stripped woman against brothers and watchmen, I make a rhetorical shift from semi-tolerant yet grounded critic (conscious of the ways in which the Song evades interpretive closure) to the passionate advocate. The movement to advocacy may *seem* as though it moves from the 'passive' voice of the interpreter to the 'active' voice of the activist/preacher, but as I have tried to demonstrate, that passive interpreter isn't so very passive after all! Choices are being made in the very *desire* to interpret, and these come to fruition in that deceptively 'objective' presentation of any meaning. Without choice there can be no ethical action; without ethical action, the Bible cannot achieve relevance in a dying world. When I assert that the Beloved, the woman cloaked by culture, has embraced love as a deliberate choice in order to confront Death with the only power equal to it, I, too, am choosing. I make a deliberate hermeneutical choice, opting for one plausible interpretation against other plausible interpretations, including the reasonable interpretation that the Beloved does *not* choose love against patriarchy but is simply following ordinary desire in what happens to be a patriarchal setting that frustrates her romantic pursuits.

Ironically, at least for the advocate in me, the one part of the Song that seems least susceptible to multiple interpretations is the brutal fact of the patriarchy itself. Apart from details, nothing strikes me as indeterminate about the brothers, the watchman or the stripped garment. The 'feminist Southern Baptist' in me could wish that these signs of patriarchy were ambiguous or at least that the suggestions of a woman's revolt against brothers, watchman and stripping were definite, incapable of being misread. But it is precisely the other way around. The signs of patriarchy appear unambiguous, while the suggestions of opposition to it are more fragile, variable signs, susceptible to other readings. And how could it be otherwise? For those fragile signs speak, if at all, only from behind the cloak that patriarchy imposes, obscuring the speaking woman.[55]

None of this is to suggest that if we could tear away the outer garment of the text, a *single* perspective or reality would be exposed to us. Gender can be constructed as a site of conflicting codes about the meaning of biological 'difference', such that there is no one female *or* male 'subject' position. The Beloved *may* think that her brothers are nitwits whom she easily outsmarts time and again, the watchmen familiar family friends who take away her garment because it isn't flattering or is impractical for evening wear. But her language, 'angry at me' (brothers, 1.6),

---

55. *Can* a cloak/wrapper/mantle obscure the face as a veil does? For a view of an ancient woman in a mantle that *also* covers her hair (and may reasonably be used to cover her nose and mouth during bad weather), see my *Smooth Words*, p. 21, fig. 1.

'they beat me, they wounded me' (watchmen, 5.7), statements in the text for which an interpreter must account, suggests to me that my readings have done a better job of trying to listen to the text, its nuances and omissions, than others have done in simply shooting past these disruptive verses in pursuit of a wonderful wedding song.

In the end, we choose. For me this hermeneutical decision between competing interpretations can only be a choosing in solidarity with those who have no voice for their own choices, those who have been taught that they may not choose![56] I cannot lift the veil of the text, at least not in a way that makes the face and voice behind the veil stand out unambiguously. But I can read with those whose lives are cloaked as a way of listening through the veils. I owe it to the text and the community of interpreters to be honest about the signal coming from behind that garment: honest about its uncertainty, its openness to a mundane (if romantically charming) or an extraordinary (and politically challenging) interpretation. I owe it to the woman in the cover-up – and all the women whose lives are enshrouded by gendered meanings – to advocate that extraordinary interpretive possibility, to partner the text into a reading that affirms life and love in all their forms against the tyrannies of domination and social death.

56. This insight is one of the considerations that help us to distinguish between an interpretation in support of veiled women and one, say, in support of Ku Klux Klan readings: the KKK has voice, access, power, technology. The veiled ones do not, so this is one place where our Western ambiguity about support of the Other, so often tinged with a suspect cultural imperialism, can be put 'on hold': we are absolutely required to support those without access, because they have no other entry into the dialogue at present.

PAUL AS LIBERATOR AND OPPRESSOR
HOW SHOULD WE EVALUATE DIVERSE VIEWS OF FIRST CORINTHIANS?

Robert C. Tannehill, Methodist Theological School, Ohio, USA

Pauline studies are no longer immune to the methodological ferment within biblical studies in general. New interpretations of Paul are appearing that may radically affect our evaluation of Paul and his work. In this article I will concentrate on two recent interpretations of Paul and 1 Corinthians that share a common concern – to demonstrate that New Testament studies can support movements of liberation from social oppression – yet result in quite different pictures of Paul. We can start by using the broad labels 'political' and 'feminist' for these two types of interpretation. Specifically, I will focus on the recent work of Richard A. Horsley and Neil Elliott, on the one hand, and Elisabeth Schüssler Fiorenza and Antoinette Clark Wire, on the other.

Although one may debate whether the two approaches are strictly incompatible, they are distinctly different, particularly in their evaluations of Paul's role for or against movements of liberation from social oppression. In the one case, Paul stands for liberation from the power of the Roman empire and the social structures that support it; in the other case, Paul is acting to limit the freedom of Corinthian women who have begun to claim their new freedom in Christ.

In this essay it is not my purpose to support one view against the other. Rather, I will point to some of the significant strengths of each. The underlying issue is how we should respond to two types of interpretation – both of them plausible but neither of them certain – that reach such different results. I will argue that both are valuable. As historical interpretations, neither of them (nor other competing interpretations) reaches the level of certainty, since our knowledge of Paul and his churches is limited to what we know from Paul's letters. Even so, they are valuable as hermeneutical exercises, demonstrating clearly how the same text can have different functions as the situation addressed changes, a lesson that continues to apply to the use of scripture today. Specifically, they demonstrate how the same texts can either support or oppose the liberation of particular social groups, depending on how we understand Paul's interactions with other persons.

Introductory Issues

Conflicting readings may result from differing conceptions of the situation being addressed by Paul. The learned reader should be aware of options and the consequences of those options for understanding the impact of the Pauline text on the lives of people. Consideration of these options is likely to raise ethical issues for interpreters with strong ethical commitments. These ethical commitments might interfere with sound historical judgment. Awareness of this possibility should lead the interpreter to weigh argument and evidence carefully. One option may seem preferable because of the interpreter's commitments and values, but he or she must always ask whether a substantial case can be made for this option. 'Substantial' is not the same as 'air tight', for on the basis of available evidence it is unlikely that we can declare that all other options are impossible. Nevertheless, the scholarly interpreter must always carry the burden of providing substantial argument and evidence.

Our ethical commitments will influence the interpretive process, even though we usually do not acknowledge them in academic circles. These commitments need not interfere with balanced historical judgment. Indeed, along with our other commitments, we have an ethical obligation to the scholarly community to present a reasonable account of a historical text, one that can be examined by persons who do not share all our presuppositions. Ethical commitment does not release the scholar from the responsibility to present reasons for a particular interpretation of a historical text, which prevents us from turning the text into a simple mirror of our desires. Yet our interests and commitments appear in our interpretations, whether we acknowledge them or not.

If an interpreter appears to have a personal interest in the outcome or to be an advocate for a cause, some would be inclined to dismiss the results. Such suspicions are aroused by the two interpretations of Paul that I will discuss in this essay. Yet a fundamental interest of some kind must motivate our work. All of our work is 'interested'; that is, there is some motivation behind it. Otherwise, we would not do it. The motivation may be religious or ethical, in a great variety of forms. It may be anti-religious – directed against religion in its historic and popular expressions. In so far as academic life has been professionalized, religious motivations may have weakened, but the result is not 'disinterested' scholarship. Professional motivation takes over – the desire to advance one's standing in the profession through gaining an academic appointment, tenure and recognition as an outstanding scholar. This motivation is just as likely to interfere with creative and sound scholarship as religious and ethical motivations. On the one hand, it can stifle creativity and critical thinking because of a fear of censure by those who presently hold the leading positions in one's field. On the other hand, it can lead to unfair criticism of previous work and exaggerated claims to uniqueness in an effort to present one's work as new and creative – 'the latest thing'. It can also lead to excessive attachment to one's own theory, which must be defended at all costs. All scholars need to be self-critical, not through denying their personal motivations but through awareness of the ways that these motivations may impinge on their scholarship, for good and ill. On ethical grounds one might argue, however, that a purely professional motive – the advancement of one's own career – is inferior to motives that aim at a larger good.

A consideration of the motives behind scholarship must also recognize the role of interpretive communities. In church history we can recognize that different denominations commonly represent interpretive communities, with different views of the significance of scripture and the meaning of the Christian gospel. (This is a simplification, for denominations that maintain organizational unity over time may conceal considerable diversity and fluctuation in their roles as interpretive communities.) Those who belong to these groups tend to interpret scripture as the group does.

American biblical scholarship is influenced by interpretive communities of a different type. A proliferation of methodologies and interests has resulted in a diversity of seminars and work groups that meet over a series of years as part of the Society of Biblical Literature. These seminars and work groups both reflect and form interpretive communities within biblical scholarship. They represent distinct methodologies or distinct goals in scholarship. They are valuable because they promote intense and focused work and allow scholars with a common focus to stimulate each other. They also demonstrate how group interests guide scholarship. These groups promote the value of a particular method or goal. If they appear to be successful, they attract members to their group. Personal relationships develop. These relationships change attitudes about which ideas and which publications are worthy of attention. Members promote each other's careers. In particular, older members in the more respected academic positions become mentors to younger, less secure members because they share common interests. Thus, the interests of the group are promoted, perhaps at a loss to some equally worthy task and with the accompanying danger of developing an insular perspective. It has become increasingly difficult for members of different groups to engage in profitable dialogue. Some members who are institutionally less secure may hesitate to question the views of the influential leaders of the group.

Doing scholarship in the midst of multiple and conflicting interests is not an easy task, but these interests are the constant life context of our work. Good scholarship is promoted not by denying the existence of such motivating interests but by testing whether they lead to reasonable interpretations in light of textual and historical evidence. Furthermore, ignoring such interests divorces the scholarly vocation from our higher calling – living for the good. A life devoted to the good requires us to sort out and adhere to the best motivations. These can be compatible with good scholarship and good teaching, which become ways of fulfilling our life vocation of living for the good.

The way in which many academic essays are written disguises the actual function of these interests. Academic essays concentrate on the arguments and evidence for a particular interpretation. Frequently there is no explanation of why the interpreter is interested in presenting such an interpretation. If there is any explanation, it is commonly confined to brief remarks about the implications of the interpretation at the end of the essay, as if these implications arose through subsequent reflection on established conclusions. In actual research our interests and ethical commitments are frequently the stimulus to seek a new interpretation. They are present at the beginning of our work and lead to new acts of historical imagination, so that a hypothesis begins to take shape. The desire for a more satisfying interpretation – satisfying in light of our values and interests – is the origin of much of biblical and theological scholarship that is most significant for human life. The resulting new hypothesis must be tested through detailed study of textual and historical evidence. This study usually leads to modification of the hypothesis, sometimes in ways that defeat our original hopes, sometimes through the discovery of an even more attractive possibility. In the course of this work there is constant interaction between our motivating desires and the constraints of textual and historical evidence.

Current interpretation of the Pauline letters begins with the belief that they are situation-specific communications. Therefore, interpretation depends heavily on an understanding of the situation that Paul is addressing, although all specific information about this must be drawn from the Pauline letter itself. Recent development of a rhetorical perspective in Pauline studies, as represented, for instance, by Elisabeth Schüssler Fiorenza's recent work,[1] complicates an already difficult task.[2] Rhetoric views communication as persuasive action. Paul wants to persuade his audience, that is, to modify its thinking and acting. Our understanding of how Paul is seeking to influence his audience – the communicative force or human impact of Paul's words – depends on our understanding of the situation to which Paul is responding. These matters will, in turn, influence our evaluation of Paul. Was Paul doing the right thing in responding as he did? Although many scholars may want to avoid this question, it is a real and important question for those with ethical commitments. This question is especially forced upon us by recent feminist interpretation.

We are dependent on Paul's letters for our understanding of the situation in Paul's churches. However, definition of the church's problems requiring intervention is already a part of Paul's rhetoric. Definitions of situations are perspectival, and conflicts arise because perspectives differ. Speakers and writers try to persuade by getting others to see the situation from their perspective. It is likely that some of the Corinthians would deny that the problems Paul sees are real problems; they would contest his understanding of their situation. Rather than assuming that we can infer the 'actual' situation directly from Paul's words, we must recognize that there was no commonly accepted definition of the actual situation but only Paul's definition and various competing definitions that reflect motivations about which we can only guess.

If there was no common understanding of the situation, even by the original participants, and our knowledge is limited to inferences from Paul's letters, it is unlikely that we will be able to reach final conclusions about the situation in the Corinthian church. The proliferation of views in the history of scholarship is already testimony to the difficulty of the task,[3] although past scholarship has generally ignored the fact that we have access only to Paul's rhetorical perspective. Yet, as already noted, our understanding of the communicative force of Paul's

---

1.   Elisabeth Schüssler Fiorenza, *Rhetoric and Ethic: The Politics of Biblical Studies* (Minneapolis: Fortress Press, 1999).

2.   See especially Schüssler Fiorenza's discussion of the 'rhetorical situation' in *Rhetoric and Ethic*, pp. 108–109.

3.   For a recent attempt to explain the 'Corinthian theology' through a critical examination of themes from previous scholarship, see Wolfgang Schrage, *Der erste Brief an die Korinther*, I (EKKNT VII/1; Zürich: Benziger Verlag, 1991; Neukirchen–Vluyn: Neukirchener Verlag, 1991), pp. 38–63.

words, their impact in the rhetorical situation, is dependent on our understanding of the situation. The result is a high degree of indeterminacy. This observation conflicts with the still prevailing assumption that there is one correct solution. The task of the scholar, then, is to prove that one's own solution is the correct one, thereby eliminating other possibilities. Our accomplishments are actually more modest, I believe. Although one interpretation may temporarily seem to rule (it may be attractive because it appears new, creative and detailed), a rival is likely to appear or reappear. It is useful to discuss arguments and evidence for each position. Yet it is likely that the currently favored position will be only marginally better than the alternatives, which prevents us from eliminating them as possibilities, since no interpretation should assume that we are provided with full information. The large gaps in our knowledge will continue to permit various interpretations of the force of Paul's words.

This may appear to be a counsel of despair, especially for concerned church members who turn to biblical scholars to provide a true understanding of Paul's words so that their faith and life may be nourished. It would seem that no one can really say what is implied for believers today because no one can be sure of the purpose or likely effect of Paul's words in the original situation. I would suggest that the implications are actually more positive. In considering the significance of a biblical text for life today, it is always necessary to ask: Does this text apply to our situation? If so, to what aspects of our situation? Answers will depend on our understanding of the situation to which Paul's words are appropriately addressed. The situation appropriately addressed may or may not be similar to the situation Paul actually addressed. That decision depends on whether Paul was acting appropriately. However, hypotheses concerning the original situation will help us to think about this issue, suggesting various possibilities that may have positive or negative effects for human life. It is useful to consider the various options because any one, or several, may illuminate our situation. Consideration of options may make us aware of possible negative effects, in certain situations, and encourage us to seek applications that will have positive effects.

We may find Paul's definition of the situation, as explained by various interpreters, to be the best guide for understanding how his words should relate to issues in our own time. However, we may decide that the tables have turned and now we need to listen to the voices of the Corinthian women prophets, who were problems for Paul but who have something to say to us.[4] We may even acknowledge the original historical context but decide that Paul's words in context are not appropriate guidance for us, perhaps because Paul's application is severely limited by the social practices of his time. Nevertheless, when placed in a new context, with a corresponding shift in their force, Paul's words become illuminating and powerful. We cannot predict with certainty how the illuminating word will be found.

By what criteria should such decisions be made? This is a question to which I cannot give an adequate answer. It would require probing our deepest religious and ethical commitments. I would note, however, that the double love commandment is

---

4.   See Antoinette Clark Wire, *The Corinthian Women Prophets: A Reconstruction through Paul's Rhetoric* (Minneapolis: Fortress Press, 1990).

presented in the New Testament not only as a guide to salvation (in Lk. 10.25-28) but also as a hermeneutical principle for interpretation of scripture,[5] for Mt. 22.40 adds, 'On these two commandments all the law and the prophets depend'. Paul agrees in that he, too, presents the command to love neighbor as a hermeneutical principle, central to understanding the whole law (Rom. 13.8-10; Gal. 5.14). So I suggest that, following this fundamental scriptural principle, we give scripture force in our lives in ways that consistently foster love of God and neighbor. This critical principle applies to our use of scripture but is also a self-critical principle for scripture itself; there are some things in scripture that cannot be positive guidance for us because they conflict with this scriptural principle. Of course, the double love commandment does not solve all our problems. Love is easily weakened to sentimentality. Furthermore, any implementation of love of neighbor depends on views of what is good for the neighbor, and there is much disagreement on this issue. Nevertheless, the double love commandment is a helpful criterion for deciding how scripture should be used.

Now we need to consider the two recent perspectives on Paul and 1 Corinthians mentioned at the beginning of this essay, the 'political' and the 'feminist'. They share a common concern: to integrate biblical scholarship with support of emancipatory social movements. Yet they reach quite different conclusions about Paul's attitude toward social emancipation. In general, they differ at the following key points:

1. Horsley and Elliott are inclined to find value in Paul's position (although Horsley is critical of Paul at certain points), but Schüssler Fiorenza and Wire listen for the voice of the Corinthians – especially the Corinthian women – behind Paul's words and attribute primary value to this alternate voice.

2. Horsley and Elliot are more inclined to base their understanding of the situation in Corinth on Paul's statements and evaluations, while Schüssler Fiorenza and Wire subject Paul's statements to a hermeneutic of suspicion and arrive at a contrasting understanding of what is happening.

3. Although both parties are concerned with the social status of the Corinthians, they use their conclusions differently. Wire believes that the Corinthians, especially the women, are persons of low social status who are being lifted up in Christ. Paul's social roots and religious experience are quite different.[6] Paul addresses the Corinthians in light of his own experience, which is largely alien to them. Horsley,

---

5. I discussed this previously in my essay, 'Freedom and Responsibility in Scripture Interpretation, with Application to Luke', in R.P. Thompson and T.E. Philips (eds.), *Literary Studies in Luke–Acts* (Macon, GA: Mercer University Press, 1998), pp. 265–78 (276–78). See also Charles H. Cosgrove, *Appealing to Scripture in Moral Debate: Five Hermeneutical Rules* (Grand Rapids: Eerdmans, 2002), pp. 158–61 and Charles H. Cosgrove, *Elusive Israel: The Puzzle of Election in Romans* (Louisville, KY: Westminster/John Knox Press, 1997), pp. 43–44; Ulrich Luz, *Matthew in History: Interpretation, Influence, and Effects* (Minneapolis: Fortress Press, 1994), pp. 82–97.

6. Wire, *The Corinthian Women Prophets*, p. 45 and, against Horsley, Wire, 'Response: The Politics of the Assembly in Corinth', in Richard A. Horsley (ed.), *Paul and Politics: Ekklesia, Israel, Imperium, Interpretation* (Harrisburg, PA: Trinity Press International, 2000), pp. 124–29 (125–26).

too, believes that most Corinthians came from the lower classes, yet, in the competition for status typical of the time and place, some had begun to claim for themselves a high spiritual status.[7] In this context, Paul's strong criticism of the 'puffed up' Corinthians may seem justified.

4. Both sets of interpreters probably share a broad commitment to the emancipation of oppressed social groups, including women, slaves and the poor. Elliott and Horsley have introduced a new perspective, however, through their emphasis on the importance of the imperial cult and imperial propaganda, viewed as methods of social control. Unlike many interpreters, they believe that Paul's gospel has a political edge in opposition to this cult and propaganda.

Paul and the Corinthian Women Prophets

Elisabeth Schüssler Fiorenza continues to reflect in depth on the task of transforming biblical interpretation, as practiced in the past, into 'emancipatory interpretation', a task that reflects her ethical commitment to the liberation of oppressed groups. Her reflections have evolved through a number of stages. I will focus on her recent summary of 'seven interpretive strategies' in *Rhetoric* and *Ethic*.[8]

Rather than referring to patriarchy, Schüssler Fiorenza now speaks more broadly of 'kyriarchal systems of domination' that appear both in the biblical text and in past interpretive practices. In order to carry out her vocation as a 'public' or 'transformative' intellectual[9] – one committed to liberative social change – she engages in 'seven interpretive strategies'. Beginning with a 'hermeneutics of experience and social location' that makes the interpreter aware of the ways in which biblical texts, functioning within present religious and social contexts, have shaped the experience of victimized groups, she moves to an 'analytic of domination' – an analysis of the ideological functions of texts in 'legitimating the kyriarchal order' – and a 'hermeneutics of suspicion' that 'seeks to demystify structures of domination that are inscribed in the text and in contemporary contexts of interpretation'. These tasks flow into a 'hermeneutics of ethical and theological evaluation' that explores both 'the cultural-religious internalizations and legitimations of kyriarchy and... the values and visions that are inscribed as countercultural alternatives in biblical texts'.[10]

This process is supported by a 'hermeneutics of remembrance and re-construction' that 'aims at making the subordinated and marginalized "others" visible again and their repressed arguments and silences "audible" '. This hermeneutics 'is fully conscious of the rhetoricity of its own re-constructions' and does not confuse them with 'reality itself'. It is inspired by a 'hermeneutics of imagination' that 'seeks to generate utopian visions... and to "dream" a different world of justice and well-being'. 'Imagination', she explains, 'enables us to fill in the gaps, empty spaces,

---

7.   Richard A. Horsley, *1 Corinthians* (ANTC; Nashville: Abingdon Press, 1998), pp. 32, 38.
8.   The following summary of Schüssler Fiorenza's hermeneutic is based on *Rhetoric and Ethic*, pp. 48–54.
9.   Schüssler Fiorenza, *Rhetoric and Ethic*, p. 81.
10.   *Rhetoric and Ethic*, pp. 48–51.

and silences, and thereby to make sense out of the text'. Imagination is as neces-sary to history and science as it is to art. The final goal and climax of the entire interpretive process is a 'hermeneutics of transformation and action for change'.[11]

I respect Schüssler Fiorenza's ethical commitments and her efforts to integrate those commitments with her profession as a biblical scholar. I also think that she is correct in emphasizing the importance of imagination in historical reconstruction. Recognizing the importance of imagination does not mean that biblical scholars can ignore textual and historical evidence. We still must accept the task of inter-preting texts within a definable historical context. Yet the text and the historical context are seldom such 'hard' evidence that they can be interpreted in only one way. Schüssler Fiorenza links her hermeneutics of imagination in historical recon-struction with the generation of a 'dream' of a 'different world of justice and well-being'.[12] She does not ignore evidence in this task, but she seeks through her scholarship a nourishing and transforming vision that can be acted upon today, in spite of the structures of domination and rhetoric of oppression embedded in the biblical texts and their world. It may seem that there is a bias toward reconstruction of the early church as a utopian community, even if the biblical texts fall far short of Schüssler Fiorenza's standards. However, I do not see this as a fault, so long as her reconstruction is still a possibility when all relevant evidence has been exam-ined, for there is an ethical purpose behind her work. Nevertheless, one cannot claim that her reconstructions eliminate other reconstructions that fill in the gaps differently through a different use of imagination. These alternatives might, in their own way, support a nourishing and transforming vision that provides a worthy guide to action today.

Antoinette Clark Wire's interpretation of 1 Corinthians, with a focus on the Corinthian women prophets, fits Schüssler Fiorenza's agenda. Wire seeks to reconstruct the religious experience of the Corinthian community, in which, she believes, the women prophets played an important role. She understands the women to be throwing off the restrictions imposed by society through claiming new freedom in Christ. She evaluates their thought and actions positively, with a correspondingly negative interpretation of Paul's efforts to restrain and correct them. Although there is a plausible basis for her emphasis on the Corinthian women prophets, as I will indicate below, Wire must use historical imagination to fill in what would otherwise be a murky picture. She does so by positing an alternative to the positions that Paul takes and describing the situation in ways that suggest that the women prophets' position was reasonable for them.[13] Thus, the

---

11. *Rhetoric and Ethic*, pp. 51–54.

12. In spite of sharp negative statements about Paul and other biblical writers, Schüssler Fiorenza also hopes to find 'biblical values and visions' that are liberative (*Rhetoric and Ethic*, pp. 9, 45).

13. Wire provides supporting argument for her approach to 1 Corinthians. The subtitle of her book is 'A Reconstruction through Paul's Rhetoric'. Paul seeks to be persuasive and therefore shapes his arguments to the audience (*The Corinthian Women Prophets*, p. 3). Thus, 'On whatever points Paul's persuasion is insistent and intense, showing he is not merely confirming their agreement but struggling for their assent, one can assume some different and opposite point of view in Corinth from the one Paul is stating' (*The Corinthian Women Prophets*, p. 9). I agree that

women prophets 'are able to tolerate more variety of opinion and practice than Paul'.[14] They understand themselves to be 'a new creation in God's image'[15] and seek to give full expression to this new reality. Paul fears that human glory will infringe on the glory of God, but the Corinthian women have a different view of God. 'They do not see God on the defense, vindicating the divine glory by capital punishment, but on the offense, giving people gifts whose exercise glorifies both themselves and God'.[16] The Corinthians regard eating sacrificial food as a 'public witness... that the sacrificed meat will not harm them... because there is no God but one'.[17] While Paul emphasizes the importance of restraint and listening in the assemblies, for the Corinthians it is important that many people 'freely speak... expressing their own faith back and forth'.[18]

Wire's interpretation of 1 Corinthians provides a good illustration of the way that historical reconstruction can radically change our understanding of the impact of a text in its historical context. For instance, a passage where Paul seems to be very careful to treat women and men equally (1 Cor. 7.3-4) takes on a different meaning for Wire. She suggests that the women prophets were claiming authority over their own bodies so that they could abstain from sexual relations and dedicate themselves to prayer and prophecy. In spite of Paul's rhetoric of equality, then, he is intervening on the side of the men when he asserts that no married person has authority over his or her own body. Paul's intervention is the result of his fear that husbands will be led into extra-marital sexual relations because of their wives' withdrawal.[19]

Wire presents an interesting, detailed and thought-provoking study of 1 Corinthians. Although she does not start with this passage, 1 Cor. 11.2-16 provides a solid basis for saying that women prophets had a role in the Corinthian community. Rather than viewing this passage as an odd comment about a side issue, it is plausible to take it as a basis for reconstructing the Corinthian situation. The references to praying and prophesying in 1 Cor. 11.4-5 provide a link to the further discussion of spiritual gifts, especially prophecy and tongues, in 1 Cor. 12–14, and the issues of these chapters, in turn, can be linked to claims to 'wisdom' and 'knowledge' in 1 Cor. 1.17–3.3; 3.18-20; 8.1-2. Wire offers a variation on the view that the Corinthian 'spirituals' celebrated their spiritual gifts, including divine wisdom, claimed freedom from social inhibitions, and felt that they enjoyed salvation in the present. There is this striking difference: Wire uses all of the indications of this behavior to describe the women prophets, and she, unlike most interpreters, presents these

---

the intensity of Paul's words provides clues to the issues that he believes to be important in the Corinthian situation and, presumably, indicates that someone in Corinth was thinking or acting in a contrary way. This does not mean, however, that the Corinthian view was 'opposite' in a precise way. There are likely to be a number of ways of interpreting the position that causes Paul's comment.

14. Wire, *The Corinthian Women Prophets*, p. 22.
15. *The Corinthian Women Prophets*, p. 126.
16. *The Corinthian Women Prophets*, p. 27.
17. *The Corinthian Women Prophets*, p. 103.
18. *The Corinthian Women Prophets*, p. 144.
19. *The Corinthian Women Prophets*, pp. 82–83.

spirituals sympathetically. Discussion of the low status of most women in Corinthian society undergirds her sympathetic portrayal.[20] Wire's interpretation provides a useful correction of the tendency to dismiss the people Paul was addressing and devalue their religious experience.

Both Wire and Schüssler Fiorenza accept the command that women be silent in the assemblies (1 Cor. 14.34-35) as an original part of 1 Corinthians.[21] Unlike many male interpreters, Wire and Schüssler Fiorenza are not inclined to defend Paul as a model of gender inclusiveness. Instead, they approach Paul with suspicion on gender issues. In spite of her extensive discussion of 1 Cor. 14.34-35 in *The Corinthian Women Prophets*, Wire does not, in my opinion, give adequate attention to the seeming inconsistency between 14.34-35 and 11.2-16, where Paul regulates but does not prohibit women praying and prophesying. Against those who point to this inconsistency as a chief argument for declaring that 14.34-35 is a non-Pauline insertion, she makes the point that '[t]hey neglect the good possibility that Paul develops his argument as the letter proceeds, increasing restrictions on women's worship participation until he feels able to demand their silence',[22] but it is hard to understand how Paul could hope to be convincing if his position is not consistent.

Most of Wire's statements in *The Corinthian Women Prophets* are measured and cautious, with appropriate reference to the uncertainty of some of her proposals. The implications of her study for women, however, are strongly expressed in her short commentary on 1 Corinthians in *Searching the Scriptures*, where she states that the women prophets 'are the group whose power he [Paul] is most persistently destabilizing',[23] and she refers to 'Paul's stranglehold move on these women's voices'.[24] Similarly, Schüssler Fiorenza, in her response to the work of Richard Horsley, Neil Elliott and others, stresses the importance of the 'public health' aspect of her work, that is, her commitment to protect the public from the damage that the Pauline texts can do.[25]

Paul and Empire

A different view of Paul emerges when Neil Elliott and Richard Horsley consider Paul, placing him against a different background. They argue that proper assessment of Paul's gospel requires us to recognize the tension between it and the ideology of the Roman empire. Past interpretation has assumed, for the most part, that Paul is concerned with the salvation of individuals or with the church as a

20. *The Corinthian Women Prophets*, pp. 62–66.

21. See Elisabeth Schüssler Fiorenza, '1 Corinthians', in James L. Mays (ed.), *The Harper-Collins Bible Commentary* (San Francisco: HarperSanFrancisco, 2000), pp. 1074–93 (1090); Wire, *The Corinthian Women Prophets*, pp. 149–58, 229–32.

22. Antoinette Clark Wire, '1 Corinthians', in Elisabeth Schüssler Fiorenza (ed.), *Searching the Scriptures*, vol. 2: *A Feminist Commentary* (New York: Crossroad, 1994), pp. 153–95 (187).

23. Wire, '1 Corinthians', p. 156.

24. Wire, '1 Corinthians', p. 188.

25. Elisabeth Schüssler Fiorenza, 'Paul and the Politics of Interpretation', in Richard A. Horsley (ed.), *Paul and Politics: Ekklesia, Israel, Imperium, Interpretation* (Harrisburg, PA: Trinity Press International, 2000), pp. 40–57 (40–53).

community, while showing little concern for political issues beyond the church. It may seem that Elliott and Horsley have a difficult case to make.

Neither Elliott nor Horsley believes that Paul was leading a rebellion or protest movement intended to cause the fall of the Roman empire. They do believe, however, that Paul was proclaiming an alternative king and kingdom destined, in God's plan, to replace the empire, and Paul was already forming an alternative society in anticipation of this change. Furthermore, Paul was more sharply conscious of the incompatibility of the two societies than has commonly been recognized.

In support of the view that Paul proclaimed a counter-imperial gospel, Horsley draws on the recent work of Roman historians who assert that the emperor cult was much more important than past New Testament scholarship has recognized, especially in Greece and Asia Minor, the areas of Paul's mature ministry.[26] Rome was able to control these areas of the empire with a remarkably small standing army and spare administrative structure. Control was maintained by the emperor cult and a patronage system with the emperor at the top. Local oligarchs were willing participants in this cult and patronage system, through which they received privileges. The emperor cult was an effective propaganda device supporting an ideology that helped unify the empire, an ideology projected by iconography, monumental buildings, public religious ceremonies and persuasive rhetoric. Past religious scholarship ignored this reality because of the tendency to separate the religious from the political, while these structures are inherently religious and political.[27]

In this context, a gospel that proclaims a different κύριος who is served by an 'international alternative society'[28] is not 'politically innocuous'.[29] In proclaiming his gospel, Paul uses terms that would be recognized, in the context of the emperor cult, as representing the honorific attributes and benefits of Caesar;[30] and, in the Greek context, the term ἐκκλησία itself was primarily a political term, referring to the local assembly of citizens.[31]

Neil Elliott agrees with Horsley and provides further support by highlighting Paul's use of the terms 'cross' and 'crucify'(σταυρός and σταυρόω). Paul does not simply refer to Jesus' death but speaks of the cross, and does so emphatically

26. Richard A. Horsley, 'General Introduction', in Richard A. Horsley (ed.), *Paul and Empire: Religion and Power in Roman Society* (Harrisburg, PA: Trinity Press International, 1997), pp. 1–8 (3–4).

27. Richard A. Horsley, 'The Gospel of Imperial Salvation: Introduction', in Richard A. Horsley (ed.), *Paul and Empire: Religion and Power in Roman Society* (Harrisburg, PA: Trinity Press International, 1997), pp. 9–24 (11–13); Richard A. Horsley, 'Rhetoric and Empire – and First Corinthians', in Richard A. Horsley (ed.), *Paul and Politics: Ekklesia, Israel, Imperium, Interpretation* (Harrisburg, PA: Trinity Press International, 2000), pp. 72–102 (75–78).

28. Horsley, 'General Introduction', p. 8.

29. Horsley, 'The Gospel of Imperial Salvation', p. 24.

30. See Dieter Georgi, 'God Turned Upside Down', in Richard A. Horsley (ed.), *Paul and Empire: Religion and Power in Roman Imperial Society* (Harrisburg, PA: Trinity Press International, 1997), pp.148–57; Helmut Koester, 'Imperial Ideology and Paul's Eschatology in 1 Thessalonians', in Richard A. Horsley (ed.), *Paul and Empire: Religion and Power in Roman Imperial Society* (Harrisburg, PA: Trinity Press International, 1997), pp. 158–66.

31. Horsley, 'General Introduction', p. 8.

(e.g., Gal. 3.1, 6.14; Phil. 2.8; 1 Cor. 1.17–2.2). Crucifixion was an instrument of public terrorism and social control, employed at that time by the Romans.[32] It would be imprudent to use such language if Paul wished to hide the fact that Jesus died a victim of the political violence of the Roman empire. Furthermore, in 1 Corinthians, following his provocative description of his message as 'the word of the cross' concerning 'Christ crucified' (1 Cor. 1.18, 23; 2.2), Paul attributes Christ's crucifixion to 'the rulers of this age' (2.8). The context shows that Paul is thinking in apocalyptic terms, and the reference to 'rulers' should be understood by means of the apocalyptic passage in 1 Cor. 15.24-26, which describes a coming transfer of 'royal authority (βασιλεία)' through the destruction of 'every rule and every authority and power'. Elliott rejects the view that these are spiritual powers unconnected with political systems.[33] Rather, as in Daniel and other apocalypses, the threatening apocalyptic powers are manifest in earthly kingdoms who use the earthly instruments of 'persecution' and 'sword'.[34]

Horsley also believes that Paul's apocalyptic is fundamentally 'anti-imperial' and emphasizes the importance of the apocalyptic perspective in 1 Corinthians.[35] Horsley finds 'the fundamental counterimperial agenda of Judean apocalyptic' in 'the underlying structuring components of Paul's arguments', most strikingly in 1 Cor. 1–4 and 15, but elsewhere in 1 Corinthians as well.[36] Indeed, apocalyptic expectation repeatedly appears in the midst of Paul's detailed instructions (see 1 Cor. 6.2; 7.29-31; 10.11; 11.26). It is Paul's task to help shape the Corinthian believers into an alternative society distinct from its social context. From this perspective the discipline Paul seeks to impose on the community – which may appear as oppressive limits on the community's freedom, from the perspective of Schüssler Fiorenza and Wire – is necessary in order to 'maintain solidarity over against the dominant imperial society'.[37] Thus, Paul wants the Corinthians to withdraw from the local court system (1 Cor. 6.1-11), participate in the world with a consciousness that they are not really part of it (7.29-31), and avoid the religious observances that are part of the social fabric of Corinthian society (10.14-22).[38] According to Horsley, 'In 1 Corinthians Paul was arguing with a religiosity of indi-vidual spiritual transcendence focused on personal devotion to and/or possession of

32. Neil Elliott, *Liberating Paul: The Justice of God and the Politics of the Apostle* (Maryknoll, NY: Orbis Books, 1994), pp. 95–96.

33. Elliott, *Liberating Paul*, pp. 109–31.

34. See Rom. 8.35-39, and Elliott, *Liberating Paul*, p. 122.

35. Horsley, 'Rhetoric and Empire', pp. 96–101.

36. 'Rhetoric and Empire', p. 98.

37. 'Rhetoric and Empire', p. 100; see Richard A. Horsley, '1 Corinthians: A Case Study of Paul's Assembly as an Alternative Society', in Richard A. Horsley (ed.), *Paul and Empire: Religion and Power in Roman Imperial Society* (Harrisburg, PA: Trinity Press International, 1997), pp. 242–52 (252).

38. 'Paul's prohibition of the Corinthians' eating of "food sacrificed to idols"... cut the Corinthians off from participation in the fundamental forms of social relations in the dominant society... Sacrifice was integral to... community life... at every social level from extended families to guilds and associations to citywide celebrations, including imperial festivals' (Horsley, '1 Corinthians', p. 247).

heavenly Sophia, very similar to that articulated in' Wis. 6–10 and Philo.[39] According to Elliott, Paul in 1 Corinthians is 'challenging the ideology of privilege'[40] as
he addresses the divisions between 'the relatively lower status "charter members"
of the congregation and the more recent converts of Apollos whose wealth, power,
and status have subtly introduced new standards and expectations for community
life'.[41] Horsley and Elliott clearly favor Paul when he is understood to be working
against these dangerous tendencies in the Corinthian community. Here again we
can see how reconstruction of the situation in the church fits with a particular
evaluation of Paul's work.

Certain Pauline passages seem to conflict with the view that Paul preached an
anti-imperial gospel. Foremost among these is Rom. 13.1-7. To maintain the position of Elliott and Horsley, the grant of divine authority to rulers in Rom. 13 must
be reduced to a Pauline stratagem in dealing with a particular issue. According to
Elliott, Paul's underlying concern is the safety of the Jewish community in Rome,
whose delicate situation would worsen with civil unrest.[42] The view that Paul is
committed to a new society that removes the distinctions of the old may also be
challenged on the basis of 1 Cor. 7.17-24 and Paul's instructions to women in
11.2-16 and 14.34-35. To be sure, Elliott chides Schüssler Fiorenza and Wire for
accepting 14.34-35 as Pauline,[43] and 7.17-24 may be instruction for the interim
which, even in the interim, is not meant as a hard and fast rule.

Conclusion: The Hermeneutical Value of Diverse Theories about the Situation in Corinth

In founding and instructing the Corinthian church, was Paul a liberator or an
oppressor?

Possibly both, for the 'feminist' and 'political' interpretations of Paul's work,
discussed above, tend to view Paul's work against different backgrounds, in the
one case, the Roman empire as an ideological system, in the other case, the early
church as a place of liberation for women. But tension remains between the two
interpretations because a different evaluation of Paul results from the different
factors that each group highlights, and they have different views of the situation in
the Corinthian church. How should we respond to these diverse views?

After the provocative work of Schüssler Fiorenza and Wire, we can no longer
begin study of the Corinthian correspondence with the assumption that Paul is
correct and fair in all his judgments, while those he sought to correct, including the
Corinthian women prophets, were necessarily in the wrong. But neither can we

---

39. Horsley, 'Rhetoric and Empire', p. 85; Horsley, *1 Corinthians* (ANTC; Nashville:
Abingdon Press, 1998), pp. 35–36, 51–56.

40. Elliott, *Liberating Paul*, pp. 204–14.

41. *Liberating Paul*, p. 205.

42. Neil Elliott, 'Romans 13.1-7 in the Context of Imperial Propaganda', in Richard A. Horsley
(ed.), *Paul and Empire: Religion and Power in Roman Imperial Society* (Harrisburg, PA: Trinity
Press International, 1997), pp. 191–204.

43. Elliott, *Liberating Paul*, pp. 52–54.

begin with the assumption that Wire's reconstruction of the situation in Corinth is the only plausible one and, by itself, yields a sufficient account of Paul's work. The view that Paul's gospel is, in important respects, 'counter-imperial', and that this aspect of his convictions shapes his response to the Corinthians, is also plausible.

Feminist interpreters modify the traditional view of biblical authority. Wire states that we should no longer begin with the assumption that the biblical author's view is authoritative; rather, we should conceive the text's authority 'more broadly as that of the full range of voices which speak through it',[44] including the voices of women. Although some might want to replace Paul's authoritative voice with that of the Corinthian women prophets, I would advocate a more balanced view, which Wire also seems to support.

Wire rightly points to the close 'relation of social experience and theological confession' in the religious life,[45] and she advances the interesting hypothesis that the differences between Paul and the Corinthian women prophets reflect their different social experience. Paul's encounter with Christ meant giving up social privileges; the Corinthian women began with a low status and few privileges but experienced exaltation in Christ.[46] Wire concludes, 'Where conflicts with a religious tradition are understood in light of the different social experience of each party, it may be possible to move toward genuine mediation of the conflicts'.[47] I take this to mean that neither of the two theologically-interpreted social experiences will be rejected. Furthermore, they will be set in dialogue with each other, as they were in the Corinthian situation, according to Wire, with the hope that deeper understanding and mutual acceptance may result. This may involve each party listening to and correcting the other. Taking multiple voices seriously means beginning with the assumption that both Paul and the Corinthians have something important to say but that the truth on each side must be understood and applied with due consideration for the insights and experience of the other party. Schüssler Fiorenza may also be open to this approach. In introducing her brief commentary on 1 Corinthians, she remarks, 'The following commentary seeks to understand the debates in Corinth as legitimate discussions within the *ekklesia*. Paul is understood as only one partner, although in retrospect a very significant one, in the theological discourse of the early Christian missionary movement'.[48]

Horsley recognizes the value of Schüssler Fiorenza and Wire's work in reconstructing multiple voices[49] and also recognizes that there will be multiple interpretations of Paul even by interpreters who share a liberationist concern. These diverse approaches, he says, are 'to be valued rather than avoided'.[50]

---

44. Wire, '1 Corinthians', p. 157.

45. Wire, *The Corinthian Women Prophets*, p. 71.

46. *The Corinthian Women Prophets*, pp. 63–69.

47. *The Corinthian Women Prophets*, p. 71.

48. Schüssler Fiorenza, '1 Corinthians', p. 1076.

49. Horsley, 'Rhetoric and Empire', pp. 85–86.

50. Horsley, 'Introduction: Krister Stendahl's Challenge to Pauline Studies', in Richard A. Horsley (ed.), *Paul and Politics: Ekklesia, Israel, Imperium, Interpretation* (Harrisburg, PA: Trinity Press International, 2000), pp. 1–16 (15).

Some may view this openness as a counsel of despair: We are stuck with conflicting interpretations, and we may as well make the best of it. I have a more positive view of the situation. On the one hand, there is value in scholarly attempts at historical reconstruction. Through this reconstructive work, seemingly bland and general statements may become telling remarks, words on target. We gain a sharper sense of their purpose and power. On the other hand, we must recognize that the voices of Paul's dialogue partners are muffled. Paul's letters indicate their presence, but the sounds are indistinct and subject to various interpretations. Therefore, historical reconstructions are necessarily interpretive experiments, some more convincing than others, but none likely to be so convincing as to eliminate all other possibilities (unless we foolishly succumb to fascination with the 'latest thing' or attribute undue authority to the views of influential mentors). As Schüssler Fiorenza has said, historical reconstruction does not result in a 'report of "what actually happened"', for our reconstructions are always products of historical imagination that must fill in significant gaps.[51]

Therefore, it is appropriate to be tolerant of competing interpretations that have been developed with rigor (and even to consider whether undeveloped suggestions could be worked out with rigor), and it is appropriate to consider a number of options as we seek to read the text in historical context, recognizing that these remain possibilities, not certainties. Shifting perspectives on the situation will result in shifting views of the force of Paul's words and different evaluations of Paul's words and work.

This thought process is similar to the thinking required when we seek an appropriate application of Paul's words in our own time, and flexible historical imagination can contribute to our thinking about appropriate application. Since Paul's letters were written not to us but to churches far distant from us in time and space, it is always necessary to ask what situations today, if any, might be appropriately addressed by Paul's words (and with what adaptations). These decisions will be influenced by our faith commitments, theological understanding and ethical values. Consideration of the multiple possibilities of understanding the original situation can play an ancillary role, making us more keenly aware of the ways that varying situations affect the force of Paul's words.

In my opinion, our preferences in interpreting the historical context of Paul's words should not strictly control our decisions about the appropriate application of those words today. It is quite possible to decide that a particular historical situation is most likely but that Paul's words in that context were damaging or dangerous. As a result, we may need to add warnings or seek an altogether different context where the results will not be damaging. Members of Christian churches will apply Paul's words in various ways. It is important to think about the possible effects of these applications in various situations today. Acquaintance with the interpretive experiments of historical scholars can be a stimulus to this thought process. Multiple experiments in historical reconstruction will help us imagine the range of contexts in which Paul's words might have been written and gain a sense of the

---

51. Schüssler Fiorenza, *Rhetoric and Ethic*, p. 52.

good and evil consequences, revealing useful applications we might not have considered, warning us of dangerous applications we might ignore, and suggesting necessary adaptations so that the words of scripture might fulfill their purpose of promoting the love of God and neighbor.

We will, of course, make these judgments in light of our commitments and values, our varying visions of what is good. The four scholars studied in this essay are not to be faulted for operating in this way, for we are all obliged to follow the best that we know. Of course, our insight into the good is faulty and incomplete. We must remain open to learning more both from scripture and from other sources. Paul rightly reminds us that we see only puzzling reflections in a distorting mirror (1 Cor. 13.12) and will never achieve perfect knowledge in this life, for there is a truth beyond our truth to which finally we must yield.

VIOLENCE FOR THE SAKE OF SOCIAL JUSTICE?
NARRATIVE, ETHICS AND INDETERMINACY IN MOSES'
SLAYING OF THE EGYPTIAN (EXODUS 2.11-15)

Dennis T. Olson, Princeton Theological Seminary, New Jersey, USA

'Today the choice is no longer between violence and nonviolence. It is either nonviolence or nonexistence.' – Martin Luther King, Jr[1]

'There is a violence that liberates, and a violence that enslaves; there is a violence that is moral and a violence that is immoral.' – Benito Mussolini[2]

'What is most powerful about [Emmanuel] Levinas' writing is his insistence on ethics as a challenge to the subject rather than as a solution to its problems.' – Colin Davis, *Levinas, An Introduction*[3]

Various interpreters have seen the narrative of Moses' slaying of the Egyptian foreman in Exod. 2.11-15 as a story about the use of violence and civil disobedience for the sake of social justice on behalf of the vulnerable and oppressed.[4] The purpose of this essay is to test that perception in the light of the ambiguities of the text in its context.

The story recounts the first episode in the young adult life of Moses before he was called by God to lead the Israelites out of Egypt. The narrative is told in two scenes.

Scene 1:
[11] One day, after Moses had grown up, he went out to his people and saw their forced labor. He saw an Egyptian beating a Hebrew, one of his kinsfolk. [12] He

---

1. Martin Luther King, Jr, *Stride Toward Freedom: The Montgomery Story* (New York: Harper & Brothers, 1958), p. 224.

2. From a speech in Udine, Italy, September 20, 1922, as quoted in George Seldes (ed.), *The Great Quotations* (New York: Simon & Schuster, 1967), p. 950.

3. Colin Davis, *Levinas, An Introduction* (Notre Dame, IN: University of Notre Dame Press, 1996), p. 143. Davis notes that 'for Levinas, commentary is a form of encounter with the Other; and, just as texts do not offer simple, unambiguous messages, neither do ethical encounters provide a stable set of rules to govern moral behavior. Ethics, in Levinas's sense, does not provide a path to knowledge of right and wrong, Good or Evil; it is a point of contact with that which challenges me most radically, and through that challenge my identity and relation with the world are thrown into question' (p. 143).

4. I am indebted to Brevard S. Childs, 'Moses' Slaying in the Two Testaments', *Biblical Theology in Crisis* (Philadelphia: Westminster, 1970), pp. 164–83, for stimulating my own thinking on this text. See also Brevard S. Childs, *The Book of Exodus, A Critical, Theological Commentary* (OTL; Louisville, KY: Westminster Press, 1974), pp. 27–46.

looked this way and that, and seeing no one he killed the Egyptian and hid him in the sand. (NRSV[5])

Scene 2:
[13] When he went out the next day, he saw two Hebrews fighting; and he said to the one who was in the wrong, 'Why do you strike your fellow Hebrew?' [14] He answered, 'Who made you a ruler and judge over us? Do you mean to kill me as you killed the Egyptian?' Then Moses was afraid and thought, 'Surely the thing is known'. [15] When Pharaoh heard of it, he sought to kill Moses. But Moses fled from Pharaoh. He settled in the land of Midian.

Was Moses ethically justified in killing the Egyptian? This question has been debated over the many centuries of this text's interpretation in both Jewish and Christian traditions. A brief review of this history of interpretation will be a helpful way into the details of the story. We begin with the New Testament.

The New Testament cites this story in two major contexts: (a) Stephen's martyrdom speech in Acts 7 and (b) the roll call of faithful Old Testament figures in Hebrews 11. Stephen's martyrdom speech in Acts 7.23-29 focuses on the scene in Exodus 2 on the day after Moses kills the Egyptian. Moses attempts to intercede in a dispute between two Hebrews, but Moses' attempt at reconciliation is rudely rejected by his fellow Israelites so that Moses is forced into exile. In Acts 7, Moses is used as one of many examples of Israel's rejection of God's anointed agent of redemption. For the writer of Acts 7, the Hebrew slave's rejection of Moses mirrors the Jewish leaders' rejection of Jesus in his crucifixion as well as the Jewish leaders' rejection of Stephen in his martyrdom. In its paraphrase of the story, Acts 7 portrays Moses' killing of the Egyptian as a positive act in which Moses 'defended an oppressed man' (v. 24) and acted as an agent of God's deliverance: 'God through [Moses] was rescuing them' (v. 25).

The expansive retelling of the story in Heb. 11.23-28 is equally positive in its evaluation of Moses killing the Egyptian but from a somewhat different angle. In the original Old Testament version of the story in Exodus 2, we are told little of Moses' interior thoughts and motivations. Hebrews 11, however, generously fills this narrative gap:

> By faith Moses, when he was grown up, refused to be called a son of Pharaoh's daughter, choosing to share ill-treatment with the people of God rather than enjoy the fleeting pleasures of sin. He considered abuse suffered for the Christ to be greater wealth than the treasures of Egypt, for he was looking ahead to the reward. By faith he left Egypt, unafraid of the king's anger (vv. 24-27).

There is no explicit mention of the killing of the Egyptian here, but the writer of Hebrews characterizes Moses during the period of his departure from Egypt as a praiseworthy example of righteous suffering and faith.

These two New Testament readings achieve their positive interpretations of Moses' act of killing the Egyptian by filling in major gaps in the narrative and by ignoring crucial elements that are clearly narrated in the Old Testament version of

---

5. Unless otherwise indicated, all translations are from the NRSV.

the story. The first element that is passed over in silence by these New Testament readings is Moses' *secrecy* in killing the Egyptian. Recall the story as it is told in Exodus 2. Moses 'looked this way and that, and seeing no one he killed the Egyptian and hid him in the sand' (Exod. 2.12). We see here no intention of committing a courageous and public act of open defiance and self-sacrifice which will mean the inevitable sacrificing of his status as a son of Pharaoh's daughter. He acts secretly, believing no one will know and therefore believing he will suffer no consequences for his action.

The second element present in the Exodus version of the story but deleted by Acts 7 and Hebrews 11 is Moses' *fear* when Pharaoh puts a death sentence on his head. On the day after the killing of the Egyptian, the quarreling Hebrews reveal that in spite of Moses' attempt to keep the act secret, they know. One of the Hebrews asks Moses, 'Do you mean to kill me as you killed the Egyptian?' The narrative plainly reveals Moses' response: 'Then Moses was afraid and thought, "Surely the thing is known". When Pharaoh heard of it, he sought to kill Moses. But Moses fled from Pharaoh' (Exod. 2.14-15). The fear of Moses in Exodus 2 is passed over and even contradicted by Hebrews 11 when it claims of Moses that '[b]y faith he left Egypt, unafraid of the king's anger' (Heb. 11.27).

The Jewish rabbinic *midrashim* on our story share with the New Testament readings a similar desire to fill in gaps and overlook other elements of the narrative in order to portray Moses' act positively. The Jewish interpreters, however, are obviously not interested in seeing Moses' experience of rejection or self-sacrifice as a prefiguring of the sacrifice or rejection of Jesus or his followers. One midrashic tradition argues that Moses killed the Egyptian out of genuine zeal for God and only after Moses had consulted with the angels, who had approved his action (*Exod. R.* 1.29). Another tradition depicts Moses prophetically divining that no proselyte (or just man) would ever arise from that Egyptian, the apparent implication being that these future facts exculpated Moses or at least mitigated any guilt he might carry for his act (*Frag. Targ.*, *Targ. Neof.* and *Targ. Ps.-J.* for Exod. 2.12). Philo comments on this event in Moses' life, stressing the cruelty of the Egyptian foreman and Moses' judgment that the killing was a righteous act (*Vit. Mos.* 1.44).

Most later Christian commentators continued this positive line of interpreting Moses' act. However, they tended to be less interested in the christological type of interpretations evident in Acts 7 and Hebrews 11 and more interested in the ethical issues of justice and ethics along the lines of Jewish midrash. Church fathers such as Gregory of Nazianzus (*Ep.* 76), Tertullian (*Adv. Marc.* 4.28) and Ambrose (*Off.* 1.36) sought to explain how Moses' killing was justified in accord with biblical revelation, reason, God's special command given to Moses in this one particular instance or some combination of these.[6] The Protestant Reformers tended to follow a similar line. Calvin, for example, in his commentary on Exodus, writes that Moses 'was armed by God's command, and, conscious of his legitimate vocation,

---

6.   See the discussion in Childs, *Biblical Theology in Crisis*, 177–79.

rightly and judiciously assumed that character which God assigned to him'.[7] This stream of positive evaluation of Moses continues to the present day. One modern interpreter notes the parallels in Exodus between Moses 'seeing' (רְאָה, 2.11) the misery of the Israelite slaves and 'striking' (נכה, 2.12) the Egyptian and God 'seeing' (2.25) the Israelites' suffering and 'striking' (12.29) the Egyptians with the final plague, the violent death of the first born of Egypt.[8] According to this modern interpreter, Moses' valiant act positively foreshadows the future deliverance of God.

There have been some dissenters among Christian commentators. Augustine, for example, condemned Moses' act of killing. Augustine compared Moses' slaying to the disciple Peter's impulsive and violent act when Jesus was arrested in the garden of Gethsemane. When Jesus was being arrested, Peter unsheathed his sword and cut off the ear of the high priest's slave. Jesus instantly condemned Peter for his action and ordered him to put his sword away (Jn. 18.10-11; see also Mk 14.47 and Lk. 22.50). Augustine viewed Moses' killing as the same sort of immature act of unreflective impulse.[9] Other interpreters have condemned the action of Moses as premature because it comes before God's call of Moses as an agent of liberation in Exodus 3.[10] Still others have condemned Moses because his secrecy, 'looking this way and that' (v. 12), suggests to them a troubled psychological state. He was acting out of a guilty or bad conscience, they argue, which nullified any possible redeeming ethical value to Moses' act of killing.[11]

What do we make of these contrasting evaluations of Moses in light of our larger question about the justification of the use of violence for the sake of social justice for others? Does the narrative condemn or praise Moses for his act of killing the Egyptian? We have noted that the answers to this question depend on filling in details where there are gaps in the story and overlooking certain details that are plainly present in the narrative. Moreover, some of the interpretations depend on which intertextual associations we make with this story. Acts 7 and Hebrews 11, for example, seek to reconstruct a series of parallel narratives from the Old Testament that all fit a similar pattern. Acts 7 interprets Moses' slaying by creating an intertextual web of stories about Israel's repeated rejection of God's appointed deliverers and leaders. Hebrews 11 creates another intertextual grid of Old Testament heroes of faith who fit a similar profile of courage, hope and self-denial. Augustine, on the other hand, interpreted the Moses story negatively in an intertextual dialogue with John 18 and the story of Peter's violent swordsmanship that was condemned by Jesus.

7. John Calvin, *Commentaries on the Last Four Books of Moses* (Grand Rapids: Baker Book House, 1989), I, p. 48.

8. Frederic Holmgren, 'Violence: God's Will on the Edge – Exodus 2.11-25', *Currents in Theology and Mission*, 16 (1989), pp. 425–29 (426).

9. Augustine, 'Reply to Faustus the Manichean [XXII.70]', in *Writings in Connection with the Manichean Heresy* (trans. Richard Stothert; Edinburgh: T. & T. Clark, 1872), p. 459.

10. C.F. Keil, *Commentary on the Pentateuch* (Edinburgh: T. & T. Clark, 1864), pp. 279–80.

11. S.R. Driver, *The Book of Exodus* (Cambridge: Cambridge University Press, 1911), pp. 30–32.

Exod. 2.11-15 and Its More Immediate Literary Context in Exodus 2

Perhaps we ought to start our intertextual dialogue a bit closer to home with the narrative of Exodus 2 itself and the stories that immediately surround it. I do not want to suggest that bringing intertexts that are further afield, whether elsewhere in the Bible or from disciplines or realms outside the Bible, including stories and events of our own day, is not a legitimate enterprise. But paying closer attention to the details of the immediate literary context of Exodus 2 may provide some helpful insights on how to read this story in light of the many other possible intertextual conversations we might have from elsewhere.

We begin with the narrative itself in Exod. 2.11-15. Is there anything in the narrative that either condemns or exonerates Moses in his act of killing the Egyptian? I think Brevard Childs is right in his answer to that question when he writes as follows in his book, *Biblical Theology in Crisis*:

> The Old Testament does not moralize on Moses' act of violence. Nowhere is there an explicit evaluation that either praises or condemns it. Rather, a situation is painted with great realism and sensitivity, and the reader is left to ponder on the anomalies of the deed... The ambiguity of the situation is that the act does not carry only one meaning. It is open to misunderstanding and a variety of possible interpretations. Moses supposed that his motivation was obvious, but the Hebrew who was abusing his fellow attributed a totally different intention from that which Moses has envisioned. 'Who made you a ruler over us?'[12]

The story alone provides no clear verdict on whether Moses' act of killing was right or wrong, justified or flawed, a model to emulate or an example of what not to do.

If we expand the circle of interpretation a bit wider and examine the narratives that immediately precede and follow the story of Moses killing the Egyptian, do we find any help in evaluating Moses' use of violence for the sake of social justice and advocacy for others? The story that immediately follows about Moses in the land of Midian (Exod. 2.15-22) is closely tied to the story of Moses killing the Egyptian through a series of parallels and contrasts. The narrative picks up after Pharaoh has threatened Moses with death and Moses has fled in fear to Midian as a political fugitive.

> [Moses] sat down by a well. [16] The priest of Midian had seven daughters. They came to draw water, and filled the troughs to water their father's flock. [17] But some shepherds came and drove them away. Moses got up and came to their defense and watered their flock. [18] When they returned to their father Reuel, he said, 'How is it that you have come back so soon today?' [19] They said, 'An Egyptian helped us against the shepherds; he even drew water for us and watered the flock'. [20] He said to his daughters, 'Where is he? Why did you leave the man? Invite him to break bread'. [21] Moses agreed to stay with the man, and he gave Moses his daughter Zipporah in marriage. [22] She bore a son, and he named him Gershom; for he said, 'I have been an alien [Hebrew גר] residing in a foreign land'.

12. Childs, 'Moses' Slaying in the Two Testaments', p. 182.

This narrative parallels the story of Moses' killing the Egyptian in that Moses again enters into another conflict to save a vulnerable party. The question of Moses' identity – whether he is a Hebrew or an Egyptian – is raised again as well. But there are also contrasts. Moses is successful in his intervention to rescue the Midianite women, and his act is interpreted positively by the ones he sought to help. The women report to Reuel, 'An Egyptian helped us against the shepherds' (v. 19). At the end of the story of Moses killing the Egyptian, he was forced to flee his home. Here, at the end of this Midianite story, Moses finds a home.

Do the contrasts between this seemingly more positive Midianite story and the story of Moses killing the Egyptian suggest that the narrator intends to condemn Moses' act of violence by what we might call a strategy of 'narrative juxtaposition', placing Moses' killing side by side with this more non-violent intervention of Moses on behalf of the Midianite women? Does this narrative juxtaposition seek to teach us that non-violent adjudication of conflict succeeds while violent intervention does not? That conclusion is not at all self-evident. We are told that Moses intervened with the mean-spirited shepherds and 'saved' (the Hebrew verb (יָשַׁע) the Midianite women. But the precise manner and details of that rescue are not narrated. Did Moses use violence again in order to 'save' the women? The Hebrew verbal root, יָשַׁע ('to save/deliver/help/rescue/defend'), occurs over 240 times in the Hebrew Bible. The great majority of uses involve conflicts of violence, war and killing, especially in Joshua, Judges, Samuel, Kings and the prophets. But sometimes the verb involves a simple request for peaceful intervention into a conflict in order to prevent further violence. For example, the woman of Tekoa requests the king to 'save' her and to prevent the killing of her son (2 Sam. 14.4-8). David praises God for protecting him from Saul, singing, 'My Savior, you saved me from violence' (2 Sam. 22.3). Thus, the particular verb used in Exod. 2.17 to describe Moses' intervention or rescue does not clearly resolve the question of whether Moses resorted to violence in chasing off the shepherds. The verb יָשַׁע is most often used in situations of violent conflict but not always. The story in vv. 15-22 is indeterminate in its use of this verb and thus does not provide a clear contrast with the violence of the preceding story when Moses killed the Egyptian foreman.[13]

Moreover, it should be noted that Moses' status as a fugitive and exile at the end of the killing episode is essentially unchanged when we reach the end of the well episode. Although Moses finds a home of sorts with the Midianites, his identity remains as an exile and alien, a status embodied in the name of his son Gershom: 'For he said, "I have been an alien [גֵּר] in a foreign land"' (Exod. 2.22). The juxtaposition of the two narratives, Moses' killing and the rescue of the Midianite women, leaves the reader without a clear ethical message regarding the use of violence for the sake of social justice. Both stories end with Moses in a

13. Moreover, one could argue that the narrative juxtaposition of the two stories (Moses' slaying and the Midianite rescue) has the effect of bringing the slaying story into the more positive orbit of the Midianite rescue story. Thus, the literary dynamic could be read as less contrasting and more assimilating, an approving association of two more or less successful rescue stories. The plausibility of this reading only increases the sense of the text's indeterminacy.

kind of exile as a foreigner in a strange land. Moses' identity here mirrors the reader's experience of indeterminacy in evaluating Moses' use of violence to defend the vulnerable and less powerful. Like Moses, whose identity straddles blurred boundaries of Hebrew or Egyptian or Midianite, the reader also straddles murky boundaries of right and wrong in contemplating Moses' slaying of the Egyptian. Can an act of justice ever be done secretly and with violence? Today would we call Moses a terrorist or a freedom-fighter? It may depend in part on one's perspective, whether one is a 'Hebrew' or an 'Egyptian'.

And yet the narrative that immediately precedes the story of Moses slaying the Egyptian also prevents us from turning ethical decision-making simply into an 'us versus them' conflict of perspectives alone. The preceding story of Moses' birth includes the scene where Moses as a baby is adopted by the daughter of Pharaoh when she finds him in a basket floating in the Nile River. Significantly, here it is an Egyptian, Pharaoh's own daughter, who performs an act of civil disobedience against her own father's decree that all Hebrew male babies be killed. Like Moses, she intervenes in a morally ambiguous situation in which her familial and civil obligations to father and nation clash with her obligation to save the life of an endangered child. Like Moses, she places herself at risk as she crosses boundaries. The narrative says nothing of the events following her adoption of Moses, other than that Moses had 'grown up' in Pharaoh's household. Did she keep Moses' identity as a Hebrew a secret, just as Moses had tried to keep his action a secret? Did she suffer any consequences when her father, Pharaoh, 'heard' and 'sought to kill Moses'? Did she, too, in effect become an exile in a foreign land? Again, the narrative is told with large gaps of indeterminacy. But what the narrative of Pharaoh's daughter does accomplish is to give the reader a dramatic example of one Egyptian who acted bravely, righteously and intentionally (she knew it was a *Hebrew* baby she was saving – Exod. 2.6).

At the beginning of the Exodus narrative, the story of Pharaoh's daughter prevents any easy painting of all Egyptians as evil. And the narrative of Moses' killing, which includes a Hebrew slave's mistreatment of a fellow Hebrew, reminds us that the Hebrew people were themselves capable of violence and wickedness (the Hebrew 'who was in the wrong' – Exod 2.13). One is reminded of the account of the Egyptian slave woman, Hagar, who was 'oppressed' (ענה) by Sarah and Abraham, the ancestors of the Hebrews (Gen. 16.6). This is the same verb, 'to oppress', that Exodus uses to describe what the Egyptians did to the Israelite slaves (Exod. 1.11-12).[14] The inclusion of the Hagar story, which describes her oppression and eventual exile into the wilderness with her son Ishmael, is a remarkably self-critical reminder to the Israelites that they are as capable of doing evil unto others as others have done to them. And the story of Pharaoh's daughter reminds us similarly that the supposed 'evil enemy' may be just as capable of genuine goodness, compassion and righteousness as the best and noblest leaders of Israel.

---

14. Terence Fretheim, 'Genesis, Introduction and Commentary', *The New Interpreter's Bible* (Nashville: Abingdon Press, 1994), I, p. 452.

Remarkably, the Old Testament often foregrounds the righteousness of certain individuals belonging to peoples whom Israel often considered their enemies in the Pentateuch. Among Israel's traditional foes, the Canaanites, there is Rahab the harlot in Joshua 2 and the Canaanite king Abimelech in Genesis 20. Joseph marries an Egyptian wife (Gen. 41.45). A previous Egyptian Pharaoh under whom Joseph works graciously welcomed Joseph's extended family into Egypt, granting to them 'the best part of the land' (Gen. 47.6). The righteous daughter of Pharaoh in Exodus 2 falls into this same category of the righteous ones, God-fearers, who live among a traditionally enemy people, in this case, the Egyptians. These righteous exemplars put cautionary brakes on any moral generalizing about a whole people or group as uniformly evil.

Let me now conclude with some final observations concerning the story of Moses slaying the Egyptian and its relationship to the question of the justification of violence in the cause of social justice on behalf of the weak and the vulnerable.

1. Some readers assume that every narrative of the Bible has one ultimate lesson to teach, a definitive position to take on a given issue, a behavior or attitude either to recommend or condemn. The long and varied history of the interpretation of this text in Exodus 2 testifies to this prevalent assumption among many readers of the Bible. Thus, gaps in the story are filled in. Certain narrative details are ignored. And a wide range of intertexts from elsewhere, whether from within the Bible itself or outside the Bible, are used as the basis to adjudicate the singular meaning or verdict rendered by the narrative. Is the story of Moses killing the Egyptian best compared to Peter's condemned act of violence in the garden of Gethsemane, which Jesus rejects? Or is Moses' act of killing the Egyptian best compared as a positive parallel to God's seeing the oppression of Israel and violently striking the Egyptians in the tenth plague of the death of the first born, an act which the narrator of Exodus seemingly approves as tragic but justified? In either case, the interpreter yearns to find a singular meaning and verdict related to Moses' act of violence.

2. My decision to begin an exploration of this Moses narrative by focusing on the details of the narrative itself as well as its most immediate literary context produced a reading that heightened the complexity of the story and avoided drawing a straightforward moral conclusion from the text by resolving its ambiguities. My decision to begin there does not preclude others from bringing a wide set of intertexts into dialogue with the narrative in Exodus 2. But I have sought to show that the surrounding narrative context also provides a suggestive intertext, helping us see the complexity of the issues involved and to be wary of prematurely trying to resolve all their ambiguities.

3. Indeed, I noted that the cluster of three short narratives in Exodus 2 – the story of Pharaoh's daughter rescuing the baby, Moses' attempt to rescue the Hebrew slave and Moses' rescue of the Midianite women – serve to blur and make complex the character and identities of the Egyptians, the Hebrews and Moses himself. Moses is an alien, not really at home anywhere whether among the Egyptians, the Hebrews or the Midianites. Pharaoh's daughter defies her Egyptian and familial boundaries by bringing Moses into her household in violation of the edicts of her

father and her nation. Moses' action in killing the Egyptian is done in secret and in fear. He believes his intentions are clear and honorable, but his own Hebrew people perceive them otherwise. This dissonance can create in the reader the impression that the character of Moses himself may be divided, consciously or subconsciously, in his intentions and motivations. Is he acting out of unthinking impulse, a bad conscience, social protest, survivor's guilt, genuine compassion, arrogant rage, divinely-inspired faithfulness, ethnic identification, sacrificial self-denial or some complex combination of two or more of these? The gap remains unfilled in the narrative, and the reader is simply left to wonder and reflect on the questions that linger once the story ends. Like Moses, the reader does not feel fully 'at home' with any one solution or verdict regarding Moses and his use of violence for the sake of social justice.

4. Exodus 2 provides an important illustration of how some Old Testament narratives may function in ethical deliberation and reflection. The narrative does not offer up a final verdict; instead, it prompts the reader to ask difficult questions and, by means of important gaps, draws the reader into the story as almost another character who must wrestle with the ambiguities, complexities and ragged edges that characterize ethical decision-making in the realities of everyday life. There seems to be, for the narrator of this story, no easily generalizable or abstract principle to apply in all cases in regard to the use of violence for the sake of social justice in advocacy for the weak. If we too quickly fill in the gaps or read this story with other intertexts far removed from its closer literary setting, we may lose important insights that the story may teach us about the nature of ethics and reality.

5. Allowing a biblical narrative like Moses' slaying of the Egyptian to remain unresolved and open with all its jagged edges may help us to see in part how and why the Bible remains a vibrant and dynamic resource in what many call our present postmodern environment, an environment in which authority is questioned and monologic truth is suspect. In his book, *Postmodern Ethics,* ethicist Zygmunt Bauman writes:

> What the postmodern mind is aware of is that there are problems in human and social life with no good solutions, twisted trajectories that cannot be straightened up, ambivalences that are more than linguistic blunders waiting to be corrected, doubts which cannot be legislated out of existence, moral agonies which no reason-dictated recipes can soothe, let alone cure. The postmodern mind does not expect any more to find the all-embracing, total and ultimate formula of life without ambiguity, risk, danger, and error, and is deeply suspicious of any voice that promised otherwise... The postmodern mind is reconciled to the idea that the messiness of the human predicament is here to stay.[15]

What this study of Exodus 2 may help us remember is that the ancient scriptures knew something of this twisted and corrupt character of humans and reality long before postmodernism ever arrived on the scene. The unrelenting tragedy of human violence against other humans lies at the core of the biblical portrait of the sinful

---

15. Zygmunt Bauman, *Postmodern Ethics* (Oxford: Basil Blackwell, 1993), p. 245.

nature of the human animal. The complex and varied voices of scripture reflect the complexities, ambiguities and provisionality of our human knowledge of ourselves, our world and our God. And yet the rich voices of scripture, like the narrative of Moses' slaying of the Egyptian, provide sufficient resources for the people of God to make adequate, if not always perfectly satisfying, decisions in particular contexts and situations.

I wish to end with a personal reflection from my own Christian (and Lutheran) tradition. One well known contextual example of a struggle to make a faithful decision about the use of violence in an attempt to save vulnerable victims from tyrannical oppression involved the German theologian Dietrich Bonhoeffer. At the time of his death, Bonhoeffer was at work on a book on Christian ethics and knew well the ambiguities and complexities of the moral life. He also knew well the worldly realism of the Bible, especially the Old Testament, a literature which grew in importance for Bonhoeffer as he struggled with an ethical response to the horrors of Hitler's Nazi terror. In the pre-war years, Bonhoeffer had strong leanings toward pacifism,[16] but during the war he actively participated in a plot to assassinate Hitler in an attempt to use violence for the sake of social justice. Bonhoeffer reasoned that there are situations where violence is morally necessary, even though those who take up violence in defense of justice become guilty by their shedding of blood. Personal innocence must be sacrificed for the sake of others.[17] As was the case with Moses slaying the Egyptian, the failed plot against Hitler seemingly accomplished little. For Bonhoeffer, as for Moses, the use of violence in advocacy for others ended in an exile of sorts; Bonhoeffer was imprisoned by the Nazis and eventually executed. But Bonhoeffer died secure in his faith in God, knowing that the fate of the world did not finally depend on his courage, wisdom or action. In the midst of the agony and complexity of real-world decisions, risks and dangers, Bonhoeffer trusted finally in God's victory, a victory already won at the cross but not yet fully actualized. Yet that trust in God did not render him passive but thrust him headlong into the hard realities of a world that, though sinful and violent, he knew as a world still loved by God.

The story of Moses' slaying of the Egyptian does not resolve for me the question of whether it is right to use violence in defense of social justice; instead it drives me into the hard, complex and morally ambiguous questions that people like Bonhoeffer asked and had to resolve for themselves under the press of trying circumstances. In our world of 9/11 and random sniper attacks and terrorist bombings and disputes over nuclear and biological weapons, a world with an abundance of wars and rumors of wars, we wait and pray in earnest hope for glimpses of God's promised future when the wolf will lie down with the lamb and every sword will be beaten into plowshares and war and death will be no more. In the

---

16. See Eberhard Bethge, *Dietrich Bonhoeffer: Man of Vision, Man of Courage* (ed. Edwin Robertson; trans. Eric Mosbacher *et al.*; New York and Evanston: Harper & Row, 1970), pp. 154–55, 160, 254.

17. See Bonhoeffer's reflection, 'The Acceptance of Guilt' in his *Ethics* (ed. Eberhard Bethge; trans. Neville Horton Smith; New York: Macmillan, 1963), pp. 240–41.

meantime, we humbly continue to struggle with Moses and Bonhoeffer and all the people of God over the ages to 'see in a mirror, dimly' (1 Cor. 13.12). We strive to do what is good and right and in accord with God's will, and yet we confess that we have fallen short of the glory of God. In this age and in this world, we, like Moses, will always die outside of – but also within sight of – the promised land (Deut. 34.1-8).

DEALING WITH RAPE (IN) NARRATIVE (GENESIS 34): ETHICS OF THE OTHER AND A TEXT IN CONFLICT

Frank M. Yamada, Seabury-Western Theological Seminary, Illinois, USA

Genesis 34, which describes the rape of Dinah and the subsequent retaliation on Shechem by the sons of Israel, is a story thick with ethical consequences. Within the text itself there are difficult ethical and moral decisions that confront the characters of the story. How should Jacob and his sons deal with the violent act that Shechem perpetrated against Dinah? How should they react to Shechem and his father when the former asks for her hand in marriage? The narrative becomes more complex ethically when the sons take vengeance into their own hands, slaying the inhabitants of the village by the sword. Jacob responds to his sons' actions with dismay, though Simeon and Levi justify their actions, saying, 'Should he treat our sister like a whore?' (v. 31).[1] Thus, within the text of Genesis 34 itself, there are differences of opinion and ethical ambiguities. Interpreters of Genesis 34 have also wrestled with the ethical and moral implications of the text. Not surprisingly, we find interpreters siding with the different characters in the story. Some, such as Meir Sternberg, assert that Simeon and Levi are in the right since they avenge the shattered honor of their sister.[2] Others, such as David Gunn and Danna Nolan Fewell, argue that to side with Simeon and Levi is to condone the brothers' inappropriate violence and disregard for social implications.[3] Gunn and Fewell propose a more favorable reading of Jacob and Shechem. In fact, they suggest that if the narrator is sympathetic toward any character in the story it is Shechem, the one who perpetrated the rape in the first place. Genesis 34 clearly is a text fraught with ethical tension both within and without, both in the story it tells and in the way interpreters tell the story. How does one deal with the ethical dilemma found here? How does an interpreter navigate through the moral differences of characters, narrators and other interpreters?

Traditionally, ethicists and biblical theologians would answer the above questions by proposing a method or ethic(s) that would enable the reader to work through such moral difficulties. Such proposals assume that Genesis 34 presents

---

1. All translations from the Hebrew Bible are mine, unless otherwise indicated.

2. Meir Sternberg, *The Poetics of Biblical Narrative: Ideological Literature and the Drama of Reading* (Bloomington, IN: Indiana University Press, 1985), pp. 445–75.

3. David M. Gunn and Danna Nolan Fewell, 'Tipping the Balance: Sternberg's Reader and the Rape of Dinah', *JBL*, 110 (1991), pp. 193–211.

the reader with the need to make an ethical determination about the action or inaction of the characters in the story and that interpreters should make ethical decisions within a coherent ethical, moral or interpretative system. While the first assumption is a given – ethically difficult texts like Genesis 34 demand a response from their readers – the second is far from certain. As Stanley Fish has argued, theory and method, though they masquerade themselves as foundational(ist) solutions to difficult problems, do not determine interpretative decisions. At the end of his essay, 'Antifoundationalism, Theory Hope, and the Teaching of Composition', Fish concludes that theory or method cannot save us from indeterminacy. In fact, 'practice has nothing to do with theory, at least in the sense of being enabled and justified by theory'.[4] More fundamentally, Jacques Derrida, when asked about the question of ethics, proposes that undecidability and not decision is at the heart of ethics:

> Far from opposing undecidability to decision, I would argue that there would be no decision, in the strong sense of the word, in ethics, in politics, no decision, and thus no responsibility, without the experience of some undecidability. If you don't experience some undecidability, then the decision would simply be the application of a programme, the consequence of a premiss or of a matrix. So a decision has to go through some impossibility in order for it to be a decision.[5]

Derrida concludes, 'Ethics and politics, therefore, start with undecidability'.[6] Contrary to what traditional ethicists would argue, undecidability is not reflective of moral paralysis, but is the very possibility of ethical living and acting.[7] This does not mean that readers should suspend making moral decisions about Genesis 34 or other ethically difficult texts. On the contrary, interpreters have made and will make ethical judgments on such texts. To what extent, however, these interpretative decisions are based in or constrained by moral or ethical systems remains to be seen. In fact, when undecidability is taken into account in one's reading, Genesis 34 can function as a parable that illustrates what can go wrong when moral imperatives and cultural norms betray the values of justice and community that they claim to embrace and protect. Genesis 34 is a story about what happens when the 'Other' is neglected for the sake of establishing one's own position.

---

4.   In Stanley Fish, *Doing What Comes Naturally: Change, Rhetoric, and the Practice of Theory in Literary and Legal Studies* (Durham, NC, and London: Duke University Press, 1989), p. 355.

5.   Jacques Derrida, 'Hospitality, Justice and Responsibility: A Dialogue with Jacques Derrida', in Richard Kearney and Mark Dooley (eds.), *Questioning Ethics: Contemporary Debates in Philosophy* (London and New York: Routledge, 1999), pp. 65–83 (66).

6.   Derrida, 'Hospitality, Justice and Responsibility', p. 66.

7.   For a discussion of postmodern ethics or ethics beyond foundationalism, see John D. Caputo, *Against Ethics: Contributions to a Poetics of Obligation with Constant Reference to Deconstruction* (Bloomington and Indianapolis: Indiana University Press, 1993); Simon Critchley, *The Ethics of Deconstruction: Derrida to Levinas* (Edinburgh: Edinburgh University Press, 2nd edn, 1999); Zygmunt Baumann, *Postmodern Ethics* (Oxford and Cambridge: Basil Blackwell, 1993); Jacques Derrida, 'Hospitality, Justice and Responsibility'; Frank M. Yamada, 'Ethics', in A.K.M. Adam (ed.), *Handbook of Postmodern Biblical Interpretation* (St Louis, MO: Chalice Press, 2000), pp. 76–84.

Negotiating Differences of Opinion in the Text:
The Rape of Dinah and the Conflicts of Men in Genesis 34

Genesis 34 begins with Dinah, daughter of Jacob, going out to visit the women of the land. Dinah's going out, from the Hebrew root, יצא, represents danger in that she is leaving the security of her own tribe to mingle with outsiders.[8] This danger is realized when Shechem, son of Hamor, 'takes', 'lies with' and 'rapes' Dinah.[9] The narrator uses three verbs in succession to suggest the escalating violence of Shechem's act.[10] Thus, at the very beginning of this story, the reader is confronted with sexual violence, an act that requires an ethical response. In fact, one can read the rest of the chapter as a series of male responses to the initial sexual violation.

Shechem provides the first response. The narrator counters Shechem's three successive verbs of violence with three expressions of affection from the prince in v. 3: 'his soul *clung* to Dinah, daughter of Jacob', 'he *loved* the girl', and '*spoke kindly* to her' (literally, 'he spoke to the heart of the girl'). The ethical decision confronting the reader at the beginning of the chapter is made more problematic by Shechem's response. The prince follows his act of sexual violence with a response of love for Dinah. Though the verbs and expressions balance out in symmetrical triads, the reader must ponder the appropriateness of Shechem's affection, especially since the relationship between Dinah and Shechem began

---

8. For example, in *Midrash Tanḥma*, an interpretation of Ps. 45.14 is used proverbially to explain Dinah's going out: '"The king's daughter is all glorious within" (Psalm 45.14). When a woman keeps herself secluded at home she is worthy to marry a high priest' (as quoted in Mishael Maswari Caspi, 'The Story of the Rape of Dinah: The Narrator and the Reader', *Hebrew Studies*, 26 [1985], p. 29).

9. See Lyn M. Bechtel, 'What If Dinah Is Not Raped? (Genesis 34)', *JSOT*, 62 (1994), pp. 19–36. Bechtel contends that Dinah is not raped but socially humiliated. Using cultural anthropological research on group-oriented societies, Bechtel claims that most scholars interpret Genesis 34 mistakenly as a rape text. She argues that the key word, ענה in the Piel, is a term that describes shaming rather than rape. What makes Shechem's sexual encounter with Dinah shameful is the fact that he is an outsider. Thus, she prefers to translate ענה in the Piel, 'to humiliate' (see esp. pp. 23–31). While Bechtel's analysis of the group dynamics in Genesis 34 is helpful, her interpretation of Shechem's actions, including her analysis of ענה, is inadequate. The three successive verbs in v. 2 suggest escalating violence (see n. 10 below). Bechtel's translation also does not take into account the violent potential within the root ענה. For discussion on ענה in the Piel as meaning 'to rape', see Susanne Scholz, 'Was It Really Rape in Genesis 34? Biblical Scholarship as a Reflection of Cultural Assumptions', in Harold C. Washington, Susan L. Graham and Pamela L. Thimmes (eds.), *Escaping Eden: New Feminist Perspectives on the Bible* (Sheffield: Sheffield Academic Press, 1998), pp. 182–98. My doctoral dissertation also treats this question: Frank M. Yamada, 'Rape Narratives as Cultural Critique: A Narrative and Cultural Analysis of Old Testament Rape Texts' (PhD dissertation in progress; Princeton Theological Seminary).

10. See Nahum M. Sarna, *Genesis: The Traditional Hebrew Text with the New JPS Translation* (JPS Torah Commentary; Philadelphia: Jewish Publication Society, 1989), p. 234; and Susanne Scholz, *Rape Plots: A Feminist Cultural Study of Genesis 34* (Studies in Biblical Literature, 13; New York: Peter Lang, 2000), p. 136.

with sexual violation.[11] Shechem proceeds to act on his desire for Dinah by asking his father to get Dinah as his wife.

It is interesting to note that there is no response from Dinah. The biblical text is not unfamiliar with female responses to sexual violation, as laws in Deuteronomy show (Deut. 22.23-27).[12] In fact, in these laws, the woman's crying out is fundamental in determining who is culpable. Also, in 2 Samuel 13, a text with vocabulary similar to that of Genesis 34, Tamar voices dismay to her half-brother Amnon at his desire to lie with her. The narrator concludes this story by describing Tamar's response of mourning, as she puts ashes on her head and rips her clothing. She leaves crying aloud as she exits the narrative. It is not important here to argue whether one of these texts is dependent on the other, though this is probably the case with Deuteronomy 22 (cf. vv. 28-29) and the Genesis 34 narrative. What is significant is that the narrator in Genesis 34, unlike the laws in Deuteronomy and the story in 2 Samuel 13, leaves out the response of Dinah altogether. We will explore the implication of this omission below. Here it is important simply to note that Dinah's response is missing. Though the act of sexual aggression is perpetrated against Dinah, we do not hear from her. The rape has erased her voice. Within the structure of the narrative, she has become the object first of Shechem's violence and second of his affection. The remainder of the narrative tells the story of other male responses to the rape. The rape of this woman will turn into negotiations and conflicts between men.

The narrative proceeds by describing the different responses of Jacob and his sons in Gen. 34.5-7. Jacob, upon hearing the news that Dinah had been defiled, 'keeps silent' (וְהֶחֱרִשׁ) and waits for his sons to return. The reader is uncertain about how to understand Jacob's silence. Is he, as the NRSV suggests, 'holding his peace', or does his silence reflect indecisiveness?[13] The first proposal suggests that Jacob is using discernment and a level head in order to make the best possible decision. The second points to an aging patriarch wavering with indecision who must wait for his sons' return before a judgment can be made. While Jacob's response is ambiguous, his sons' reaction to the situation is clear. They are indignant and angry that their sister has been defiled. As they see it, Shechem has committed a disgraceful act in Israel, a thing that should not have been done (v. 7). The different responses of

---

11. Gunn and Fewell suggest that this string of verbs expressing affection points to a change in Shechem's attitude toward Dinah. She has become for him a person rather than an object of his desire ('Tipping the Balance', p. 197). Claus Westermann sees this string of verbs as an intensification of Shechem's feelings for Dinah. See Claus Westermann, *Genesis 12–36* (A Continental Commentary; Minneapolis: Augsburg Publishing House, 1985), p. 538. By contrast, Scholz argues that Shechem's behavior is consistent with a rapist; accordingly, her translation of the verbs minimizes the tone of affection (*Rape Plots*, pp. 138–42).

12. But see Carolyn Pressler, 'Sexual Violence and Deuteronomic Law', in Athalya Brenner (ed.), *A Feminist Companion to Exodus and Deuteronomy* (FCB, 6; Sheffield: Sheffield Academic Press, 1994), pp.102–12. Pressler argues that Deut. 22.25-27 and 22.28-29 (and subsequently Genesis 34) are not about rape but about 'involuntary adultery' in the case of the betrothed woman and 'financial injury' in the case of the unbetrothed woman.

13. See the discussion of Gunn/Fewell and Sternberg below for their different characterizations of Jacob.

Jacob and his sons will manifest themselves in conflicting attitudes toward the inhabitants of the city as the story moves toward its conclusion. Within the context of the story, opinions about how to act or react will make the difference between peace and vengeance, life and death.

In Gen. 34.8-17, Hamor and Shechem negotiate with Jacob and his sons. They come to an agreement, though the sons of Israel act deceitfully in the proceedings. Jacob's sons tell Hamor and Shechem that they will consent to allow Shechem to marry Dinah and for the two tribes to intermarry on the condition that all the males of the village become circumcised. The text is explicit, describing the sons' words as deceitful in v. 13 (במרמה, which means literally 'in deceit'). In this way, the narrator frames the reader's understanding of the sons and their intention. They are acting underhandedly. Their words cannot be taken at face value, and their actions must be read suspiciously. In this way, the sons' motivation and future deeds are determined by the moral judgment of the narrator. Regardless of what their plan might be, the reader understands their actions under the umbrella of deceit. The sons' tainted motivation stands in contrast to what appears at the beginning of the bargaining to be the forthright negotiations of Shechem and Hamor. Though Shechem's initial act of rape is violent, his negotiations with Jacob and his sons are exemplary. Hamor and Shechem suggest that the two tribes intermarry and that Jacob and his sons live in the land (v. 10). Shechem himself offers to pay as much as Jacob and his sons demand for the bride price (v. 12). Finally, Hamor and Shechem are willing to comply with the Israelites' desire for them to be circumcised (vv. 18-19). The narrator adds to the reader's sense that Shechem is acting in good faith by characterizing Shechem as being more honorable than all those in his family (v. 19). The portrayal of Shechem and Hamor as being honest in their dealings with Jacob and his sons, however, is shaded by the scene that follows. Hamor and Shechem, after appealing to the men of the city to comply with the Israelites' demands, provide the men with a motivation for carrying out the stipulations of the agreement. They say, 'Their livestock, their property and all of their animals, will they not be ours?' (v. 23). Thus, though Shechem and Hamor handle themselves honorably in negotiations, their willingness to adhere to the agreement is colored by a motivation to plunder the Israelites through assimilation in marriage. The sons of Israel act deceitfully while Shechem and Hamor are driven by an ulterior motive. The pact between Israel and the inhabitants of this city is doomed to fail.

The inhabitants of the city agree to the demands of Jacob's sons, and all the men are circumcised. On the third day, while the men of the city are still 'in pain', Simeon and Levi attack the city with the sword and kill all the males (v. 25). By mentioning that the men were still in pain from being circumcised and that the city had settled into a secure state (בטח), the narrator highlights both the vulnerability of the inhabitants and the unexpected nature of the attack. The narration emphasizes the deceptive and brutal nature of the two brothers' retribution. The two men kill Hamor, Shechem and all of the males and proceed to take Dinah out of Shechem's house. Ironically, the verb translated, 'they took' (from the root, לקח), is the same one used in v. 2 to describe Shechem's taking of Dinah. The brothers then proceed by going out (וַיֵּצְאוּ) of the city. These last two *waw*-consecutive verbs in v. 26 (from the roots לקח, 'to take', and יצא, 'to go out') provide an inclusio for Dinah's role in the story. Dinah began by *going out* (וַתֵּצֵא) to visit with the women of the land and was subsequently *taken* (וַיִּקַּח) by Shechem and raped. The story ends as her brothers *take* (וַיִּקְחוּ) her out of Shechem's house and then proceed to *go out* (וַיֵּצְאוּ) of the city with her. In both cases, Dinah is the object of male seizure, represented by the verb לקח. At the beginning she is forcefully *taken* by Shechem, and at the end she is *taken* back by her brothers. Where the story began with her own exploration, *going out* to meet the women of the land, the story ends with the brothers *going out* of the city with Dinah. In each case, the fate of her journey is determined by the actions of men. Dinah's response is not heard in either 'taking'. She does not speak. Not only does Dinah lack voice, her fate through the negotiations and in the end is in the hands of men. Though the story begins with Dinah's self-initiated departure from her family, it finishes as a tale of male disputes and seizures, of men taking her in and men leading her out.

The scene deteriorates as the sons of Jacob come upon the slain men and proceed to pillage the city (v. 27). The narrator adds that the plundering is motivated by the fact that Shechem has defiled their sister. However, this motivation, based in revenge, is stained as reflected in the detailed way that the narrator describes the pillaging of the city, highlighting the excessive nature of the looting: 'They took their flocks, their herds, their donkeys and whatever was in the city or the field. They took captive and carried off as spoil all their wealth, all their little ones, their wives and all that was in the houses' (vv. 28-29).[14] The sons of Jacob leave the city in waste. The narrator has made clear to the reader that the sons' motivation stems from revenge; however, the excess with which the retaliation is carried out causes the reader to question whether the punishment fits the crime. Not only is the demolition of the city excessive, the attack, as noted above, is carried out under the cloak of deception. The sons of Jacob have fooled and made fools of Hamor, Shechem and the inhabitants of the city. The sons waited until the city was at its most vulnerable point – when all the men were in pain from their circumcision – and proceeded to make the city pay excessively for the crime that Shechem committed.

The brothers' deception surprises not only Shechem and Hamor; Jacob himself is shocked and grieved by his sons' actions. He tells Simeon and Levi that they have brought trouble on him by giving him a bad reputation among the peoples of the land (Gen. 34.30). The verb used is from the root באשׁ, which literally means, 'to stink'. Thus, his reputation has become an unbearable stench among the inhabitants of Canaan. Because of the deeds of his sons, Jacob has become 'odious to the inhabitants of the land, the Canaanites and the Perizzites' (NRSV, v. 30). Jacob's response to his sons also suggests that he is fearful that the people of the land will rise up against him because of the violence his sons have committed. He says, 'I am few in number, and if they gather against me and attack me, I shall be destroyed, both I and my house' (v. 30). It is clear to the reader that Jacob's sons

---

14. The direct objects of plunder occur first in the sentence structure, emphasizing the extent of the spoil that the sons of Jacob carry off from the city.

have acted in opposition to the will of their father. Because of their desire for vengeance, the sons have done things that will make it difficult for Jacob and his clan to live peaceably in the land.[15] The reader recognizes through Jacob's response that the patriarch desired to make peaceful negotiations with Shechem and Hamor. Jacob's disposition is consistent with his earlier dealings with the inhabitants of this city, when he purchased a plot of land from the sons of Hamor (Gen. 33.18-19).[16] The reader, however, is also left to question Jacob's motivation about the events that have transpired. Has he been concerned about the welfare of his daughter? If so, his words do not convey this concern clearly. In fact, Jacob's primary worry seems to be about his reputation in the land. Nowhere in his comment is there evidence of his thoughts about Dinah and her situation. What is clear is that he is angry with his sons, Simeon and Levi, because they have ruined his reputation and threatened his security and the security of his family. He will carry this anger with him to the grave (see Gen. 49.5-7).[17]

Simeon and Levi's response to Jacob in v. 31 mirrors the reader's thoughts about Jacob's apparent lack of concern for Dinah. They counter their father's charges by posing the question, 'Should he treat our sister like a whore?' (v. 31). Thus, they justify their actions against Shechem, Hamor and the inhabitants of the city within the framework of retribution. They have acted from a desire to vindicate the lost honor of their sister. Dinah has been defiled and Shechem must pay. It is significant that Simeon and Levi are singled out as instigators in this event since both are the sons of Leah. At the beginning of Genesis 34, in an uncharacteristic move for the biblical text, Dinah is described as the daughter of Leah (v. 1). In a narrative where most of the characters are designated by their relationship to another and where sons and daughters are usually identified through their fathers (e.g., 'the sons of Jacob', 'Shechem, son of Hamor', etc.), it is meaningful that Dinah is mentioned as the daughter of Leah. The significance of this characterization becomes clearer when it is two sons of Leah, Simeon and Levi, who instigate the violent retribution against Shechem and the inhabitants of the city. Family politics have contributed to the courses of action that these two sons have taken.

---

15. Walter Brueggemann, *Genesis* (Interpretation; Atlanta: John Knox, 1982), p. 279.

16. The congenial atmosphere of the negotiations is highlighted by the narrator's description of Jacob's entrance into the land as 'safe' or 'peaceful' in v. 18. This description sets up the narrative in Genesis 34 so that the reader perceives the inhabitants of Shechem as friendly and open to inter-action with Jacob and his family. Thus, Dinah's initial going out to meet the women of the land, though creating the potential for danger, is set within a context where peaceful interchange is expected.

17. Most scholars suggest an early date for Genesis 49, due to its archaic language and its similarity to other tribal blessings (e.g., Deuteronomy 33). The narrative context of this poem, however, frames Genesis 49 as a deathbed blessing. For discussion on the date and language of Genesis 49, see David Noel Freedman, '"Who is Like Thee Among the Gods?" The Religion of Early Israel', in Patrick D. Miller, Paul D. Hanson and S. Dean McBride (eds.), *Ancient Israelite Religion: Essays in Honor of Frank Moore Cross* (Philadelphia: Fortress Press, 1987), pp. 315-35; and David Noel Freedman and Frank Moore Cross, *Studies in Ancient Yahwistic Poetry* (Grand Rapids: Eerdmans, 1997), pp. 69-96.

Genesis 34 ends abruptly with the rhetorical question that Simeon and Levi pose to Jacob, 'Should he treat our sister like a whore?' (v. 31). The reader is left to ponder the meaning and significance of the conclusion. While Jacob is clearly angry with his sons because of how their actions have affected his reputation (v. 30) and while the sentiments and opinions of the two brothers, Simeon and Levi, are clear (v. 31), the ethical consequences of the characters' words and actions leave the reader in a quandary. As our examination of the text has shown, no male character in Genesis 34 is clearly in the right. All the male characters are conflicted and morally questionable at different points in the story. Shechem acts honorably in his transactions with the sons of Jacob. The narrator even characterizes him as honorable (v. 19). His words in negotiation and his willingness to comply are tainted, however, by his initial act of violence against Dinah. The rape, though countered by three phrases of affection in v. 3, remains as a brutal fact. The story depicts this most clearly through Simeon and Levi, who cannot forget that Shechem has defiled their sister. The character and motivation of Shechem and his father are also called into question when the reader recognizes that the two men desire to take the property and livestock of Jacob's tribe through intermarriage (v. 23). Thus, the character of Shechem is ethically questionable. He is a rapist who falls in love with his victim and is willing to go to any length to get the woman that he wants, even if his whole tribe has to be circumcised. When we turn to Jacob, his desire to have peaceful interactions with the inhabitants of the land (cf. Gen. 33.18-19 and 34.30) is not bad in and of itself. However, his preoccupation with his reputation in the land at the end of Genesis 34 is obtuse and morally questionable in light of the violence committed against his daughter. The story leaves the reader with a perception of Jacob as a man who is overly concerned with his own honor and reputation, a flaw that clouds his moral and ethical senses. As for Simeon and Levi, they are motivated to act by the damaged honor of their sister, but their deceitful interactions with Shechem and Hamor, coupled with the excessive violence with which they carry out their vengeance, turn their motivation into a shameless act of aggression. Even the men of the city, who are characterized as victims of Jacob's sons and holy war, are motivated to circumcise themselves so that the women, livestock and property of Israel might be theirs (v. 23).

The narrative started out as a story about the rape of Dinah, an act that requires an ethical response from the reader and the characters in the story. What the story becomes is a tale depicting the questionable reactions of men, responses that complicate, if not exacerbate, the situation. Shechem cares for Dinah and is willing to negotiate with Jacob and his sons to make her his wife, but only after he has raped her. Simeon and Levi are concerned that Dinah not be treated as a prostitute, but they turn her humiliation into an act of excessive retaliation against a vulnerable city. Dinah's shame has become a springboard for her brothers' twisted plan of retribution – a tribal castration and ethnic cleansing. The reader is left to ponder. But what about Dinah? She is the one who was victimized by rape. Shechem's lust has shattered her personhood and future as a woman, and yet we do not hear from her. The story degenerates after the rape into a series of male negotiations and conflicts. The family of Jacob is divided. The sons' reckless behavior has created a stench around the name of Jacob/Israel. The city of Shechem lies in waste, dead bodies strewn throughout. At the conclusion of the story, Dinah remains in her desolate state. In a male-dominated society, she is damaged goods. At the end of Genesis 34, no one wins. The rape of a woman calls for an ethical response concerned with the victim, but this story of rape deteriorates into a contest of male honor and reputation. The result is violence (against Shechem and the city), fragmentation (of the Jacobite family) and desolation (of Dinah).

The ethical questions surrounding the text of Genesis 34 are numerous. How is a reader to respond to a text that has so many ethical ambiguities? How does one evaluate a rapist who falls in love with his victim, a father who neglects the fact that his daughter has been raped, while obsessing over his own reputation, or two blood brothers whose desire for vengeance turns into excessive violence? More importantly, how does a reader address a raped woman's need for justice when the story itself degenerates into a contest over male honor, moving her to the margins of the text? Before addressing these questions, I will turn to discussions of Genesis 34 and the attempts of interpreters to find their way through the ethical confusion in this text. I will focus on a particularly contentious exchange between Meir Sternberg on the one hand and Fewell and Gunn on the other.

Negotiating Differences of Opinion in Interpretation: Texts Imitating Reality and Readers Imitating Texts

My reading of Genesis 34 highlights that the male characters in the story are conflicted and ethically questionable. All have interests and intentions that cause them to respond to the rape of Dinah differently. All the responses are morally questionable. It should not be surprising, therefore, that interpreters of Genesis 34 have differing opinions about the morality and immorality of the characters in the story. An exchange between Meir Sternberg and David Gunn and Danna Nolan Fewell will provide a useful illustration of how interpreters attempt to navigate the ethical ambiguities of Genesis 34. My intention is not to suggest which argument is right and which one is wrong but to show how each attempts to work through the ethical difficulties within Genesis 34.

Sternberg, in his influential work, *The Poetics of Biblical Narrative*, argues that Genesis 34 is a story about rhetorical persuasion and balance.[18] He suggests that the narrator, rather than telling the tale in clear categories of right and wrong, makes the job more difficult and interesting by intentionally telling the story in a more complex way. He writes as follows:

> It is not that [the narrator] saddles himself with another inflexible value system but that he spurns the appeal to ready-made codes that would smooth the way of persuasion. He chooses to complicate his rhetorical task by entangling the moral issues and going counter to stock response.[19]

---

18. Sternberg's discussion of the rape of Dinah occurs in his chapter, 'The Art of Persuasion' in *The Poetics of Biblical Narrative*, pp. 445–75.

19. Sternberg, *The Poetics of Biblical Narrative*, pp. 444–45.

For Sternberg, part of the art of biblical narrative lies in how the narrator makes the story more complex. He argues that Genesis 34 is a tale of balance in that the narrator works to balance out morally two acts of violence – the rape of Dinah and the revenge of her brothers on Shechem and the inhabitants of the city. He acknowledges that the latter act of retaliation by Dinah's brothers is disproportionate to the crime that Shechem commits. Hence, the narrator faces a problem. How can the reader be persuaded that Simeon and Levi have acted rightly when it is likely that the reader will have sympathy for the victims of their violent retribution? Sternberg suggests that the narrator amasses enough sympathy for the brothers through the telling of the story, so that, in the end, the reader clearly stands on their side. Sternberg structures the story in three phases. In the first phase, vv. 1-12, the narrator accumulates 'maximal sympathy for Jacob's sons'.[20] In contrast to Shechem's rape of Dinah and Jacob's wavering indecision, the reader identifies with the brothers' indignation at the defilement of their sister. Thus, at the beginning of the story, the narrator has created an accumulation of sympathy for the brothers. In the second phase, vv. 13-26, the narrator complicates the issue through the disproportionate act of violence that the brothers commit against Shechem and the inhabitants of the city. Their actions balance the scale of sympathy, returning it to a state of equilibrium. Sternberg, describing this rhetorical structure and strategy, states, 'That initial accumulation tips the scales of judgment so heavily on the brothers' side (as victims) that their following excesses (as victimizers) only produce emotional and moral equilibrium'.[21] In the final phase, vv. 27-31, Simeon and Levi are the protagonists in the eyes of the reader, since they are the only ones who maintain their principles and attempt to right the wrong that was committed against Dinah. Jacob is overcome by an egocentric pragmatism that is concerned only with his safety and the potential of materialistic gain from interaction with the Hivites. Simeon and Levi, however, are guided by what Sternberg calls their 'idealism'.[22] They say, 'Damn the consequences'.[23] The brothers will do whatever they must to stay true to their principles and vindicate their own reputation and their sister's.

Sternberg concludes that Simeon and Levi are the heroes of the story. Though their violent retribution against Shechem and the Hivites is disproportionate to Shechem's crime, the narrator has stored up enough sympathy with the reader to balance the excesses of their violence. In Sternberg's reading, Shechem is a dubious character. Not only has he raped Dinah; in his negotiations with Jacob's sons, he has failed to mention any sense of the wrong that he has committed. Sternberg characterizes the bargaining speech of Hamor and Shechem as showing 'brazen disregard of antecedents'.[24] Sternberg is also critical of Jacob. His failure to act or speak on behalf of his daughter is unconscionable. At the end of his analysis, Sternberg characterizes Jacob as acting out of pragmatism and egocentric

---

20. *The Poetics of Biblical Narrative*, p. 446.
21. *The Poetics of Biblical Narrative*, p. 446.
22. *The Poetics of Biblical Narrative*, p. 474.
23. *The Poetics of Biblical Narrative*, p. 474.
24. *The Poetics of Biblical Narrative*, p. 456.

self-preservation.[25] Thus, while Jacob, Shechem and Hamor are all drawn by self-centeredness or greed, Simeon and Levi act out of a principled 'national-religious framework'.[26]

Gunn and Fewell, in their article, 'Tipping the Balance: Sternberg's Reader and the Rape of Dinah', contend with Sternberg's poetics, which is grounded in the concept that he terms 'foolproof composition'.[27] For Sternberg, the Bible, which he calls ideological literature because it is always interested in persuading its reader to a particular point of view, is 'difficult to read, easy to underread and overread and even misread, but virtually impossible to, so to speak, counterread'.[28] The competent reader, when attentive to the text, cannot miss the point that the story is trying to make. Gunn and Fewell argue that Sternberg's poetics and his concept of a competent reader are informed by his own value system – an androcentric one – that is different from their own. Thus, they offer an alternative reading of Genesis 34, one that is self-consciously grounded in a feminist value system. Rather than going through every point of disagreement between Gunn/Fewell and Sternberg, I will focus on the differences in interpretation of key characters and events in Genesis 34, and the ethical implications that Gunn and Fewell attach to these differences.

Contrary to Sternberg, Gunn and Fewell argue that the initial scene in Genesis 34 does not generate sympathy for the brothers but casts Shechem in a complex ethical light. They suggest that the expressions of affection in v. 3 – 'his soul clung', 'he loved' and 'he spoke to the heart' – characterize Shechem positively. His attitude toward Dinah has changed to the point of seeing her as a person. In v. 2, Dinah is the object of his desire. In v. 3, 'the woman becomes for Shechem a real person: his soul clings to *Dinah*, he loves *the young woman*, and he speaks to *the young woman's heart*'.[29] Hence, if the narrator is generating sympathy for a character, Gunn and Fewell argue that it is for Shechem and not the unmentioned brothers as Sternberg asserts.

Jacob's response to the rape of Dinah is another point of divergence between Sternberg and Gunn and Fewell. Sternberg labels Jacob's initial silence as indifference to the harm that has come upon his daughter. He contrasts Jacob's silent response to the indignation that the brothers show upon hearing the news. For Sternberg, Jacob's silence is hard to understand. His daughter has been raped. In response, he does nothing and says nothing. He does not care. Gunn and Fewell

---

25. *The Poetics of Biblical Narrative*, p. 474.

26. *The Poetics of Biblical Narrative*, p. 457. Sternberg uses the phrase, 'national-religious framework', to characterize the brothers' idealism, which is signified by circumcision. They have taken the 'higher ground' by refusing to agree to the economic pragmatism represented by the negotiations of the Hivites *(The Poetics of Biblical Narrative*, pp. 457–58).

27. 'Tipping the Balance', 193. For a discussion of 'foolproof composition' in Sternberg, see *The Poetics of Biblical Narrative*, pp. 41–57 (esp. pp. 50–51). See also Sternberg's reply to Gunn and Fewell in Sternberg, 'Biblical Poetics and Sexual Politics: From Reading to Counterreading', *JBL*, 111 (1992), pp. 463–73.

28. *The Poetics of Biblical Narrative*, p. 50.

29. Gunn and Fewell, 'Tipping the Balance', p. 197 (emphasis original).

offer another plausible interpretation of Jacob's silence. They suggest that the silence could reflect Jacob's determination to keep his peace in a potentially volatile situation. They propose that Sternberg's characterization of Jacob is driven by the Western cultural ideal of 'action-oriented heroics'. For Gunn and Fewell, 'Jacob's silence derives from caution rather than apathy'.[30] At the end of the story, Jacob speaks out against his sons. He fears that their reckless behavior will create trouble for him and his family. Sternberg, consistent with his earlier characterization, sees Jacob's comments as reflective of the patriarch's egocentrism and self-preservation. Gunn and Fewell emphasize that Jacob's response includes the expression, 'I and my house', suggesting that Jacob cares not only about his own reputation and safety but also about the reputation and safety of his entire house.[31] Where Sternberg sees Jacob as indifferent, pragmatic and self-absorbed, Gunn and Fewell see a father who is keeping a level head while trying to make the best of an already broken situation.

Simeon and Levi are the protagonists, in Sternberg's judgment, because they act out of principles and from concern for their sister's condition rather than from a materialistic pragmatism. The brothers' speech in vv. 13-17 illustrates this. They are not lured by the possibility of land and property that would come through intermarriage with the Hivites. Instead they hold to their principles: 'We cannot do this thing, to give our sister to one who is uncircumcised, for that would be a disgrace to us' (v. 14). Gunn and Fewell, however, argue that the brothers' speech cannot be taken at face value, since the narrator clearly labels it as deceitful (v. 13). The brothers never say 'no' to the offer made by Hamor and Shechem. They simply add the stipulation of circumcision. The brothers' speech and their 'socio-religious motivation' cannot be trusted, since all of it is framed with deceit. Gunn and Fewell add that the brothers' motivation is driven not out of concern for their sister but out of an interest in preserving their own honor. As the brothers' speech suggests, they cannot give their sister to an uncircumcised man, 'for it would be a disgrace to us' (v. 14). At the end of the story, after the massacre at Shechem, Sternberg's reading finds moral balance and equilibrium, enabling the narrator to uphold Simeon and Levi as heroes. By contrast, Gunn and Fewell characterize the actions of Simeon and Levi as reckless and without regard for larger social implications. Gunn and Fewell's conclusion about Simeon and Levi is clear: 'Their

---

30. 'Tipping the Balance', p. 198.

31. Gunn and Fewell realize that Sternberg acknowledges Jacob's concern for his family but say that he does so 'reluctantly' (see 'Tipping the Balance', p. 207, n. 24). The paragraph in Sternberg to which they point is an interesting one. It concludes his discussion of Genesis 34. Rather than reaffirming his position of the narrator's clear preference for Simeon and Levi, he suggests that in the end '(t)he narrator no more pronounces judgment on this family quarrel than he did on the conflict with the Hivites. He seems to leave the issue open for the reader to decide' (Sternberg, *The Poetics of Biblical Narrative*, p. 475). While Sternberg makes clear later in the paragraph that the narrator's sympathy clearly lies with Simeon and Levi, he acknowledges complexity in the different characters (specifically Jacob, Simeon and Levi) that his earlier reading did not emphasize. Jacob is not completely self-serving, because he rightly has concerns for the safety of his house. Even Simeon and Levi, Sternberg's protagonists, act out of 'disregard for consequences rather than out of trust in God's providence' (p. 475).

grossly disproportionate response remains just that. If they are to be defended as upholders of high principle, then we need to look more closely at the particulars of that principle'.[32]

The last character that Gunn and Fewell mention is Dinah. They argue that for Sternberg, Dinah is simply a function of plot. Gunn and Fewell suggest a couple of ways that Dinah's presence can be seen in the text or reconstructed back into the story. First, though Dinah does not have voice within the story, she has narrative presence through the mentioning of her name and through her relation to other men in the story (e.g., as Jacob's daughter and the brothers' sister). Second, Gunn and Fewell suggest a way that readers might consider the rights of Dinah by looking at the different ways that male characters care for her. By having sexual relations with Dinah, Shechem has already defiled her. By offering to marry her, he has provided Dinah with a way to live. Thus, Gunn and Fewell see Shechem's offer to marry Dinah as a viable, albeit messy, solution. Jacob's apparent agreement to Hamor's offer may reflect his acceptance of this reality.

Gunn and Fewell end their article on an ethical note, comparing the value systems of their reader over against Sternberg's. Their comment is worth quoting at length:

> First, that where Sternberg's reader sees admirable principles, our reader sees culpable neglect of responsibility. If Simeon and Levi are Sternberg's heroes, they are certainly not ours.
>
> Second, that where Sternberg's reader expresses contempt for the characters Jacob, Hamor, and Shechem, our reader expresses a measure of sympathy for them, not as heroes but as complex characters making the best of a flawed world.
>
> Third, that where Sternberg's reader sees Dinah as a helpless girl to be rescued, our reader sees a young woman who could have made her own choices – limited though they might have been – had she been asked.[33]

The conclusion of Gunn and Fewell's article brings us to a point of contact with the present essay. What is at stake for Gunn and Fewell is the ethics of reading and the differences that our interpretations make for arriving at moral judgments about texts and about interpretations of texts. I will address this issue more specifically below, but first we must see what we can learn from the interchange described above. Time and space do not permit us to consider Sternberg's lengthy response to Gunn and Fewell.[34] Our goal, however, is not to exhaust the dialogue between these two parties but to highlight how each interpreter navigates differently the ethical ambiguities within Genesis 34. The present sample is more than sufficient for us to make some observations about how these readers come to judgments about this text.

When we explore the differences between Sternberg's interpretation and the interpretation of Gunn and Fewell, we come to some significant conclusions about the ways in which these readers read. Both interpretations argue from the text but

32. 'Tipping the Balance', p. 205.
33. 'Tipping the Balance', p. 211.
34. 'Biblical Poetics and Sexual Politics'.

also from competing value systems. Their conclusions differ and at many points are diametrically opposed to each other. This is especially clear in their evaluation of the different characters in the story, as Gunn and Fewell make clear in their conclusion.[35] Both interpretations agree that the rape is wrong. Sternberg and Gunn/ Fewell disagree, however, on the appropriateness and inappropriateness of the men's responses to the incident. Sternberg's heroes are reckless and violent to Gunn and Fewell. Gunn and Fewell's complex characters are examples of ineptitude and greed for Sternberg.

The interpreters, like the text of Genesis 34, are in conflict and conflicted. Gunn and Fewell take Sternberg to task for a reading that they argue is informed by an androcentric value system. Sternberg offers his own riposte in a later article, 'Biblical Poetics and Sexual Politics: From Reading to Counterreading', in which he produces a lengthy apology of his work, chiding Gunn and Fewell for their readerly incompetence and inadequate scholarship.[36] The interpreters are not only in conflict; their interpretations are also ethically conflicted. Both readings attempt to portray certain characters as acting ethically, though these characterizations have a difficult time deflecting criticism. Looked at apart from the narrative, the notion of Simeon and Levi's idealism is morally appealing. Often, ethical decisions are made not out of expediency or pragmatism, but out of determination to stay true to what one believes. Dietrich Bonhoeffer's life and writings are a testament to such ethical acting and thinking. Within the context of Genesis 34, however, Simeon and Levi are presented as complex characters, whose idealism leads to excessive violence and ethnic cleansing. To compensate for this complexity, Sternberg reads the beginning of Genesis 34 as the narrator's strategy to accumulate sympathy for Simeon and Levi, characters who have not yet entered the scene, as Gunn and Fewell correctly point out. Sternberg must also go to great lengths to explain how the reader can suspend judgment on the brothers' 'deceit' in v. 13.[37] The less-forced explanation would be to read the brothers' words as the narrator describes, as deceitful. Similarly, Gunn and Fewell portray Shechem, Hamor and Jacob as characters who do their best to navigate the ethical complexities of a 'flawed world'.[38] This ethic, which they call an 'ethic of responsibility', when examined on its own, is also noble and good. Womanist scholars have often described black women's experience as 'making a way out of no way'. The ability of human beings to forge their way through the complexities and conflicts of life is surely a virtue. Within

---

35. See the similar observations about the debate between Gunn/Fewell and Sternberg in Paul R. Noble, 'A "Balanced" Reading of the Rape of Dinah: Some Exegetical and Methodological Observations', *BibInt*, 4 (1996), pp. 173–204.

36. Sternberg concludes his article, 'So my answer is categorical. No, by the standards to which it aspires, this performance will hardly qualify as competent. It has no poetics to offer, no theory of reading, no coherent enterprise or argument, no sense of history, cultural norms, and the difference they make to understanding, no eye for detail, not even linguistic expertise worthy of the Bible's art – only a cause that serves it ill and it ill serves in turn. If this is how women's liberation stands to the reader's, then politics and professionalism must never mix for the good of both' ('Biblical Poetics and Sexual Politics', p. 488).

37. *The Poetics of Biblical Narrative,* pp. 458–63.

38. 'Tipping the Balance', p. 211.

the narrative world of Genesis 34, however, Hamor and Shechem's proposal, coupled with Jacob's acquiescence, puts Dinah in a situation where her means of survival is to live with her rapist as a husband, a decision that is determined by the choices of men. This solution, as Gunn and Fewell admit, is ethically questionable.[39] Thus, in the end, navigating one's ethical way through interpretations of Genesis 34 proves to be just as difficult as reading one's way through the ethical ambiguities within the text itself. With the exception of Gunn and Fewell's reconstruction of an absent Dinah, this scholarly debate has become an argument over the merits or demerits of different men in the text. So what is a reader to do?

Reading for the Other:
Emmanuel Levinas and the Ethics of the Other in Genesis 34

I offer in closing not a conclusion or 'way out' of the ethical entanglements described above, for to do so would be to suggest that a methodology, system of reading or a particular interpretation is what puts Humpty Dumpty back together again. What I have suggested is that Genesis 34 demands a response from readers precisely because it is ethically complex and difficult. Genesis 34 has created the possibility for ethics. The story itself describes different and conflicted responses from characters to an act of violence – the rape of Dinah. With each response from the characters, the story gets more perplexing and convoluted. The complicated ethical environment that emerges is reflected in the conflicting and conflicted interpretations of Genesis 34, illustrated by the exchange between Sternberg's poetics and Gunn and Fewell's ethics of responsibility. Our interpretations and reflections have brought us to a point of undecidability. Thus, we have returned to Derrida's point that undecidability is the very possibility of ethics. The text of Genesis 34 and the texts of its interpreters have created an ethical occasion, an opening through which we might consider some ethical considerations. It is to ethics, Emmanuel Levinas' ethics of the Other, that we will now turn and face, if only for a brief moment.

Levinas' ethics of the Other, which raises a critical response to existential philosophy and the privileging of Being (*Dasein*), has been summarized well in other places.[40] In short, Levinas reverses the traditional order of ontology and

---

39. Gunn and Fewell are aware of this danger and suggest that their own reading runs the risk of being patriarchal in this respect, ironically, the very issue for which they fault Sternberg. In the end, they lay blame on the world of the story. 'Justice', they say, 'cannot be served in a society where men, men's rights, and men's honor control women's lives. To advocate a woman's marrying her rapist might itself seem to be a dangerous and androcentric advocacy. And so it would be if the story world offered other liberating alternatives' ('Tipping the Balance', p. 211). Such a conclusion is interesting, especially since Gunn and Fewell's reading strategy emphasizes the role of readers in shaping interpretation.

40. For useful introductions to Levinas see Colin Davis, *Levinas: An Introduction* (Notre Dame, IN: University of Notre Dame Press, 1996); Critchley, *The Ethics of Deconstruction*, esp. pp. 4–9; and Seán Hand, 'Introduction' to *The Levinas Reader* (ed. Seán Hand; Oxford: Basil Blackwell, 1989), pp. 1–8. Biblical scholars have also sought to work with Levinas when

ethics by proposing 'ethics as first philosophy'.[41] What is prior to Being is the experience of the Other, an infinite alterity, which beckons us to responsibility. This Other is not something that can be objectified or subsumed into the self or into a relation of the self. As Critchley suggests, 'Ethics, for Levinas, is critique; it is the critical *mise en question* of the liberty, spontaneity, and cognitive emprise of the ego that seeks to reduce all otherness to itself'.[42] Ethics, says Levinas, is 'the putting into question of my spontaneity by the presence of the Other'.[43] Thus, Levinas proposes that ethics is an encounter with the face of the Other. Face-to-face with the Other, I am confronted with an original alterity, something that refuses to be subordinated to my own self-understanding. Thus, it is alterity or otherness that compels me to respond ethically.

If we approach Genesis 34 with 'otherness' in mind, we can begin to see how one might hear the text ethically, in a Levinasian sense. The alterity or otherness experienced in Genesis 34 emerges through an encounter with the text's presentation. It is that which is excluded through the text's (or interpreters') objectification that opens a space for ethics, for an encounter with the face of the Other.[44] It is that which we consciously, unconsciously or subconsciously push to the margins that must be heard. In the text of Genesis 34 we are first confronted with Shechem's violent rape of Dinah. This horrible act demands a response from the reader and the characters in the story. As I have already suggested, the story quickly degenerates into a tale about the desires, negotiations and conflicts of men. Ironically, in a system where men decide and determine things, the most obvious issue of justice – the justice of a raped woman – gets lost among the different motivations, responses and arguments of men. The text excludes Dinah by narrating the story as a tale of male honor and vengeance. Her voice is silenced, she does not cry out, nor is her response narrated. All that the narrator communicates to the reader, intentionally or unintentionally, are the different male responses and attitudes to Shechem's crime. The reader stands appalled at this narratively constructed world, where the rape of one of Israel's daughters is turned into excessive violence, family dissension and,

---

considering the ethics of interpretation. See Danna Nolan Fewell and Gary A. Phillips, 'Ethics, Bible, Reading As If', *Semeia*, 77 (1997), pp. 4–10; Gary A. Phillips, 'Levinas', in A.K.M. Adam (ed.), *Handbook of Postmodern Biblical Interpretation* (St Louis: Chalice Press, 2000), pp. 154–59; Frank M. Yamada, 'Ethics', in A.K.M. Adam (ed.), *Handbook of Postmodern Biblical Interpretation* (St Louis: Chalice Press, 2000), pp. 76–84.

41. Emmanuel Levinas, *Totality and Infinity: An Essay on Exteriority* (trans. Alphonso Lingis; Pittsburgh: Duquesne University Press, 1969), esp. pp. 194–219; and Levinas, 'Ethics as First Philosophy', in Hand (ed.), *The Levinas Reader*, pp. 75–87.

42. Critchley, *The Ethics of Deconstruction*, p. 5.

43. As quoted in Critchley, *The Ethics of Deconstruction*, p. 5.

44. Levinas, when describing how ethics works within the language of ontology (e.g., 'ethics is X'), differentiates between the Saying and the Said. The Saying is that performative aspect of ethics in which one encounters the face-to-face relation to the Other. The Said is the objectification of truth and experience into propositions. Thus, the Saying is always betraying the representations of the Said, refusing to be reduced to its particulars. See Levinas, *Otherwise Than Being: Or Beyond Essence* (trans. Alphonso Lingis; Pittsburgh: Duquesne University Press, 1999), esp. pp. 5–8.

in the final account, the woman's desolation and isolation. The world becomes a strange place when a woman's defilement turns into the wars of men. Hence, it is Dinah's plight and her exclusion from justice that create the lacuna that opens up this text toward ethical possibility. The experience of the text and the otherness that it creates, like classical or Shakespearean tragedy, beckons us to consider a different world with a different story to tell – a script where ethical practice is not confined to violent retribution, ethnic suspicion or even silent acquiescence. In such a story, a woman's defilement will not become an opportunity for men (or interpreters) to establish their own cause or to vindicate their own honor. To the extent that our interpretations and world reflect the brokenness of Genesis 34, the Other will continue to beckon us and call us to responsibility and ethics.

ABRAHAM'S 'HERETICAL' IMPERATIVE:
A RESPONSE TO JACQUES DERRIDA

Mark G. Brett, Whitley College, University of Melbourne,
Victoria, Australia

In exploring the agenda of *The Meanings We Choose*, I will focus on Jacques
Derrida's reading of the Abraham story in *The Gift of Death*.[1] My argument will
suggest that Derrida has not opened up Genesis 22 in a way that a deconstructive
reading might have,[2] but his work does raise, indirectly, a significant question for
all biblical interpretation: to what extent does the practice of reading scripture
entail a conflict of responsibilities?

Beyond Ethics?

In developing my response to *The Gift of Death*, it will be necessary to provide a
brief summary of its main arguments, especially those concerning Søren Kierkegaard's *Fear and Trembling*,[3] since Derrida's work is shaped in conversation
with Kierkegaard. The key questions in this conversation are whether there are
forms of ethics or faith that can be purified of self-interest and the quest for
rewards. Derrida and Kierkegaard's interest in the biblical narrative stems from
their perception that Abraham's sacrifice of Isaac cannot be reduced to an
'economy of exchange' – to a system of material or metaphysical rewards. The
divine test is designed specifically to see whether Abraham can sacrifice his invest-
ment in the future.[4] Yet the extremity of this faith, according to Kierkegaard and

---

1.   Jacques Derrida, *The Gift of Death* (trans. D. Willis; Chicago: University of Chicago Press,
1995); *Donner la mort* (Paris: Galilée, 2nd edn, 1999).
2.   Derrida opposed the 'indispensable guardrail' of commentary to the 'opening up' of deconstructive reading in *Of Grammatology* (trans. G. Spivak; Baltimore: The Johns Hopkins University
Press, 1976), p. 158; *De la grammatologie* (Paris: Minuit, 1967), p. 227. As a strategy of reading,
deconstruction tends to open up tensions and aporia in a text – even within texts that biblical critics
may regard as belonging to a single literary source. For a secondary account, see especially Simon
Critchley, *The Ethics of Deconstruction: Derrida and Levinas* (Oxford: Basil Blackwell, 1992).
3.   Søren Kierkegaard, *Fear and Trembling, and Sickness unto Death* (trans. W. Lowrie; Princeton, NJ: Princeton University Press, 2nd edn, 1954).
4.   Kierkegaard includes metaphysical rewards as part of Abraham's test: 'If his faith had been
only for a future life, he surely would have cast everything away in order to hasten out of this
world to which he did not belong. But Abraham's faith was not of this sort' (*Fear and Trembling*,
p. 34). Derrida's critique of Matthew 6 shows how Christian faith can be seen as a calculation of

Derrida, moves beyond any conventional sense of ethics. Abraham did not give what the tragic hero has characteristically given – one's own life for the sake of others. If he had been the tragic hero, Derrida agrees with Kierkegaard, he would have sacrificed his own wishes for the sake of duty[5] – duty towards his family or some other group. He could, for example, have sacrificed *himself* in order to protect his family from the appalling demand of God. Genesis 22, on the other hand, does not describe this kind of hero or any kind of conventional responsibility. The narrative is concerned not with one who sacrifices desire for the sake of duty but with one who sacrifices both desire and duty as well. Abraham does not incite disciples to go and do likewise.[6] The kind of faith depicted in Genesis 22 does not establish a tradition or conventional ethic of responsibility. Hence, Derrida can conclude that 'there is no language, no reason, no generality or mediation to justify this ultimate responsibility'; it cannot be reduced to ethical generalities or 'transmitted from generation to generation'.[7]

Up to this point, Derrida's argument overlaps with Kierkegaard's, but Derrida goes one step further. *The Gift of Death* puts forward the sweeping claim that 'there is no responsibility without a dissident and inventive rupture with respect to tradition, authority, orthodoxy, rule, or doctrine'.[8] This claim, that *all* responsibility is essentially 'heretical',[9] is an unfortunate generalization, since it threatens to obscure the difference that heretical responsibility might make. Indeed, Derrida elsewhere maintains a distinction between different kinds of responsibility: we are encouraged to maintain the difference between an ethical form of duty and an *absolute* duty that competes with universalizable ethics. Thus arises the paradox that 'the absoluteness of duty, of responsibility, and of obligation certainly demands that one transgress ethical duty, although in betraying it one belongs to it, and at the same time, recognizes it'.[10] In other words, heretical responsibility may override ethical responsibility, but for the heresy to be transgressive we must accept that the ethical sphere has its own validity. Thus, unless Abraham loved his son and was compelled by the conventional ethical commitments of parenthood, there would have been nothing sacrificial about following the divine demand.[11] In short, not all forms of responsibility are essentially heretical, and one could therefore wonder why Derrida made the claim that the heretical imperative is universal.

heavenly rewards, but our discussion here will be restricted to Genesis. In response to Derrida's reading of Matthew 6, John Caputo draws attention to the 'uncalculating' aspects of vv. 25-34 (John Caputo, 'Instants, Secrets and Singularities: Dealing Death in Kierkegaard and Derrida', in Martin J. Matustík and Merold Westphal [eds.], *Kierkegaard in Post/Modernity* [Bloomington: Indiana University Press, 1995], pp. 216–38).

5.   *Fear and Trembling*, p. 88. Cf. Derrida's comments on Kant's *Critique of Practical Reason*, in *The Gift of Death*, p. 93; *Donner la mort*, p. 128.

6.   *Fear and Trembling*, p. 42.

7.   *The Gift of Death*, pp. 71, 80; *Donner la mort*, pp. 101, 112–13.

8.   *The Gift of Death*, p. 27; *Donner la mort*, p. 47.

9.   Derrida borrows the term from Patocka in *The Gift of Death*, pp. 1–34; *Donner la mort*, pp. 15–56.

10.   *The Gift of Death*, p. 66; *Donner la mort*, p. 95.

11.   Cf. *The Gift of Death*, p. 64; *Donner la mort*, p. 94.

Before exploring the implications of this critique, it is also worth noticing that the text of Genesis is potentially more complex than even Kierkegaard or Derrida imagines. They both focus on the sacrifice of Isaac in isolation from the surrounding literary context. If, however, we read Genesis 22 in parallel with Genesis 21, then a number of questions are raised about the relative significance of Abraham's two sons. In Genesis 21, we find another story of sacrifice: the expulsion of Ishmael. Why have the editors placed these two 'sacrifice' stories side by side?[12]

It is widely agreed that the Persian period is the most likely historical setting for the final editing of Genesis, but the implications of this consensus are disputed. Recent analyses of the final editing have come to diametrically opposed hypotheses as to what might have motivated the editors. Christopher Heard's work reads the narratives of Genesis 12–36 as amounting to a series of 'dis-elections' in which the marginal characters (in this case, Ishmael) are excluded from the covenant by an omniscient narrator who carries divine authority: the diselect can have an ambiguous character; whether they are given positive or negative construals is neither here nor there as far as the narrator is concerned, because their personal character is, in the end, almost completely irrelevant.[13] On this account, the narrator provides divine legitimation for the editors, who are to be seen as ethnocentric mediators of Persian imperial interests.[14]

Heard's proposal forms a useful contrast to my own work on Genesis, since our interpretative interests are so compatible: we both read the 'final' text as shaped by the politics of the Persian period, and we both explore the ambiguity of the narratives in ideological terms. My hypothesis, taking a cue from post-colonial studies, is that different traditions are juxtaposed by the editors in such a way as to undermine the dominant voice, including the voice of the omniscient narrator. The editors are thereby subtly resisting the ethnocentric ideology of the imperial governors. This interpretation suggests that Abraham's 'heretical' moment is part of an editorial *reductio ad absurdum* that, far from sacrificing ethics on the altar of the omniscient narrator, embodies a key focus of the Israelite legal traditions regarding concern for the stranger.[15] This will be the argument developed below.

---

12. In asking this question about what the editors 'intended', I do not mean to exclude the validity of other exegetical questions. Nor do I imagine that 'intention' is an unproblematic concept. In my recent work on Genesis, I position this question methodologically against the background of other interpretive interests, arguing that 'editorial intention' is a useful shorthand for speaking about the historical agency that may lie behind the making of the 'final' text. Mark G. Brett, *Genesis: Procreation and the Politics of Identity* (Old Testament Readings; London: Routledge, 2000), pp. 1–23 ('The Contest of Methods'). The discussion below in section 2 revises portions of this earlier work.

13. R. Christopher Heard, *Dynamics of Diselection: Ambiguity in Genesis 12–36 and Ethnic Boundaries in Post-Exilic Judah* (Semeia Studies, 39; Atlanta: Society of Biblical Literature, 2001), p. 183.

14. Heard, *Diselection*, p. 184.

15. See, e.g., Frank Crüsemann, '"You Know the Heart of a Stranger" (Exodus 23.9): A Recollection of the Torah in the Face of New Nationalism and Xenophobia', *Concilium*, 4 (1993), pp. 95-109.

Genesis 21–22 may well relate to the issues surrounding the divorces of foreign women prescribed by the imperial governors of the Persian period.[16] The prohibition of foreign marriages would have clarified the administration of property, since land tenure based on purity of birth could exclude competing land claims. As Kenneth Hoglund's work has demonstrated, what appears on the surface as theological discourse may actually reflect issues of social control. The property claims of the 'holy seed' who returned from Babylon, for example, could well have been made on the basis of genealogical connections designed to demonstrate prior ownership, and these claims would inevitably have come into conflict with those who had never gone into exile and who are represented as having intermarried with the 'people of the lands' (Ezra 9.1). My hypothesis is that this theological discourse in Ezra is a distortion of Priestly tradition.[17]

Heard's reading, on the other hand, sees Genesis as covertly supportive of the governors' attempts at social control. In the discussion of Genesis 21–22 that follows, I defend my reading against Heard's proposals, firstly on exegetical grounds. Even if, however, the exegetical options that we have proposed turn out to be equally defensible, there are ethical reasons why I have chosen to read Genesis as resistance literature. I will discuss these reasons with reference to Derrida's meditations on the biblical texts.

Characters, Narrators and Editors in Genesis 21–22

It is appropriate to begin this re-reading of Genesis by pointing out that both Derrida and Kierkegaard succumb to the claim of the divine speech in Genesis 22.2 that Isaac is Abraham's 'only son'.[18] In so doing, they allow the narrator of Genesis 22 to displace the narrator in Genesis 21. In 21.13, the divine voice makes clear that Abraham does have another son, Ishmael. Since it is through Ishmael that Arab Muslims trace their lineage back to Abraham, we may wonder whether Derrida has over-looked the deconstructive potential in his own question about the patriarch: 'But is this heretical and paradoxical knight of faith Jewish, Christian, or Judeo-Christian-Islamic?'[19] Ishmael's name is ironic: although his name means 'El hears'

16. This connection is made independently both by Heard, *Diselection*, and by Brett, *Genesis*, drawing in particular on the work of Kenneth Hoglund, *Achaemenid Imperial Administration in Syria-Palestine and the Missions of Ezra and Nehemiah* (SBLDS, 125; Atlanta: Scholars Press, 1992).

17. This hypothesis accords with Mary Douglas' reading of Priestly traditions in *In the Wilderness: The Doctrine of Defilement in the Book of Numbers* (Sheffield: JSOT Press, 1993); Mary Douglas, *Leviticus as Literature* (Oxford: Oxford University Press, 1999); cf. Rolf Rendtorff, 'The Ger in the Priestly Laws of the Pentateuch', in Mark G. Brett (ed.), *Ethnicity and the Bible* (Leiden: E.J. Brill, 1996), pp. 77–88.

18. *Fear and Trembling*, p. 35; *The Gift of Death*, p. 95; *Donner la mort*, p. 131.

19. *The Gift of Death*, p. 64, cf. pp. 69–70; *Donner la mort*, p. 95; cf. pp. 99–100. This potential is still overlooked in the second French edition of *Donner la mort*, which has some additional references to Ishmael and to Islamic tradition. Cf. Gil Anidjar, '"Once More, Once More": Derrida the Arab, the Jew', introduction to Jacques Derrida, *Acts of Religion* (New York: Routledge, 2002), p. 10 n. 29.

(16.11), it seems that the narrator's God of Genesis 22 does not hear Ishmael's voice; the divine discourse does not even recognize Ishmael's existence. Heard's argument also follows the tradition of ignoring the contradiction in the divine voice,[20] representing the narrator as advocating the dis-election of Ishmael.

Heard suggests that even if the ambiguities of the text allow us to read Ishmael more positively and Sarah more negatively, these differences of character are irrelevant to the overriding point that Ishmael is divinely destined for exclusion. The sight of Ishmael 'laughing' provokes Sarah to assert in Gen. 21.9-10 that Hagar's son will not share the inheritance of Isaac. Some translations have Ishmael 'mocking' in v. 9, rather than 'laughing', but not only is this negative connotation an unnecessary imposition on the Hebrew, it also obscures the verbal connection between the catalyst for Sarah's malice – Ishmael's laughter – and the name Isaac: יצחק means 'he laughs', and hence Isaac's name recalls the incongruity of his birth. Sarah's meditation in 21.6 elaborates the comic theme of childbirth at an impossibly old age: 'Laughter has God made for me; whoever hears will laugh at me'.[21] Even though Sarah has been incongruously blessed with a son in her old age, it seems that the question of inheritance is beyond a joke. It is possible to read her as ungraciously self-interested and Ishmael as an innocent victim, but Heard's argument is that these ambiguities are irrelevant from the divine point of view.

If Sarah's complaint to Abraham in Gen. 21.9-10 can be read in some sense as a political allegory of events in the Persian period, then it is noticeable that the editors have allowed Sarah's speech to render the driving away of a foreign woman purely in economic terms; from Sarah's point of view the issue is inheritance, and there is no theological veneer obscuring this fact. Hagar's and Ishmael's fate in Genesis 21, we may agree, stands for the dispossession of many others who have intermarried. But do the editors legitimate the politics of dispossession, or do they not? In attempting to answer this question, we need to consider some of the details of Genesis 22 as well.

The story in Genesis 22 defies domestication within any conventional code of obedience to divine command.[22] God's demand to sacrifice Isaac is a chilling display of exclusivist ideology, tortuously trying to cover up the reality of the one excluded. The staccato syntax at the beginning of v. 2 points to much larger problems of identity: 'Take now your son, your only one, whom you love, Isaac, and take yourself to the land of Moriah and offer him up as a burnt offering...' Classical Jewish commentary has explicated the problem here exquisitely by expanding the biblical narrative with a dialogue between Abraham and God:

20. Heard, *Diselection* (pp. 135–36), touches on the possibility of an unreliable narrator, without recognizing that this possibility actually undermines his overall thesis.

21. Here and elsewhere, translations from the Hebrew Bible are my own. For alternative translations of Gen. 21.6, see Heard, *Diselection*, p. 85.

22. While there are fragmentary clues that point to child sacrifice in early Israelite experience, such an act would be unthinkable to an audience in the Persian period. See Exod. 22.29 and contrast Exod. 34.19-20. The relevant traditions are discussed by Jon D. Levenson, *The Death and Resurrection of the Beloved Son: The Transformation of Child Sacrifice in Judaism and Christianity* (New Haven: Yale University Press, 1983); cf. Brevard S. Childs, *Biblical Theology of the Old and New Testaments* (Minneapolis: Fortress Press, 1993), pp. 325–36.

'Your son'. Abraham said to Him, 'I have two sons'. God said to him, 'Your only one'. He said, 'This one is the only one to his mother, and this one is the only one to *his* mother'. He said to him, 'Whom you love'. Abraham replied, 'I love them both'. He said to him, 'Isaac'.[23]

The rabbis could have avoided this complexity by resorting to the fact that Ishmael has already been sent away in the previous chapter, and in this sense he is already out of the picture, but the rabbinical retelling of the story has not availed itself of such an easy solution to the problem. There is indeed a profundity to this re-writing that surpasses much of the modern scholarship on the chapter. The sequence of identity descriptions in 22.2 has opened up all the old wounds: Abraham has two sons, not one, and indeed it is precisely God who emphasizes in the previous chapter that Ishmael is Abraham's seed (21.13). Moreover, whatever elements of self-interest may be reflected in Abraham's advocacy of Ishmael in 17.18 and in his negative response to Sarah's exclusivist concern with Isaac in 21.10-11, it is never suggested in the narrative that Ishmael is not loved by his father.

One wonders why the editors have allowed the divine voice to contradict itself within such a short stretch of text. It is surely no accident that the difference between 21.13 and 22.2 turns on the significance of Ishmael. God's positive reference to Ishmael as Abraham's seed in 21.13 is all too swiftly occluded by the divine command in 22.2. Moreover, the editors have chosen not to provide a simple identification of Isaac at the beginning of ch. 22 (along the lines, perhaps, of 'take your son, the son of the covenant'). Evidently the story in ch. 22 was not originally attached to the expulsion of Ishmael in ch. 21, and the editors may simply be preserving a traditional form of words in 22.2, but such a diachronic hypothesis does not exhaust the question of why the editors have structured chs 21–22 the way they have. The idea that they have juxtaposed the stories for purely antiquarian reasons, without regard to the narrative tensions they have created, seems implausible. Taken together with all the other evidence of subtle editing in Genesis,[24] the significance of ch. 22 may well be suggested by its literary context.

In both chapters, 21 and 22, Abraham is called on to sacrifice a son. In the first case, the sacrifice comes at Sarah's initiative, not God's; it is she who wants to cut off Ishmael's inheritance by sending him away, and Abraham sees Sarah's agency as evil (21.11). God's part in the drama is restricted to comforting Abraham, assuring him that Ishmael is his seed and that the slavewoman's son will become a great nation. In the second case, ch. 22, the sacrifice *is* God's initiative.

In both stories, Abraham's silence is excruciating. In this respect, Derrida's focus on the silence of the second story is incomplete. There is no dialogue at the sending away of Hagar and Ishmael, but the dramatic tension in Genesis 22 is what usually captures commentators: the journey is done, the wood is cut, the young servants are instructed to wait behind, the fire and the knife are in the father's hand, and in the most poignant detail of all, the wood is carried by Isaac, the intended

---

23. *Gen. Rab.* 55.7. See Brett, *Genesis*, pp. 73–78; Heard, *Diselection*, pp. 90–94.

24. See Brett, *Genesis,* which treats the whole of Genesis. Heard's work deals only with Genesis 12–26.

victim (22.6). Only after all these details are recorded is silence broken, and the dialogue is Isaac's initiative: 'My father... Here is the fire and the wood, but where is the sheep for the burnt offering?' Even at this point, the father can speak only by using a misleading metaphor: 'God will see to the sheep for the offering, my son'. There is no dialogue, then, as the altar is built, the wood is laid out, Isaac is bound, he is placed on the altar, and finally the father takes the knife in his hand as the narrator confirms the patriarch's intention – 'in order to slaughter his son' (22.10). There is no argument with God, as in the case of Sodom, and the narrator does not even portray Abraham's repulsion, as in his response to Sarah's directive to drive out the slavewoman and her son. There is neither an expression of anger against God nor a pious speech of acquiescence; just silent obedience.

At the highpoint of horror, a divine messenger calls out from the heavens, just as when Hagar was at breaking point in 21.16-17. In ch. 21, Hagar is sitting 'a bowshot' away from Ishmael, unwilling to watch her child die, and the heavenly messenger assures her that God has heard her son's weeping. The voice of the innocent victim is heard, as the reader would expect from the naming of 'Ishmael' earlier in 16.11. In ch. 22, on the other hand, Abraham has the instrument of death in his own hand; he could not have been closer to his son. This time when the divine messenger calls out from the heavens, it is not in response to the weeping of the innocent victim, the son near death. The narrator has chosen not to focus on any human despair, whether that of the parent or of the child. This cannot be because the Genesis narrator has no interest in emotions, since feelings of anger and despair are powerfully depicted elsewhere. But these emotions are simply not the focus in the immediate context. What is at issue, apparently, is solely the extraordinary obedience of Abraham:

> Because you have done this thing and have not held back your son, your only one, I will greatly bless you and will greatly multiply your seed, as the stars in the heavens and as the sand on the shore of the sea, and your seed shall seize the gate of their enemies. And all the nations of the earth will be blessed through your seed because you have listened to my voice. (22.16-18)

This divine speech, however, still leaves some significant questions hanging: why is it, for example, that the editors have retained the reference to Abraham's 'only' son – reiterating 22.1 – when the intertextual connections with the Ishmael narratives are so clear? Not only do we find the common themes linking ch. 22 to the expulsion of Hagar in ch. 21, but when Abraham names the place of Isaac's deliverance 'Yahweh Yireh' ('Yahweh sees') in 22.14, this naming scene parallels Hagar's naming of God in 16.13-14 ('El who sees me'). The theme of divine sight permeates both 16.13-14 and 22.14, linking Hagar's experience of divine perception with Abraham's. Moreover, in both chapters 16 and 22 the naming scenes are associated with the divine deliverance of Abraham's sons, as well as with divine promises. These connections make it all the more puzzling to find that Yahweh's promises in 22.16-18 mention Abraham's 'only' son. The divine speech seems to be written within the terms of reference defined by an exclusivist ideology, one which would regard Isaac as the only relevant son since he is the one circumscribed by the covenant in 17.18-22. Given the numerous allusions to Ishmael in ch. 22, however, this ideology need not be identified with the final editors' point of view. It is just as likely that the joining of chs 21 and 22 is designed to undermine such exclusivism.

The concluding verses of ch. 22 might seem relatively insignificant, and we may not expect them to contribute much to the discussion of the weighty issues of covenant theology. But Gen. 22.19-24 may indeed be related to the subversive editorial intentions evidenced by the juxtaposition of chs 21 and 22. There are at least two aspects worth noting: the reference to a journey in 22.19 and the genealogical notes in 22.20-24. After the dramatic test of faith in ch. 22, v. 19 says that Abraham returns to Beersheba, the very place where, according to 21.14, the divine promise concerning Ishmael was delivered to his mother Hagar. Historicist scholarship may treat this as the accidental collocation of originally separate traditions, but for the careful reader of the final form, this geographical irony is simply too great to dismiss; Beersheba is the site where God promised that Abraham's other son would become a great nation. Ishmael is the son confirmed by God as the seed of Abraham (21.13), and Ishmael is the son whom Abraham himself circumcised, marking him with the sign of the covenant (17.23-27). As the son of an Egyptian, he is the product of a foreign marriage, but the editors have planted numerous clues to suggest that this is no impediment to divine blessing.

The second aspect of 22.19-24 worth noting is that the genealogical details provide the identity of a certain Rebekah, who is destined in ch. 24 to become Isaac's wife. Rebekah, we discover here for the first time, is the granddaughter of Abraham's brother Nahor. In line with the exclusivist ideology of the divine speeches in ch. 22, the marriage of Isaac and Rebekah is foreshadowed as endogamous.[25] In short, the son explicitly circumscribed by the covenant, Isaac, is associated already in ch. 22 with endogamy. Yet 22.19 implies that Isaac lives with his father in Beersheba, the very place where Abraham's son through an exogamous marriage received a divine promise. In short, the names of Hagar and Ishmael are mentioned nowhere in ch. 22, but the traces of their presence are everywhere. The reader is faced with a choice: either we hear their voices, or we read with the exclusivist ideology of ch. 22 and ignore them. The editors of Genesis, it seems, have provided several reasons for hearing them.

In the historical setting of the Persian period, the intertextual connections between chs 21 and 22 would have had quite clear social implications. The model of holiness promoted by the imperial governors suggested that all foreign women should be sent away, including Egyptians (Ezra 9.1-2). The expulsion of Hagar and her son can, in this sense, be read as one paradigm of holiness. Yet, as we have seen, a careful reading of the final form of Genesis suggests that the editors thought

25. For the purposes of this discussion, 'endogamous' describes marriage within a particular kinship group, while 'exogamous' refers to marriage outside this kinship group. Note, however, that Isaac's marriage to Rebekah has been undermined in advance by the divine command in Gen. 12.1, which would stand against endogamous marriage, and by the lack of divine blessing on the wooing of Rebekah in Genesis 24. See Brett, *Genesis*, pp. 49–51, and cf. Heard, *Diselection*, pp. 28–29, who once again notes the narrator's ambiguity without recognizing that this weakens his overall argument.

otherwise. While not explicitly attacking the ideology of endogamy, they arranged the narratives such that Hagar and Ishmael emerge equally as recipients of divine grace, and exogamous marriages are thereby covertly defended. The exclusivist ideology of the divine speeches in ch. 22 can pass without question only if one is willing to deny the reality of Ishmael's existence and his status as Abraham's son. In effect, the narrow conception of covenant is not just dishonest; it is blind to the wider dimensions of divine action in the world. The post-exilic reader of Genesis is invited not to succumb to the paradigm of holiness suggested by Ezra 9.1-2.

Nevertheless, the detail and the drama of Genesis 22 cannot simply be dismissed as exclusivist ideology. There is a theological profundity in the chapter that deserves further reflection. By this point in the narrative, we should remember, Isaac has become the focus of all Abraham's hopes for blessing and fame (21.12). If a test of faith is to be a test of self-interest, it will need to address the son who represents that self-interest, Isaac. The editors seem to have used the narrative of Genesis 22, even with its exclusivist ideology, to address the most rigorous question for piety: will Abraham follow God's instructions only because the rewards of progeny and land are so desirable, or is God intrinsically worthy of obedience? The question is never framed in such philosophically abstract terms, but by putting the life of Isaac at risk, the narrative has indeed evoked precisely this issue (cf. the parallel issue in Job 1.9).

In effect, the editors have placed two tests of faith side by side in Genesis 21 and 22. The first, the sacrifice of Hagar and Ishmael, is the kind of test proposed by the imperial governors of the Persian period. Yet this test does not actually touch the core issue of self-interest: if the quest for purity is simply a means to gain divine rewards, then God has been honored not as intrinsically worthy but only as the giver of desirable goods. In Derrida's terms, the economy of exchange is still firmly in place. Genesis 22, on the other hand, implies that the only true test for disinterested piety would be to sacrifice Isaac – the medium through which all the future gifts of progeny and land would be grasped. Given the system of rewards and punishments outlined elsewhere in legal traditions of Israel (e.g., in Deuteronomy 28), it is appropriate that Abraham's supreme test of faith should be contrary to the law. If his obedience to God was simply meant to foreshadow legal obedience, then once again the issue of self-interest would not have been addressed: since keeping the law is also a means to acquiring divine blessings, no test of legal obedience could demonstrate that Abraham was capable of disinterested piety. Keeping the law does not entail the conviction that God is intrinsically worthy of obedience. While none of this is stated explicitly in the book of Genesis, there is enough evidence to suggest that the editors have undermined Ezra's test of piety (which represents purity in marriage as obedience to the law) by proposing a more profound theological test in the narrative of Genesis 22.

The sacrifice of Isaac presents a model of faith that is completely removed from any economy of exchange. On this point we can follow Kierkegaard and Derrida. It discloses the superficiality of more conventional sacrifices, yet it is a hard act to follow, or perhaps, an impossible act to follow. Hence, it can be understood as a *reductio ad absurdum* in literary form. In socio-political terms, it unmasks the strategy of social control that the imperial governors have dressed up in theological discourse. The narrative is not designed as a model of responsibility that can be imitated and generalized. The point of the literary strategy, however, is not to empty ethics of any value; it is to provoke a reevaluation of what might count as ethics.

As it turns out, although Ezra represents the expulsion of an Egyptian woman like Hagar as a mark of holiness, the law in Deut. 23.7-8 allows for the cultic inclusion of Egyptians only three generations after Moses. In narrative terms, this exclusion expired long before the Persian period. Moreover, Mary Douglas and Rolf Rendtorff have shown how Priestly tradition opposes the ethnocentrism of Ezra-Nehemiah.[26] In short, we have enough evidence to suggest that the governors of the Persian period distort the law as a means of imperial social control. The heretical sacrifice of Isaac has the heuristic function of provoking an ethical response that would question the motivation of dispossessing foreign women. And thus responsibility toward foreign wives returns as a viable ethic, and indeed, one that stands firmly within the legal traditions of Israel: 'You shall not wrong or oppress an alien, for you were aliens in Egypt' (Exod. 22.21).

Re-interpreting Derrida's Paradox

Kierkegaard and Derrida were not engaged, of course, in exegesis (given his attitude to biblical scholars, Kierkegaard could well have been offended at the very thought). We may concede to them that they have shed light on the most pure form of a gift. But does it follow that Abraham's extreme example can lead to generalizing conclusions, for example, that authentic faith lies beyond ethics (Kierkegaard) or that all responsibility is essentially heretical (Derrida)?

Derrida himself provides an edifying critique of Kierkegaard, building on the work of Emmanuel Levinas. Levinas objected to Kierkegaard's assumption that ethics must be understood in terms of universalizable abstractness, and argued on the contrary that ethics begins in a respect for 'absolute singularity'.[27] Levinas says, for example, that 'Ethics as the conscience of a responsibility towards the other... does not lose one in the generality; far from it, it singularizes, it posits one as a unique individual'.[28] His stress on the innate otherness of every human being applies equally to God, and in this sense, Kierkegaard's rigid opposition between the ethical and the religious can be deconstructed.[29]

But whether we side with Kierkegaard or with Levinas, it is intriguing to notice the paradoxical tension in Derrida's own arguments concerning the universalizing and particularizing forms of ethics. *The Gift of Death* distinguishes between the local concerns and duties of everyday life, on the one hand, and an equally valid concern for universality, on the other. What makes the sacrifice of Isaac most offensive is not so much the fact of sacrifice as such, but the fact that the narrative

---

26. See the literature cited in n. 17 above.

27. *The Gift of Death*, p. 84; *Donner la mort*, p. 117.

28. *The Gift of Death*, p. 78, citing Emmanuel Levinas, *Noms propres* (Montpellier: Fata Morgana, 1976), p. 113.

29. *The Gift of Death*, p. 84; *Donner la mort*, p. 117,

concerns the sacrifice of Abraham's own. In effect, Derrida also reads Genesis 22 as a provocation to reformulate ethics. And the reformulation is startling. Sacrifice, far from being the exception, 'is the most common event in the world'.[30] We do not recognize its ubiquity, because we are attuned to local – rather than universal – forms of duty and ethics. When, for example, justice is habitually domesticated within nationalist ideologies, we fail to see its most radical demands. Thus, Derrida can write:

> By preferring my work, simply by giving it my time and attention, by preferring my activity as a citizen or as a professorial and professional philosopher, writing and speaking here in a public language, French in my case, I am perhaps fulfilling my duty. But I am sacrificing and betraying at every moment all my other obliga-tions: my obligations to the other others whom I know or don't know, the billions of my fellows... who are dying of starvation or sickness... every one being sacri-ficed to every one else in this land of Moriah that is our habitat every second of every day.[31]

It is not that authentic religious faith always transgresses ethical universals, as Kierkegaard argues; for Derrida, the more significant point is that *local* forms of ethics (duties toward family and nation, etc.) always transgress *universal* forms of ethics (the concern for those 'other others'). He suggests that '[a]s soon as I enter into a relation with the other, with the gaze, look, request, love, command, or call of the other, I know that I can respond only by sacrificing ethics, that is, by sacri-ficing whatever obliges me to also respond, in the same way, in the same instant, to all the others'.[32] For this claim to be meaningful, he cannot be suggesting that the development of local relationships means the death of ethics as such; he also acknowledges that the duties of family and nation have their own ethical validity. If these duties did not have this validity, then there would be no sacrifice. Derrida's paradox therefore seems to leave us on the horns of a dilemma: either we address our local forms of obligation and duty, in which case we act heretically in respect of universal obligations, or we address the *other* others, beyond our local forms of commitment, in which case we act heretically in respect of our local duties.

Against this background, we might be tempted to accept Derrida's claim that all responsibility can be seen as 'heretical' – not because, as he says in a moment of modernism, 'there is no responsibility without a dissident and inventive rupture with respect to tradition',[33] but because the 'heretical' imperative arises in the tension *between* local and universal commitments, both of which are defined by tradition.[34] Biblical tradition, for example, affirms both particular and universal

---

30. *The Gift of Death*, p. 85; *Donner la mort*, p. 19.

31. *The Gift of Death*, p. 69; *Donner la mort*, pp. 98–99.

32. *The Gift of Death*, p. 68; *Donner la mort*, p. 98.

33. *The Gift of Death*, p. 27; *Donner la mort*, p. 47.

34. This tension cannot be resolved by formal logic, but in virtue ethics it has characteristically been resolved by accounts of practical reasoning. Among the exponents of virtue theory, Alasdair MacIntyre has highlighted the conflict, within a single tradition, of good with good. See, e.g., *After Virtue* (London: Gerald Duckworth, 1981), ch. 12. MacIntyre describes the conflict of good with good in terms of Sophoclean 'tragedy', rather than 'heresy'.

commitments. On my reading of Genesis, the editors have structured their material in ways that reflect precisely this tension. The first divine promise to Abram moves between the promise of a 'great nation' and a blessing to 'all the families of the earth' (Gen. 12.2). And even Gen. 22.18 re-affirms a blessing to 'all the nations of the earth'. The Hagar and Ishmael traditions can be read as one of many examples of how the ethnocentric pole is transgressed by the editors' concern for the 'other others'.

Transposing this tension into the contemporary world of biblical interpretation, I could perhaps reformulate Derrida's paragraph cited above: by preferring my version of biblical scholarship, simply by giving it my time and attention, by preferring my activity as a citizen or as a professional biblical critic, writing and speaking here in a particular language, English in my case, I am perhaps fulfilling my duty. But I am sacrificing and betraying at every moment all my other obligations: my obligations to the other others whom I know or don't know, each one being sacrificed in this land of Moriah that is our habitat every second of every day.

Our conflict of responsibilities is partly an implication of being finite human beings, and in this respect, there is nothing peculiar about being biblical scholars. Those of us who read and teach texts, rather than say, work for an aid organization, have already made a certain kind of choice. Those of us who work for an aid organization, in one relief or development project and not another, have equally sacrificed the 'other others'.

There are also choices that arise specifically within the profession of biblical studies. Post-colonial theories have, for example, raised questions about how different voices are included or excluded by the institutional structures of power that shape our work. We may see ourselves as accountable to many scholars within our discipline, but how do we see accountability to those 'other others' on the edge of our disciplinary structures, e.g., to colleagues in the Third World, or to the poor and marginalized whose lives are shaped, at least in part, by the Bible?[35]

I have argued elsewhere[36] that there are good reasons within my own local context to provide a reading of Genesis that sees it as a challenge to ethnocentrism, e.g., in debates about asylum seekers and inter-religious dialogue. In the current political climate in Australia, in which asylum seekers from Muslim countries are subject to paranoid strategies of exclusion, there are especially good reasons not to see Ishmael as subject to divine dis-election. This is clearly not just a local issue,

---

35. See, e.g., Fernando Segovia and Mary Ann Tolbert (eds.), *Reading from This Place: Social Location and Biblical Interpretation in Global Perspective* (Minneapolis: Fortress Press, 1996); Fernando Segovia, 'Racial and Ethnic Minorities in Biblical Studies', in Mark G. Brett (ed.), *Ethnicity and the Bible*, pp. 468–92; Gerald West, *The Academy of the Poor: Towards a Dialogical Reading of the Bible* (Sheffield: Sheffield Academic Press, 1999); Steve Charleston, 'The Old Testament of Native America', in Susan Brooks Thistlethwaite and Mary Potter Engel (eds.), *Lift Every Voice: Constructing Christian Theologies from the Underside* (San Francisco: HarperCollins, 1990), pp. 49–61; Brett, 'Canto Ergo Sum: Indigenous Peoples and Postcolonial Theology', *Pacifica* 16 (2003), pp. 247–56.

36. Brett, 'Self-criticism, Cretan Liars and the Sly Redactors of Genesis', in Ingrid Kitzberger (ed.), *Autobiographical Biblical Criticism: Between Text and Self* (Leiden: DEO, 2002), pp. 114–32.

and, for example, some aspects of my work have been drawn in a Christian-Muslim dialogue project in Lebanon.[37] Given the range of possible interpretations that are equally defensible in cognitive terms, I have chosen a reading of Genesis that provides hermeneutical possibilities in the present.

There are also autobiographical reasons lying behind my choices,[38] and my Protestant dispositions led me to envisage the possibility that such an emancipatory interpretation of Genesis could have an impact on communities for whom the Bible still carries some weight. An interpretation such as Heard's, on the other hand, seems to deprive Genesis of political potential. If it was clearly the best account of all the relevant evidence, I might be compelled to adopt it on grounds of intellectual integrity (noting that what counts as 'integrity' is culturally specific). For the reasons outlined above, I do not feel compelled to adopt it. Biblical interpreters are, however, always faced with – or implicated in – a constant series of ethical choices, and Derrida has demonstrated that there is no easy formula for resolving our competing responsibilities.

In any conflict of interpretations – not just in cases where the options turn on finely balanced probabilities – our moral responsibilities are necessarily engaged. Yet our responsibilities are not always commensurable, and, in particular, the tension between local and global ethics cannot be resolved by reference to logical calculations. We are never able to fulfill all our obligations, yet our finitude does not dictate that we need only attend to the most convenient and local responsibilities. Genesis 22 does not present us with such cheap grace.

---

37. See Mazhar Mallouhi *et al.* (eds.), *The Beginnings of the World and Humanity: A Contemporary Study in Genesis* [in Arabic] (Beirut, Lebanon: Dar Al Jil, 2001), pp.149–367.
38. The relevance of these autobiographical reasons is discussed in Brett, 'Self-criticism'.

CHOOSING BETWEEN TWOS:
APOCALYPTIC HERMENEUTICS IN SCIENCE FICTION, THE
RADICAL RIGHT AND RECENT HISTORICAL JESUS SCHOLARSHIP

Jeffrey L. Staley, Seattle University, Washington, USA

This essay explores the dualistic hermeneutics and ethics of ancient Jewish and Christian apocalyptic as it is found in three diverse contemporary contexts: science fiction films, the radical Christian Right and recent historical Jesus scholarship as typified by the Jesus Seminar.[1] I will argue that these three very different contemporary responses to ancient biblical apocalyptic have adopted its dualistic perspective on the world. This is due, in part, to a shared, determinate understanding of ancient apocalyptic that never significantly challenges apocalyptic's hermeneutical and ethical underpinnings. Apocalyptic, for them, seems to preclude indeterminacy.

In view of the terrorist attacks of September 11 and recent US 'Homeland Security' responses, is it possible for professional interpreters of scripture to find ways of complicating these canonical apocalyptic texts in ethically and hermeneutically responsible ways? Can we re-vision them as indeterminate? Or are there always only two ways, two choices, only determinate meanings for interpreters of biblical apocalyptic? And what about the church's theological engagement with biblical apocalyptic? Do we tend to read the Bible 'apocalyptically', operating with a concept of scriptural authority that is 'apocalyptic' and 'determinate' and requires a commensurate reading approach? Or can a concept of scriptural authority function within a certain range of meanings, accommodating different reading strategies?

An Apocabiography

I was born just a few years after the end of World War II into a devout Plymouth Brethren family of itinerant fundamentalist preachers and missionaries. The Plymouth Brethren (non)denomination began in England in the 1830s when revivals were sweeping Great Britain with apocalyptic hopes, evangelical fervor and yearnings for Christian unity. John Nelson Darby was its patron saint (a 'born again' Irish Anglican), and he, along with later 'Brethren', disseminated the peculiar

---

1.   An earlier version of this essay entitled 'Brains and Pens, Brawn and Bodies: Contemporary North American Appropriations of Christian Millennialism', was presented as part of the Distinguished Speakers Lecture Series, January 30, 2000, at the Centre for Studies in Religion and Society, University of Victoria, Canada.

eschatology of dispen(sen)sationalism and its pretribulational rapture to Canada, the United States and Europe. These beliefs gained a particularly firm hold in the hearts of North American Protestants through the publication of the Scofield Reference Bible in 1909.[2]

The doctrine of a pretribulational rapture was so deeply ingrained in my soul that as a child I can remember occasionally waking up in the morning to an unearthly silence in my house and being terrified that Jesus had come in the night. Had he taken my parents and siblings to heaven and left me behind (Mt. 24.40-41; cf. 1 Thess. 4.17; Dan. 7.25; Rev. 13.5)? In those brief anxious moments I was convinced that I was an orphan, left alone to face the awfulness of the end-time catastrophes summarized in sermons on Mark 13. No amount of fervent praying could dislodge this paralyzing fear and convincingly confirm for me that I was 'on the right side' of the end-time cosmic battle. Thankfully, my parents' or siblings' voices, or the soft shuffle of feet heading to the bathroom, always broke through the eerie morning silence, reassuring me that the last trump had not yet sounded.

In June of 1967, just after I finished my sophomore year of high school, I could be found huddled over my little transistor radio listening to the hourly updates of the Arab-Israeli Six Day War, wondering if the Rapture of the church would occur by the end of the week. My family and I waited breathlessly, on kitchen stools, as the Israelis captured the old city of Jerusalem and prayed at the Wailing Wall. Surely the rebuilding of the Jewish temple could be only a few years down the road! Would the wildly popular US (Roman Catholic) president, John F. Kennedy, with his mortal head wound miraculously healed (Rev. 13.12), reappear as the Antichrist and stride into the Jerusalem temple to proclaim himself to be God (2 Thess. 2.3-4)?[3] Rumors were circulating in fundamentalist Christian circles that Kennedy's body had been whisked away from Dallas Parkland Hospital in November, 1963, and had been cryogenically preserved, awaiting the day when medical technology would be able to heal his assassin's fatal bullet wound. Perhaps the day for Kennedy's resuscitation had finally arrived, now, three and a half years after his shocking death.

During that momentous week in June of 1967, my mother recalled her evangelist father sitting in their Kansas City living room in May 1948, transfixed by other radio reports – of the United Nations' vote to partition Palestine. Ezekiel's prophecy of the dry bones (Ezek. 37) was being fulfilled in his own lifetime. My grandfather, along with countless other interpreters of biblical prophecy, firmly believed that Jesus would come again within a generation of that 1948 date. (So how many years *is* a generation? Twenty years? Thirty years?)

---

2.   Timothy P. Weber, *Living in the Shadow of the Second Coming: American Premillennialism, 1875–1982* (Chicago: University of Chicago Press, 1983), pp. 16–17, 21–22; see also James M. Efird, *End-Times: Rapture, Antichrist, Millennium* (Nashville: Abingdon Press, 1986), pp. 17–37; and David Van Biema, 'The End: How it Got that Way', *Time Magazine* (July 1, 2002), pp. 46–47.

3.   For example, see http://www.raptureme.com/rr-antichrist.html (accessed June 28, 2002).

It was no mere coincidence that in 1970, three years after the Six Day Arab–Israeli War and twenty-two years after Israel's independence, Hal Lindsey's multimillion best seller, *The Late Great Planet Earth*,[4] popularized Darby's apocalyptic theories for the next generation of Bible novices and religious enthusiasts. In the summer of 1971, with Larry Norman's popular Christian rock lament, 'I Wish We'd All Been Ready', and his call to arms, 'Right Here in America', playing over and over in my head, I devoured Lindsey's sensationalist writings and transposed them into a study guide on the book of Revelation for fireside Christian camp devotionals. But contrary to Lindsey's whimsies, the seventies passed without Armageddon's onslaught.

Fifteen years later I had finished a PhD in New Testament, joined the United Presbyterian Church and begun a university teaching career. I thought I had left my adolescent apocalyptic imagination in the dust of Ezekiel's mythic valley. But in fact only a fragment of it lay buried there. As I grow older I find myself forming new friends from the mounds of Ezekiel's bleached bones. Our pasts never quite leave us. Like Ezekiel's bizarre vision, apocalyptic imagery has reappeared in mainstream American conversation and life, reconfiguring and reconstituting its bony frame in imaginative and surprising ways.

Apocalyptic rhetoric dominated the international politics of 'Desert Storm' in the early 1990s, the Y2K scare of 1999, and has reached a fever pitch in our present, patriotic post-September 11 'War on Terrorism'.[5] Apocalyptic metaphors have invigorated recent Hollywood blockbusters like *The Matrix*[6] and *Independence Day*, and have resurfaced in New Testament scholars' reassessments of the Jesus tradition.[7] Having seen US popular culture yank the beasts of apocalyptic dualism out of the primordial seas of Near Eastern mythology one more time, biblical interpreters are being forced to confront its political rhetoric and wild-eyed hermeneutics with renewed vigor. In light of September 11, it has become imperative that biblical scholars become ethically sensitive to ways in which these dualisms get translated into the popular political rhetoric of 'us against them', and the blameless and good against the cowardly and evil 'other'. Are there ways to interpret ancient apocalyptic narratives without giving in to the

---

4. (Grand Rapids: Zondervan, 1970). Like McDonald's Hamburgers' neon marquees, each new printing proudly listed how many copies had been gobbled up by a hungry public. See Weber, *Living in the Shadow of the Second Coming*, pp. 211–17.

5. See for example, Nancy Gibbs, 'Apocalypse Now', *Time Magazine* (July 1, 2002), pp. 40–48.

6. Two sequels to the immensely popular *The Matrix* are set for release in 2003 (http://keanuweb.com/credits/movie.matrix2.html, accessed June 28, 2002; and http://www.norcalmovies.com/TheMatrix2/, accessed June 28, 2002).

7. For example, see John P. Meier, *A Marginal Jew: Rethinking the Historical Jesus*, vol. 2: *Mentor, Message, and Miracles* (New York: Doubleday, 1994); N.T. Wright, *Jesus and the Victory of God*, vol. 2: *Christian Origins and the Question of God* (Minneapolis: Fortress Press, 1997); Bart D. Ehrman, *Jesus: Apocalyptic Prophet of the New Millennium* (New York: Oxford University Press, 1999); Marcus J. Borg and N.T. Wright, *The Meaning of Jesus: Two Visions* (San Francisco: Harper, 2000); and Dale C. Allison and Robert J. Miller (eds.), *The Apocalyptic Jesus: A Debate* (Santa Rosa, CA: Polebridge, 2001).

binary oppositions that are so easily assimilated by nationalism and theological dogmatism? Biblical interpreters must address this question if they hope to have a voice in contemporary US politics and the ideological battles over globalization and postcolonialism.[8]

Images of Ancient Apocalyptic Dualism in
Contemporary North American Culture

My own interest in ancient Jewish and Christian apocalyptic traditions is thus framed by personal and professional issues, by ethical and hermeneutical questions. It arises out of my own autobiographical roots in Christian apocalyptic sectarianism, and it continues to be challenged by the resurgence of dualistic apocalyptic rhetoric in popular culture and US politics. By analyzing how biblical scholars have appropriated (or failed to appropriate) this tradition over the past century, I believe that we may find ways to evaluate critically its dualisms for contemporary American culture and Christian communities.

In order to grasp the pervasiveness of apocalyptic dualism in contemporary North American culture and in order to construct a framework for reading beyond that ideology, I propose the following two theses. The first is that the apocalyptic dualisms of late twentieth-century, secular North American culture are found most explicitly in science fiction films and the militant Radical Right[9] and reflect two recurring responses to an ancient apocalyptic phenomenon. The second is that liberal Protestant (and more recently, liberal Roman Catholic) reconstructions of Jesus – regardless of their critical stance to the biblical tradition – stand as dualistic antidotes to the popular, eschatological hopes of secular North American culture and science fiction, fundamentalist Protestantism, and the militant Radical Right.

To a certain extent, my understanding of the role of apocalyptic dualism in twentieth-century North American culture is rooted in a provocative quote from John Dominic Crossan's book, *Jesus: A Revolutionary Biography*.[10] Crossan writes: 'Apocalypticism, which is usually called millennialism or millenarianism within the wider scope of comparative anthropology, comes in two main types, one stemming ... from the Retainers, who support the Governors with their brains and pens; and the other from the Peasants, who support it with their brawn and bodies'.[11] To put my first thesis in Crossan's words, I believe science fiction as a literary genre reflects the 'brain and pen' dualisms of contemporary apocalyptic, while militant Radical Right groups and such represent a 'brawn and bodies' response to contemporary expressions of apocalyptic dualism.

---

8.   For example, see R. Alan Culpepper, *The Gospel and Letters of John* (Nashville: Abingdon Press, 1998), pp. 299–305.

9.   Robert Jewett describes their ideology as a 'Captain America Complex'. See Jewett, *The Captain America Complex* (Santa Fe, NM: Bear, 1984).

10. (San Francisco: HarperSanFrancisco, 1994).

11. *Jesus: A Revolutionary Biography*, p. 40.

Ancient Apocalyptic Dualism, Contemporary
Science Fiction and the Radical Right

Frederick Kreuziger's 1982 monograph, *Apocalypse and Science Fiction: A Dialectic of Religious and Secular Soteriologies*,[12] has been largely overlooked by scholars of biblical apocalyptic.[13] But it is a provocative book, and one of the earliest attempts to argue that there is a correspondence between ancient apocalyptic views of salvation and modern science fiction. Kreuziger believed that if scholars of religion studied the social and literary origins of science fiction, they would be better able to contextualize ancient apocalyptic socially, theologically and literarily. Although his attempt to draw a clear line of connection between the ancient genre of apocalyptic and the modern genre of science fiction is perhaps overstated, there is a provocative, postmodern edge to the way he juxtaposes the ancient literary genre with a contemporary one.

Kreuziger has surprisingly little to say about science fiction films,[14] but within a few years a number of scholars were connecting the two apocalyptic media forms. One of the earliest scholars to look at the relationship between science fiction films and ancient apocalyptic was Ron Large. In an insightful essay entitled 'American Apocalyptic',[15] Large used James Cameron's vastly popular *Terminator* movies[16] to show how apocalyptic dualism carried over into science fiction and interpenetrated American politics. Before long, a number of writers – both secular and religious – joined in the conversation.[17] These scholars have opened up an entirely new way of thinking about how ancient Jewish and Christian apocalyptic continues to influence North American culture. Taken out of an explicitly Christian context, the secularization of dualistic apocalyptic motifs and ideology, along with apocalyptic's fantastic visions and graphic violence, have found fertile grounds for growth in Hollywood and popular culture.

---

12. (AARAS 40; Chico, CA: Scholars Press, 1982).

13. Surprisingly, Kreuziger's name is not found in the index of Joel W. Martin and Conrad E. Ostwalt Jr (eds.), *Screening the Sacred: Religion, Myth, and Ideology in Popular American Film* (Boulder, CO: Westview, 1995) or in the index of George Aichele and Richard Walsh (eds.), *Screening Scripture: Intertextual Connections Between Scripture and Film* (Harrisburg, PA: Trinity Press International, 2002), despite the fact that both books draw connections between science fiction films and biblical apocalyptic.

14. Kreuziger, *Apocalypse and Science Fiction*, pp. 84, 193, 213, 215.

15. Ron Large, 'American Apocalyptic', *The Fourth R*, 4 (1991), pp. 1–8.

16. *Terminator 3* is set for release in July 2003. (http://www.upcomingmovies.com/terminator3.html. Accessed June 29, 2002).

17. See especially, Conrad E. Ostwalt Jr, 'Hollywood and Armageddon: Apocalyptic Themes in Recent Cinematic Presentation', in *Screening the Sacred*, pp. 55–63; Kevin Pask, 'Cyborg Economics: Desire and Labor in the *Terminator* Films', in Richard Dellamora (ed.), *Postmodern Apocalypse: Theory and Cultural Practice at the End* (Philadelphia: University of Pennsylvania Press, 1995), pp. 182–98; and Richard Walsh, 'On Finding a Non-American Revelation: *End of Days* and the Book of Revelation', in *Screening Scripture*, pp. 1–23.

Ancient Apocalyptic Dualism

Although it is little known outside the realm of biblical scholarship and was not part of Kreuziger's or Large's analysis,[18] the book of *1 Enoch* is one of the most useful apocalyptic texts for drawing comparisons between the ancient dualistic genre and modern science fiction. This book, which scholars have divided into five distinctive parts, was most likely the creation of 'brain and pen' scribes of Qumran, and was probably written over a period of about two hundred years, from around 150 BCE down to 50 CE.[19] The literary connections between ancient apocalyptic and modern science fiction can be seen most easily in Book One (*1 En*. 1–36) and Book Four (*1 En*. 83–90). Book One, 'The Book of Watchers', begins with Enoch's prophecy of a future cataclysmic judgment and is followed by a narrative section that describes the fall of the angels or 'watchers'. As a result of angels cohabiting with human women, catastrophic evil enters the world through a cosmic invasion of fallen angels or 'watchers' (cf. Gen. 6.1-5). Besides teaching humans immoral acts, these creatures teach humanity all forms of technology. For example, they instruct humans in the art of making weapons, mining, writing and in the crafts related to beautifying the body – jewelry, cosmetics and dyes. They also teach humans the natural 'sciences', that is, the skills necessary for healing: medicinal herbs, magical spells and astronomy (*1 En*. 8; see also 65 and 69.1-11).

For Enoch, then, 'science' and technology enter our world through the reckless misuse of otherworldly power. And although Enoch himself will use these same scientific and technical skills to write and to navigate through the cosmos, science and technology are clearly not benign powers. Only the wisest can use them with impunity (cf. Rev. 18.11-24). As a result of the evil that invaded the earth, Enoch was told to warn the fallen watchers of the judgment that would soon befall them (*1 En*. 12–13). He does this by taking tours of the judgment places above, within and beyond the edges of the earth (*1 En*. 14–21).

The 'Book of Watchers' by itself, apart from the later parts of *1 Enoch*, plays a central role in subsequent developments of Jewish and Christian apocalyptic. And its significance for the development of science fiction should not be overlooked. First, the invasion of the earth by hostile outside forces – an invasion that alters the course of humanity – is one of the most common motifs in science fiction today. Second, the destructive potential of science and technology is a dominant theme in our everyday lives, as well as in science fiction. The Y2K crisis is the most obvious recent example of this, along with our fears of germ warfare and a nuclear holocaust. These three crises are of our own making, and all three have had worldwide destructive, apocalyptic language associated with their misuse. Third, otherworldly journeys – not merely as dreams or visions, but as actual ascensions and tours of physical places that are full of sights and sounds – prefigure contemporary cosmological narratives of events on distant planets and in far-off galaxies.

---

18. Kreuziger quotes briefly from *1 Enoch* (*Apocalypse and Science Fiction*, p. 184). Large does not.

19. Geza Vermes, *The Complete Dead Sea Scrolls in English* (New York: Penguin, 1997), pp. 513–14; D.S. Russell, *The Old Testament Pseudepigrapha: Patriarchs and Prophets in Early Judaism* (Philadelphia: Fortress Press, 1987), pp. 24–43.

'The Book of Dreams' comprises chs 83–90, or Book Four of *1 Enoch* and is a section of the book that compares most favorably with modern science fiction. It is a survey of Israel's history in the form of *ex eventu* prophecy, whereby the fictional character, Enoch, looks down into the distant 'future' (which is the real author's actual past) and prophesies what 'is to come'. This section of *1 Enoch* can be dated fairly easily to about 164 BCE, shortly after the *ex eventu* prophecy of Daniel 8–12.[20] The importance of the 'Book of Dreams' for science fiction is threefold. First, as many scholars have noted, prophecy 'after the event' gives the audience a powerful sense that 'all things have been determined'. Second, *ex eventu* prophecy works toward a climactic earthly battle (e.g., the battle of Armageddon), which pits the forces of good against the forces of evil. This, then, culminates in a third important motif common to much of science fiction – a divine intervention that rescues the embattled, righteous, earthly minority at the moment when circumstances look their bleakest.

Although it is not my purpose here to show how these central motifs and dualisms are found, elaborated upon and revised in later Christian apocalyptic texts such as Mark 13, 1 Thessalonians or Revelation, it is important to note at least a few differences between Christian apocalyptic texts and Jewish apocalyptic texts. By and large, surveys of successive world empires in the guise of *ex eventu* prophecy are absent from apocalypses composed by Christians. For example, while the 'Little Apocalypse' of Mark 13 (cf. Revelation 13) is probably *ex eventu* prophecy, 'Jesus' does not give an expansive overview of human history leading up to the destruction of the Jerusalem temple. There is no mention of the four world empires of Daniel in Mark 13, in Paul's letters, the book of Revelation or the *Shepherd of Hermas*.[21] It is interesting to note, however, that classic dispensational interpretations of the book of Revelation have viewed the letters to the seven churches (Revelation 2–3) typologically, as representing seven periods of church history from Jesus to 1900.[22] Feeling the need for an expansive survey of history in the New Testament's only full-fledged apocalypse, some fundamentalists have invented one: John's seven letters to the churches of Asia.

---

20. See H.F.D. Sparks (ed.), *The Apocryphal Old Testament* (Oxford: Clarendon Press, 1984), p. 176. Science fiction films that deal with *ex eventu*-like phenomena are *Back to the Future*, the first three *Terminator* films, and *Twelve Monkeys*.

21. For an elaboration of the differences between Christian and Jewish apocalyptic, see John J. Collins, 'Pseudonymity, Historical Reviews, and the Genre of Revelation', *CBQ*, 39 (1977), pp. 328–43; and D.S. Russell, *Divine Disclosure: An Introduction to Jewish Apocalyptic* (Minneapolis: Fortress Press, 1992), pp. 128–40.

22. Recognizing that there will be some variation among interpreters of Bible prophecy, the serious student can still roughly distinguish the following seven periods of church history in Rev. 2.1–3.22. The church at Ephesus represents the Apostolic Church (30–100 CE); the church at Smyrna represents the Church of the Roman Persecution (100–313 CE); the church at Pergamum represents the Constantinian Church (313–600 CE); the Church at Thyatira represents the Papal Period (590–1517 CE); the church at Sardis represents the Reformation Age (1517–1730 CE); the church at Philadelphia represents the Church of the Great Missionary Movement (1648–1900); and the church at Laodicia represents the Apostate Church (1900–?). See 'The Seven Churches', http://www.prophecyupdate.com/the_seven_churches.htm (accessed June 30, 2002).

Secondly, in contrast to Jewish apocalypses, their Christian counterparts tend to spend much more time describing the cosmic savior figure who intervenes in human history at its moment of deepest crisis.[23] Of course, in the Christian tradition, this figure is Jesus Christ himself. Finally, Christian apocalypses all characterize the faithful as non-violent resisters to the ever-present evil forces pervading the world.[24] Ancient Jewish apocalypses have mixed responses to confronting evil. In other words, the 'brawn and body', proactive, militant-resistant category of apocalypticists is a later development within Christianity. Mark's gospel is an excellent example of an early Christian non-violent response to an apocalyptic crisis. It juxtaposes Barabbas and Jesus in such a way that Jesus, the nonviolent liberator, is killed, while Barabbas, the violent resister to Roman hegemony, is released by Pilate (Mk. 15.7). Nevertheless, it is not Barabbas but the nonviolent Jesus who brings ultimate salvation in Mark's story.

In an early effort to define the literary genre 'apocalypse', John Collins argued that ancient Jewish and Christian apocalypses fall into two main categories: temporal apocalypses and spatial apocalypses.[25] Interestingly, both elements are present in *1 Enoch*. In *1 Enoch*, the Book of Watchers is primarily a spatial apocalypse, since most of it describes Enoch's tour of heaven, while the Book of Dreams is a temporal apocalypse, since it is a survey of human history that culminates in God invading this world and radically changing it.

Contemporary Science Fiction

Although neither Collins nor Kreuziger applies these two categories of ancient apocalypses – spatial and temporal – to contemporary science fiction, they fit the genre quite well. Indeed, Tim LaHaye's vastly popular Christian science fiction/ apocalyptic *Left Behind* series[26] (he and his wife hit it big in 1976 with their Christian sex manual)[27] combines science fiction and an explicit dispensational view of history. But, there are other obvious 'temporal' science fiction films such as *2001, Close Encounters of a Third Kind, Superman, Cocoon 1, Cocoon 2, The Abyss, Independence Day* and *Men in Black*,[28] where our world is invaded by either benevolent or malevolent powers. Then there are the 'spatial' science fiction films like *Star Wars, Alien* and *Star Trek: First Contact*, which take place entirely in other galaxies or planets that have no physical connection to our earth. Like their ancient prototypes (the spatial, tour-of-the-heavens apocalypses), this sub-genre of

---

23. For example, cf. Dan. 7.13-14; *1 En.* 46, 48; Rev. 1.12-18.

24. Walter Wink, *The Powers That Be: Theology for a New Millennium* (New York: Doubleday, 1998), pp. 128–44.

25. John J. Collins (ed.), 'Apocalypse: The Morphology of a Genre', *Semeia*, 14 (1979).

26. With Jerry B. Jenkins, *Left Behind* (Wheaton, IL: Tyndale, 1996); *Tribulation Force*, (Wheaton, IL: Tyndale, 1997); *Nicolae* (Wheaton, IL: Tyndale, 1998); *Soul Harvest* (Wheaton, IL: Tyndale, 1999); *Apollyon* (Wheaton, IL: Tyndale, 1999); *Assassins* (Wheaton, IL: Tyndale, 2000); *The Indwelling* (Wheaton, IL: Tyndale, 2001); *The Mark* (Wheaton, IL: Tyndale, 2001); *Desecration* (Wheaton, IL: Tyndale, 2002); *The Remnant* (Wheaton, IL: Tyndale, 2002). See also, John Cloud, 'Meet the Prophet', *Time* (July 1, 2002), pp. 50–53.

27. Tim LaHaye and Beverly LaHaye, *The Act of Marriage* (Grand Rapids: Zondervan, 1976).

28. *Men in Black 2* was released in July 2002.

science fiction film seems to be a bit less common than the 'earth invasion' type. But contemporary science fiction often mixes the temporal and spatial elements in ways that ancient Jewish and Christian cosmology did not. For example, the first two *Terminator* films, *Twelve Monkeys* and *The Matrix Trilogy*, have someone from the future invade the present world. That is, there is no hint of another spatial plane beyond this world in the films. The fiction is completely temporal and non-spatial. On the other hand, *The Alien* movies and some of the *Star Trek* films (most notably the *The Search for Spock*) have humans invading other planets and radically affecting them or being affected by them. The closest equivalent to this latter motif in the Bible would be Satan's invasion of Heaven (Rev. 12.7-9).

Just as ancient apocalyptic speculates on the nature of the savior figure who invades human history, so also does modern science fiction. It is no coincidence that the intitials 'JC' are connected with the savior figures of many contemporary science fiction films. For example, in the *Terminator* films the hero is 'John Connor' and in *Twelve Monkeys*, James Cole.[29] And at the beginning of *The Matrix*, Thomas Anderson, the future hero 'Neo', is greeted with 'You're my own personal Jesus Christ, man'. But is the hero a human look-alike with 'superhuman', otherworldly powers – like Superman? Or is the person an ordinary human with special gifts as in *Terminator*, *Twelve Monkeys*, *The Matrix* and *Spiderman*? And what of technology? Is it a gift from a world beyond our own or simply a projection of human ingenuity into the future? Does it have the power to destroy and deceive (*2001*, *Star Trek*, *Terminator*, *The Matrix*)? Or does it have the ability to save humanity (*2001*, *Star Trek IV: The Voyage Home*, *Men in Black*)? Is technology harnessed to an evil impulse that comes from within humans as in the apostle Paul, *The Matrix*, the *Terminator* films, *Twelve Monkeys* and the Y2K crisis? Or does it come from outside humanity, as in *First Enoch* and *Independence Day*?

My point in this brief listing of motifs and themes is simply to show that on the level of literary genre, there is a deep connection between the ancient dualistic world of biblical apocalyptic and our present world. And while the contemporary expressions of apocalyptic in 'brains and pens' is most obvious in the wildly popular science fiction films of the entertainment industry rather than in the esoteric myths of an ancient priestly aristocracy, the dualistic symbolic world of apocalyptic must resonate deeply within our psyche if Hollywood can return to it time and again and continue to reap high profits. Writing about James Cameron's first *Terminator* film, Ron Large wrote, 'One reason why the film [and I would add, most science fiction] works so well is its connection to apocalyptic motifs in American life. The relationship between American self-understanding and God's plan for the future is a central component of American identity and sense of purpose. It is ultimately a desire for hope and meaning. This is not an unworthy goal; however, one problem is that it may also serve to further establish the association between the apocalyptic vision and present violence'.[30]

---

29. In *End of Days*, a film whose plot is explicitly dependent upon the book of Revelation, the hero's name is 'Jericho Cane'.

30. 'American Apocalyptic', p. 7. See also James H. Smylie, 'A New Heaven and New Earth:

The Radical Right

The connection between apocalyptic and two distinct social classes is an important component of John Dominic Crossan's two-pronged analysis. His quick brush strokes place the writers and the doers, the upper class and the lower class in binary opposition.[31] But generally speaking, biblical scholars have argued one way or the other. *Either* ancient apocalypticists were among the elite, writing class of priests and royal retainers, *or* they were numbered among the illiterate, disenfranchised peasants and the destitute. In Crossan's more complex social analysis of Second Temple Judaism, both 'brains and pens' and 'brawn and body' apocalyptic responses are common cultural reactions to perceived crises.

As noted earlier, Crossan has argued that there is a 'brawn' element to ancient apocalyptic that is the complement to the elite 'brain' component that I have just been analyzing. The 'brawn' side of apocalyptic is usually represented by a lower social class that is literally willing to embody its apocalyptic ideology by giving over physical body and life to the cause. In our contemporary world, 'brawn' is symbolized in the cyanide-laced Kool-Aid of The People's Temple in Guyana, the lethal cocktail mix of phenobarbital and vodka taken by Southern California's Heaven's Gate group, and the exploding jet airliners of September 11.

Over the past seven years, The Southern Poverty Law Center has devoted a number of its publications to the relationship between Radical Right groups and Christian apocalypticism.[32] The Law Center's intent is to help educators and church leaders understand the ideological basis for some of the violence perpetrated by apocalyptic groups and to give educators and church leaders the tools to deal with these ideologies when confronted with them in schools and churches.

As documented by the Center, Christian and non-Christian apocalyptic hate groups grew enormously in the United States in the 1990s. They began to decline shortly after the year 2000 – no doubt due to the failure of the Y2K crisis to materialize – but they have begun to mushroom once again in the aftermath of September 11. Fueled in part by a growing economic disparity between upper-middle class whites and lower middle class to lower class whites, by internet communication and crisis events like September 11, these groups have found the relatively isolated, sparsely populated, predominantly white, 'inland empire' of the US Pacific Northwest a particularly hospitable place to settle down. Consequently, the geographical region I call home (Washington, Idaho and Montana) has become a hotbed of Radical Right groups that are heavily indebted to apocalyptic interpretations of the Bible.

Uses of the Millennium in American Religious History', *Int*, 53 (1999), pp. 143–57; Hal Lindsey, *The 1980's: Countdown to Armageddon* (New York: Bantam, 1980), pp. 131–58; John F. Walvoord, *Armageddon, Oil and the Middle East Crisis: What the Bible Says about the Future of the Middle East and the End of the Western Civilization* (Grand Rapids: Zondervan, 1990), pp. 53–64.

31. *Jesus*, p. 40.

32. The Southern Poverty Law Center is a non-profit organization based in Montgomery, Alabama, 'internationally known for its tolerance education program, its legal victories against white supremacist groups, its tracking of hate groups and its sponsorship of the Civil Rights Memorial' (http://www.splcenter.org/; accessed June 30, 2002).

Like the various Zealot groups in the first Jewish Revolt (66–73 CE), Radical Right groups are not easily categorized theologically or ideologically. In Crossan's terms, this is because they are more focused on 'brawn and body' strategies than 'brain and pen' ideas.[33] However, most make some claim of being rooted in Christianity – even if, for them, that 'authentic' Christian tradition was quickly corrupted. The Southern Poverty Law Center has identified 'Christian Identity' as one of the most violent and explicitly 'Christian' groups of the radical right. For example, Timothy McVeigh, the man responsible for the Oklahoma City bombing on the anniversary of the Branch Davidian conflagration, had ties to Christian Identity groups in the Midwest. Hence, I will focus on 'Christian Identity' as a way to briefly introduce the contemporary 'brawn and body' apocalyptic groups of the US Radical Right. According to an intelligence report of the Southern Poverty Law Center,

> Identity's apocalyptic roots are British-Israelism, a curiosity of mid-Victorian England that maintained that the Anglo-Saxons were the true lost tribes of Israel. In America these beliefs were transformed into a fiercely anti-Semitic, racist theology... The American Identity doctrine maintains that whites will be pitted against evil non-white satanic forces in an apocalyptic battle. Identity professes that Adam was a white man, the product of a second creation. In Identity's system, God's first creation produced people of color, 'the beasts of the field,' or 'mud people'. Jews, according to Identity, are literally children of Satan, the descendants of a union between Eve and the serpent. These individuals mated with the 'beasts' to produce the Edomites, mongrel people who are the embodiment of Satan and the source of the world's evil.[34]

Like ancient apocalyptic (*1 Enoch*) and much of science fiction, the origin of evil – especially in terms of miscegenation – plays an important role in the ideology. The Southern Poverty Law Center's description of Christian Identity goes on to note that its eschatology is also rooted in apocalyptic language. But unlike most of apocalyptic Protestant fundamentalist groups, Christian Identity is 'postmillennial',

> meaning that in order for the Second Coming [of Christ] to occur, God's law on Earth must first be established through a great battle, Armageddon. In this battle, the forces of good – the white 'Israelites' – will be pitted against the armies of Satan, represented by the Jewish-controlled federal [U.S.] government. Identity followers will wage an all-out war against ZOG (the Zionist Occupied Government), 'race-traitors' [especially whites who intermarry with other racial groups] and anyone else who stands in their way.[35]

Many of the proponents of Christian Identity are virulently opposed to the pre-millennial, pretribulational apocalypticism represented by much of Protestant fundamentalism.[36] And although many adherents of the ideology grew up with

---

33. Crossan, *Jesus*, pp. 43–44.

34. Southern Poverty Law Center, 'Racist Identity Sect Fuels Extremist Movement', Intelligence Report #79 (August 1995), p. 3.

35. Southern Poverty Law Center, 'Racist Identity Sect Fuels Extremist Movement', p. 3.

36. Interestingly, Hal Lindsey's 1980 sequel to *The Late Great Planet Earth, The 1980s:*

Darby's dispensationalism and the Scofield Reference Bible as I did, they are
now committed to Identity Pastor Peter J. Peters's point of view, which

> criticizes 'Judeo-Christian churches in America' for planning to 'leave earth via
> the "rapture"' and for listening to '*doomsday* date setters (like Hal Lindsey) who
> predict the end of the world and who always miss'. [Peters] has little regard for
> those who 'want to escape the corruption in the world rather than expose it'.
> These are the people, Peter observes, who have an 'I just want to go home to
> Jesus mentality rather than stay and fight for Jesus'. Instead of complacently
> waiting for the end, Peters counsels his listeners and readers against letting the
> last days (i.e. the end of this period) be 'yours or your family's last days'. The
> goal for Christians, according to Peters, is learning 'how to survive, overcome
> and be victorious'.[37]

Of course, not all Radical Right groups share Peter J. Peter's theological roots
and agenda. There are hundreds of Radical Right groups hunkered down in the
United States today, and a look at any of their websites quickly reveals their
differences.[38] Some do not claim to be Christian at all. Yet all do share a certain
apocalyptic view of the future, of a nation and a people spiraling downward toward
disaster – a disaster that the chosen ones have been called to oppose, body and
soul. But biblical scholars have generally argued that ancient apocalypticists were
either among the disenfranchised, elite, writing class of priests and royal retainers,
or they were numbered among the illiterate, disenfranchised peasants and the
destitute. From John Dominic Crossan's more complex social analysis of Second
Temple Judaism and from my quick survey of contemporary American culture, it is
clear that a dualistic hermeneutic is at work in both the 'brain and pens' and the
'brawn and body' forms of apocalyptic. But more than that. As we shall see below,
the same hermeneutic is at work in this past century's two most prominent scholarly views of the historical Jesus.

Apocalyptic Dualism and Historical Jesus Studies

In *Jesus: A Revolutionary Biography*, Crossan writes that John the Baptist preached
'the imminent advent of the avenging apocalyptic God',[39] who would 'restore a
terribly disordered world' through 'some massive and world-shaking divine
intervention'.[40] And although Jesus was baptized by this same John, a 'peasant
apocalypticist',[41] Crossan argues that Jesus became 'almost the exact opposite of
the Baptist'.[42] That is to say, Jesus was non-apocalyptic and this-worldly in his

Countdown to Armageddon, weds pretribulational apocalypticism to a Christian Right political
agenda (pp. 131–75). See also Weber, *Living in the Shadow of the Second Coming*, pp. 218–26.

   37. Linda Schearing, 'Millennialism, Mayhem, and the Year 2000: Apocalypticism and the
Radical Right' (unpublished paper), p. 12.

   38. For example, see http://personalwebs.myriad.net/steveb/mil.html (accessed February 25,
2000).

   39. http://personalwebs.myriad.net/steveb/mil.html, p. 38.

   40. http://personalwebs.myriad.net/steveb/mil.html, p. 32.

   41. http://personalwebs.myriad.net/steveb/mil.html, p. 38.

   42. http://personalwebs.myriad.net/steveb/mil.html, p. 48.

understanding of God's activity and human responsibility. He did not speculate about the end of the world or God's imminent, dramatic intervention in human history. His message was not intended for non-Jews, and it was not about his own role as divine savior or about a repentance focused on salvation from hell. While Crossan's description of Jesus sounds scandalous to many people raised in the church, that is not what I find most interesting about his work. What intrigues me about Crossan's Jesus research is the fact that his conclusions stand in complete contrast and opposition to the view of Jesus promulgated by Albert Schweitzer at the beginning of the twentieth century. And Schweitzer's view of Jesus was what dominated the first half of that just completed century. While newer theories of oral sources, reevaluations of the biographical importance of Mark, the discovery of the *Gospel of Thomas*, and developments in the sociology of ancient Palestine all combine to play a role in Crossan's historical reassessment of Jesus, I believe that there are also underlying theological and apologetical reasons for the shift in his emphasis. And thus my argument below shall be that the shift in 'liberal' New Testament scholars' assessments of Jesus' relationship to apocalyptic is a litmus test for the role apocalyptic plays in the North American cultural consciousness. And it is no less dualistic than the views these scholars seek to overturn.

Written in 1906 and translated into English in 1910, just a few years before the outbreak of the 'Great War', Albert Schweitzer's *The Quest of the Historical Jesus*[43] brought to life a new vision of Jesus. It was one that spoke in a prophetic voice against the eschatological hopes of those Christians standing on the threshold of the second millennium's last century. *The Christian Century*, a liberal Protestant magazine founded shortly before the end of the nineteenth century, recently reflected back over its one hundred years of publication and quoted from its first printing in the twentieth century. The editors wrote: 'Expressing hope "in God and Christian people, and especially the God-fearing, liberty-loving brotherhood that pleads for the unity of God's children", they dared to believe that "the most Christian of all the centuries so far" lay ahead of them. And they wanted to turn that vision into reality'.[44] For the early editors of the magazine, their hope and conviction was that the twentieth century would indeed be *the* Christian century, a century when Christ's message of God's Kingdom – a kingdom of love, peace and harmony between all peoples – would empower humanity to new heights of virtue and perfection. But Schweitzer's bombshell would show how the preceding two centuries' liberal views of Jesus – views so eloquently expressed in the pages of *The Christian Century* – had misconstrued the message of Jesus, turning it into a this-worldly message of God-blessed human potential.

After first outlining eighteenth and nineteenth century critical investigations into the Jesus of history, Schweitzer took pains to show that those portraits of Jesus said more about the scholars doing the research than they said about the historical Jesus. It is a masterful book, and perhaps the time is ripe to redo what Schweitzer did one

---

43. *The Quest of the Historical Jesus: A Critical Study of Its Progress from Reimarus to Wrede* (New York: Macmillan, 1973).

44. *The Christian Century* 117/3 (January 26, 2000), p. 77.

hundred years ago. But Schweitzer does not stop with an analysis of one hundred years of Jesus scholarship. He goes on to unveil a Jesus who was radically apocalyptic, who was expecting God to break into human history in some powerful new way through his own mission. Jesus was, in a word, not a wimpy, liberal-minded Protestant preaching pious platitudes about the 'brotherhood of man'. In language bordering on poetry, Schweitzer writes of Jesus:

> There is silence all around. The Baptist appears and cries: 'Repent, for the Kingdom of Heaven is at hand'. Soon after that comes Jesus, and in the knowledge that he is the coming Son of Man lays hold of the wheel of the world to set it moving on that last revolution which is to bring all ordinary history to a close. It refuses to turn, and He throws Himself upon it. Then it does turn; it crushes him. Instead of bringing in the eschatological conditions, He has destroyed them. The wheel rolls onward and the mangled body of the one immeasurably great Man, who was strong enough to think of Himself as the spiritual ruler of mankind and so bend history to His purpose, is hanging upon it still. That is His victory and His reign.[45]

It is clear that Schweitzer's interpretation of Jesus looked in two directions. Schweitzer looked both at his Western culture's scholarly presentations of Jesus and at (the historical) Jesus himself. And in his reconstructed historical Jesus, Schweitzer found a person who prophetically spoke *against* the prevailing ethos of his day, against 'the Messiah who preached the ethic of the Kingdom of God [and]… founded the Kingdom of Heaven on earth'.[46] *That* Jesus of Nazareth, he writes, 'never had any existence'.[47]

The recent spate of non-apocalyptic Jesuses floating around in North American biblical scholarship does not make explicit mention of Radical Right groups like Christian Identity or contemporary science fiction films. Instead, Crossan and other founders of the Jesus Seminar are pointedly directed toward exposing the errors of fundamentalist Protestant portraits of Christ as typified in their literalistic, dualistic interpretations of biblical prophecy.[48] But in so doing, Crossan and the Jesus Seminar radically undercut not only the apocalyptic Christ so dear to the heart of Protestant fundamentalism but also the apocalyptic Jesus of Albert Schweitzer, science fiction, and the Radical Right.

A Non-Apocalyptic Jesus for an Apocalyptic Age

Schweitzer's apocalyptic Jesus dominated the first half of the twentieth century. It successfully weathered a world war and the decades immediately following that war, during a time when Jesus' and the early church's apocalyptic words seemed more and more profoundly attuned to the unraveling of human history – another world war, genocide, the dawning of the atomic age and the emerging of the Cold War. But the end of Schweitzer's apocalyptic Jesus was foreshadowed in Rudolf

---

45. *Quest of the Historical Jesus*, pp. 370–71.
46. *Quest of the Historical Jesus*, p. 398.
47. *Quest of the Historical Jesus*, p. 371.
48. For example, see Walsh, 'On Finding a Non-American Revelation', pp. 5–6, esp. n. 15.

Bultmann's New Testament theology, which stood at the century's midpoint.[49] Bultmann's New Testament hermeneutical project took Schweitzer's emphasis on apocalyptic seriously, so seriously that his student, Ernst Käsemann, could later argue that 'apocalyptic [was] the mother of Christian theology'.[50] However, Bultmann's research into Christian origins led him to attribute Schweitzer's apocalyptic worldview primarily to the early Christian communities rather than to Jesus himself. Because of liberal Protestantism's misguided preoccupation with the life of Jesus, Bultmann had little to say about the physical details of Jesus' life or the internal workings of Jesus' mind. Instead, having taken the first-century apocalyptic worldview seriously, Bultmann understood his task to be primarily and profoundly hermeneutical. Here, the Christian interpreter's goal was to 'demythologize' the apocalyptic world of Jesus and the early church and appropriate its existential center for contemporary theology, for a European world that knew the meaning of crisis but for whom the language of demons, angels and the Second Coming of Jesus held little meaning.

As the twentieth century drew to a close, New Testament scholars – particularly those from the United States – continued to be interested in Jesus, despite the relative skepticism of the 'Second Quest' with its focus on Jesus's words over his deeds. This late twentieth-century, largely North American movement is sometimes called 'the Third Quest' (Schweitzer to Bultmann being the First Quest and Bultmann's students having initiated the Second Quest), but it removes Bultmann and his followers' explicit hermeneutical questions from the Jesus equation. The self-proclaimed voice of this 'Third Quest', Robert Funk's Jesus Seminar, has sought to refocus scholarly attention on Jesus for the public at large and in a context outside any church or parachurch organization. In its evaluation of the Jesus tradition, a non-apocalyptic (or as Marcus Borg argues, I think incorrectly, a non-eschatological Jesus)[51] is revealed.

The purpose of the Jesus Seminar has never explicitly been to 'reinvent Jesus'. It is based largely upon a reassessment of the gospels' saying material, or 'Q', especially in light of the 1946 discovery of the *Gospel of Thomas*, more thorough archaeological work in Galilee and the refinement of sociological models for studying first-century Palestine. Nevertheless, Robert Funk writes in the introduction to the *Five Gospels*:

> In the aftermath of the controversy over Darwin's *The Origin of Species* (published in 1859) and the ensuing Scopes 'monkey' trial in 1925, American biblical scholarship retreated into the closet. The fundamentalist mentality generated a climate of inquisition that made honest scholarly judgments dangerous. Numerous biblical scholars were subjected to heresy trials and suffered the loss of academic posts. They learned it was safer to keep their critical judgments private.

49. *Theology of the New Testament* (trans. Kendrick Grobel; New York: Charles Scribner's Sons, 1951, 1955).

50. As quoted in Klaus Koch, *The Rediscovery of Apocalyptic* (trans. Margaret Kohl; London: SCM Press, 1972), p. 14.

51. *Meeting Jesus Again for the First Time: The Historical Jesus and the Heart of Contemporary Faith* (San Francisco: HarperSanFrancisco, 1994), p. 2; cf. Crossan, *Jesus*, pp. 52–53.

However, the intellectual ferment of the century soon reasserted itself in colleges, universities and seminaries. By the end of World War II, critical scholars again quietly dominated the academic scene from one end of the continent to the other. Critical biblical scholarship was supported, of course, by other university disciplines which wanted to ensure that dogmatic considerations not be permitted to intrude into scientific and historical research. The fundamentalists were forced, as a consequence, to found their own Bible colleges and seminaries in order to propagate their point of view. In launching new institutions, the fundamentalists even refused accommodation with the older, established church-related schools that dotted the land.

One focal point of the raging controversies was who Jesus was and what he had said.[52]

As the Jesus Seminar has made clear through its many press releases and publications, it has uncovered a Jesus who was an illiterate Galilean peasant, a charismatic teacher, healer and exorcist, who, in Marcus Borg's words, was a boundary-crosser, breaking purity boundaries in the name of a compassionate God.[53] Eventually Jesus went to Jerusalem – why, we cannot be sure – confronted the entrenched priestly elite in the temple, was arrested and crucified.

In outward appearances, then, Jesus at the end of the twentieth century looks radically different from Schweitzer's Jesus at its beginning. Or different even from Bultmann's Jesus at the middle of the century. In contrast to Bultmann and his followers, the 'Third Quest' has no explicit interest in the hermeneutical questions that sought to relate the past world of Jesus to the present world. There is no attempt to 'get into the mind of Jesus', to relate Jesus to the world outside the Judaism of the Roman empire or to construct a detailed sequence of the events in his life. And there is a radical rejection of Schweitzer's apocalyptic Jesus. However, on a deeper pastoral and prophetic level, there are some remarkable points of connection between the first quest, the second quest and the third quest. The 'Third Quest' for Jesus, as typified by Crossan, Funk and Borg, argues that Jesus was non-apocalyptic. His message was centered not on issues of the end of the world, or the end of an age, but rather on the revitalizing of the Jewish people and their covenant with their God.

All this may sound radical and revolutionary to the outsider who is unfamiliar with the last hundred years of research on the historical Jesus. But there is an important connection between the seemingly disparate perspectives of Schweitzer and the Jesus Seminar. Writing in a non-apocalyptic period of Western European cultural history, Schweitzer's historical and critical research – or should we say his *faith*? – led him to find in the Jesus tradition an 'authentic' person and voice that spoke against the prevailing ethos of his day, a person and voice that challenged the false optimism in the human spirit and the blindness to colonial and racial

52. *The Five Gospels*, p. 1.

53. *Meeting Jesus Again*, p. 58. See my analysis of Borg's 'boundary crosser' metaphor in *Reading with a Passion: Rhetoric, Autobiography, and the American West in the Gospel of John* (New York: Continuum, 1995), pp. 122–27.

oppression, a voice opposed to an optimism that believed human effort could usher in the kingdom of heaven on earth. Similarly, toward the end of the twentieth century (beginning in the mid-1980s with President Reagan's apocalyptic predictions of Soviet power and a disinterest in ecological issues, in a period of radical fear and pessimism in the lower middle class over issues of economics and race), we find liberal Protestants and liberal Roman Catholics discovering a non-apocalyptic Jesus, a Jesus who can speak powerfully and pointedly against other-worldly copouts from the messiness of day-to-day living. This 'new' Jesus is a 'this-worldly' Jesus, one who does not speculate about the future or wring from history a catastrophic end where only the 'faithful' survive. This Jesus, like Schweitzer's before it, is a counter-cultural Jesus, one who is at odds with the social angst of late twentieth-century politics, one who can call – despite the absence of religious commitment – all people to recommit themselves to the world and its earthbound problems. In this sense, then, both the 'First Quest' and the 'Third Quest' share an implicit connection to the 'Second Quest', that is, a commitment to the hermeneutical (and spiritual) task of connecting the world of Jesus to one's own day.[54] And finally, these quests often share with their apocalyptic pretexts and cultural precursors a dualistic, determinate hermeneutic of adversarial response, an 'us against them' mentality that tends to replicate the problematical binarisms of apocalyptic rather than moving beyond them to a more broadly-based literary indeterminacy and ethical pluralism.

Complicating Apocalyptic (Determinate) Dualisms

Can the non-apocalyptic, historical Jesus of John Crossan, Marcus Borg and Robert Funk 'save' North America from the apocalyptic-fed, post-September 11 dualisms of a new millennium? It would be nice to think so. But if Schweitzer's study were used as a test case, the answer could turn out to be more negative. 'Brawn and bodies' tend not to listen very attentively to the 'brains and pens' of the 'priestly', 'scribal' world of academe.

In light of my analysis of science fiction, the Radical Right and historical Jesus studies, there is evidence to suggest that the Jesuses of liberal Protestantism – whether that of the first, second or third quest – all share a religious or faith commitment: to find a Jesus in the Christian tradition who speaks counter-culturally to their contemporary worlds. Interestingly, Schweitzer's prophetic, apocalyptic Jesus was heavily indebted to the Markan tradition, while the Jesus of the third quest is heavily dependent upon the less apocalyptically-driven Lukan Jesus. It remains to be seen whether New Testament scholars and church folk can find (or will want to look for) in the Christian canon, at the beginning of the third millennium, a portrait of Jesus that can speak prophetically, existentially, beyond the determinate dualisms of apocalyptic, to the issues of postcolonialism, globalization, re-entrenched religious dogmatism, nationalism and personal alienation.

---

54. Cf. Staley, *Reading with a Passion*, pp. 14–15.

If Schweitzer was right in arguing that John's gospel was the favorite of the early nineteenth-century liberal lives of Jesus,[55] perhaps a positive reassessment of Johannine historical traditions will reinvigorate Jesus and apocalyptic studies at the beginning of the third millennium.[56] But even a diehard Johannine scholar like myself is not holding his breath on that possibility. However, I do think that Johannine scholars have been forced, by the very nature of the texts they investigate, to deal creatively with the hermeneutical challenges of Johannine dualism. And perhaps the lessons learned from problematizing and complicating its determinate dualisms may infiltrate historical Jesus studies and apocalyptic studies.[57] Whatever our resources will be, the shadow of post-September 11 apocalyptic rhetoric demands that biblical scholars and pastors find ways to complicate its dualistic oppositions in ethically life-giving, productive ways.

Is It Possible to 'Befriend' an Apocalyptic Dualism When We Find One?

One way to avoid the determinate dualisms of apocalyptic is to read apocalyptic in ways that undermine these dualisms. Various hermeneutical strategies, including those associated with deconstruction, offer inviting escape routes. Nevertheless, apocalyptic texts, like propagandistic rhetoric (which apocalyptic in many ways resembles), is much more difficult than other kinds of literature to read as 'subject to indeterminacy'. For example, *Mein Kampf*, I would think, is more difficult to read as 'subject to indeterminacy' than Joyce's *Ulysses*. And since *Mein Kampf* is not a canonical text for me, it is not worth the effort to read it for its literary indeterminacies. It is easier to dismiss it on other grounds. Since Revelation is a canonical text for me, I will work harder to 'find' literary indeterminacies in it or to create a context for reading the book as indeterminate despite its rather pervasive determinate dualisms.

But finding indeterminacy in Revelation (and biblical apocalyptic more generally) is not the only way to reread apocalyptic dualism. Another avenue for rereading Revelation (and biblical apocalyptic more generally) against the grain of determinate dualism is suggested by Adele Reinhartz's recent book on the Fourth Gospel, *Befriending the Beloved Disciple: A Jewish Reading of the Gospel of John*. Reinhartz proposes a thought-provoking, fourfold model for reading beyond that book's determinate binarisms. Taking a cue from Wayne Booth's *The Company We Keep: An Ethics of Fiction*,[58] Reinhartz focuses on the ethical implications of

---

55. *The Quest of the Historical Jesus*, pp. 58–67, 86–89.

56. For example, see Robert T. Fortna and Tom Thatcher (eds.), *Jesus in the Johannine Tradition* (Louisville, KY: Westminster/John Knox Press, 2001).

57. Here I am thinking particularly of Adele Reinhartz, *Befriending the Beloved Disciple* (New York: Continuum, 2001) (see below), and the collection of essays edited by Musa Dube and myself entitled *John and Postcolonialism: Travel, Space, and Power* (New York: Continuum International, 2002). See also Tina Pippin, *Apocalyptic Bodies: The Biblical End of the World in Text and Image* (New York: Routledge, 1999) and Stephen D. Moore, 'Revolting Revelations', in *God's Beauty Parlor and Other Queer Spaces in and around the Bible* (Stanford, CA: Stanford University Press, 2001), pp. 173–99.

58. (Berkeley, CA: University of California Press, 1988).

what she terms 'compliant reading', 'resistant reading', 'sympathetic reading' and 'engaged reading' as she explores the Johannine metaphor of the Beloved Disciple in four roles: the reader's mentor, opponent, colleague and 'other'. With each type of reading she asks two interrelated questions: (1) What kind of 'friend' is the Beloved Disciple to the different types of readings, that is, does the 'implied author' 'encourage' compliant, resistant, sympathetic, or engaged readings of 'his' text? and (2) What kind of reader do we become when we read the text in these various modes?[59] Reinhartz's choice of metaphor opens up the reader's imagination to multiple active reading strategies and challenges the normal understanding of what counts as a 'faithful', 'friendly' reading of the Bible, where the faithful reader is the one who 'submits' to the determinate, ideological perspective of the text without a critical engagement of its ethos or its literary indeterminacies. So what might her fourfold reading metaphor look like in relation to the binary oppositions of apocalyptic literature and the apocalyptic/non-apocalyptic Jesuses of academic discourse?

Reinhartz defines a 'compliant reading' as one where readers accept the implied author's 'gift *in the terms in which he offers it*… They comply with the directions that the implied author describes'.[60] If one were to apply Reinhartz's description of compliant reading to contemporary North American cultural readings of ancient apocalyptic texts, my dispensationalist childhood experience of biblical apocalyptic, most science fiction's re-imaging of ancient apocalyptic themes, and the Radical Right's apocalyptic reworking of biblical texts would all generally reflect compliant readings of ancient biblical apocalyptic. And in terms of recent historical Jesus studies, N.T. Wright's *Jesus and the Victory of God* would typify a reconstructed Jesus that is generally compliant and accepting of the canonical gospels' portrayals. That is, none of these approaches challenges the implicit or explicit 'determinate' binary oppositions that seem to dominate the texts' ideologies.

Reinhartz's resistant reading is the mirror image of a compliant reading. She argues that it 'entails the effort systematically to read from the point of view of the Other as defined by the text or genre under discussion'.[61] Applied to apocalyptic and to Jesus, Radical Right groups like Christian Identity vie for sensationalist headlines with their violent, resistant readings against the grain. If the Jew is the persecuted faithful remnant of ancient biblical apocalyptic, suffering under the pervasive power of pagan *Gentiles*, then Christian Identity and the like paint the world with theories of *Jewish* world domination (Zionist Occupied Government) and conspiracies drawn from the fraudulent *Protocols of the Elders of Zion*. They, the Gentile, white faithful, along with their white, Gentile Jesus become the purified remnant of the last days, standing guard against the mud race of Jews, Africans, Arabs and Asians.

From Reinhartz's perspective, the problem with resistant readings is that they 'cannot overcome or bypass the rhetoric of binary opposition… but rather reproduce

---

59. *Befriending the Beloved Disciple*, pp. 54, 82, 99, 131.
60. *Befriending the Beloved Disciple*, p. 54 (emphasis added).
61. *Befriending the Beloved Disciple*, p. 81.

them in reverse'.[62] Her observation is correct. But the Radical Right's resistant readings of Jesus and apocalyptic can also have a positive effect on disengaged readers who might otherwise dismiss these ancient texts out of hand. When *resistant* readers find racism, sexism, violence and hatred at the core of biblical texts, disengaged readers are sometimes able to see for the first time that the same sorts of ethical problems arise from *compliant* readings. In the name of 'orthodoxy' and evangelical fervor, these readings also often vilify the 'Other' as Arab, Chinese, Roman Catholic or Russian.[63]

The final pairing of readings is the most interesting and challenging for contemporary Christians. Reinhartz defines a sympathetic reading as one in which the implied author is a 'colleague... a peer who struggles with similar issues in similar ways [as I do]',[64] but without being engaged 'over the issues that divide us'.[65] An engaged reading, on the other hand, is one that 'attempts to engage seriously and directly with the fundamental content of the Beloved Disciple's gift [or for us, the apocalypticist's gift] as well as with [one's]... own inability, or if you like, unwillingness, to accept it'.[66] For me, most scholarly readings of ancient Jewish apocalyptic and Jesus fail precisely at this point: We are not honest in dealing with our inability to accept the apocalypticist's 'gift'. Finding ourselves in a corner where we must deal with canonical apocalyptic texts that dismay or repel us, we invent ways to reject what we dislike in the name of some overarching methodological or hermeneutical consistency. For the scholar, disengagement with the text often begins to occur at the point where theory begins to dominate. Rather than straightforwardly saying, 'I don't like this apocalyptic Jesus because', or 'I can't accept this view of the world for the following reasons, but I can work with this', we cover up our own ethical misgivings with the biblical text through complex historical reconstructions and theoretical constructs. But an engaged reading of ancient apocalyptic writers and the Jesus tradition would entail, in Reinhartz's words, 'fac[ing] the challenge of opening up [our] own understanding[s] of the world to include... [them] without at the same time abdicating [our] right to judge the ethos, and the ethical criteria, that... [they] support'.[67]

Reinhartz's models of reading raise important questions regarding the kind of reading approach that is appropriate for scripture. Does the concept of scriptural authority require a particular kind of reading approach, or can a concept of scriptural authority function within a certain range of types, accommodating different reading strategies? Perhaps scriptural authority is a somewhat indeterminate concept, one which believers too often reduce – through binary thinking – to the model of an apocalyptic oracle that demands a forced choice between compliant

---

62. *Befriending the Beloved Disciple*, p. 98.

63. E.g., Lindsey, *Countdown to Armageddon*, pp. 43–45, 67–68, 95–96; cf. Pippin, *Apocalyptic Bodies*, pp. 13–31, 100–16.

64. *Befriending the Beloved Disciple*, p. 130.

65. *Befriending the Beloved Disciple*, p. 130.

66. *Befriending the Beloved Disciple*, 131.

67. *Befriending the Beloved Disciple*, p. 162. However, Reinhartz recognizes that honest ethical judgment of canonical texts can present problems for communities of faith (p. 166).

reading (submissive to scriptural authority) or resistant reading (rejecting scriptural authority). Space does not permit an extended discussion of these questions. It is enough to note that the kinds of genres that seem to call for this forced choice – apocalypse and prophetic oracle – are not the only genres in scripture. Hence, it is fair to ask whether the presence of other genres in the Bible – wisdom, poetry, romance, historical narrative – may call for a rethinking of what kind(s) of reading approaches the Bible 'wants'. If we let some of those other genres shape our conception of the kind of 'book' the Bible is, then we may also consider it appropriate to read biblical apocalyptic not submissively but in a sympathetic and engaged way.

So what would a sympathetic or 'engaged' reading of ancient apocalyptic look like? Would we know a befriended dualism if we saw one? Would Reinhartz count the work of Walter Wink,[68] Tina Pippin,[69] Stephen Moore[70] or Catharine Keller[71] as 'engaged readings' of Jesus and apocalyptic? Or do these readings of biblical texts merely reflect unsympathetic, idiosyncratic, ideological critiques without real 'engagement'? It is not clear what Reinhartz would make of postmodern, ethically interested readings of Jesus and apocalyptic. However, from my point of view, insofar as these authors lead us to engage, critically and constructively, the determinate dualisms of apocalyptic and at the same time reveal those features of the apocalyptic texts that are indeterminate or give cause for questioning the determinate dualism of the apocalyptic vision, they can foster conversations and communities that move beyond the ethical binarisms of 'my protestations of innocence' and 'your obvious guilt'.

Reinhartz's metaphor of 'befriending the Beloved Disciple' complicates biblical hermeneutics in an ethically responsible manner and pushes beyond the traditional norms of reading approved by historical critical methods. But I believe that reading apocalyptic – or reading Jesus reading apocalyptic – is still more complex than her fourfold metaphor appears to presume. Reinhartz herself hints at this in her conclusion when she writes, 'as real readers, even as real scholars, we float freely among these [four] perspectives and draw on two or more at once in the process of interpreting or explaining the texts to ourselves and to others'.[72] Furthermore, she acknowledges that her own 'particular identity and family history' has molded her perception of Johannine dualisms.[73] And since she never fully engages the Johannine text on the level of *her own* 'particular identity and family history', there is still an air of academic objectivity to her argument. She reads the Johannine text the way she does because she has an adult *theory* to back up her reading, not because of any peculiar childhood memory or adolescent trauma. The same is even more obvious, of course, in historical Jesus research,

---

68. *The Powers that Be.*

69. *Apocalyptic Bodies.*

70. *God's Beauty Parlor.*

71. *Apocalypse Now and Then: A Feminist Guide to the End of the World* (Boston: Beacon Press, 1996).

72. *Befriending the Beloved Disciple*, p. 165.

73. *Befriending the Beloved Disciple*, p. 166.

where 'reading Jesus' appears under the rhetorical guise of antiseptic, germ-free interpretation. If John Dominic Crossan or Marcus Borg have ever had apocalyptic nightmares where a giant, fire-breathing Jesus destroys the world, they wouldn't get caught telling us about it. Even if it were to become the basis of a revolutionary new theory and book.

An Apocabiographical Postscript

I awoke on September 10, 2001, in a dark funk of depression. I am not a person given to wide mood swings, but a certain unquantifiable weight lay heavy on my shoulders that day. After a quick breakfast, I turned on my computer and pretended to start writing. In an ironic moment of bemused whimsy (or was it merely procrastination?), I typed into my favorite search engine something like 'incredible weight of sadness'. I don't remember the exact phrase. By the end of the day I had erased it from my computer and my memory. I don't like my family finding my more bizarre search histories on my hard drive. So I typed something like 'incredible weight of sadness' and hit 'enter'. Up popped part of a poem by John Donne, one I didn't recognize. I was looking for a sign from God that life was worth living. For the moment, John Donne had done it. The next day was September 11, 2001. I heard about the planes on my way to Gold's Gym to work out. The story was live on National Public Radio, but I just thought I was listening to the review of a new Tom Clancy novel. Then I walked into the gym and saw the TV images. Two monstrously huge towers collapsing into Manhattan dust. Dry, choking. Thousands dead. Is there a Jesus out there who can save us from the twos of ancient apocalyptic, science fiction, the Radical Right and the rubble of Ground Zero? Maybe one Jesus isn't enough anymore. Canonical *and* otherwise. Pluriform *and* monochrome. Jesus! We are desperate. We need more than one of you.

I want to be an ethically responsible postmodern person. I seek to write about apocalyptic in a postmodern mode, one that keeps endings 'open', 'indeterminate', without losing sight of apocalyptic's notion that actions matter or apocalyptic's warning against complacency and its protest against dominant power. In our postmodern, post-September 11, postcolonial culture, I am looking for a hermeneutical third way, a fourth plane – a fifth for the third to wonder about and plan and weigh and find lurking behind the I AM-big pentameter loins a sonnet set free, escaped, alive[74]

---

74. With apologies to Frank Kermode, this essay has no 'tock'. Kermode, *The Sense of an Ending: Studies in the Theory of Fiction* (New York: Oxford University Press, 1967), pp. 51–52.

BIBLIOGRAPHY

Achtemeier, Elizabeth, *The Old Testament and the Proclamation of the Gospel* (Philadelphia: Westminster Press, 1973).

Adam, A.K.M., 'The Future of Our Allusions', *Society of Biblical Literature Seminar Papers*, 31 (1992), pp. 5–13.

—*Making Sense of New Testament Theology: 'Modern' Problems and Prospects* (Studies in American Biblical Hermeneutics, 11; Macon, GA: Mercer University Press, 1995).

—'The Sign of Jonah: A Fish-Eye View', *Semeia*, 51 (1990), pp. 177–91.

—'Twisting to Destruction: A Memorandum on the Ethics of Interpretation', *Perspectives in Religious Studies*, 23 (1996), pp. 215–22.

—*What Is Postmodern Biblical Criticism?* (Minneapolis: Fortress Press, 1995).

Adam, Margaret B., 'This Is My Story, This Is My Song… A Feminist Claim on Scripture, Ideology, and Interpretation', in Harold C. Washington, Susan Lochrie Graham and Pamela Thimmes (eds.), *Escaping Eden* (Sheffield: Sheffield Academic Press, 1998), pp. 218–32.

Aichele, George, *et al.*, *The Postmodern Bible: The Bible and Culture Collective* (New Haven and London: Yale University Press, 1995), pp. 272–308.

Aichele, George, and Gary A. Philips (eds.), 'Intertextuality and the Bible', *Semeia*, 69/70 (1995).

Aichele, George and Richard Walsh (eds.), *Screening Scripture: Intertextual Connections Between Scripture and Film* (Harrisburg, PA: Trinity Press International, 2002).

Allison, Dale C., and Robert J. Miller (eds.), *The Apocalyptic Jesus: A Debate* (Santa Rosa, CA: Polebridge, 2001).

Anderson, H. George, T. Austin Murphy and Joseph A. Burgess (eds.), *Justification by Faith* (Lutherans and Catholics in Dialogue, VII; Minneapolis: Augsburg, 1985).

Anidjar, Gil, ' "Once More, Once More": Derrida the Arab, the Jew', introduction to Jacques Derrida, *Acts of Religion* (New York: Routledge, 2002).

Ash, Beth Sharon, 'Jewish Hermeneutics and Contemporary Theories of Textuality: Hartman, Bloom, and Derrida', *Modern Philology*, 85 (1987), pp. 65–80.

Augustine, *Writings in Connection with the Manichean Heresy* (trans. Richard Stothert; Edinburgh: T. & T. Clark, 1872).

Aulén, Gustaf, *Christus Victor: An Historical Study of the Three Main Types of the Idea of Atonement* (trans. A.G. Herbert; New York: Macmillan, 1951).

Bahti, Timothy, 'Ambiguity and Indeterminacy: The Juncture', *Comparative Literature*, 38 (1986), pp. 209–23.

Bakhtin, M.M., *The Dialogic Imagination* (ed. Michael Holquist; trans. Caryl Emerson and Michael Holquist; Austin, TX: University of Texas Press, 1981).

Bal, Mieke, *Death and Dissymmetry: The Politics of Coherence in the Book of Judges* (Chicago: University of Chicago Press, 1988).

Barnstone, Willis, *The Poetics of Translation: History, Theory, Practice* (New Haven: Yale University Press, 1993).

Barr, James, *The Concept of Biblical Theology: An Old Testament Perspective* (Minneapolis: Fortress Press, 1999).

—'The Literal, the Allegorical, and Modern Biblical Scholarship', *JSOT*, 44 (1989), pp. 3–17.

Barrett, C.K., *The Epistle to the Romans* (London: A. & C. Black, 1973).

Barthes, Roland, *Image, Music, Text* (New York: Hill & Wang, 1977).

Barton, John, *Holy Writings, Sacred Text: The Canon in Early Christianity* (Louisville, KY: Westminster/John Knox Press, 1997).

Bauman, Zygmunt, *Postmodern Ethics* (Oxford and Cambridge: Basil Blackwell, 1993).

Beare, Frank W., *The Gospel according to Matthew: Translation, Introduction, and Commentary* (San Francisco: Harper & Row, 1981).

Bechtel, Lyn M., 'What If Dinah Is Not Raped? (Genesis 34)', *JSOT*, 62 (1994), pp. 19–36.

Bechtel, Trevor, 'How to Eat Your Bible: Performance and Understanding for Mennonites', *Conrad Grebel Review* (forthcoming).

Beker, J. Christiaan, *Paul the Apostle: The Triumph of God in Life and Thought* (Philadelphia: Fortress, 1980).

—*Paul's Apocalyptic Gospel: The Coming Triumph of God* (Philadelphia: Fortress Press, 1982).

Bernard of Clairvaux, *On the Song of Songs IV* (trans. Irene Edmonds; Kalamazoo, MI: Cistercian Publications, 1980).

Betz, Hans Dieter, *The Sermon on the Mount: A Commentary on the Sermon on the Mount, including the Sermon on the Plain (Matthew 5.3–7.27 and Luke 6.20-49)* (Hermeneia; Minneapolis: Augsburg Fortress Press, 1995).

Black, Fiona C., 'Nocturnal Egression: Exploring Some Margins of the Song of Songs', in A.K.M. Adam (ed.), *Postmodern Interpretations of the Bible – A Reader* (St Louis, MO: Chalice Press, 2001), pp. 93–104.

Booth, Wayne C., *The Company We Keep* (Berkeley: University of California Press, 1988).

Borg, Marcus J., *Meeting Jesus Again for the First Time: The Historical Jesus and the Heart of Contemporary Faith* (San Francisco: HarperSanFrancisco, 1994).

Borg, Marcus J., and N.T. Wright, *The Meaning of Jesus: Two Visions* (San Francisco: Harper, 2000).

Bornkamm, Günther, 'Das Doppelgebot der Liebe', in *Neutestamentliche Studien für Rudolf Bultmann* (Berlin: Alfred Töpelmann, 2nd edn, 1957), pp. 85–93.

—*Paul* (trans. D.M.G. Stalker; New York: Harper & Row, 1971).

Brenner, Athalya, 'Introduction', in Athalya Brenner (ed.), *A Feminist Companion to the Latter Prophets* (FCB, 8; Sheffield: Sheffield Academic Press, 1995), pp. 21–37.

Brett, Mark G., *Genesis: Procreation and the Politics of Identity* (Old Testament Readings; London: Routledge, 2000).

—'Self-criticism, Cretan Liars and the Sly Redactors of Genesis', in Ingrid Kitzberger (ed.), *Autobiographical Biblical Criticism: Between Text and Self* (Leiden: DEO, 2002), pp. 114–32.

—'Canto Ergo Sum: Indigenous Peoples and Postcolonial Theology', *Pacifica* 16 (2003), pp. 247–56.

Brown, Joanne Carlson, and Carole R. Bohn (eds.), *Christianity, Patriarchy and Abuse: A Feminist Critique* (Cleveland: Pilgrim Press, 1989).

Bruce, F.F., *The Epistle of Paul to the Romans* (NICNT; Grand Rapids: Eerdmans, 1963).

Brueggemann, Walter, *Genesis* (Interpretation; Atlanta: John Knox Press, 1982).

—'A Text That Redescribes', *TTod*, 58 (2002), pp. 526–40.

—*Theology of the Old Testament: Testimony, Dispute, Advocacy* (Minneapolis: Augsburg-Fortress, 1997).

Bultmann, Rudolf, 'Is Exegesis without Presuppositions Possible?', in Schubert M. Ogden (ed. and trans.), *Existence and Faith: Shorter Writings of Rudolf Bultmann* (London and Glasgow: Collins, 1964), pp. 342–51.

—'Das Problem der Ethik bei Paulus', *ZNW*, 23 (1924), pp. 123–40.

—*Theology of the New Testament* (2 vols.; trans. Kendrick Grobel; New York: Charles Scribner's Sons, 1951 and 1955).

Calvin, John, *Commentaries on the Last Four Books of Moses* (Grand Rapids: Baker Book House, 1989).

Campbell, William S., *Paul's Gospel in an Intercultural Context: Jew and Gentile in the Letter to the Romans* (Frankfurt and New York: Peter Lang, 1991).

Caputo, John D., *Against Ethics: Contributions to a Poetics of Obligation with Constant Reference to Deconstruction* (Bloomington and Indianapolis: Indiana University Press, 1993).

—'Instants, Secrets and Singularities: Dealing Death in Kierkegaard and Derrida', in Martin J. Matustík and Merold Westphal (eds), *Kierkegaard in Post/Modernity* (Bloomington: Indiana University Press, 1995), pp. 216–38.

—*The Prayers and Tears of Jacques Derrida: Religion without Religion* (Bloomington, IN: Indiana University Press, 1997).

Carson, Donald A., *Jesus' Sermon on the Mount and His Confrontation with the World: An Exposition of Matthew 5–10* (Toronto and Grand Rapids: Global Christian Publishers, 1999).

—*The Sermon on the Mount: An Evangelical Exposition of Matthew 5–7* (Grand Rapids: Baker Book House, 1978).

Caspi, Mishael Maswari, 'The Story of the Rape of Dinah: The Narrator and the Reader', *Hebrew Studies*, 26 (1985), pp. 25–45.

Charleston, Steve, 'The Old Testament of Native America', in Susan B. Thistlethwaite and Mary Potter Engels (eds.), *Lift Every Voice: Constructing Christian Theologies from the Underside* (San Francisco: HarperCollins, 1990), pp. 49–61.

Childs, Brevard S., *Biblical Theology in Crisis* (Philadelphia: Westminster, 1970).

—*Biblical Theology of the Old and New Testaments* (Minneapolis: Fortress Press, 1993).

—*The Book of Exodus, A Critical, Theological Commentary* (OTL; Louisville, KY: Westminster Press, 1974).

Cloud, John, 'Meet the Prophet', *Time Magazine* (July 1, 2002), pp. 50–53.

Collins, John J. (ed.), 'Apocalypse: The Morphology of a Genre', *Semeia*, 14 (1979).

Confucius, *The Analects of Confucius (Lun Yu)* (trans. Chichung Huang; New York: Oxford University Press, 1997).

Conzelmann, Hans, *An Outline of the Theology of the New Testament* (trans. John Bowden; New York: Harper and Row, 1969).

Cosgrove, Charles H., 'Advocating One Reasonable Interpretation of Paul against Other Reasonable Interpretations: A Theological Approach to the *Sonderweg* Question', in Robert Gagnon (ed.), *Another Way? Pauline Soteriology for Jews and Gentiles in Romans* (Grand Rapids: Eerdmans, forthcoming).

—*Appealing to Scripture in Moral Debate: Five Hermeneutical Rules* (Grand Rapids: Eerdmans, 2002).

—*Elusive Israel: The Puzzle of Election in Romans* (Louisville, KY: Westminster/John Knox Press, 1997).

—'The Justification of the "Other": An Interpretation of Rom. 1.18–4.25', in Eugene H. Lovering (ed.), *Society of Biblical Literature 1992 Seminar Papers* (Atlanta: Scholars Press, 1992), pp. 613–34.

—'Rhetorical Suspense in Romans 9–11: A Study in Polyvalence and Hermeneutical Election', *JBL*, 115 (1996), pp. 271–87.

Critchley, Simon, *The Ethics of Deconstruction: Derrida and Levinas* (Oxford: Basil Blackwell, 1992).

Crossan, John Dominic, *Jesus: A Revolutionary Biography* (San Francisco: HarperSanFrancisco, 1994).

Crüsemann, Frank, ' "You Know the Heart of a Stranger" (Exodus 23.9): A Recollection of the Torah in the Face of New Nationalism and Xenophobia', *Concilium*, 4 (1993), pp. 95–109.

Culler, Jonathan, *On Deconstruction: Theory and Criticism after Structuralism* (Ithaca, NY: Cornell University Press, 1982).

Culpepper, R. Alan, *The Gospel and Letters of John* (Nashville: Abingdon Press, 1998).

Dahl, Nils A., 'Trinitarian Baptismal Creeds and New Testament Christology', in Donald H. Juel (ed.), *Jesus the Christ: The Historical Origins of Christological Doctrine* (Minneapolis: Fortress Press, 1991).

Dauber, Kenneth, 'The Bible as Literature: Reading Like the Rabbis', *Semeia*, 31 (1985), pp. 27–48.

Davies, W.D., and Dale C. Allison, Jr, *A Critical and Exegetical Commentary on the Gospel according to Matthew*, vol. 3: *Commentary on Matthew XIX–XXVIII* (Edinburgh: T. & T. Clark, 1988).

Davis, Colin, *Levinas: An Introduction* (Notre Dame: University of Notre Dame Press, 1996).

Delitzsch, Franz, *Commentary on the Song of Songs and Ecclesiastes* (trans. M.G. Easton; Grand Rapids: Eerdmans, 1950).

Derrida, Jacques, *Donner la mort* (Paris: Galilée, 2nd edn, 1999). ET: *The Gift of Death* (trans. D. Willis; Chicago: Chicago University Press, 1995).

—'Hospitality, Justice and Responsibility: A Dialogue with Jacques Derrida', in R. Kearney and M. Dooley (eds.), *Questioning Ethics: Contemporary Debates in Philosophy* (London and New York: Routledge, 1999), pp. 65–83.

—'Living on/Border Lines' (trans. James Hulbert), in Harold Bloom *et al.*, *Deconstruction and Criticism* (New York: Seabury, 1979), pp. 75–176.

—*Of Grammatology* (trans. Gayatri Spivak; Baltimore: The Johns Hopkins University Press, 1976).

Dilthey, Wilhelm, *Selected Writings* (ed. and trans. H.P. Rickman; New York: Cambridge University Press, 1976).

Dodd, C.H., *The Epistle of Paul to the Romans* (New York: Harper, 1970).

Donaldson, Terence L., 'The Law That Hangs (Matthew 22.40): Rabbinic Formulations and Matthean Social World', *CBQ*, 57 (1995), pp. 689–709.

Donfried, Karl P. (ed.), *The Romans Debate* (Peabody, MA: Hendrickson, rev. and expanded edn, 1991).

Douglas, Mary, *In the Wilderness: The Doctrine of Defilement in the Book of Numbers* (Sheffield: JSOT Press, 1993).

—*Leviticus as Literature* (Oxford: Oxford University Press, 1999).

Driver, S.R., *The Book of Exodus* (Cambridge: Cambridge University Press, 1911).

Dube, Musa, and Jeffrey L. Staley (eds.), *John and Postcolonialism: Travel, Space, and Power* (New York: Continuum International, 2002).

Dunn, James D.G., 'The Formal and Theological Coherence of Romans', in Karl P. Donfried (ed.), *The Romans Debate* (Peabody, MA: Hendrickson, expanded edn, 1977 and 1991), pp. 245–50.

—'The New Perspective on Paul', in Karl P. Donfried (ed.), *The Romans Debate*, exp. edn (Peabody, MA: Hendrickson, 1991), pp. 299–308.

—*Romans 1–8* and *Romans 9–16* (WBC 38a & b; Waco, TX: Word Books, 1988–89).

—*The Theology of Paul the Apostle* (Grand Rapids: Eerdmans, 1998).

Dworkin, Ronald, *Law's Empire* (Cambridge, MA: Harvard University Press, 1985).

—'The Model of Rules', *The University of Chicago Law Review*, 35 (1967), pp. 14–46 (reprinted in *Taking Rights Seriously* [Cambridge, MA: Harvard University Press, 1977], pp. 14–45).

Efird, James M., *End-Times: Rapture, Antichrist, Millennium* (Nashville: Abingdon Press, 1986).

Ehrman, Bart D., *Jesus: Apocalyptic Prophet of the New Millennium* (New York: Oxford University Press, 1999).

Elliott, Neil, *Liberating Paul: The Justice of God and the Politics of the Apostle* (Sheffield: Sheffield Academic Press, 1995).

—*The Rhetoric of Romans: Argumentative Constraint and Strategy and Paul's Debate with Judaism* (JSNTSup, 55; Sheffield: Sheffield Academic Press, 1990).

—'Romans 13.1-7 in the Context of Imperial Propaganda', in Richard A. Horsley (ed.), *Paul and Empire: Religion and Power in Roman Imperial Society* (Harrisburg, PA: Trinity Press International, 1997), pp. 191–204.

Elyon, Ari, 'The Torah as Love Goddess', in Michael Chernick (ed.), *Essential Papers on the Talmud* (New York: New York University Press, 1994), pp. 463–76.

Exum, J. Cheryl, 'Ten Things Every Feminist Should Know about the Song of Songs', in Athalya Brenner and Carole R. Fontaine (eds.), *A Feminist Companion to the Song of Songs* (A Feminist Companion to the Bible, Second Series, 6; Sheffield: Sheffield Academic Press, 2000), pp. 24–35.

Felder, Cane Hope (ed.), *Stony the Road We Trod: African American Biblical Interpretation* (Minneapolis: Fortress Press, 1991).

Fetterley, Judith, *The Resisting Reader: A Feminist Approach to American Literature* (Bloomington, IN: Indiana University Press, 1978).

Fewell, Danna Nolan and Gary A. Phillips, 'Ethics, Bible, Reading As If', *Semeia*, 77 (1997), pp. 1–21.

Fingarette, Herbert, *Confucius: The Secular as the Sacred* (New York: Harper & Row, 1972).

Fish, Stanley, *Doing What Comes Naturally: Change, Rhetoric, and the Practice of Theory in Literary and Legal Studies* (Durham, NC, and London: Duke University Press, 1989).

Florovsky, Georges, 'The Function of Tradition in the Ancient Church', in *Bible, Church, Tradition: An Eastern Orthodox View* (Belmont, MA: Norland Publishing Company, 1972), pp. 73–92.

Fontaine, Carole R., ' "Go Forth Into the Fields": An Earth-Centered Reading of the Song of Songs', in Norman C. Habel and Shirley Wurst (eds.), *The Earth Story in the Wisdom Traditions*, Earth Bible, 3 (Sheffield: Sheffield Academic Press, 2001), pp. 126–42.

—' "Many Devices"(Qoheleth 7.23–8.1): Qoheleth, Misogyny and the *Malleus Maleficarum* ', in Athalya Brenner and Carole R. Fontaine (eds.), *A Feminist Companion to the Wisdom and Psalms* (A Feminist Companion to the Bible, Second Series, 2; Sheffield: Sheffield Academic Press, 1998), pp. 137–68.

—*Smooth Words: Women, Proverbs and Performance in Biblical Wisdom* (Sheffield: Sheffield Academic Press/Continuum, 2002).

Fortna, Robert T. and Tom Thatcher (eds.), *Jesus in the Johannine Tradition* (Louisville, KY: Westminster/John Knox Press, 2001).

Fowl, Stephen, *Engaging Scripture: A Model for Theological Interpretation* (Oxford: Basil Blackwell, 1999).

Fowl, Stephen, and Gregory L. Jones, *Reading in Communion: Scripture and Ethics in the Christian Life* (Grand Rapids: Eerdmans, 1991).

Fox, Michael V., 'The Uses of Indeterminacy', *Semeia*, 71/2 (1995), pp. 173–92.

Freedman, David Noel, ' "Who is Like Thee Among the Gods?" The Religion of Early Israel', in Patrick D. Miller, Paul D. Hanson, and S. Dean McBride (eds.), *Ancient Israelite Religion: Essays in Honor of Frank Moore Cross* (Philadelphia: Fortress Press, 1987), pp. 315–35.

Freedman, David Noel, and Frank Moore Cross, *Studies in Ancient Yahwistic Poetry* (Grand Rapids: Eerdmans, 2nd edn, 1997).

Frei, Hans W. 'The "Literal" Reading of Biblical Narrative in the Christian Tradition: Does It Stretch or Will It Break?', in Frank McConnell (ed.), *The Bible and the Narrative Tradition* (New York: Oxford University Press, 1986), pp. 36–77.

Fretheim, Terence, 'Genesis, Introduction and Commentary', *The New Interpreter's Bible* (Nashville: Abingdon Press, 1994), I, pp. 321–674.

Gabler, Johann Philipp, 'An Oration on the Proper Distinction between Biblical and Dogmatic Theology and the Specific Objectives of Each' (trans. John Sandys-Wunsch and Laurence Eldridge), *SJT*, 33 (1980), pp. 133–44.

Gadamer, Hans-Georg, *Truth and Method* (rev. trans. Joel Weinsheimer and Donald G. Marshall; New York: Crossroad, 2nd edn, 1994).

Gager, John G., *Reinventing Paul* (New York: Oxford University Press, 2000).

Gaston, Lloyd, 'Paul and the Torah', in Alan T. Davies (ed.), *Antisemitism and the Foundations of Christianity* (New York: Paulist Press, 1979), pp. 48–71.

—*Paul and the Torah* (Vancouver: University of British Columbia Press, 1987).

Georgi, Dieter, 'God Turned Upside Down', in Richard A. Horsley (ed.), *Paul and Empire: Religion and Power in Roman Imperial Society* (Harrisburg, PA: Trinity Press International, 1997), pp.148–57.

Gerhardsson, Birger, 'The Hermeneutic Program in Matthew 22.37-40', in R. Hammerton-Kelly and Robin Scroggs (ed.), *Jews, Greeks, and Christians* (Leiden: E.J. Brill, 1976), pp. 129–50.

Gibbs, Nancy, 'Apocalypse Now', *Time Magazine* (July 1, 2002), pp. 40–48.

Gonzalez, Justo, *Out of Every Tribe and Nation: Christian Theology at the Ethnic Roundtable* (Nashville: Abingdon Press, 1992).

Graff, Gerald, 'Determinacy/Indeterminacy', in Frank Lentricchia and Thomas McLaughlin (eds.), *Critical Terms for Literary Study* (Chicago and London: University of Chicago Press, 1990), pp. 163–76.

Grant, Robert M. and David Tracy, *A Short History of the Interpretation of the Bible* (Minneapolis: Fortress Press, 2nd edn, 1984).

Green, William Scott, 'Romancing the Tome: Rabbinic Hermeneutics and the Theory of Literature', *Semeia*, 40 (1987), pp. 147–68.

Grenholm, Cristina and Daniel Patte, 'Overture: Receptions, Critical Interpretations, and Scriptural Criticism', in Cristina Grenholm and Daniel Patte (eds.), *Reading Israel in Romans: Legitimacy and Plausibility of Divergent Interpretations* (Romans Through History and Cultures Series, vol. 1; Harrisburg, PA: Trinity Press International, 2000), pp. 1–54.

Griswold, Wendy, *Cultures and Societies in a Changing World* (London/Thousand Oaks/New Delhi: Pine Forge Press, 1994).

Gundry, Robert H., *Matthew: A Commentary on His Handbook for a Mixed Church under Persecution* (Grand Rapids: Eerdmans, 2nd edn, 1994).

—'The Moral Frustration of Paul Before His Conversion: Sexual Lust in Romans 7.7-25', in Donald A. Hagner and Murray J. Harris (eds.), *Pauline Studies: Essays Presented to F.F. Bruce* (Grand Rapids: Eerdmans, 1980), pp. 228–45.

Gunn, David M. and Danna Nolan Fewell, 'Tipping the Balance: Sternberg's Reader and the Rape of Dinah', *JBL*, 110 (1991), pp. 193–211.

Gustafson, James M., Letter to the editor, *The Christian Century*, 119/3 (July 3–10, 2002), p. 44.

Habermas, Jürgen, *Knowledge and Human Interests* (trans. Jeremy J. Shapiro; Boston: Beacon Press, 1971).

—*Moral Consciousness and Communicative Action* (trans. Christian Lenhardt and Shiery Weber Nicholsen; Cambridge, MA: MIT Press, 1990).

Hägglund, Bengt, 'Die Bedeutung der "regula fidei" als Grundlage theologisher Aussagen', *ST*, 12 (1958), pp. 1–44.

Handelman, Susan, *The Slayers of Moses: The Emergence of Rabbinic Interpretation in Modern Literary Theory* (Albany, NY: SUNY Press, 1982).

Hanson, R.P.C., *Tradition in the Early Church* (Philadelphia: The Westminster Press, 1962).

Harnack, Adolf von, 'Über das Verhältnis des Prologs des Vierten Evangeliums zum ganzen Werk', *ZTK*, 2 (1898), pp. 189–231.

Harrington, Daniel J., *The Gospel of Matthew* (SP Series, 1; Collegeville, MN: Liturgical Press, 1991).

Hassan, Riffat, 'The Issue of Woman-Man Equality in the Islamic Tradition', in K.E. Kvam, L.S. Schearing and W.H. Ziegler (eds.), *Eve and Adam: Jewish, Christian and Muslim Readings on Genesis and Gender* (Indianapolis: Indiana University Press, 1999), pp. 463–76.

—'Women in Muslim Culture', in M. Darrol Bryant (ed.), *Muslim-Christian Dialogue: Problems and Promise* (New York: Paragon Press, 1998), pp. 187–201.

—*Women's Rights and Islam: From the I.C.P.D. to Beijing* (Louisville, KY: Publications, 1995).

Hastings, Adrian (ed.), *The Oxford Companion to Christian Thought* (Oxford: Oxford University Press, 2000).

Hays, Richard B., *The Moral Vision of the New Testament. A Contemporary Introduction to New Testament Ethics: Creation, Cross, and New Creation* (San Francisco: HarperSanFrancisco, 1996).

Heard, R. Christopher, *Dynamics of Diselection: Ambiguity in Genesis 12–36 and Ethnic Boundaries in Post-Exilic Judah* (SBL Semeia Studies, 39; Atlanta: Society of Biblical Literature, 2001).

Hirsch, E.D., 'Three Dimensions of Hermeneutics', in *The Aims of Interpretation* (Chicago and London: University of Chicago Press, 1976).

—*Validity in Interpretation* (New Haven, CT: Yale University Press, 1967).

Hoglund, Kenneth, *Achaemenid Imperial Administration in Syria-Palestine and the Missions of Ezra and Nehemiah* (SBLDS, 125; Atlanta: Scholars Press, 1992).

Holl, Karl, 'Die Rechtfertigungslehre im Lichte der Geschichte des Protestantismus', in *Gesämmelte Aufsätze zur Kirchengeschichte*, III (Tübingen: J.C.B. Mohr, 1922), pp. 525–57.

—'Was hat die Rechtfertigungslehre dem modernen Menschen zu sagen?', in *Gesämmelte Aufsätze zur Kirchengeschichte*, III (Tübingen: J.C.B. Mohr, 1922), pp. 558–67.

Holladay, Carl R., 'Contemporary Methods of Reading the Bible', in *The New Interpreter's Bible*, I (Nashville: Abingdon Press, 1994), pp. 125–49.

Holmgren, Frederick, 'Violence: God's Will on the Edge – Exodus 2.11-25', *Currents in Theology and Mission*, 16 (1989), pp. 425–29.

Hoodfar, Homa, 'The Veil in Their Minds and on Our Heads: Veiling Practices and Muslim Women', in Elizabeth A. Castelli (ed.), *Women, Gender, Religion: a Reader* (New York: Palgrave, 2001), pp. 420–46.

Horsley, Richard A., *1 Corinthians* (ANTC; Nashville: Abingdon Press, 1998).

—'1 Corinthians: A Case Study of Paul's Assembly as an Alternative Society', in Richard A. Horsley (ed.), *Paul and Empire: Religion and Power in Roman Imperial Society* (Harrisburg, PA: Trinity Press International, 1997), pp. 242–52.

—'General Introduction', in Richard A. Horsley (ed.), *Paul and Empire: Religion and Power in Roman Imperial Society* (Harrisburg, PA: Trinity Press International, 1997), pp. 1–8.

—'The Gospel of Imperial Salvation: Introduction', in Richard A. Horsley (ed.), *Paul and Empire: Religion and Power in Roman Imperial Society* (Harrisburg, PA: Trinity Press International, 1997), pp. 9–24.

—'Introduction: Krister Stendahl's Challenge to Pauline Studies', in Richard A. Horsley (ed.), *Paul and Politics: Ekklesia, Israel, Imperium, Interpretation* (Harrisburg, PA: Trinity Press International, 2000), pp. 1–16.

—'Rhetoric and Empire – and 1 Corinthians', in Richard A. Horsley (ed.), *Paul and Politics: Ekklesia, Israel, Imperium, Interpretation* (Harrisburg, PA: Trinity Press International, 2000), pp. 72–102.

Jameson, Fredric, *The Political Unconscious: Narrative as a Socially Symbolic Act* (Ithaca, NY: Cornell University Press, 1981).

Jobling, David, and Tina Pippin (eds.), 'Ideological Criticism of Biblical Texts', *Semeia*, 59 (1992).

Johnson, E. Elizabeth and David M. Hay, *Pauline Theology*, vol. 4: *Looking Back, Pressing On* (SBL Seminar Series, 4; Atlanta: Scholars Press, 1997).

Johnson, Mark, *Philosophical Perspectives on Metaphor* (Minneapolis: University of Minnesota Press, 1981).

Käsemann, Ernst, *Commentary on Romans* (trans. Geoffrey W. Bromiley; Grand Rapids: Eerdmans, 1980).

—*New Testament Questions of Today* (trans. W.J. Montague; Philadelphia: Fortress Press, 1969).

—*Perspectives on Paul* (trans. Margaret Kohl; Philadelphia: Fortress Press, 1971).

Kaser, Max, *Roman Private Law* (trans. Rolf Dannenbring; Pretoria: University of South Africa, 4th edn, 1984).

Keck, Leander E., *Paul and His Letters* (PC; Philadelphia: Fortress Press, 2nd edn, 1988).

Keel, O., *The Song of Songs: A Continental Commentary* (trans. F.J. Gaiser; Minneapolis: Fortress Press, 1994).

Keener, Craig S., *A Commentary on the Gospel of Matthew* (Grand Rapids: Eerdmans, 1999).

Keil, C.F., *Commentary on the Pentateuch* (Edinburgh: T. & T. Clark, 1864).

Keller, Catharine, *Apocalypse Now and Then: A Feminist Guide to the End of the World* (Boston: Beacon Press, 1996).

Kelsey, David H., *The Uses of Scripture in Recent Theology* (Philadelphia: Fortress Press, 1975). Reprinted as *Proving Doctrine: The Uses of Scripture in Modern Theology* (Harrisburg, PA: Trinity Press International, 1999).

Kermode, Frank, *The Classic: Literary Images of Permanance and Change* (New York: Viking Press, 1975).

—*The Genesis of Secrecy: On the Interpretation of Narrative* (Cambridge, MA: Harvard University Press, 1979).

—*The Sense of an Ending: Studies in the Theory of Fiction* (New York: Oxford University Press, 1967).

Kierkegaard, Sören, *Fear and Trembling, and Sickness unto Death* (trans. W. Lowrie; Princeton, NJ: Princeton University Press, 2nd edn, 1954).

King, Martin Luther, *Stride Toward Freedom: The Montgomery Story* (New York: Harper & Brothers, 1958).

Koch, Klaus, *The Rediscovery of Apocalyptic* (trans. Margaret Kohl; London: SCM Press, 1972).

Koester, Helmut, 'Imperial Ideology and Paul's Eschatology in 1 Thessalonians', in Richard A. Horsley (ed.), *Paul and Empire: Religion and Power in Roman Imperial Society* (Harrisburg, PA: Trinity Press International, 1997), pp. 158–66.

Kreuziger, Frederick, *Apocalypse and Science Fiction: A Dialectic of Religious and Secular Soteriologies* (AARAS, 40; Chico, CA: Scholars Press, 1982).

Lacocque, André, *Romance, She Wrote: A Hermeneutical Essay on Song of Songs* (Harrisburg, PA: Trinity Press International, 1998).

LaHaye, Tim and Beverly LaHaye, *The Act of Marriage* (Grand Rapids: Zondervan, 1976).

LaHaye, Tim, with Jerry B. Jenkins, *Apollyon* (Wheaton, IL: Tyndale, 1999).

—*Assassins* (Wheaton, IL: Tyndale, 2000).

—*Desecration* (Wheaton, IL: Tyndale, 2002).

—*The Indwelling* (Wheaton, IL: Tyndale, 2001).

—*Left Behind* (Wheaton, IL: Tyndale, 1996).

—*The Mark* (Wheaton, IL: Tyndale, 2001).

—*Nicolae* (Wheaton, IL: Tyndale, 1998).

—*The Remnant* (Wheaton, IL: Tyndale, 2002).

—*Soul Harvest* (Wheaton, IL: Tyndale, 1999).

—*Tribulation Force* (Wheaton, IL: Tyndale, 1997).

Lanser, Susan S., '(Feminist) Criticism in the Garden: Inferring Genesis 2–3', *Semeia*, 41 (1988), pp. 67–84.

Large, Ron, 'American Apocalyptic', *The Fourth R*, 4 (1991), pp. 1–8.

Lasine, Stuart, 'Indeterminacy and the Bible: A Review of Literary and Anthropological Theories and Their Application to Biblical Texts', *Hebrew Studies*, 27 (1986), pp. 48–80.

Leech, Geoffrey N., and Michael H. Short, *Principles of Pragmatics* (London and New York: Longman, 1983).

—*Style in Fiction: A Linguistic Introduction to English Fictional Prose* (London and New York: Longman, 1981).

Lehmann, Paul, '¿Que está haciendo el Dios en el mundo?', *Cuadernos teológicos*, 10 (1961), pp. 243–68.

Levenson, Jon. D., *The Death and Resurrection of the Beloved Son: The Transformation of Child Sacrifice in Judaism and Christianity* (New Haven: Yale University Press, 1983).

Levinas, Emmanuel, *The Levinas Reader* (ed. Seán Hand; Oxford: Basil Blackwell, 1989).

—*Noms propres* (Montpellier: Fata Morgana, 1976).

—*Otherwise Than Being: Or Beyond Essence* (trans. A. Lingis; Pittsburgh: Duquesne University Press, 1999).

—*Totality and Infinity: An Essay on Exteriority* (trans. A. Lingis; Pittsburgh: Duquesne University Press, 1969).

Levine, Amy-Jill, 'Anti-Judaism and the Gospel of Matthew', in William R. Farmer (ed.), *Anti-Judaism and the Gospels* (Valley Forge, PA: Trinity Press International, 1999), pp. 9–36.

—'Matthean Jesus, Biblical Law, and Hemorrhaging Woman', in D.R. Bauer and M.A. Powell (eds.), *Treasures Old and New: Recent Contributions to Matthean Studies* (SBL Symposium Series, 1; Atlanta: Scholars Press, 1996), pp. 379–97.

—'Matthew's Advice to a Divided Readership', in David E. Aune (ed.), *The Gospel of Matthew in Current Study: Studies in Memory of William G. Thompson, SJ* (Grand Rapids: Eerdmans, 2001), pp. 22–41.

Lewis, C.S., *The Screwtape Letters and Screwtape Proposes a Toast* (New York: Macmillan, 1966).

Lindsey, Hal, *The Late, Great Planet Earth* (Grand Rapids: Zondervan, 1970).

—*The 1980's: Countdown to Armageddon* (New York: Bantam, 1980).

Lloyd-Jones, D. Martyn, *Romans: An Exposition of Chapter 7.1–8.4: The Law, Its Functions and Limits* (London: Banner of Truth Trust, 1973).

Louw, J.P., *Semantics of New Testament Greek* (Philadelphia: Fortress Press, 1982).

Luz, Ulrich, *Matthew in History: Interpretation, Influence, and Effects* (Minneapolis: Fortress Press, 1994).

MacIntyre, Alisdair, *After Virtue* (London: Gerald Duckworth, 1981).

Mallouhi, Mazhar *et al.* (eds.), *The Beginnings of the World and Humanity: A Contemporary Study in Genesis* [in Arabic] (Beirut, Lebanon: Dar Al Jil, 2001).

Martin, Joel W. and Conrad E. Ostwalt Jr (eds.), *Screening the Sacred: Religion, Myth, and Ideology in Popular American Film* (Boulder, CO: Westview, 1995).

Meeks, Wayne A., 'On Trusting an Unpredictable God', in John T. Carroll *et al.* (eds.), *Faith and History: Essays in Honor of Paul W. Meyer* (Atlanta, GA: Scholars Press, 1990), pp. 105–24.

—'Understanding Early Christian Ethics', *JBL*, 105 (1986), pp. 3–11.

Meier, John P., *A Marginal Jew: Rethinking the Historical Jesus*, vol. 2: *Mentor, Message, and Miracles* (New York: Doubleday, 1994).

Midrash Rabbah, Exodus (trans. S.M. Lehrman; London: Soncino, 1988).

Moi, Tori (ed.), *The Kristeva Reader* (New York: Columbia University Press, 1986).

Moore, Stephen D., 'Revolting Revelations', in *God's Beauty Parlor and Other Queer Spaces in and around the Bible* (Stanford, CA: Stanford University Press, 2001), pp. 173–99.

Morton, Michael and Judith Still (eds.), *Intertextuality: Theories and Practices* (Manchester and New York: Manchester University Press, 1991).

Mosala, Itumelang J., 'The Use of the Bible in Black Theology', in Itumelang J. Mosala and Buti Tlhagale (eds.), *The Unquestionable Right to be Free: Black Theology from South Africa* (Maryknoll, NY: Orbis Books, 1986), pp. 175–99.

Murphy, R. E., *The Song of Songs: A Commentary on the Book of Canticles or the Song of Songs* (Hermeneia; Minneapolis: Fortress Press 1990).

Nida, Eugene A. and C.R. Tabor, *The Theory and Practice of Translation: Helps for Translators* (Leiden: E.J. Brill, 1969).

Noble, Paul R., 'A "Balanced" Reading of the Rape of Dinah: Some Exegetical and Methodological Observations', *BibInt*, 4 (1996), pp. 173–204.

O'Day, Gail R. and David Petersen (eds.), *The Access Bible: New Revised Standard Version with the Apocryphal/Deuterocanonical Books* (College Edition; Oxford and New York: Oxford University Press, 1999).

Ostriker, Alicia, 'A Holy of Holies: The Song of Songs as Countertext', in Athalya Brenner and Carole R. Fontaine (eds.), *A Feminist Companion to the The Song of Songs* (FCB, 2nd series; Sheffield: Sheffield Academic Press, 2000), pp. 36–54.

Ostwalt Jr, Conrad E., 'Hollywood and Armageddon: Apocalyptic Themes in Recent Cinematic Presentation', in George Aichele and Richard Walsh (eds.), *Screening Scripture: Intertextual Connections Between Scripture and Film* (Harrisburg, PA: Trinity International, 2002), pp. 55–63.

Pask, Kevin, 'Cyborg Economics: Desire and Labor in the *Terminator* Films', in Richard Dellamora (ed.), *Postmodern Apocalypse: Theory and Cultural Practice at the End* (Philadelphia: University of Pennsylvania Press, 1995), pp. 182–98.

Patte, Daniel, *The Challenge of Discipleship: A Critical Study of the Sermon on the Mount as Scripture* (Harrisburg, PA: Trinity Press International, 1999).

—*Discipleship according to the Sermon on the Mount: Four Legitimate Readings, Four Plausible Views of Discipleship, and Their Relative Values* (Harrisburg, PA: Trinity Press International, 1996).

—*Ethics of Biblical Interpretation: A Reevaluation* (Louisville, KY: Westminster/John Knox Press, 1995).

—*Paul's Faith and the Power of the Gospel* (Philadelphia: Fortress Press, 1983).

—*The Religious Dimensions of Biblical Texts: Greimas's Structural Semiotics and Biblical Exegesis* (SBL Semeia Studies; Atlanta: Scholars Press, 1990), pp. 1–72.

Patte, Daniel (ed.), Enrique Dussel, Cristina Grenholm, Kwok Pui-lan, Archie Chi Chung Lee, Vasile Mihoc, Jesse Mugambi and Eugene TeSelle (assoc. eds.), *The Cambridge Dictionary of Christianity* (Cambridge, UK, and New York: Cambridge University Press, forthcoming).

Phillips, Gary A., 'Levinas', in A.K.M. Adam (ed.), *Handbook of Postmodern Biblical Interpretation* (St Louis: Chalice Press, 2000), pp. 154–59.

Pilch, John J., 'Family Violence in Cross-Cultural Perspective: An Approach for Feminist Interpreters of the Bible', in Athalya Brenner and Carole R. Fontaine (eds.), *A Feminist Companion to Reading the Bible: Approaches, Methods, Strategies* (Sheffield: Sheffield Academic Press, 1997), pp. 306–25.

Pippin, Tina, *Apocalyptic Bodies: The Biblical End of the World in Text and Image* (New York: Routledge, 1999).

Pope, Marvin, *Song of Songs* (AB; Garden City, NY: Doubleday, 1977).

Pressler, Carolyn, 'Sexual Violence and Deuteronomic Law', in Athalya Brenner (ed.), *A Feminist Companion to Exodus and Deuteronomy* (FCB, 6; Sheffield: Sheffield Academic Press, 1994), pp. 102–12.

Quinn, Philip L., 'Atonement, theories of', in Adrian Hastings (ed.), *Oxford Companion to Christian Thought* (Oxford: Oxford University Press, 2000), pp. 51–52.

Quintilian, *Institutio Oratoria* (trans. H.E. Butler; Loeb Classical Library; Cambridge, MA: Harvard University Press, 1921; London: William Heinemann, 1921).

Rad, Gerhard von, *Genesis: A Commentary* (OTL; Philadelphia: Westminster Press, rev. edn, 1972).

Reinhartz, Adele, *Befriending the Beloved Disciple* (New York: Continuum, 2001).

Rendtorff, Rolf, 'The *Ger* in the Priestly Laws of the Pentateuch', in Mark G. Brett (ed.), *Ethnicity and the Bible* (Leiden: E.J. Brill, 1996), pp. 77–88.

Richards, I.A., *The Philosophy of Rhetoric* (New York: Oxford University Press, 1965).

Riches, John, *A Century of New Testament Study* (Valley Forge, PA: Trinity Press International, 1993).

Ricoeur, Paul, *The Symbolism of Evil* (Boston: Beacon Press, 1967).

Ruether, Rosemary Radforth, *Faith and Fratricide: The Theological Roots of Antisemitism* (New York: Seabury, 1974).

Russell, D.S., *The Old Testament Pseudepigrapha: Patriarchs and Prophets in Early Judaism* (Philadelphia: Fortress Press, 1987).

Sanders, E.P., 'The Covenant as a Soteriological Category and the Nature of Salvation in Palestinian and Hellenistic Judaism', in Robert Hammerton-Kelly and Robin Scroggs (eds.), *Jews, Greeks and Christians* (Leiden: E.J. Brill, 1976), pp. 11–44.

—*Paul and Palestinian Judaism: A Comparison of Patterns of Religion* (Philadelphia: Fortress Press, 1977).

Sarna, Nahum M., *Genesis: The Traditional Hebrew Text with the New JPS Translation* (JPS Torah Commentary; Philadelphia: Jewish Publication Society, 1989).

Scalia, Antonin, *A Matter of Interpretation: Federal Courts and the Law* (Princeton, NJ: Princeton University Press, 1997).

Schaberg, Jane, 'Luke', in Carol A. Newsom and Sharon H. Ringe (eds.), *The Women's Bible Commentary* (Louisville, KY: Westminster/John Knox Press, exp. edn, 1998), pp. 275–92.

Schearing, Linda, 'Millennialism, Mayhem, and the Year 2000: Apocalypticism and the Radical Right' (unpublished paper).

Schipani, Daniel, *Religious Education Encounters Liberation Theology* (Birmingham, AL: Religious Education Press, 1998), pp. 210–60.

Scholz, Susanne, *Rape Plots: A Feminist Cultural Study of Genesis 34* (Studies in Biblical Literature, 13; New York: Peter Lang, 2000).

—'Was It Really Rape in Genesis 34? Biblical Scholarship as a Reflection of Cultural Assumptions', in Harold C. Washington, Susan L. Graham and Pamela L. Thimmes (eds.), *Escaping Eden: New Feminist Perspectives on the Bible* (Sheffield: Sheffield Academic Press, 1998), pp. 182–98.

Schrage, Wolfgang, *Der erste Brief an die Korinther*, vol. 1 (EKKNT, VII/1; Zürich: Benziger Verlag, 1991; Neukirchen–Vluyn: Neukirchener Verlag, 1991).

—*The Ethics of the New Testament* (trans. David E. Green; Philadelphia: Fortress Press, 1988).

Schreiter, Robert J., *Constructing Local Theologies* (Chicago: Catholic Theological Union, 1977).

Schüssler Fiorenza, Elisabeth, '1 Corinthians', in James L. Mays (ed.), *The HarperCollins Bible Commentary* (San Francisco: HarperSanFrancisco, 2000), pp. 1074–92.

—'The Ethics of Biblical Interpretation: Decentering Biblical Scholarship', *JBL*, 107 (1988), pp. 3–17.

—*In Memory of Her: A Feminist Theological Reconstruction of Christian Origins* (New York: Crossroad, 1983).

—'Missionaries, Apostles, Coworkers: Romans 16 and the Reconstruction of Women's Early Christian History', *Word and World*, 6 (1986), pp. 420–33.

—'Paul and the Politics of Interpretation', in Richard A. Horsley (ed.), *Paul and Politics: Ekklesia, Israel, Imperium, Interpretation* (Harrisburg, PA: Trinity Press International, 2000), pp. 40–57.

—'The Praxis of Coequal Discipleship', in Richard A. Horsley (ed.), *Paul and Empire: Religion and Power in Roman Imperial Society* (Harrisburg, PA: Trinity Press International, 1997), pp. 224–41.

—*Rhetoric and Ethic: The Politics of Biblical Studies* (Minneapolis: Fortress Press, 1999).

Schweitzer, Albert, *Paul and His Interpreters: a Critical History* (trans. W. Montgomery; London: A. & C. Black, 1912).

—*The Quest of the Historical Jesus: A Critical Study of Its Progress from Reimarus to Wrede* (New York: Macmillan, 1973).

Segovia, Fernando, 'Racial and Ethnic Minorities in Biblical Studies', in Mark Brett (ed.), *Ethnicity and the Bible* (Leiden and New York: E.J. Brill, 1996), pp. 468–92.

Segovia, Fernando and Mary Ann Tolbert (eds.), *Reading from This Place: Social Location and Biblical Interpretation in Global Perspective* (2 vols.; Minneapolis: Fortress Press, 1995).

Segundo, Juan Luis, 'The Hermeneutic Circle', in *Liberation of Theology* (trans. John Drury; Maryknoll, NY: Orbis Books, 1976), pp. 7–38.

Siker, Jeffrey S., *Scripture and Ethics: Twentieth-Century Portraits* (New York and Oxford: Oxford University Press, 1977).

Simpson, William. K. (ed.), 'The Contendings of Horus and Seth', in *The Literature of Ancient Egypt: An Anthology of Stories, Instructions, and Poetry* (New Haven: Yale University Press, new edn, 1973), pp. 108–26.

Smart, James, *The Strange Silence of the Bible in the Church* (Philadelphia: Westminster Press, 1970).

Smith, James K.A., *The Fall of Interpretation: Philosophical Foundations for a Creational Hermeneutic* (Downers Grove, IL: InterVarsity Press, 2000).

Smith, Wilfred Cantwell, *What Is Scripture: A Comparative Approach* (Minneapolis: Fortress Press, 1993).

Smylie, James H., 'A New Heaven and New Earth: Uses of the Millennium in American Religious History', *Int*, 53 (1999), pp. 143–57.

Snodgrass, Klyne R., 'Matthew's Understanding of the Law', *Int*, 46 (1992), pp. 368–78.

Soskice, Janet Martin, *Metaphor and Religious Language* (Oxford: Clarendon Press, 1985).

Southern Poverty Law Center, 'Racist Identity Sect Fuels Nationwide Extremist Movement', Intelligence Report #79 (August 1995).

Sparks, H.F.D. (ed.), *The Apocryphal Old Testament* (Oxford: Clarendon Press, 1984).

Spivak, Gayatri C. 'Can the Subaltern Speak?', in G. Nelson and L. Grossberg (eds.), *Marxism and the Interpretation of Culture* (London: Macmillan, 1988), pp. 277–313.

Staley, Jeffrey L., *Reading with a Passion: Rhetoric, Autobiography, and the American West in the Gospel of John* (New York: Continuum, 1995).

Stendahl, Krister, 'Biblical Theology, Contemporary', in G.A. Buttrick (gen. ed.), *The Interpreter's Dictionary of the Bible: An Illustrated Encyclopedia*, I (Nashville: Abingdon Press, 1962), pp. 418–32.

—'A Last Word', in Daniel Patte and Eugene TeSelle (eds.), *Engaging Augustine on Romans: Self, Context, and Theology in Interpretation* (Harrisburg, PA: Trinity Press International, 2002), pp. 270–72.

—*Paul Among Jews and Gentiles and Other Essays* (Philadelphia: Fortress Press, 1976).

Steinmetz, David C., 'The Superiority of Pre-Critical Exegesis', *TTod*, 37 (1980/81), pp. 27–38.

Sternberg, Meir, 'Biblical Poetics and Sexual Politics: From Reading to Counterreading', *JBL*, 111 (1992), pp. 463–88.

—*The Poetics of Biblical Narrative: Ideological Literature and the Drama of Reading* (Bloomington: Indiana University Press, 1985).

Stowers, Stanley K., *The Diatribe and Paul's Letter to the Romans* (Chico, CA: Scholars Press, 1981).

—*A Rereading of Romans: Justice, Jews, and Gentiles* (New Haven, London: Yale University Press, 1994).

Sugirtharajab, R.S. (ed.), *The Postcolonial Bible* (Sheffield: Sheffield Academic Press, 1998).

—*Voices from the Margin: Interpreting the Bible in the Third World* (London, SPCK, 1991).

Tannehill, Robert C., 'Freedom and Responsibility in Scripture Interpretation, with Application to Luke', in R.P. Thompson and T.E. Philips (eds.), *Literary Studies in Luke–Acts* (Macon, GA: Mercer University Press, 1998), pp. 265–78.

Thiselton, Anthony, *New Horizons in Hermeneutics: The Theory and Practice of Transforming Biblical Reading* (London: HarperCollins, 1992; Grand Rapids: Zondervan, 1992).

Tillich, Paul, *Love, Power, and Justice: Ontological Analyses and Ethical Applications* (Oxford: Oxford University Press, 1954).

—*Systematic Theology*, I (3 vols. in one; Chicago: University of Chicago Press; New York and Evanston: Harper & Row, 1967).

Trible, Phyllis, *God and the Rhetoric of Sexuality* (Philadelphia: Fortress Press, 1978).

Tyler, Stephen A., *The Unspeakable: Discourse, Dialogue, and Rhetoric in the Postmodern World* (Madison, WI: University of Wisconsin Press, 1987).

Van Biema, David, 'The End: How it Got that Way', *Time Magazine* (July 1, 2002), pp. 46–47.

Vanhoozer, Kevin J., 'Body Piercing, the Natural Sense, and the Task of Theological Interpretation: A Hermeneutical Homily on John 19.34', *ExAu*, 16 (2000), pp. 1–29.

—*Is There a Meaning in This Text? The Bible, the Reader, and the Morality of Biblical Knowledge* (Leicester, England: Apollos, 1998; Grand Rapids: Zondervan, 1998).

Vermes, Geza, *The Complete Dead Sea Scrolls in English* (New York: Penguin Books, 1997).

Volf, Miroslav, *Exclusion and Embrace: A Theological Exploration of Identity, Otherness, and Reconciliation* (Nashville: Abingdon Press, 1996).

Walsh, Cary Ellen, *Exquisite Desire: Religion, the Erotic, and the Song of Songs* (Minneapolis: Fortress Press, 2000).

Walsh, Richard, 'On Finding a Non-American Revelation: *End of Days* and the Book of Revelation', in George Aichele and Richard Walsh (eds.), *Screening Scripture: Intertextual Connections Between Scripture and Film* (Harrisburg, PA: Trinity International, 2002), pp. 1–23.

Walvoord, John F., *Armageddon, Oil and the Middle East Crisis: What the Bible Says about the Future of the Middle East and the End of the Western Civilization* (Grand Rapids: Zondervan, 1990).

Watson, Francis, *Text, Church, and World: Biblical Interpretation in Theological Perspective* (Grand Rapids: Eerdmans, 1994; Edinburgh: T. & T. Clark, 1994).

—*Text and Truth: Redefining Biblical Theology* (Grand Rapids: Eerdmans, 1997; Edinburgh: T. & T. Clark, 1997).

Weber, Timothy P., *Living in the Shadow of the Second Coming: American Premillennialism, 1875–1982* (Chicago: University of Chicago Press, 1983).

Weems, Renita J., *Battered Love: Marriage, Sex, and Violence in the Hebrew Prophets* (OBT; Minneapolis: Augsburg-Fortress, 1995).

West, Gerald O., *The Academy of the Poor: Towards a Dialogical Reading of the Bible* (Sheffield: Sheffield Academic Press, 1999).

—*Contextual Bible Study* (Pietermaritzburg, South Africa: Cluster Publications, 1993).

Westerholm, Stephen, *Israel's Law and the Church's Faith: Paul and His Recent Interpreters* (Grand Rapids: Eerdmans, 1988).

Westermann, Claus, 'Beauty in the Hebrew Bible', trans. Üte Oestringer and Carole R. Fontaine, in Athalya Brenner and Carole R. Fontaine (eds.), *A Feminist Companion to Reading the Bible: Approaches, Methods, Strategies* (Sheffield: Sheffield Academic Press, 1997), pp. 584–602.

—*Genesis 12–36* (A Continental Commentary; Minneapolis: Augsburg Publishing House, 1985).

Wink, Walter, *The Powers That Be: Theology for a New Millennium* (New York: Doubleday, 1998).

Wire, Antoinette Clark, *The Corinthian Women Prophets: A Reconstruction through Paul's Rhetoric* (Minneapolis: Fortress Press, 1990).

—'1 Corinthians', in Elisabeth Schüssler Fiorenza (ed.), *Searching the Scriptures*, vol. 2: *A Feminist Commentary* (New York: Crossroad, 1994).

—'Response: The Politics of the Assembly in Corinth', in Richard A. Horsley (ed.), *Paul and Politics: Ekklesia, Israel, Imperium, Interpretation* (Harrisburg, PA: Trinity Press International, 2000), pp. 124–29.

Wright, N.T., *Jesus and the Victory of God*, vol. 2: *Christian Origins and the Question of God* (Minneapolis: Fortress Press, 1997).

Wuellner, Wilhelm, 'Paul's Rhetoric of Argumentation: An Alternative to the Donfried-Karris Debate over Romans', in Karl P. Donfried (ed.), *The Romans Debate* (Peabody, MA: Hendrickson, expanded edn, 1977 and 1991), pp. 128–46.

Yamada, Frank M., 'Ethics', in A.K.M. Adam (ed.), *Handbook of Postmodern Biblical Interpretation* (St Louis: Chalice Press, 2000), pp. 76–84.

—'Rape Narratives as Cultural Critique: A Narrative and Cultural Analysis of Old Testament Rape Texts' (PhD dissertation in progress; Princeton Theological Seminary).

Yeo, Khiok-khng, 'A Confucian Reading of Romans 7.14-25: Nomos (Law) and Li (Propriety)', *Jian Dao: A Journal of Bible and Theology*, 5 (1996), pp. 127–41.

—*Rhetorical Interaction in 1 Corinthians 8 and 10: A Formal Analysis with Preliminary Suggestions for a Chinese, Cross-Cultural Hermeneutic* (Leiden: E.J. Brill, 1995).

—*What Has Jerusalem to Do with Beijing? Biblical Interpretation from a Chinese Perspective* (Harrisburg, PA: Trinity Press International, 1998).

Ziesler, J.A., 'The Role of the Tenth Commandment in Romans 7', *JSNT*, 33 (1988), pp. 41–56.

INTERNET SOURCES

Amnesty International, 'Pakistan: Women's Rights',
http.//web.amnesty.org/ai.nsf/recent/ASA330062002?OpenDocument#top;
http.//web.amnesty.org/ai.nsf/recent/ASA330062002?OpenDocument.

Jillani, Hina, Report for Amnesty International, http.//web.amnesty.org/ai.nsf/Index/ASA330201999?OpenDocument&of=COUNTRIES\PAKISTAN

http.//www.keanuweb.com/ credits/movie.matrix2.html (accessed June 28, 2002).

http.//www.norcalmovies.com/TheMatrix2/ (accessed June 28, 2002).

http.//www.raptureme.com/rr-antichrist.html (accessed June 28, 2002).

http.//www.upcomingmovies.com/terminator3.html (accessed June 29, 2002).

http.//www.prophecyupdate.com/the_seven_churches.htm (accessed June 30, 2002).

INDEX

INDEX OF REFERENCES

OLD TESTAMENT

NEW TESTAMENT